Deepak Bhargava has been a leader, strategist, and campaigner in movements for social and economic justice for over thirty years. He is currently a distinguished lecturer at CUNY's School of Labor and Urban Studies, a senior fellow at the Roosevelt Institute, and co-founder of Leadership for Democracy and Social Justice. He was previously president of Community Change. He is co-editor (with Ruth Milkman and Penny Lewis) of *Immigration Matters: Movements, Visions, and Strategies for a Progressive Future*. He lives in New York City.

Stephanie Luce is a professor of labor studies at CUNY's School of Labor and Urban Studies and professor of sociology at the CUNY Graduate Center. She is the author of numerous books on the labor movement and the living wage, including *Labor Movements: Global Perspectives*, as well as the co-author (with Robert Pollin) of *The Living Wage*. She lives in New York City.

PRACTICAL RADICALS

SEVEN STRATEGIES TO CHANGE THE WORLD

Deepak Bhargava
and
Stephanie Luce

NEW YORK
LONDON

© 2023 by Deepak Bhargava & Stephanie Luce
Preface to the Paperback Edition and Afterword © 2025 by Deepak Bhargava & Stephanie Luce
Illustrations © 2023 by Jeffrey Phillips
All rights reserved.
No part of this book may be reproduced, in any form, without written permission from the publisher.

Requests for permission to reproduce selections from this book should be made through our website: https://thenewpress.org/contact.

First published in the United States by The New Press, New York, 2023
Paperback edition published by The New Press, 2025
Distributed by Two Rivers Distribution

ISBN 978-1-62097-821-4 (hc)
ISBN 978-1- 62097-981-5 (pb)
ISBN 978-1-62097-993-8 (ebook)
CIP data is available

The New Press publishes books that promote and enrich public discussion and understanding of the issues vital to our democracy and to a more equitable world. These books are made possible by the enthusiasm of our readers; the support of a committed group of donors, large and small; the collaboration of our many partners in the independent media and the not-for-profit sector; booksellers, who often hand-sell New Press books; librarians; and above all by our authors.

www.thenewpress.org

This book was set in Minion Pro and Serifa

Printed in the United States of America

Contents

Preface to the Paperback Edition vii
Preface ix

Part I: Foundations: Vision, Strategy, and Power   1

  1. Lineages of Change: Strategies for Underdogs. 3

  2. You Can't Build What You Can't Imagine: The Role of
     Vision in Transformational Change 17

  3. How Underdogs Win: Strategy Fundamentals 31

  4. The Change Ensemble: Forms of Power 44

  5. Setting the Stage: Six Ways Overdogs Got Us to Today 58

Part II: Notes of Change: Seven Strategies Underdogs Use to Win   73

  6.1: Base-Building—Community Organizations: Love and Rigor
      at Make the Road NY 78

  6.2: Base-Building—Labor Unions: Worker Power, the Common
      Good, and the St. Paul Federation of Educators 98

  7. Disruptive Movements: Breaking the Rules, Changing the
     Paradigm: The Welfare Rights Movement .114

  8. Narrative Shift: Changing the Common Sense: Occupy Wall
     Street. 135

9. Electoral Change: Politics from the Ground Up: Building
   Multiracial Coalitions to Take Governing Power............152

10. Inside-Outside Campaigns: Building Coalitions to Seize the
    Moment: Winning $15 in Chicago 173

11. Momentum: Distributed Organizing, Big Results: 350.org
    and the Divestment Movement 190

12. Collective Care: Personal Pain to Communal Strength:
    The Gay Men's Health Crisis Responds to AIDS.............. 209

13. Power from Below: Harmonizing Strategy Models in the
    Movement for Abolition 228

**Part III: Melodies for Movements: Underdog Strategy in the
Twenty-First Century**   **245**

14. Unity Builds Power: Addressing Conflict in Organizations
    and Movements 249

15. Strategists Are Made, Not Born: The Inner Life of Strategy 265

16. Learning from Our Opponents: How Overdogs Develop
    Strategy 277

17. Rhythms for Practical Radicals: A Long View 290

18. Learning from Lineages, Harmonizing Our Movements 305

Afterword.. 325
Acknowledgments..335
Tools, Prompts, and Resources 341
Notes..431
Index... 465

Preface to the Paperback Edition

This book was written for organizers working in dark times. Many of the stories we tell are about people who found a way to beat odds far higher than what most of us face now. Enslaved people organizing for abolition in an environment of racial terror, queer communities responding to the devastation of the AIDS crisis in the midst of a moral panic against them, and undocumented immigrants in New York fighting for their survival during Covid—all of their causes were unpopular with large swaths of the public when they began. Yet they prevailed. We live in a world that was made immensely better by their struggles and victories.

We set ourselves the task of understanding the strategies used by underdogs throughout history not as an academic exercise, but to illuminate pathways for organizers today who also confront seemingly intractable problems. As authoritarianism, climate change, and runaway corporate power grow and metastasize—alongside a rising wave of racism, sexism, and nativism—we have a responsibility to ask ourselves, as previous generations of practical radicals did: how can we make a real difference?

But since this book came out in late 2023, the times have become darker, the problems more intractable. The strategies and tactics many of us are most comfortable with don't work as well as they used to. Litigation as an offensive strategy is more challenging with many courts captured by extremists. Mass protests are less effective than they once were. Policy work is undermined when the consensus about major issues—even about basic facts—has broken down. Prevailing political models—already becoming unsustainable as government agencies became subject to corporate capture—are irrelevant as entire agencies are decimated. People have lost faith in political institutions and the capacity of political parties to solve problems. We need strategies appropriate for the new era we have entered, even if they force us outside our comfort zones.

The good news is that the large repertoire of strategies that have been developed over centuries by our movement ancestors, some of which are not well understood or have fallen into disuse, can nourish our imagination today. We recently saw the power of disruption—one of the seven strategies we feature in the book—when the United Auto Workers struck against the Big Three automakers in the fall of 2023. Since the 1980s the conventional wisdom has held that strikes are useless or counterproductive, but the UAW pushed ahead anyway, adding creative twists like targeting the most profitable plants, increasing the number of plants on strike as negotiations progressed, and using shorter strikes that were easier to sustain. There is a long tradition of nonviolent civil resistance, the use of strikes, boycotts, and other forms of disruption, that will be essential to revive in this era.

Understanding which strategies can be effective in this period of history, and which we may need to let go of, is crucial because the stakes are so high. We need to be serious about winning. Otherwise these escalating disasters can create a climate of despair, with people turning inwards, away from public life. Knowing that power can be built and wielded for good, that there *are* strategies that can win against great odds, is hugely important in a time when overdogs want us to give up.

We wrote *Practical Radicals* to generate conversation, debate, and hope for those fighting for transformative change. We hope you find what follows useful. We've also written an Afterword to apply those frameworks to our current situation.

Preface

How do oppressed people, facing far stronger opponents, sometimes win? We wrote this book about strategy to answer that question.

Understanding how movements win is more important than ever. We live in an age of people-powered social change. As everyday people's confidence in governing elites and institutions collapses, movements on the Left and Right ebb and flow.[1] The Movement for Black Lives, the youth climate movement, an upsurge of worker organizing, and the broad-based resistance to Donald Trump brought millions of people to the streets. On the Right, mass movements have brought authoritarians to power across the globe. In the United States, a growing white nationalist movement plotted with the sitting president to mount a coup, and they have not stopped plotting.

We come to the book with complementary strengths. Stephanie brings experience in the labor movement, electoral politics, and international work, as well as theoretical training and years of teaching experience. Deepak brings experience in community organizing, policy, and national campaigns for economic justice, immigrant rights, and electoral change, including sixteen years leading Community Change, a national social justice organization that strengthens organizing in low-income communities of color. We're both also lifers in movements, not just as professionals but also through volunteering, marching, canvassing, and getting arrested for good causes. Our own experiences, both triumphs and heartbreaks, are woven throughout the book.

Deepak was always interested in theory and history, unusually so for a U.S. movement practitioner. Stephanie was always deeply engaged in organizing work, unusually so for an academic. Yet both of us found the absence of compelling, comprehensive, and accessible frameworks for understanding strategy, organizing, and movements frustrating. Organizers and academics often invoke the concept of power—but don't agree about what it is. One of our goals was to synthesize the best ideas from movements and academia, worlds that are too often suspicious of each other, and offer a practical framework for people trying to change the world.

This was a humbling task, and we could not have taken it on alone. We began teaching a class on "Power and Strategy" at the CUNY School of Labor and Urban Studies in 2020. That first class brought together thirty exceptional students, many of whom had run important campaigns for labor, community, and other organizations, to workshop the ideas that became this book. There was some madness that first semester as we coped with teaching students all over the country. But there was also magic. We recruited iconic movement leaders to guest teach, like Heather Booth, Frances Fox Piven, Alan Jenkins, Cristina Jimenez, Eliseo Medina, and Maurice Mitchell. Students grappled with classic movement texts by W.E.B. DuBois, A.J. Muste, and the Combahee River Collective, as well as some of the best academic writing we found about strategy.

We interviewed dozens of organizers to write this book, read work by academics and practitioners, and reflected on our own experience in movements. And we researched how elites develop strategy in business, military, and politics.

Organizers rarely get the opportunity to step back and reflect on their work and the broader movement, because they're in a grind of crises and campaigns. Our students have been energized by engaging with colleagues working in different movements. They have been grateful for the space to think big about how to change the world. One of our favorite sessions invites students to build a thirty-year plan for the Left, modeled off the infamous Powell memorandum, a text that exemplifies the approach of the Right-wing architects whose cruel and reactionary visions shaped the world we live in today.

Surprisingly few students have had formal training in the various lineages of organizing and strategy that are, or should be, their inheritance. Instead, most have been trained in a technical craft in one particular school, not in the arts of power and strategy. This contrasts with what we have learned about how Right-wingers train leaders at business schools and in the military, which emphasize strategy and vision rather than technical know-how. The motto on the homepage of the website of the conservative Leadership Institute, which has trained over 200,000 people, is compelling and simple: "You owe it to your philosophy to learn how to win." Indeed.

We wrote this book because we think that the practice of rigorous strategy on the Left has deteriorated in recent years. Organizers debate whether you can teach strategy at all, or if the ability is mostly innate. Our view is that great strategists are made, not born. Strategy can be taught, and strategists can get better with practice. Some students learn through reading, some through lectures, but most everyone really starts to "get it" when working together in groups to put the concepts into practice. We've compiled and created tools that cross different traditions of social change, and borrowed and adapted lessons from the military and Silicon Valley too. We think the ideas in the book are most likely to stick when you use the tools.

We wrote this book for a specific audience: the segment of the Left who might embrace the label **practical radical**. These are organizers who hold big visions for transforming society *and* are willing to do what it takes to win in the real world. Legendary organizer Bayard Rustin, a consummate practical radical, criticized two other dominant ways of approaching social change: "My quarrel with the 'no-win' tendency in the civil rights movement (and the reason I have so designated it) parallels my quarrel with the moderates outside the movement. As the latter lack the vision or will for fundamental change, the former lack a realistic strategy for achieving it.

For such a strategy they substitute militancy. But militancy is a matter of posture and volume and not of effect."[2] Practical radicals are not content to be on the right side without a plan to make their vision a reality. And they are not satisfied with working on small issues without an analysis of what's wrong with society and a vision of how it could be better.

A word about what this book is not. It is not an organizing "how to" manual. While good organizing overlaps with strategy, our focus is on the latter. We occasionally refer to movement work in other countries, but for the most part we focus on the United States. The book is not for people who are dogmatic about "one right way" to make change. This cultish tendency to exalt a particular practitioner or approach, while denigrating others, is pervasive and pernicious. We don't believe any school of social change has a monopoly on effective strategy; in fact, we've found that our opponents can be worthy teachers too.

We see developing strategy as analogous to music making. That's why we've used music metaphors throughout the book, with genre-crossing musicians in mind. We imagine different models of social change as different notes in the scale, which can be played together and in different combinations as melodies and harmonies.

We seek to ground movement folk in the diverse lineages of social change. Many practitioners working today may not know the theory or history behind the strategy they use, let alone be familiar with other ones. Practical radicals can't expect to win simply by repeating what their ancestors did. But they also won't win without access to their full organizing inheritance, so they can remix strategies to meet today's challenges. Like musicians, organizers must improvise in a dialogue with inherited traditions in order to compose new freedom songs.

As we write this, compounding crises of racism, climate change, economic inequality, attacks on women's and LGBTQ+ rights, nativism, and authoritarianism have pushed us into scary and unfamiliar waters. Among our movement colleagues, there is some exhaustion and despair, but also grit, imagination, and hope that another world is possible. Some of the people and movements we write about prevailed against even greater odds than we face now. We believe in our collective capacity to imagine and build a different society. And we're inspired by the millions of people who make the choice to do that every day. This book is for them.

Deepak Bhargava and Stephanie Luce
New York City
March 18, 2023

PART I

FOUNDATIONS: VISION, STRATEGY, AND POWER

1

Lineages of Change: Strategies for Underdogs

The sun had not yet risen on May 13, 1862, when Robert Smalls navigated a steamboat through Confederate checkpoints. Smalls, born into slavery in 1839 in Beaufort, South Carolina, raised a white makeshift flag from the boat he and fifteen others had stolen, signaling that they were surrendering themselves to the Union fleet and were therefore free.[1]

Some Americans have heard of Robert Smalls; a Navy ship was even recently renamed for him. But if they have, it's almost always as part of a superficial narrative of the abolition of slavery. They may learn about how the British Parliament abolished the slave trade in 1807, about Bleeding Kansas and the desperate battles of the Civil War, about the Emancipation Proclamation and perhaps the Thirteenth Amendment, but they rarely learn about *why* these dramatic events happened. This take on history—a highlight reel of culminating events—can be compelling. But it obscures the real story—what these events were a culmination *of*.

Smalls's escape, for example. It wasn't merely a daring adventure. It was part of a much broader strategy: a high-risk, loosely coordinated mass desertion by hundreds of thousands of enslaved people. This "general strike" (in the words of scholar and activist W.E.B. DuBois) played a crucial role in breaking the Confederacy during the Civil War—more than any of the battles that fill our textbooks.[2]

And this strike was only one of the wide range of creative strategies that people, in an effort that spanned decades and continents, used to disrupt the economic, ideological, and political foundations of slavery. The international movement, with enslaved and formerly enslaved people at the heart, fought to pass laws, boycotted consumer products, rallied in mass meetings, petitioned legislatures, marched, engaged in mass public education, ran away, took up arms, operated underground railroads, and created a new common sense about the evils of slavery. Some of these strategies were legal, but many were not. Some were pursued in public, while others were necessarily clandestine. But the disparate players came together into a movement like jazz musicians come together in an ensemble. Many of the core strategies that organizers and campaigners use today have their origins in the multigenerational, multicontinental struggle to end slavery.[3]

Why Underdogs Need Strategy

Underdogs—those fighting for liberation of the oppressed—have changed the course of history in monumental ways. They did so not only by proclaiming their critiques and visions—though that was important—but also by organizing people to counter the power of wealth and repression.

Successful underdog movements exemplify two deep truths. First, transformational change isn't achieved just because it's morally right. It was strategy, not merely righteousness, that ended slavery. One of the brilliant architects of the abolition movement, Frederick Douglass, said in 1857: "This struggle may be a moral one, or it may be a physical one, and it may be both moral and physical, but it must be a struggle. Power concedes nothing without a demand. It never did and it never will."[4] Douglass sought to dispel the illusion that exposing the evils of slavery would, by itself, overthrow a system that formed the basis of society in the South, generated massive profits for banks and merchants in the North, paid taxes to governments, and provided cheap products to consumers across the globe.

Douglass's words resonate today. The failures of current systems, from climate change to economic inequality, have been exposed again and again. But critics and visionaries writing about alternatives often don't say much about *how* to achieve change. Vision, as Douglass argued, is never self-executing. Organizers need strategies that chart a path underdogs can travel, from the world as it is to the world as it could be.

Oppressed people need strategy because they lack the raw power of their opponents. We call their opponents the **overdogs**: those who hold power and maintain (or worsen) the status quo, preventing underdogs from winning their demands, whether they're big landlords kicking people out of their homes, state legislators denying voting rights, or corporations keeping workers in poverty.[5] Overdogs don't just have raw power; they also have strategy—and they need it because they are vastly outnumbered. In fact, most books about strategy—from Machiavelli's *The Prince* to Henry Kissinger's *World Order*—are written by and for overdogs so they can maintain and extend their rule. There are schools and industries devoted to training elites: business schools, military academies, union-busting firms, and massive consulting companies like McKinsey and Boston Consulting Group.

Underdogs have strategy as well, but the transmission of the diverse lineages of their wisdom has too often been interrupted or lost due to state repression and violent attacks (particularly against Black freedom movements), through moral panics like the Red Scare purges, and through the genocide of Indigenous people. Many in the U.S. Left have been skeptical of the need for reflection, study, and training. And just like we saw with the Civil War, strategy can seem less interesting than culminating events, and the events are certainly easier to teach. Martin Luther King Jr.'s "I Have a Dream" speech is far more dramatic, and easier to explain, than the decades of work that put him on that stage at that moment. As a result, many organizers arrive at this work animated with passion to correct injustice, but with limited access to the immense library of experience that could help them respond to today's challenges.

There are great underdog books available as more writers and organizers, like adrienne maree brown, Mark and Paul Engler, Lisa Fithian, Alicia Garza, Steve Phillips, Jonathan Smucker, and others, have put their wisdom into writing. But some of the classic books about organizing and strategy for underdogs are focused on only one tradition, and at times are contemptuous of the ways others go about making change. The iconic book about underdog strategy, Saul Alinsky's *Rules for Radicals,* was written over five decades ago. Alinsky urged social change practitioners to be pragmatic rather than visionary: to avoid discussion of ideology, electoral politics, and coalitions.[6] We respect Alinsky's contributions, which still have much to teach us. But based on our decades of experience working in movements, we believe good strategists will need to reject much of his rigid doctrine and borrow from a wide variety of other traditions. This goes against the grain of how social change is typically taught in the United States. By temperament or training, many experienced activists tend to be devotees of particular schools of thought and practice. And many of the younger organizers we meet have had mostly haphazard, ad hoc training that covers only narrow terrain. This brings us to the second truth about how change happens: a combination of strategies is needed to win.

It Takes Multiple, Aligned Strategies to Win Transformational Change

There is no single best approach to strategy, and in fact transformational change requires a mixture of creative strategies, working together harmoniously. But more than that, practitioners in different traditions actually depend on each other for success. For example, disruptive, raucous movements in the 1960s weren't distractions from the "real" work of building mass organization as Alinsky argued—they were essential fuel for the explosive growth of racial justice and community organizations. This was also the case in the Great Depression of the 1930s, as mass movements of workers and unemployed people protested and spurred labor law reform and massive relief programs, while flooding old unions and founding new ones. And the reverse is true too: disruptive social movements that may seem to burst on the scene spontaneously often arise out of patient organizing work over many years.

Ella Baker, a legendary organizer in the civil rights movement, famously challenged the NAACP's top-down approach to change and instead promoted a strategy of base-building in the South. This turn toward community organizing was a consequential decision that laid the groundwork for vibrant movements to emerge in the late 1950s and 1960s. She spent decades identifying and training grassroots leaders in the South, long before national attention focused on civil rights in the 1960s. This behind-the-scenes work isn't as exciting as mass mobilizations or strikes, and it isn't usually done by the charismatic leaders we see on TV, but it's the lifeblood of social change. Baker wrote regularly of this kind of work as she traveled the South in the 1940s: "I must leave now for one of those small church night meetings which are usually more exhausting than the immediate returns warrant, but it's part of the spade work so let it be."[7] There are cycles for social movements—like the movements in a symphony or concerto, not everything can be a crescendo. A lot happens in the quieter, slower parts of a piece of music that sets the stage for the climax.

The civil rights movement's breakthroughs depended on slow, patient organizing *and* dramatic actions, like the lunch counter sit-ins. It relied on working with legislators, registering voters, and sharing powerful images to make moral claims. No single strategy alone would have worked. And different moments in history call for specific combinations of methods. Good underdog strategists can sense when it's time to shift from spadework in the hard times to fanning the flames of disruption when conditions are ripe, as Ella Baker did.

You need a variety of strategies to win social change, but what people do to change the world for the better is not equally strategic at all times. Musicians rely on a diversity of notes, tempos, dynamics, and timbres, but they make choices—and so too must organizers. Organizers need methods to assess the relative strengths and weaknesses of different strategies in specific contexts. Strategy isn't just a matter of personal preference. Transformational change doesn't happen by accident.

Imagining the span of change across decades rather than campaign cycles means a shift of mindset. It requires a long-term vision, an analysis of the historical moment (conjuncture), and a strategy that bridges them. Your vision must be clear—you can't organize toward a world you can't imagine, or only against the current system. It requires soberly assessing the state of struggle between different social forces, the "common sense" of the times, and where there are openings for change. Lastly, it requires creative strategies that build a bridge from the **world as it is** to the **world as it could be**.

In this book, we describe seven strategy models that underdogs use as bridges, based on patterns and rhythms we have identified that repeat across time and place. Each of the strategies depends on the power available to underdogs. We'll describe six forms of power and explain how they shape strategy. Each form of power can be thought of as an instrument, and each strategy model, a note on the musical scale. Musicians play melodies by stringing together multiple notes. When other musicians are added, the music becomes even more multidimensional and compelling. Strategies can be combined—harmonized—when organizers draw from different models, such as when Black public-sector workers unionized in the 1960s and 1970s by drawing from both base-building labor organizing and the disruptive power of the civil rights movement.

The complexity of transformational change can be frustrating. The impulse to teach or practice a single strategy is understandable.[8] And usually people do have to learn one craft before they can innovate and synthesize elements of others. But acknowledging the multiple, intersecting, and (ideally) reinforcing paths to change can be liberating. Organizers can find ways to appreciate and synchronize different contributions and to ask, from the perspective of a whole piece of music, do we need more of this instrument and less of that one? For instance, is there too much electoral work and not enough disruption?

Many successful movements and organizers intuitively learn to combine notes in novel ways in response to changing circumstances. But most people play instruments better with training. This book aims to give practitioners access to a broad repertoire so they can compose the right melodies and harmonies for movements—to construct and participate in "meta-strategy."

Seven Strategy Models for Transformational Change

Underdogs can draw on seven lineages of strategy and combine them in new ways based on their assessment of power and the moment.

The first model we discuss in the book is **base-building**.[9] The idea is that to win anything, you need to organize people, often one by one, door by door, co-worker by co-worker, and to develop strong bonds and leadership capacity. When people come together in mass organizations, they have the power of numbers and solidarity to win concessions from overdogs. We include two chapters about base-building, one focused on community organizing and one on unions, because we believe that base-building is the key note for all strategies for social change. Base-building by community groups and unions is the dominant model used by U.S. underdogs, so it's crucial to understand the strengths and limitations of the forms we've inherited and how they must evolve to meet today's challenges. Chapters 6.1 and 6.2 tell the stories of the community organization Make the Road NY and labor union St. Paul Federation of Educators and show how each used base-building to build powerful member-led organizations.

The second strategy model is **disruptive movements**. Disruption is not the same as noisy protests, which might not have an impact. Disruption is the ability to stop those in power from doing what they want to do and to break up the status quo—in short, the "power to wound."[10] Unions strike and stop production; if the workers can't be replaced, the employer will eventually need to cave in order to start production again.[11] Disruption can occur outside the workplace as people come together to block streets, stop key meetings from happening, fill jails, or push the system past capacity in other ways. In Chapter 7, we describe how working-class Black women used disruptive power to expand the welfare system in the 1960s.

A third strategy is ideological. **Narrative shift** is about winning hearts and minds and support for your vision. In this context, *narrative* means "a Big Story, rooted in shared values and common themes, that influences how audiences process information and make decisions."[12] We focus on narrative shift strategies that are grounded in organizing and that use popular education, creative actions, periodicals, theory, literature, movies, music, and more to influence the ways in which people make sense of society. It's more than a savvy media campaign: narrative work must be based on people's lived experiences, speak to their identity, and tell a story that explains the past and provides a path to the future. Occupy Wall Street (Chapter 8) is an example of how large numbers of people were able to change the narrative on inequality.

A fourth strategy is **electoral change**. Organizations endorse candidates or run their own, develop platforms, pursue get-out-the-vote efforts, and attempt to win the power to govern. In many countries, Left political parties that unite diverse movements have been a principal strategy for social change. While that has been less true in the United States, progressive insurgents have challenged the Democratic Party and devoted more attention to winning elections to prevent authoritarian Republicans from capturing the government. We focus on a few organizations that are building power through year-round organizing using a variety of approaches, including the New Georgia Project, California Calls, and the Working Families Party (Chapter 9).

While electoral strategies focus on winning the power to govern, an **inside-outside campaign** strategy allows organizations to win major policy reform by working "inside" in alliance with sympathetic legislators, but also building "outside" pressure through grassroots organizing. "Inside-outside" can be a way to do a variety of things, such as take control of important institutions, but in this context, we use it to mean campaigns to win and enforce policy. If an organization is powerful enough, it can achieve policy gains on its own, but usually underdogs have to build coalitions to win. For example, labor unions and community groups can work together to pass higher minimum wages in city and state legislatures, using inside relationships with supportive legislators as well as outside tactics, such as marches, rallies, petitions, op-eds, and voter drives, to pressure legislators to pass the bill. Inside-outside campaigns rely on multiple forms of power and in this way are a hybrid model that builds on other strategies. In Chapter 10 we describe how the Chicago Fight for $15 and a Union campaign was able to win a major wage increase from an anti-union mayor.

Another hybrid is the **momentum model**, in which organizers combine mass protest with narrative change. Momentum-driven campaigns seek to change the political weather—to expand what's possible to win by changing the "common sense" on a particular issue. Organizers seek out polarizing fights that attract a passionate minority of intense supporters *and* build a majority of passive support for the cause among the mass public. The internet and social media are crucial tools that allow momentum-driven campaigns to grow quickly. Organizers build campaigns that can absorb large numbers of new people and use mass training to frontload a shared set of values, cultural norms, demands, and brands at the beginning of a campaign. The model features "distributed organizing"—action driven by thousands of volunteers, supported but not controlled by a movement hub. Campaigns win by undermining institutional pillars that hold up a social consensus or by delegitimizing them, just as 350.org has done in its climate change work (Chapter 11).

Finally, we describe **collective care** as a strategy model. While care—meeting people's basic needs for food, health, emotional support, or community—is part of everyone's daily lives, we highlight how caring for one another can be about more than survival; it can be strategic. When organizations prioritize collective care, they enable people to take risks, pool resources, stick with a movement for the long term, and build the capacity to organize. When systems are unresponsive and underdogs face urgent needs, collective care can be a powerful antidote to despair, change people's sense of their agency and identity, and lay the tracks for challenging those systems. When the AIDS epidemic emerged in the 1980s, the Gay Men's Health Crisis formed as a mutual aid network. While providing crucial care to those with HIV/AIDS, it went beyond basic service-provision and became a hub for activist strategy and a launching pad for other strategies, including the more well known, militant direct action group ACT UP (Chapter 12).

Our research led us to some counterintuitive conclusions about the limitations, possibilities, and potential futures of each of the strategy models, and about how they can be combined to meet this historical moment, which we discuss in the conclusion. And we find that transformational change requires all seven models. Robert Smalls used most of these strategies. After escaping slavery, Smalls continued his work advocating on behalf of Black equality. He went on a speaking tour to raise funds for the Union and he petitioned the Secretary of War to allow Black soldiers and sailors to enlist and personally helped recruit over five thousand of the Black volunteers. After the war, Smalls bought the plantation where he and his mother had been enslaved for his family to live on as free people. He eventually became a congressman and served until the end of Reconstruction. The arc of Smalls's life shows how the abolition of slavery was won, with different strategies emphasized at different times.* Today, most practitioners are trained in at best a few approaches, without guidance on how they might be harmonized. Strategists need to learn from other traditions. As trumpeter Don Cherry observed, "When people believe in boundaries, they become part of them."[13]

Unfortunately, Overdogs Strategize Too

Overdogs use strategy too. And their commitment to long-term strategy has helped them win a lot. But because they command vast armies, immense wealth, the machinery of the state, and most of the media—advantages underdogs lack—their strategies are different.[14] And overdogs don't confront daily emergencies arising from systems of oppression, so it's easier

---

* While many transformational movements have elements of violence, such as the armed revolt in Haiti, our focus is on nonviolent strategies. There are other strategies underdogs have used over the years that we've left out. For example, we cover ways in which campaigns have used legal and communications strategies and tactics, but we don't include efforts that are wholly legal or communications focused; instead, we focus on organizing people in large numbers.

for them to develop strategies that span years or even decades, and to have backup plans in case of failure.

In this book, we distinguish between **strategies from above** and **strategies from below**: between those that benefit from (and seek to protect) the status quo and those that challenge it. We use the terms *Left* or *progressive* to refer to those people and groups fighting to end systems of oppression that keep underdogs down. We use them interchangeably in the book even though in reality sometimes people make distinctions between them, particularly to distinguish a sharper critique of capitalism on the Left. We use the term *liberal* to describe those who fight for incremental reform without challenging power relations in society. Conversely, we use *Right* to refer to those people and groups who hold conservative views that either uphold systems of oppression or refuse to acknowledge that those systems exist.

Not all top-down strategies are Right-wing, and not all bottom-up strategies are Left-wing. By strategies from above, we mean situations where a relatively small number of actors (say, the billionaire Koch brothers and their network of Right-wing funders) orchestrate big changes—by starting new organizations to shape worldviews, elect politicians, or pass laws. By strategies from below, we mean decentralized efforts that engage thousands or even millions of people whose decisions contribute to an overall outcome, such as the decisions of enslaved people, workers, people of faith, and others to challenge slavery across continents. Most social change efforts don't fall neatly into either category. Most movements from below have leaders—people like Harriet Tubman, Toussaint L'Ouverture, Frederick Douglass, and William Wilberforce (who was influential precisely because he was wealthy and powerful). And they have organizations that direct strategy, like the Quakers and the New England Anti-Slavery Society in the 1800s, or unions and community groups today, which include large numbers of organized members, but also can be hierarchical in their internal structures and decision making.

And while it's easy—and not *entirely* wrong—to view Right-wing movements as fake or manufactured, Right-wing politics do have a genuine mass constituency. The authoritarian movement supporting Donald Trump isn't staged or managed from Mar-a-Lago. There are tens of thousands of people who enthusiastically work to take over school boards, to pass policy against critical race theory, and to harass and threaten violence against election officials. Similarly, successes in the anti-abortion movement relied at least in part on disruption, narrative change, and long-term grassroots mobilization by religious and other anti-abortion groups. Taking this grassroots component of Right-wing strategy seriously is crucial to understanding how to counter it.

We believe that multiple systems of oppression keep humans from reaching their full potential and liberation. These systems, which include racial, gender, and class hierarchies, have existed since long before the country was founded. The goal of underdog movements is to end these systems. We use **racial capitalism** to describe the U.S. economic and political system, which is biased in favor of overdogs. But those biases don't mean that underdogs can't fight and win. There are contradictions and cracks in the system, and overdogs and underdogs have always fought to shape the character of the system. In the 1930s, underdogs won important victories that led to a period of **managed capitalism** that shifted power in their favor.

Overdogs fought back, deploying intersecting strategies over decades to bring about **racial neoliberalism** as the reigning economic and social paradigm. Racial neoliberalism is a specific form of racial capitalism based on the idea that governments should exist primarily to enforce social control and white supremacy and help employers and investors maximize profit. It emphasizes individual responsibility, arguing that racism is simply a matter of individual attitudes.[15] We explore the case of racial neoliberalism as an example of overdog strategy in greater depth in Chapter 5, and we consider the distinctive elements of overdog strategy in business, politics, and the military—some of which we can learn from and apply—in Chapter 16.

While they have developed sophisticated strategies, overdogs are not invincible. They can be slow-moving and, convinced of their own invulnerability, often fail to take the opposition seriously until it's too late. Their privileged vantage point can make it hard for them to see reality clearly.[16] By contrast, oppressed people often must be sensitive to their surroundings just to survive. This can help them understand the psychology of their oppressors, a crucial asset.

In general, overdogs' greater resources—and the nature of the authoritarian personality—allow them to impose discipline and hierarchy, like conductors directing orchestras, which is both their strength and their weakness. By contrast, underdog movements are often more improvisational and less hierarchical, like jazz ensembles. Jazz demands intense dedication and deep cooperation—if musicians all sharing the same space each did their own thing, the result would be a painful cacophony. Instead, the jazz musician listens to others and adapts. Each musician plays a role, but together they are more than the sum of their parts. While there is a role for conductors in underdog strategy, transformational democratic social justice won't come from a single person or strategy, but rather from a variety of players improvising strategies in harmony.

Practical radicals (see Chapter 2) should devote time and resources to training strategists to build a bridge between the world as it is and the world as it could be, with an emphasis on developing leadership roles for those on the front lines of systems of oppression. It will take a combination of the seven strategy models, making use of different forms of power, to win transformational change. Organizers should learn from unfamiliar underdog traditions of strategy and find ways to harmonize with one another to meet the challenges of our time.

Book Overview

Readers can pick and choose any order they'd like to follow in the book. Part I focuses on the theory that grounds the seven models, including the six forms of power, and how strategy should start with an analysis of the world as it is and a vision of the future world as it should be.

Part II presents the seven models of social change, including case studies of each. We explore the roles of emotion, spirit, and identity in fueling social change in many of the models and consider how passion and commitment can enable underdogs to overcome what seem to be insurmountable odds. We end Part II with a look at how underdogs used the seven models of strategy and six forms of power to end slavery in the eighteenth and nineteenth centuries.

In Part III, we explore sources of innovation and challenges for strategy development. We provide insights on how to diagnose and overcome internal conflict in movements, and how underdogs can become better strategists. We explain common strategies used by overdogs, assess which of their methods underdogs can ethically use, and explore the crucial role of time in transformational change.

We end the book with reflections on the future of the seven models and how to apply our framework to the work ahead. We aren't merely diagnosing or chronicling. We share ideas for how to build more powerful, united, and effective movements at a crucial moment in history when the dominant paradigm of racial neoliberalism may be crumbling but what comes next is not yet decided.

We offer discussion prompts and tools, like worksheets and exercises, at the end of most chapters. The tools are templates that can be adapted to any campaign or movement. Our students often find the tools to be their favorite part of our class. We hope that a deeper understanding of the diversity of methods and tools can help underdogs win some of the historic fights of these times—for democracy, for justice, against authoritarianism, and for the future of humans on this planet.

Isaiah Berlin, in his essay "The Hedgehog and the Fox," argued that some writers and thinkers repeat the same formula over and over, while others do something radically different each time. As the saying goes: "A fox knows many things, but a hedgehog knows one big thing."[17] We think the complexity of the world we live in requires more foxes—practitioners who can range across a large terrain, borrow from different traditions, and mash up old elements into new winning strategies. We still need hedgehogs, but this is a book for crafty foxes.

2

You Can't Build What You Can't Imagine: The Role of Vision in Transformational Change

We ask our students to read two pieces that exemplify good strategy; they come from opposite sides of the political spectrum. On the Right, future Supreme Court justice Lewis Powell wrote the infamous "Powell memorandum" as a call to arms for the U.S. Chamber of Commerce in 1971. He laid out a plan to capture key institutions such as the media and universities to reverse the spread of radical ideas that challenged capitalism and white supremacy. On the Left, Marxist revolutionary V.I. Lenin wrote "Left-Wing Communism: An Infantile Disorder" in 1920. He argued for the necessity of alliances to achieve change and criticized purist colleagues who hoped that they could will a socialist society into being without making political compromises along the way.

Powell and Lenin have nothing in common politically, but both are icy in their critique of sloppy thinking and are ruthless about winning. They weave three elements together that are usually handled separately: a sober analysis of the world as it is (what we and others call the conjuncture), a bold long-term vision for the world as it could be, and rigorous strategy to get from here to there.

We've worked with organizers who dismiss long-range vision, arguing that the tasks at hand are too urgent to divert precious energy to fantasies.

And we've been in gatherings where Leftists weren't willing to grapple honestly with the limits of our power, preferring to criticize others for any deviation from a pure "line" rather than develop a strategy to win. Both of these tendencies—we call them pragmatism and utopianism—can be destructive, cause brutal conflict among potential allies, and lead to failure. The following examples illustrate the perils of losing sight of vision or strategy.

Given his roots in community organizing, some progressives thought Barack Obama would be a movement president. They were mistaken. Obama often invoked movements of the past—he cited "Seneca Falls, and Selma, and Stonewall" in his second inaugural address, for example. But he took the status quo mostly as a given and didn't prioritize changing the rules of the game, such as voting rights and labor law and immigration reform. His administration took the side of bankers in the foreclosure crisis that stripped working-class people, especially people of color, of wealth. Like many Democrats, he was a pragmatist who sought incremental reforms that could be achieved without stepping on entrenched interests' toes. The failures of the Obama era to deliver for people in the wake of the Great Recession helped create the conditions for Donald Trump and for an authoritarian movement to grow.[1]

On the other hand, history is filled with stories of Leftists who failed to accurately assess their current conditions, rejecting a pragmatic path that would have better enabled them to achieve strategic goals. An extreme example was the German Communist Party (KPD) in the 1930s. Rather than building an alliance with other parties to defeat Hitler, the KPD identified the Social Democrats as their leading enemy because they allegedly deceived workers with pseudo-socialist rhetoric. This led the head of the KPD to declare: "Nothing could be more fatal for us than to opportunistically overestimate the danger posed by Hitler-fascism."[2] The Social Democrats had made equally disastrous calculations in the 1910s when they decided to abandon an international worker's movement and align with German employers in WWI. The Left's failure to soberly assess the threat and make necessary alliances proved catastrophic.

In this book, we highlight practical radicals who avoided the pitfalls of pragmatism and utopianism by combining rigorous analysis, broad social vision, and sophisticated strategy.[3] Practical radicals embrace the inevitable tension between the hard realities of the world as it is and the dreams of liberation embodied in their vision of the world as it should be. This space is where they do their finest work.[4] Below, we explore vision and the concept of conjunctures.

You Can't Build What You Can't Imagine: The Role of Vision

The British cultural theorist Stuart Hall explains that vision should be grounded in what he calls **root ideas**.[5] These are not only utopian dreams or programmatic demands, but also basic understandings of how the world operates, and how humans should live, who we should love, and how we should approach work and leisure. Root ideas also address the important question: What do "the people" want? Based on these root ideas, movements and political parties tell stories of the society we should build, of the villains who block our progress, of our history and travails, and of who is legitimately part of "the people." In recent decades, Right-wing forces have been better than liberals and Leftists at casting a vision of the future that connects to lived experience.

Hall grappled with the rise of the Right and Margaret Thatcher's Conservative Party in the United Kingdom in the 1970s and 1980s. He explained how Thatcherism assembled ideas about law and order, the traditional family, personal responsibility, and British nationalism and identity that spoke to many British people. In contrast, the Labour Party offered detailed policy plans, such as how to reform the National Health Service, without projecting a moral vision. This problem persists. In recent years, Right-wingers in the United States have combined white nationalism, nativism, patriarchy, law and order, and a "you're on your own" ethic into a popular program that—in the absence of an alternative—has enabled them to assemble a formidable coalition. Meanwhile, the Democratic Party proposed a laundry list of policies without a story about the society they sought to build. There were many disparate notes, but no coherent song.

In 2021, Deepak discussed President Joe Biden's proposed American Rescue Plan legislation (which included some shockingly big ideas) with the students in his social policy class. His students followed the news but couldn't make heads or tails of the bill. They were predisposed to think it was better than what Trump had done, but what was the core idea tying all these policies together? Who were they in the story, and who were the villains? Similarly, his students met the arrival of child tax credit checks in their bank accounts not with joy, relief, or gratitude, but with suspicion. It's not surprising that working-class people, especially people of color who've experienced abuse at the hands of the government, asked: "What's the catch?" No one had given them a story to make sense of the policy, so they interpreted it through the lens of their lived experience.

It's not just the Democratic Party that gets lost in policy to the detriment of vision. Some parts of the progressive movement focus exclusively on single issues or policies, which makes it challenging to build support for transformational change. If they aspire to assemble a majority coalition, Left political insurgencies must work across issues and speak to different constituencies. One vivid example is the Bernie Sanders presidential campaign, which achieved improbable momentum in 2016 in part because of great grassroots organizing, but also because Sanders offered more than a laundry list of policies. He offered a critique that named the villains: corporations and the billionaires and millionaires who were responsible for and profited from the struggles of working people. The heroes in his story were everyday Americans who could create a better world by working together. And he painted a picture of a society in which wealth is shared rather than hoarded, in which people cooperate rather than compete. This contrasted with Hillary Clinton's campaign, which was long on policy proposals and short on vision.

Vision is not only about the future. It involves telling a story about the past. Hall argued that the Labour Party had lost a sense of history and, as a result, could not provide people a coherent narrative about where the British people came from. Today's battles over school curricula are manifestations of this struggle. The civil rights movement of the 1960s and 1970s achieved many victories, including new scholarship telling a more accurate story of U.S. history, which was then incorporated into many school textbooks. Conservatives fought back—passing laws to exclude entire portions of history from school curriculum—to challenge a history that threatened their distorted view of reality. If they aren't stopped, they will shape not only how we talk about our history, but also how we dream of our future.

Root ideas also involve an articulation of the "we"; who is the imagined community that works together to reach the promised land? Hall argues that the British Labour Party failed in part because it was stuck in an old conception of the working class that ignored the vibrancy of the women's, Black, immigrant, and LGBTQ+ movements. In contrast, Trump's politics mobilized a clear sense of the "we." He invoked a besieged white population that would be swamped by people of color in a "great replacement." His policies—the border wall, clamping down on immigration, attacks on China—flowed from the vision. Progressives must develop a coherent and robust story of "we" that is broad enough to include all oppressed groups (which, in our current winner-take-all economy, is most of the population) without losing the specificity of their histories and needs. A new Left narrative will need to tell a story of the linked fate of this new multiracial "we," not only in opposition to the Right's white nationalism, but as protagonists coming together to shape the future.

Where Does Vision Come From?

Spirituality is a taproot for visions of a new society. *Buen vivir* derives from Indigenous traditions that emphasize the interconnection and sacredness of all life. And every religion has traditions that prioritize social justice. The Black church is a crucial source of power, inspiration, and vision for its members.[6] Quakers have been disproportionately involved in struggles for

> ## Box 2.1: Two Visions:
> ## Black Liberation and *Buen Vivir*
>
> The long tradition of Black radical imagination continues today.[7] Black freedom dreams of exodus during slavery and its aftermath "represented dreams of black self-determination," writes scholar Robin D.G. Kelley.[8] Freedom dreams, shared through stories, art, and theory, provided a north star and connection to pathways for action, such as the Underground Railroad. Decades later, the Black Panther Party's first point in its ten-point program of 1966 declared: "We want freedom."[9] The party put its vision into practice through collective-care initiatives like the Free Breakfast program, which fed thousands of children around the country and represented Black self-determination and community survival.
>
> In the modern movement for abolition, organizer Mariame Kaba has inspired many to dream not only of a world without prisons, but also of an entirely different society. She writes, "It's time for a jailbreak of the imagination in order to make the impossible possible."[10]
>
> Vision also plays an important role in the concept of *buen vivir,* or "living well," which has been growing in South America for the past few decades. *Buen vivir* is an idea, vision, and ethical orientation based on Indigenous practice in the Andes and reflects how collective living can benefit people and the environment. *Buen vivir* puts human and ecological life at the center, rather than economic development and profit.[11]
>
> The ethics of *buen vivir* have been put into practice in several places. Ecuador and Bolivia have included the concept in their constitutions and require the state to seek ecological balance in economic planning. Bolivia has

> adopted the "Mother Earth" law, a multipronged approach to climate change that looks to protect humans and nature.
> Researchers have developed new indicators to measure the health of a country. Rather than prioritizing growth rates or stock market values, *buen vivir* considers measures of good collective living, from democracy to biodiversity. This not only guides a vision of a better world but helps inform strategy by giving us better information about the world as it is.

social justice, including abolition and peace. And liberation theology has inspired people throughout Latin America. *Tikkun Olam*—"repairing the world"—motivates activism in Jewish traditions, while a long progressive lineage of thought and practice in Islam emphasizes the radical equality of all humans and their duty to stand for justice. But spirituality doesn't have to come from organized religion to animate vision. Many people find the sacred through a connection to nature—giving greater meaning to their environmental activism. And even secular philosophies, like socialism or human rights, can be practiced with rituals that foster a sense of purpose and give struggles a transcendent meaning. For many, vision is rooted in ties to community, place, and lineage.

Crucially, vision isn't an escape from reality. It's born of real-world struggle.[12] The best organizers are constantly listening and observing, helping people build imagination out of their daily struggles. Vision is developed by people who are working to change the world in conversation with each other, their ancestors, and their descendants.

North Stars and Freedom Dreams

The term *north star* has many origins, including among enslaved people, who invoked it to signify the path to freedom. As our colleague Reverend Edwin Robinson says, "our enslaved ancestors weren't always clear about what freedom land looked like, but they knew it wasn't where they were, and following the North Star would get them there."[13] Today, proposals like the Green New Deal are north stars that lead us toward the vision of a sustainable planet. With a north star, organizers can develop a long-term strategy and better prepare for hazards that may knock them off course. Political upheaval, natural disasters, and war can force detours on the path toward liberation. It may be necessary to make temporary alliances and compromises along the way.

The vision for a different world doesn't have to be a blueprint describing every detail of an alternative future.[14] In fact, creating a blueprint might not be possible without first developing new capabilities in a more just society. Current society has socialized and trained people in harmful and destructive behaviors that will need to be unlearned. The project of building a more just society should include future generations, so we need to leave space for their input too. This framework is exemplified by the Haudenosaunee principle that you should consider the impact your actions will have seven generations into the future.[15]

The north star and vision don't have to be a complete overhaul of racial capitalism. It might be a smaller goal for a particular campaign. For example, in 2006, Stephanie helped her faculty and librarian union found the Public Higher Education Network of Massachusetts (PHENOM) to push for a dramatic expansion in public higher education across the state, including demands for free and accessible higher education, fully staffed universities and colleges, and democratic control of higher education. These demands were the vision that organizers knew would take years to win. Working with a long-term vision of "free higher ed," PHENOM developed short-term north star demands of free community college, more faculty, smaller class sizes, and adjunct pay increases—and subsequently won notable gains.

We live in a golden age of freedom dreams. Movements have developed new north stars over the last decade, as the system's grip on our imaginations has weakened. Proposals for reparations, a universal basic income, a jobs guarantee, a minimum wage that's a living wage, debt-free college, and universal childcare and home care could be the beginning of a "jailbreak of the imagination."[16] This proliferation of ideas creates both a challenge and an opportunity: how to connect it all into a compelling vision of a new society.

Shared Values Guide Strategy

Many organizers approach vision by engaging people in discussions of values. Shared values can act as connective tissue to bring people and ideas together. For example, in 2008, when Deepak was executive director of Community Change, the organization convened the "Campaign for Community Values," an unusual coalition of grassroots groups working with different constituencies and issues under the frame of "linked fate."[17] They believed that underneath all progressive issues lies a foundational value of interdependence, that we depend on cooperation rather than competition and on community instead of individual effort alone. The campaign connected groups and leaders working on immigration, poverty, and racial justice, and it helped people see themselves in each other through the lens of shared values. The coalition organized a presidential debate in Iowa, during a blizzard, with two thousand grassroots low-income leaders. All the major Democratic candidates for president came and took questions from the audience. Shared values changed how people spoke about their issues and the connections they made with others. Deepak was moved by how white rural farmers connected their own experience of struggle to that of undocumented workers. Both were harmed by the same set of U.S. trade policies. These shared stories forged a new sense of "we."

Conversations about values can be an organizing tool. People who might not agree on specific policy, or who identify with particular political labels, may find common ground on values, such as solidarity or democracy. This requires discussion and education, since not everyone shares the same understanding of these concepts, and values can mean different things over time and place. Once you have agreement on values, you can avoid empty labels and assumptions and have richer discussions and evaluations of future and current societies and institutions.

During the pandemic, nursing home workers were made to work on the front lines with patients, often with little or no protective equipment. Rob

Baril, president of Service Employees International Union (SEIU) 1199NE, a union that represents nursing home workers in Connecticut and Rhode Island, explains how his members' rage, fear, and frustration shifted the union's focus. "We moved from demanding what we could win to what we deserved," he said. Most of the union's members are Black and Brown women, a workforce without much traditional power. Nevertheless, they made a list of twelve bold demands, including "racial and economic justice for all workers" and "a clear, specific plan to address the racial disparities in care for Black and Brown residents that COVID-19 has exposed."[18] With these long-term demands in place, the union bargained over shorter-term demands, such as safety equipment, wage increases, and paid sick days. The union made significant gains in its contract but has not abandoned its long-term vision of racial and economic justice. Baril and 1199NE members know that winning a strong contract is vital but is only one step toward their vision for society.

Making Space to Dream: The Power of Vision

Vision can sustain people's hope during difficult times in multiple ways. *Hope can motivate people to act.* One of Stephanie's former students, Zack Exley, was hired and trained by a union that discouraged organizers from discussing long-term goals or strategy with workers. Exley broke from the orthodoxy and found that workers were more interested in taking risks to unionize when they saw their fight as part of something larger. Exley went on to put these ideas into practice when he and his colleague Becky Bond worked for Bernie Sanders's 2016 presidential campaign. They found tens of thousands of people waiting to be asked to do something big, people who were excited and motivated by the thought of transformational change, not small steps and small ideas. "You won't get a revolution if you don't ask for one," Exley and Bond write.[19]

Vision can also *develop skills and capacities that prepare organizers for an alternative world.* Activists use the term *prefigurative politics* to describe the practice of living the values and types of relationships they want to see in the future. Stephanie saw an element of prefigurative politics in the New York

State campaign to raise wages for home-care workers in 2022. She co-wrote a report for the campaign and participated in a day of lobbying and protesting at the state Capitol in Albany. Many members of the campaign are people with disabilities who are wheelchair users, vision-impaired, or otherwise need care. The activists spent weeks in Albany pressuring the state legislature to pass a higher wage for home-care workers. "We had people coming from all over the state who needed care just to be living with us at the hotel, but even just to be in the Capitol they needed support to use the bathroom. We had to help people eat," Ilana Berger, co-director of New York Caring Majority, told Stephanie afterward, reflecting on what she had experienced. The campaign hired aides and a driver with an accessible van. "We had members say things like, 'this is the first time in sixteen months that I've gotten three meals a day, that I've been able to take a shower when I needed to in the morning, that I've been able to sleep in a bed.' So, we literally were doing the prefigurative thing by providing care and support. By showing how well people could thrive if they actually had the care they need."[20] The campaign's organizing prefigured its vision by centering the needs of both people with disabilities and low-wage home-care workers.

Third, *vision keeps leaders and organizers fresh, inspiring, and inspired.* It's easy for organizers and leaders to focus solely on immediate tasks since most are urgent and important. This is understandable. But without taking time to dream big, their goals will become more and more narrow, less and less liberatory. Elected leaders, whether on the city council or in union office, may come in with lofty goals but quickly get sucked into figuring out budgets, debating small policy changes, or defending prior gains. Union leaders will see only as far as the next contract unless they make time and space for discussing long-term vision and strategy. Overworked organizers will forget the connection between their day-to-day work and the larger freedom struggle.

Fourth, *vision reminds us of our potential—not just as individuals, but collectively, as humanity.* In a paper on transformative organizing, Steve Williams argues that developing human capacity is vital to any liberation or justice movement. This should come with the "acknowledgement that in addition to creating conditions of war, poverty, and climate catastrophe, the dominant systems stunt the full development of all people," Williams writes. The system limits us, and then we believe we're limited. Vision is a reminder that growth is possible.[21]

Naming the Moment: The Conjuncture

As important as it is, a bold vision alone is insufficient to achieve social change. Movements need a shared analysis of the world as it is and a bridge to get to the world as it could be. Hall pointed to the importance of **conjunctural analysis**—understanding the actual, specific, and concrete trends in different spheres of society, including politics, culture, and economy, that together create the current situation (the "historical conjuncture"). These currents might contradict one another and give rise to new opportunities; together, they create a terrain of struggle. For example, while we've lived under a system of racial capitalism for centuries, the dominant ideas, economic arrangements, and political structures have changed. A system of formal democracy where most people have a vote is different from a system where whole categories of people are excluded by race or gender. A slave owner is different from a factory boss or a private equity fund. Even when a long-term vision like Black liberation is constant, different historical situations demand different strategies. Conjunctural analysis is a tool that helps us identify openings for change and answer the question of under what conditions certain strategies might succeed. As Dolly Parton put it, "We cannot direct the wind, but we can adjust the sails."[22]

There are times when a dominant set of ideas is questioned because it no longer represents people's experiences. Thatcherism was a political and ideological project to seize the opportunity during a rupture in the 1970s when the Labour Party's ideas seemed to have failed. The country was in crisis, facing economic slowdown and rising prices. Unions launched big strikes but failed to win gains for members.

The 2008 financial crisis created another rupture, this time a crisis of legitimacy for racial neoliberalism. The establishment in both political parties was discredited. The shock of the crisis created an opening for a new popular morality about the economy. The racial neoliberal paradigm came under attack from two sides. The Right seized the moment: the Tea Party emerged to blame Obama, big government, unions, and people of color. The Left, disoriented or waiting to follow Obama's lead, was slow to fight back. But eventually Occupy Wall Street, the Fight for $15 and a Union, and Sanders's campaign were all responses to this opening.

Your choices depend on your analysis of the conjuncture. For example, in 2020 some Left groups thought Trump and Biden were similar enough in their support of neoliberal policies that members of the Left should devote themselves to movement work outside of elections. But the vast majority of Leftists, us included, believed Trump—and the white supremacist, authoritarian movement he represented—posed existential threats to underdog movements and demanded that the Left join a broad electoral alliance with other forces.

There's no simple template for analyzing the historical situation. We've created a conjunctural analysis worksheet for our students (Tool 3), which requires a close study of the ways in which overdogs and underdogs use ideological, economic, political, and military networks to maintain power; alliances and tensions within the ruling forces; cracks in the ideological narrative; forms of power available to liberation movements; strategies available to movements based on those forms of power; and openings for new narratives or a new common sense to explain the crisis. There are other tools such as LeftRoots' Toolkit for Liberatory Strategy, SCOPE's Power Analysis (Tool 33), and Bill Moyers's Movement Action Plan (MAP).[23]

Unlike pragmatists, practical radicals will not settle for the small reforms that can be won by taking current power relationships as given. But unlike utopians, practical radicals make strategic alliances with people and groups with differing views. Lenin argued against dogmatic short-term approaches—organizers must be flexible in their tactics while also firm in their commitment to the north star. Crucially, he argued, good leaders will know when they have to accept a compromise, not because they sold out, but because the compromise was "forced upon them by the necessity of the objective conditions and the balance of forces."[24] In other words, unless you have enough power and the conditions are right, you will have to make compromises.

Conjunctural analysis leads us away from formulaic strategies—everything depends on context. Over the centuries, overdogs and underdogs have developed methods and frameworks—bridges—to help them move from the world as it is to the world as it could be. Those bridges are what we call strategy models. We turn next to building blocks of strategy and seeing how the strategy models relate to vision and conjuncture. Treated separately, these three elements clash in harsh dissonance. When skillfully harmonized, they power transformational social change.

Tools

To apply the concepts in this chapter, see the Tools section for the following:

Tool 1 Shared Values
Tool 2 Prompt: Envisioning a Future World
Tool 3 Conjunctural Analysis

3

How Underdogs Win: Strategy Fundamentals

Practical radicals know that ideas alone won't change the world. A vision of the future and an analysis of the present are necessary, but not sufficient, for transformational change. Strategy is the bridge. There are many definitions of *strategy*. For our purposes, we mean a plan to achieve a goal, under conditions of uncertainty, with limited resources, facing opposition.

This definition assumes that you have a goal in the first place. This is why vision is so essential—strategy without vision is a bridge to nowhere. The definition also assumes that you don't have complete control of the situation.

Unpredictability and the actions of other actors, including your opponents, matter. Military historian Lawrence Freedman says that strategy is about getting more out of a situation than might be expected given the starting balance of power. Strategy "is the art of creating power."[1]

Regardless of whether it's being used in business, politics, war, or for social change, strategy has five common elements:

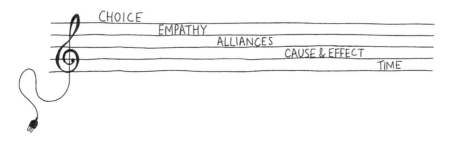

Choice: Strategy involves choosing to use scarce resources—people, time, and money—in a specific way. Every strategy involves a choice *not* to do something else.

Empathy: Strategy depends on the ability to understand and share the feelings of another. When we use this term in class, some of our students find it jarring. You don't have to agree with someone to empathize with them. Strategy does require imagining how others might respond to particular actions, assessing individuals and groups as potential opponents or allies, and understanding their motivations. Women, people of color, and other oppressed groups often develop a strong intuition for understanding others, including their oppressors.[2]

Alliances: All strategy involves forming temporary or lasting coalitions between individuals, groups, or countries. A crucial element of strategy is exploiting divisions within the opponent's coalition and weakening the alliances that hold them together. Underdogs often focus on building unity among oppressed people, but creating wedges among overdogs can be decisive.

Cause and Effect: As we'll explore, all strategy comes down to a theory of cause and effect—that Action A will produce Outcome B, directly or indirectly.

Time: The strategy models in this book work on different time horizons.

Some strategies unfold over decades, like abolition and the campaign to install racial neoliberalism. Others aim to seize a moment. Good strategists are wizards of time—they may seek to compress time to force a confrontation when underdogs are at their strongest. Alternatively, in slower periods they may engage in "spadework," developing grassroots leaders for opportunities in the future.

Some common polarities define a strategy, as follows:

Attrition or annihilation? Does a strategy aim to get the opponent to the bargaining table for a negotiated solution, or does it seek to attain total power, or even to destroy the opponent? For example, a labor union doesn't want to destroy the opponent (the employer), because in our current system that would also destroy jobs. However, employers often seek to destroy unions, viewing them as an obstacle to maximum profits.

Top-down or bottom-up? U.S. history gives the credit for great strategies to individuals, often (because we live in a racist and sexist society), a singular white man. But in fact, strategy is often the product of group deliberation. It may be decided through a top-down process, a democratic one that engages many people in a community, or a combination of the two.

Force or guile? Machiavelli famously contrasted the approach of the lion—relying on overwhelming strength and favoring direct attack—to that of the fox, who favors deception and surprise.

> Since a ruler . . . needs to know how to make good use of beastly qualities, he should take as his models among the animals both

the fox and the lion, for the lion does not know how to avoid traps, and the fox is easily overpowered by the wolves. So you must be a fox when it comes to suspecting a trap, and a lion when it comes to making the wolves turn tail. Those who simply act like a lion all the time do not understand their business.[3]

Variants of this polarity include an orientation to compulsion or persuasion, strength or smarts, courage or imagination, and direct or indirect means. In general, overdogs tend to favor force, while underdogs specialize in guile, but both elements are present in many strategies.

Detailed plans or improvisation? All strategies involve some premeditation and calculation. Some strategies map out a campaign from beginning to end, including the sequencing of particular tactics. Others begin with an analysis of the balance and forms of power and respond in a more free-flowing way.

Some military scholars have argued that it's not possible to develop strategy because "no plan survives contact with the enemy," as Prussian general Helmuth von Moltke famously said.[4] Some scholars and generals have continued to be skeptical of strategy. "Because strategy is necessary, however, does not mean that it is possible," writes war scholar Richard K. Betts.[5] Yet military leaders continue to strategize. To address the challenge of changing conditions, the U.S. Army developed a concept called Commander's Intent (CI), which is the idea of sharing the general goal of a mission, or what success would look like. The CI is the outcome, the vision. It's up to those on the ground to determine the specific maneuvers to get to the outcome, depending on the conditions. This approach allows subordinates to carry out the vision of a top general. In social justice work, such hierarchies are less common, but the CI idea allows us to see a relationship between the end goal and strategy. The cross-organizational Fight for $15 and a Union campaign is an example of how campaigns from various cities found different ways, based on local context and their opponent's response, to achieve the vision of a $15 minimum wage.

We believe the best strategy for underdogs unfolds in a *process*, developed in struggle by people most-impacted and close to the ground and revised as conditions change and assumptions are tested. This contrasts with the "master plan" approach to strategy, which some on the Left have wrongly attributed to the Right and tried to copy.[6]

Strategies and Tactics

A famous dictum attributed to Sun Tzu, the famous Chinese military strategist is "Strategy without tactics is the slowest route to victory. Tactics without strategy is the noise before defeat."[7] Fundamentally, strategy involves identifying your group's form of power (Chapter 4) and then finding ways to concentrate it to achieve your goals. Tactics are activities that mobilize a type of power, directed at a target, and intended to achieve a specific objective.[8]

Midwest Academy, a national training institute, developed the Strategy Chart, which helps organizers choose appropriate tactics, but only after clarifying long-term goals and analyzing organizational resources, opponents, allies, and targets.[9] This is in contrast to the process activists often take—choosing tactics, rather than developing them based on the conjuncture and power available.

The brilliant Birmingham campaign to end segregation illustrates the difference between strategy and tactics. In 1963 Rev. Wyatt Tee Walker, executive director of the Southern Christian Leadership Conference (SCLC) and a close aide to Dr. Martin Luther King Jr., and his colleagues created Project Confrontation (Project C), which aimed to end segregation in one of the most racist cities in the country.

Walker explained the core of Project C's strategy: "I knew that two things would move Birmingham: Mess with the money and make it inconvenient for the white community. That was the way to make change come."[10] Walker's strategy depended on using people power to disrupt the routines of everyday life and the profitability of segregation. His analysis showed four distinct factions in the white power structure—businessmen and industrialists, political elites (including the notorious Sheriff Bull Connor), white extremist groups like the Ku Klux Klan, and the white public (there was considerable overlap among these groups). He concluded that if you could break the business faction away from the rest through a sustained boycott of white businesses, segregation could fall. Walker expressed the strategy as a matter of cold math:

> We know that in most businesses 6 percent is the margin of profit. Black folks made up 35–40 percent of the consumer population [in Birmingham]. So all we felt we had to do was get a 50 percent response from the black community. We didn't think that all blacks would go along with it.[11]

The strategy of dividing the white power structure depended on tactics such as a boycott and demonstrations that disrupted business in downtown.

Most accounts of the Birmingham campaign focus on the dramatic moments. For example, thousands of children and young people were trained in civil disobedience to lead the Children's Crusade. In response, police sprayed these children with powerful water hoses, hit them with batons, menaced them with police dogs, and jailed them.

The dramatic tactics built on a foundation of years of unheralded organizing by groups like the Alabama Christian Movement for Human Rights, led by Rev. Fred Shuttlesworth. The tactics succeeded because they grew out of a careful analysis of the situation. Walker carefully scoped out Birmingham, even down to details like how many stools, tables, and chairs were in downtown stores, so that he knew how many protestors it would take to have an impact—and developed a strategy that went right to the heart of the opponent's vulnerability. He developed an "arc of escalation"—phases of the campaign that would intensify, leading to a crescendo and forcing a crisis that would garner national attention and force a rupture in the overdog coalition. Without the tactics, the strategy would have been a dead letter. Without the underlying strategy, the tactics would not have been so precisely calculated.

Walker was clear-eyed and specific in his calculus of how the struggle would be won and had no illusions that mass demonstrations and the boycott would change hearts and minds:

> The [white] people there would never have talked to us were it not for the fact that our movement was so powerful that the city

ground to a screeching halt, there was no way they could operate business. They couldn't open up because the movement was so powerful. They didn't talk to us on a moral ground. They wanted to do business. And they had to solve the problem of how they gonna do business and stop the demonstrations.[12]

Cause and Effect

Walker's theory was that Action A (a disciplined boycott together with dramatic noncooperation with segregation) would lead to Outcome B (cracking the opposition coalition). Viewed this way, strategy is a series of logical propositions and a process of developing and testing hypotheses.

At first glance, cause and effect may seem simple: A causes B. Many of the frameworks and tools we explore in this book, such as Silicon Valley's "lean startup," assume that if you look hard enough, you'll find this simple relationship. **Reverse engineering** is a method that demands that you examine what conditions are necessary to achieve a desired outcome and what conditions would be nice to have. By rigorously paring down the list, a group can identify the essential success factors (Tool 4). Thinking this way is useful because it forces teams to consider choices. What are we *not* going to do so we can pour all our resources into the strategy we think will win?

Yotam Marom, a core Occupy Wall Street activist, argues that Left groups often fail at strategy because they are unwilling to have hard, rigorous conversations and make difficult choices.[13] He quotes Richard Rumelt, a business theorist, who wrote:

> Having conflicting goals, dedicating resources to unconnected targets, and accommodating incompatible interests are the luxuries of the rich and powerful, but they make for bad strategy. Despite this, most organizations will not create focused strategies. Instead, they will generate laundry lists of desirable outcomes and, at the same time, ignore the need for genuine competence in coordinating and focusing their resources. Good strategy requires leaders who are willing and able to say no to a wide variety of actions and interests. Strategy is at least as

much about what an organization does not do as it is about what it does.[14]

There are, however, more holistic approaches to causation as well. Paradigms as diverse as systems theory, cybernetics, complexity and chaos theory, and the Buddhist idea of interdependent origination deny that you can separate elements of a complex system. Everything affects everything else, so changes in any one part of a complex system will have (often unpredictable) effects on the rest of the system. Mathematician and meteorologist Edward Norton Lorenz described the "butterfly effect"—how a small perturbation (like a butterfly flapping its wings) could shape the timing and path of a tornado weeks later.[15] adrienne maree brown developed an influential framework called "emergent strategy" that sees systems as interdependent, complex, and fractal (meaning that the same patterns recur at small and large levels). brown invites activists to consider how even small shifts at a local level can reverberate and produce systemic change.[16] Theory U, developed by Otto Scharmer and others in business schools, invites practitioners to let go of habitual patterns of understanding the world, take in the whole field of experience with fresh eyes, and find new ways of acting that can disrupt dysfunctional systems.[17] These approaches are important because they encourage us to look at the whole system, and at all the actors and interactions that sustain and threaten it.

brown describes an experience familiar to many people involved in progressive strategy:

> Creating more possibilities is my favorite part of emergent strategy—this is where we shape tomorrow towards abundance. Creating more possibilities counters the very foundational assumptions of strategy. The word "strategy" is a military term which means *a* plan of action towards *a* goal. . . . Reducing the wild and wonderful world into one thing that we can grasp, handle, hold onto, and advance. . . . I have been in countless meetings where there was a moment of creative abundance and energy, and then someone said we need to pick one thing to get

behind, or a three- or five- or a ten-point plan. What came next was sometimes very compelling and visionary. Other times—often times—it was reductionist, agreeing on the lowest common denominator, the least exciting thing, because it was the only place there was unity.[18]

In our class, we ask our students whether Marom's or brown's approach resonates more with them. Usually, students are equally divided. And we ask them to reflect on their own gifts: are they inclined toward the linear or the holistic approach to strategy? Our view is that both ways of looking at the world are essential because most winning strategies involve a holistic view and linear logic. Practicing less-familiar approaches can expand your repertoire and stretch your strategic imagination.

Box 3.1 Lineages of Strategy from Below

Most of the famous texts on strategy are written for overdogs. But there are long lineages of underdog strategy. Some have been passed down orally, while others have been documented in training manuals and guides for activists, like Midwest Academy's *Organizing for Social Change*. Walker drew upon a "trickster" tradition of strategy that has been passed down orally in the Black community—Br'er Rabbit was a mythical figure who outsmarted stronger foes. Coyote is a similar character in Indigenous cultures. These diverse traditions, spanning constituencies, eras, and ideologies, are underdogs' collective inheritance.

The United States has a rich tradition of community organizing. Faith-based groups were some of the first to fight to abolish slavery. Today's community- and faith-based organizations work on issues ranging from housing to the environment, to immigrant rights and racial justice. Labor unions also have a long and rich history. We draw upon all of these traditions, as well as upon the lineage of nonviolent social

> movements, which have played a large role in U.S. politics. Some movement practitioners adhere to nonviolence on principle, grounded in either religious or moral tradition, or in a view that good ends cannot justify violent means. Others adopt nonviolence based on the belief that, if it comes to violence, the underdogs simply don't have the firepower of the overdogs.
>
> Knowledge of these different lineages will help ensure that organizers don't talk past each other. Practitioners may use the same words—*organizing* or *power*, for example—but have totally different definitions for them. What looks like success in one tradition may be a failure in another. For example, community organizing tends to emphasize scripted actions, with a clear sense of how many people will show up and who will say and do what. The thinking is that you're more likely to get a target to do what you want if people are acting in a disciplined way. Some of the more disruptive traditions favor wildness and unpredictability, under the theory that overdogs will be unnerved by the threat of social disorder and make concessions to avoid it.

The Relationship Between Vision, Conjuncture, and Strategy

The process of combining a bold vision, an analysis of the current situation, and rigorous strategy is neither sequential nor mechanical. All three elements influence each other simultaneously. In a given conjuncture, specific horizons of vision open up, like the Green New Deal as a response to climate change. Vision also shapes how we understand a conjuncture, like how the dream of Black liberation inspired hundreds of thousands of enslaved people to view the Civil War as an opportunity.

Your vision of the future also affects your strategies and tactics. For example, many believe that we must be democratic in our organizations today if we want to build a democratic tomorrow, and that we must build multiracial movements now to achieve a multiracial future. However, an ecological perspective of movements suggests it could be possible to have some organizations with different structures in the same movement, such as organizations of largely white people within a larger multiracial movement, or hierarchical institutions (like universities) within a larger democracy movement.

Your strategies may alter your vision—successful ones may expand your vision of what is possible. Many people report that participating in actions such as strikes or marches changes their political consciousness. Workers who go on strike, or activists in civil rights protests, deepen their commitment to their cause and to its values, such as solidarity and justice. This might happen if a strike wins and they see the power of collective action. Or if a protest fails, participants may decide they need to deepen their political commitment.[19] Large protests and strikes can also shift public opinion in support of the movements.[20]

We've discussed how strategy is limited without vision. Vision without strategy is equally a dead end. The moral vision of the Black freedom movement was essential, but without strategists like Walker, who soberly assessed power relationships and developed inventive strategies and tactics, the vision would not have been realized.

Finally, strategy must be embedded in an analysis of the real-world situation (the conjuncture). Strategy is a process that requires adapting to the context, just as a jazz musician improvising must listen carefully to the music others are playing around them. As organizer Kevin Simowitz says, "Strategy happens in motion, not when Smart People write Strategy Memos."[21] Walker's strategy derived from his sophisticated analysis of the potential fissures in the white power structure in Birmingham, which appeared to most observers to be a monolith, and also from his analysis of the failure of a recent campaign in Albany, Georgia, to break segregation. The German Communist Party's failure to see fascism as a dire and unique threat led to the disastrous decision to target rather than ally with the Social Democrats (Chapter 2). It was based on a poor analysis, and the resulting decision in turn shaped how the conjuncture unfolded.

Practical radicals work at the intersection of vision, conjuncture, and strategy. As Nina Simone said about jazz, it's "not just music, it's a way of life, it's a way of being, a way of thinking."[22] Thinking across these three dimensions simultaneously has important implications. First, *it should motivate organizers to consider their tendencies, as both individuals and groups.* Some organizers lean toward bold vision, others toward brass-tacks strategy, and still others toward analyzing the landscape. You need all three, in constant dialogue and balance, to make progress. Any good strategy will need to be revised and adjusted based on the situation, while the vision anchors the long-term plan. When Deepak came to organizing, the field was steeped in pragmatism—it was long on strategy, but short on vision. Organizer Gary Delgado wrote an article in 1998 called "The Last Stop Sign" that challenged colleagues to ask the question: "Power for whom and to do what?" He pushed the field to prioritize vision and racial justice.[23] Today, bold visions for transformational change are animating organizers. But in our experience, strategic muscles have atrophied. The world needs organizers who are both righteous and bold in vision and rigorous and imaginative about strategy.

Second, this understanding *should also inspire you to take a longer view.* brown teaches us that organizing is like time travel: "it is a way of saying we are going to put our hands directly on the future." At the same time, she says, organizing allows you to travel back in time as you learn from your ancestors.[24] Similarly, we think visioning is a project that builds from the past to travel to the future.

brown's emphasis on time is telling. Our dominant culture prioritizes short-term thinking. Sometimes you need to focus on the tasks in front of you, but that can disconnect you from the deep past and the far future and hinder social change. Black and Indigenous visionaries stretched their imaginations across many generations, learning from their ancestors and acting to nurture the future of descendants they would never know. We have to cultivate that kind of spaciousness if we want to build transformative visions and effective strategies.

Finally, the framework we propose is liberating because *it emphasizes the importance of the choices that organizers make.* Underdogs inherit conditions and circumstances that they didn't choose or create. But how they assess the situation, the visions they set their compass to, and the strategies they develop are up to them. The distance between the world as it is and the world as it could be is the space where movements make history.

Tools
Tool 4 Reverse Engineering
Tool 5 Prompt: Strategy Fundamentals
Tool 6 Resources: Strategy Toolkits and Training Organizations
Tool 14 Resource: Holistic Strategy Development
Tool 29 Lean Startup for Social Change
Tool 34 Strategy Chart

4

The Change Ensemble: Forms of Power

In the 2000s, Deepak frequently traveled to Arizona to support immigrant rights activists facing a powerful nativist movement. Fifteen armed far-Right activists crashed one of their gatherings in Tucson and threatened to perform "citizens arrests" and to call Customs and Border Patrol. Some of the immigrant leaders at the meeting were undocumented. Playing for time, Deepak and a few others got the armed white guys outside and asked them questions. It turned out that a few of them were part of law enforcement agencies and had close ties to Republican lawmakers. They believed Arizona was being "invaded" and that they were heroes, not terrorist vigilantes. Undocumented movement colleagues were able to leave through a back entrance while the militia members were distracted. The Right-wing activists relied on multiple forms of power to break up the meeting: their numbers, physical force, the power of the state, and a popular ideology that legitimized the persecution of immigrants. Later, activists debriefed and gained insight from the experience about how different parts of the state's white power structure were connected.

To win transformational change, organizers must study overdogs to learn how they gained power and what they do to maintain it. But it's not enough to understand how to react to power from above. Organizers and movement builders must also assess and build their own power. Some activists have an aversion to power, viewing it as inevitably corrupting. Many people's experience with power is abusive, so a distaste for it is understandable. But power exists, and to not name or fight for it means ceding it to the overdogs. As Dr. Martin Luther King Jr. famously put it, "What is needed is a realization that power without love is reckless and abusive and that love without power is sentimental and anemic. Power at its best is love implementing the demands of justice. Justice at its best is love correcting everything that stands against love."[1] The truth alone will not set us free.

Choosing the Right Instrument

Political theorists have debated power for centuries. Some focus on levels of power, others on sources (Box 4.1). In our movement work, we've been struck by the lack of clarity and agreement on what power even means. After teaching organizers about power for several years, we found combining the work of sociologists Michael Mann, Erik Olin Wright, and Beverly Silver to be most useful.[2]

Part of the confusion is that power takes many different forms; we believe that it's useful to look at these forms separately. We suggest a framework of six forms of power: ideological, political, economic, military, solidarity, and disruption. These are not neatly divided, and often overlap.[3] For example, corporations in the United States have relied on political power to enhance their economic power. They've rigged trade rules so they can easily move jobs or investments across borders, while workers face high barriers (legal and financial) to moving between countries. And when workers tried to organize a union at the Amazon warehouse in Bessemer, Alabama, workers and the union had to follow strict regulations, while Amazon flagrantly broke the law.

The War of Ideas: Ideological Power

We use *ideology* to refer to how people make sense of the world—the system of values, beliefs, and norms that shape how people make meaning, from explicitly ideological beliefs to "common sense" to unexamined habits of thought. Ideological power is the ability to affect ideology. Such power can be exercised subtly. The Italian theorist Antonio Gramsci described how those in power could run society in a way that made underdogs believe it was in their best interest to participate in the system. He used the term *hegemony* to describe the political and cultural domination of one group over another through norms and common sense. In this way, rulers maintain power through (manufactured) consent of the population.[4]

Organized religion, such as the Catholic Church, has been a key source of ideological power over the course of centuries. Ideological power can also be expressed as dominant political perspectives, like nationalism, liberalism, or socialism.

It isn't enough to come up with ideas: you need to spread them as well. You can use tools such as books, newspapers, television, social media, and public speaking to spread your ideas and amass ideological power. Overdogs have a definite upper hand here; they're more likely to control large institutions that affect our beliefs, from Fox News to radio stations and social media networks. We swim every day in an ocean of overdog ideas that justify existing systems and divert our attention away from injustice. As literary critic Terry Eagleton puts it, "The most efficient oppressor is the one who persuades his underlings to love, desire and identify with his power."[5]

But underdogs can still influence culture, education, and common sense. They can develop ideological power by finding fissures in the common sense and bringing them to the fore. An entire country is not ideologically consistent. Even individuals may not be consistent in their beliefs. For example, many Americans never understood the government's role in Medicare and the cost that it entailed—a confusion nicely illustrated by a constituent's angry letter to Representative Pat Schroeder urging her to "keep the government's hands off my Medicare."[6] Many on the Right hate bankers and Wall Streeters even as they vote for Wall Street's puppet politicians. And, as Gramsci argued, some workers may have a consciousness that reflects their connection with fellow workers based on their lived experiences, but also believe in hegemonic ideas uncritically. Underdogs can lift up these contradictions and provide alternative explanations to make sense of reality.

Underdogs do have one essential advantage: a vision of liberation, justice, and equality is simply more attractive than anything overdogs can honestly offer. Many on the Right understand this; they spend a lot of effort making sure their vision is never expressed honestly. Underdogs can undermine the legitimacy of the status quo by spreading their vision, providing alternative explanations about how the world works, and exposing the lies or myths overdogs tell. This ideological work lays the groundwork to build and use other forms of power.

The Sioux Tribe of Standing Rock demonstrates the power of ideology. Beginning in 2016, they worked with allies to defend their land against the Dakota Access Pipeline. They called themselves Water Protectors to show they were not just opposing the pipeline; they were fighting for life, people, and the planet. The simple term *Water Protectors* and courageous organizing allowed for the history of Indigenous people as stewards of the land to be told. And the movement's simple but powerful slogan, "Water Is Life," helped shift the narrative from a story of oppression to a story of liberation.[7]

The marriage equality movement challenged and changed ideology as well. Only 27 percent of Americans supported same-sex marriage in 1996; by 2022, 71 percent did.[8] Winning marriage equality required a variety of ideological strategies, such as refraining from relying only on a rights-based framework that could reinforce an "us versus them" mentality.[9] Instead, the idea that "love is love" invoked shared values of commitment, care, and freedom that appealed to a wide base and allowed the space for the common sense to shift.

Winning by Governing: Political Power

Political power is what many people mean by the term *power*. It includes the power to punish and discipline (through laws, courts, and police), to set the rules of the game, and to provide (or withhold) many goods and services—from public education and roads to Social Security.[10]

The most obvious way to gain political power is to run for office and win. Overdogs have the advantage here as well, particularly in the United States where money plays such a crucial role in elections, and the rules of the electoral game have often excluded or debilitated underdogs. There are many examples of underdogs winning elections, but there are fewer examples of underdogs obtaining real governing power in U.S. cities or states. There are some, however, such as the so-called sewer socialists who took control of dozens of cities in the early 1900s, most notably in Milwaukee, Wisconsin, where Emil Seidel was elected as the first socialist mayor in the United States in 1910, along with a number of socialists in other city positions.[11] More recently, Harold Washington built a progressive multiracial coalition to govern Chicago as its first Black mayor from 1983 to 1987. Since then, progressives have won majorities in a few cities for limited periods. We can also see that periods of major social reform were made possible in part by the presence of organized Leftists in government who could influence ideologically diverse coalitions, such as the Left wing of the New Deal coalition.

Another source of political power comes through gains won by prior struggles that set the rules of the game—"frozen power."[12] For example, when worker movements were strong, they won the 1935 National Labor Relations Act (NLRA), which recognized workers' right to form unions. Similarly, the civil rights movement won the Voting Rights Act of 1965. Both acts have been attacked and weakened, yet they continue to affect the rules of the game decades after passage.

Of course, laws on the books can be poorly enforced, and contracts can be broken, so political power requires a state strong enough to enforce laws as well as social movements that demand enforcement.

Capital and Labor: Economic Power

Economic power comes primarily through controlling the production of goods and services, though it is also reflected in wealth and access to resources. Bosses usually have far more economic power than do workers. When workers strike, they face the possibility of losing their job and means of survival. Even a temporary loss of income can be disastrous, given that workers usually start with few resources, particularly in a country with a limited safety net. Employers can more likely afford to wait out a strike.

Even though underdogs are vastly disadvantaged, they do have some economic power. First, while they may not own the factory, most do own their labor and can withhold it. Sometimes this can be done with very few people. For example, a worker who's the only person in the company who knows how to use the bookkeeping software has a decent amount of power. If a small group of workers control which ships get unloaded at a port, they have more power. The International Longshore Workers Union (ILWU) controls twenty-nine ports on the west coast of the United States, and the fourteen thousand workers handle about $1 trillion worth of goods per year. The ILWU called a nine-month slowdown in 2014–2015, which was estimated to have cost the economy $2 billion per day, and helped the union maintain health benefits and job security.[13] And small numbers of workers can multiply their power with alliances. In 2013, thirty workers at a Walmart warehouse outside of Chicago walked off the job to protest unfair working conditions. Working with the Warehouse Workers for Justice, backed by the United Electrical Workers, the workers joined with six hundred community and labor allies to shut down the facility for a day, keeping goods from entering or leaving, costing the company about $8 million.[14]

Underdogs can also use their economic power as consumers or shareholders. Boycotts are difficult to pull off in today's complex global economy, but they can have an impact, particularly when highly organized and strategic, as in the case of the legendary grape boycott organized by the United Farm Workers.[15]

Finally, underdogs can build alternative institutions that make it more difficult for private investors to make money. This includes making and keeping schools, libraries, transit systems, utilities, or even entire industries publicly owned rather than for private profit. It also includes credit unions, worker and consumer cooperatives, communal housing, and collective farms.

Guns and Fear: Military and Police Power

Military power rests on the direct use or threat of violence. Mann argues that militaries should be considered separate from states because historically they have been separately organized and operate under different rules than the rest of society. Around the world, military generals have broken from political leaders to lead coups or take independent action. We saw how important the distinction between military and political power can be during Donald Trump's attempted coup after losing the 2020 election. The military, including General Mark Milley, chairman of the Joint Chiefs of Staff, had planned to disobey the president if he tried to use them to maintain power.

Mann also distinguishes police from military power, asserting that police forces answer to civilian leaders rather than military generals. It's true that most military and police operations we discuss here have been under the direction of political leaders, but while this is mostly true in the United States, it's not always clear in other countries. And even in the United States, there are examples of military, security agencies, and police disregarding procedures and acting on their own accord. A growing segment of the U.S. police has militarized. In some cases, the chief of police and police unions are powerful enough to punish elected officials who try to curtail police power. In this book, when we talk about military power from above, we include the police, border patrol, National Guard, FBI, CIA, and the National Security Agency (NSA).

The military and police have repeatedly propped up the interests of the powerful. Some of the most visible examples include using the military to displace and commit genocide against Indigenous people, the use of military and police to crush strikes and break unions, using the National Guard to break up civil rights and student protests, and the FBI's COINTELPRO program.[16]

The United States has also deployed military force in support of underdogs, such as when the federal government sent in the National Guard and active-duty military to escort the Little Rock Nine to attend their first day in a desegregated school in 1957. These are important exceptions, and they are responses both to mass movements and to conflicts between federal and state governments.

There have also been instances in which underdogs used military power directly. In the United States, the idea that underdogs could use military power against the most powerful military in the world seems far-fetched at best, particularly if we consider police, border guards, and new forms of technological repression in the overdogs' arsenal. But military power has played a role in underdog liberation struggles in other countries, whether in the form of a formal rebel army like in Zimbabwe, the use of guerilla tactics in several countries, or Chileans creating their own homemade shields and weapons to fight police repression in 2019. However, social-movement scholars Erica Chenoweth and Maria Stephan found that of 627 liberation struggles that took place between 1900 and 2019, those that used nonviolent methods such as civil disobedience, voting, general strikes, and other mass action were twice as likely to succeed than those that used armed resistance.[17]

Unity Is Strength: Solidarity Power

The power to work together is at the heart of each source of power we've discussed so far. Mann takes solidarity power for granted in his framework; he argues that power of any kind occurs only through organizing with others. But we include solidarity power separately in part because it's one of the most important forms of power for underdogs—and one they can deliberately and measurably grow over time.

By solidarity power we mean the ability to form associations, networks, and alliances that advance one's interests. People often associate organizing with underdogs, but overdogs build solidarity power too (Chapter 5).

Underdogs rely heavily on solidarity power because they're at a disadvantage when they act on their own. For example, a boss has more power than any one worker. It's easy to fire a worker who complains. But a boss will likely think twice before firing all the workers at once. Or think how one tenant threatening to withhold rent until a boiler is fixed will have less power than all the tenants united. This is the power of solidarity.

Usually, solidarity power grows with greater numbers (the share of workers in a workplace, for example), but it's not only the number of people—their level of participation also matters, as does the depth of the bonds between them. And of course, people aren't just numbers; individual talents, interests, knowledge, and ideas should be valued, developed, and used to advance the struggle.

Underdogs have access to resources that can help build solidarity power. Meeting spaces are invaluable, particularly in environments with little access to public space. Free childcare and food make it easier for people to attend events. With a budget, groups can hire organizers and reach more people. Internal democracy can improve membership participation and organizational functioning, some argue, by reducing the potential for group-shattering divisions.[18]

There is a dark side to solidarity power. It has been used by groups of underdogs to exclude other underdogs, such as labor unions that gained power by keeping Black people or women or immigrants out of the union. They used solidarity power to keep tight control over their jobs. Nationalism is another form of solidarity that can lead one group of underdogs to join in coalition with overdogs and keep underdogs in other nations down. Underdogs must ask, "solidarity for whom?"

Care is an aspect of solidarity power. Care work is often undervalued by theorists and organizers, yet generations of activists have understood that social movements and organizations depend on interpersonal and emotional labor. Changemakers need to develop skills to truly listen to one another, discuss different ideas, and deal with conflict—and ideally organizations should create cultures that emphasize collective care. They also need to develop a collective capacity to survive when facing the harsh realities of daily life as well as repression from the opposition. The more that community is fostered, the better individuals are prepared to take the risks needed to fight for transformational change. It's no coincidence that many social movements on both the Left and the Right have been based in churches (such as the Black church and white evangelical churches), which provide community, care, and connection to a larger purpose. Scholar Deva Woodly argues that the Movement for Black Lives intentionally focused on the politics of care for that reason. When done well, care work enables more people to participate in the movement and engage in healthy ways.[19]

Political scientists also point out that this kind of care work is not just an individual issue, or a movement issue, but a social one too. Democracies are healthier and stronger when people have their basic needs met and the tools to deal with trauma, conflict, and difference.

We have found in our teaching and working with organizers that although solidarity is foundational to all forms of power, it's easy to overlook. Identifying it as a separate form of power encourages organizers to consider the ways in which they can, or need to, build it.

Shut It Down: Disruptive Power

Like solidarity power, disruption is a fundamental tool for underdogs—the status quo is good for overdogs by definition, and disrupting it will usually hurt them. Italian sociologist Luca Perrone used the concept *potere vulnerante*: the power to wound.[20] Disruptive power often works alongside other forms of power. Strikes, for example, involve disruptive, solidarity, and economic power.

Disruptive power includes resisting or practicing noncooperation with the status quo. As social movement scholar Frances Fox Piven explains, underdogs' ultimate power is the power to withhold consent. It can be difficult to refuse to cooperate by yourself, but strategic organizing can create the conditions in which refusing consent to the status quo is easier.[21]

Even small groups may have disruptive power if they control key technologies, resources, or chokepoints. For example, hackers who shut down U.S. oil pipelines in 2021 created an immediate and costly impact.[22] In other words, disruptive power is the power to stop business as usual, or to make a credible threat to do so. Sometimes it's a carefully planned action, like a strike, and sometimes disruptive action can spread virally into a disruptive movement (Chapter 7).

Underdogs frequently use nonviolent tactics where masses of people block roads, fill jails, or stop key meetings from happening. Because racialized capitalism depends on maintaining a system of racial hierarchy, disruptive power might also include ways to prevent economic elites from perpetuating white supremacy, such as when civil rights activists sat at whites-only lunch counters. Nearly every Black person in the city joined the Montgomery bus boycott, threatening the financial viability of segregated bus companies. And thousands of white workers have attempted to disrupt racial hierarchies by working to build multiracial unions.

Sometimes these acts are more symbolic than truly disruptive. Symbolic actions can still have an impact. For example, measured by its disruptive power, the 2003 International Day of Protest against the Iraq War was a blip—it took place on a weekend day and made no effort to block commerce or other activity. But it helped galvanize generalized anger against the war into a global movement. However, it's essential that organizers understand the difference between a protest that seeks to garner press coverage or recruit more people to the cause and a disruptive action that stops an oppressive system from functioning.[23]

True strategic disruption requires disrupting the actual system targeted for change for a sustained period, and in a way that inflicts costs so high that the target is forced to give in. This can be hard to do. It requires identifying vulnerabilities such as where key goods are produced (factories) or distributed (ports); where money or information flows; or where ideology is generated and enforced. It's also hard to do because disruption can alienate allies. Other underdog organizations, union leaders, or progressive legislators may attempt to tame or forbid disruptive actions because of economic or legal implications. And it's risky—disruptive actions are often met by violence and repression.

Overdogs also use disruptive power. Again, this can overlap with other forms of power, like how police power has been used to disrupt organizations, with tactics ranging from infiltration and informants to murder. In labor disputes, employers combine disruptive and economic power in the form of "lockouts"—keeping workers from their place of work. Employers and investors also threaten to, or actually do, take their money and jobs out of a region, or out of the country entirely. But since overdogs have more resources and are able to rule by obtaining (often manufactured) consent, they have less need for disruption. This makes disruptive power all the more valuable for underdogs.

Putting It All Together: Power to Rule and Power for Liberation

To understand your power, you need to consider the larger system in which you operate and the nature of the particular moment, because power is not finite. Both overdogs and underdogs can hold power from various sources, and in different networks, at the same time.

Each form of power can be used to reinforce others. Indeed, it can be hard to draw clear lines. And the quest to build power in any arena will come in fits and starts. Savvy strategists draw on multiple and overlapping sources of power. Overdogs know this well. Practical radicals must work with the power available to them, and in a fight for survival that may only be solidarity power. But underdogs sometimes focus too much on only one form of power, forgetting to look for ways to bring them together, and the necessity of doing so. We aren't advocating for underdogs to simply emulate overdogs. Vision and values should guide underdog strategy, and that is true when thinking about power as well.

In the next chapter, we turn to an examination of the ways overdogs have used all six forms of power as instruments to bring about our current economic and political order.

> **Box 4.1 Other Theories of and Frameworks for Power**
>
> There are many frameworks for defining and categorizing power. While most offer useful insights, we developed our own framework, which builds from some of these approaches, in an effort to find a framework that was comprehensive and useful to organizers.
>
> A *pluralist* theory of power views people as having power through citizenship—the power to vote for politicians that do the best job, or the power to join groups that lobby politicians to pass the best laws. Under this theory of power, there is no hierarchy or systems of oppression that create an unlevel playing field.
>
> *Marxist* theories of power tend to focus on the economic sphere. In this view, political power is an expression of economic power: who owns the tools, land, and factories that produce the goods and services people need for survival? Marxists debate whether the state exists to service individual capitalists, or to keep the overall system of capitalism functioning, such as through macro-economic policies or with regulations that could negatively impact individual capitalists.
>
> The *post-structuralist* school, associated with theorists such as Michel Foucault and Judith Butler, views power independent of social actors. In other words, instead of power existing in an economic or political system, it's found in language, ideas, and institutional practices that together shape the "discourse."
>
> Another strand of theory privileges the *role of elites* in

explaining power from above. In this view, elites are those with the power to control government, corporations, unions, and other large institutions in society.[24]

While these schools of thought analyze power in general, several theorists have developed specific frameworks to understand power for liberation, or underdog power:

The *Power Resources Approach* is a framework that describes the kinds of power workers may build or wield. It uses structural power to describe power that comes from one's location in the economy or labor market, and associational power for the power that comes from acting in solidarity. They add institutional power, which comes from past gains, such as labor law or collective bargaining agreements, and societal power, which includes coalitional power—strength from working in coalitions with community organizations or other unions—and discursive power, the ability to influence the common sense.[25] This maps closely with our framework, but we've modified some of the terms to be more accessible.

Sociologist Patricia Hill Collins developed the *matrix of domination*, which includes four domains of power: structural, disciplinary, hegemonic, and interpersonal.[26]

Political scientist Archon Fung categorizes *power for liberation* into everyday power, policy power, structural power, and ethical power.[27]

Richard Healey, Sandra Hinson, and the Grassroots Power Project have defined *three faces of power* as organizing people, building institutions, and the battle of big ideas.[28]

Tools

Tool 3 Conjunctural Analysis
Tool 7 Power for Underdogs
Tool 33 Power Analysis

5

Setting the Stage: Six Ways Overdogs Got Us to Today

The New Deal policies passed in the Great Depression of the 1930s allowed policymakers and underdogs to restrain capitalism. This is why the economy of the 1930s to 1970s is known as managed capitalism—workers made significant gains, and income inequality declined. Social justice organizers also made tremendous advances in those years—winning voting rights and equal employment opportunity laws, shifting the common sense around racial equality, and making advances in women's, disability, and gay rights.

But in the 1970s another global economic crisis hit. Neoliberal thinkers took advantage of the crisis to argue that laissez-faire was superior to New Deal managed capitalism. But the conservative movement that emerged in the United States in the 1970s was about more than economic policy and theory; it also came out of a political backlash against the gains won by the civil rights, women's, and other social justice movements of the 1960s and 1970s. We use the term **racial neoliberalism** to highlight that neoliberalism was about restoring racial hierarchy as well as Wall Street power. (This term isn't perfect; it ignores how the movement also harnessed resentment toward women, LGBTQ+ people, immigrants, and other marginalized groups.) We believe a movement based on economics alone would not have succeeded.

In this chapter, we tell the stories of six overdogs who, using the six forms of power, helped shape our current order. This isn't a story of a conspiracy. While there *were* secret meetings and deliberate plans to trick and mislead, the reigning neoliberal order would have never come to be through these efforts alone.[1] It took a variety of thinkers, strategists, organizers, and grassroots movements that sometimes were at odds but eventually came together in an alliance. Their efforts helped create the "world as it is"—the conditions that underdogs have struggled against for the past fifty years.

Capturing the Common Sense: Ideological Power

In 1971, a corporate lawyer from Virginia, Lewis Powell Jr., wrote "Attack on the American Free Enterprise System" (the Powell Memo). Powell saw the growing move to regulate private business, as well as the social movements of the time, like the anti–Vietnam War movement, as Trojan horses for the spread of communism and an attack on the "American way." He wrote:

> No thoughtful person can question that the American economic system is under broad attack. . . . What now concerns us is quite new in the history of America. We are not dealing with sporadic or isolated attacks from a relatively few extremists or even from the minority socialist cadre. Rather, the assault on the enterprise system is broadly based and consistently pursued. It is gaining momentum and converts.[2]

The memo sketched out a sophisticated plan to challenge perceived liberal dominance in universities and the media. He implored businesses to invest in electing politicians sympathetic to Right-wing causes and to install conservative judges in the courts. Powell exhorted business leaders to work to influence the public by surveilling school curriculum and media, sending speakers to college campuses, and writing op-eds and books, disseminating pro-business ideology.

This document helped sow the seeds for the Right's decades-long "war of ideas" to overturn the reigning New Deal paradigms. Wealthy conservatives funded think tanks, programs, and research initiatives at universities to legitimize neoliberalism and its tenets through academic scholarship. CEOs began to include political statements alongside earnings statements. Organizations such as the Business Roundtable were developed to promote business interests in the political sphere. By the late 1970s, the neoliberals had made significant inroads in policy debates.

But again, a movement based on economics alone would have failed. In addition to having a pro-business agenda, the movement tapped into a resurgence of racism and patriarchal ideas. The successes of the civil and women's rights movements and others of the 1960s and 1970s incited fear and resentment. Neoliberal strategists were able to exploit and magnify this backlash. Powell had already denounced Martin Luther King Jr., claiming that his movement's civil disobedience was at odds with American democracy and law.[3] The neoliberals emerging in the 1970s began to tie racist backlash and pro-market, anti-government policies together through the concept of individualism. The idea was that it's up to you to make your own life better, and if things don't work out, it's your fault. If you're a worker and you can't make your rent, it's because you don't work hard enough. If you're Black and rejected for a job, it's because you're not qualified.

The connection between white supremacy and conservative economics continues today, as Right-wingers foster the idea that "hard-working Americans" are paying taxes for programs that "lazy people" and undocumented immigrants are taking advantage of. The solution? Cut social spending.

The success of Powell's plan may obscure how the conservative backlash wasn't only imposed from above. Everyday people, organized in mass membership organizations like the Moral Majority, Focus on the Family, and the National Rifle Association (NRA), and in institutions such as white evangelical churches, worked for it as well. These conservative grassroots movements have lost on some issues (for example, marriage equality), but they have been enormously successful overall.

Divide and Conquer: Political Power

The Great Depression led many to ask whether we needed not just reform, but also radical change. Rather than allow support for communism or other radical agendas to grow, President Franklin D. Roosevelt's administration put forth the New Deal, which proposed social programs and regulations to stabilize and rebuild the system. Roosevelt's team also believed it could restore capitalism. Capitalists who might have opposed such programs at other times were more open to the New Deal, partly because the existing system had clearly failed and partly because they found the alternatives more frightening. The following decades were called the "liberal consensus"—most Democrats *and* Republicans supported the New Deal programs.

Not all Republicans, however. The Republican Party included reactionaries—people who saw the New Deal as unwise at best and communist at worst. And by the 1960s, white supremacist Southerners, who had been Democrats since the Civil War, were becoming Republicans.

As late as Richard Nixon's presidency, the Republican Party didn't have a coherent political strategy or ideology. But ruthless political strategists like Lee Atwater worked to take over the party in the 1970s, pushing moderates out of leadership. By the time Ronald Reagan was elected president, the Republican Party had managed to harness racial resentment and neoliberal policy into a cohesive agenda.

Atwater, born in 1951, got active in politics in high school, where he used fake materials and physical intimidation to help his friend get elected student body president. "I learned how to organize," Atwater later wrote of the experience. "And I learned how to polarize."[4] He quickly rose up through the ranks of the South Carolina Republican Party in the 1970s and 1980s.[5] Credited as one of the architects of "dog whistle" politics, Atwater strategically talked about racial issues without using overtly racist language.[6] As he told an interviewer in 1981, "You say stuff like forced busing, states' rights and all that stuff. You're getting so abstract now [that] you're talking about cutting taxes, and all these things you're talking about are totally economic things and a byproduct of them is Blacks get hurt worse than whites."[7]

Atwater is only one of the scores of political operatives responsible for racial neoliberalism's electoral gains, but his ruthless approach to manipulating political rules and employing racial divide-and-conquer strategies had great influence. As investigative journalist Jane Mayer notes: "Atwater's tactics were a bridge between the old Republican Party of the Nixon era, when dirty tricks were considered a scandal, and the new Republican Party of Donald Trump, in which lies, fear-mongering, and winning at any cost have become normalized."[8] This strategy contributed to a massive power shift. The Democratic Party dominated in the postwar decades, but starting with Reagan's election in 1980, the Republicans steadily built Right-wing power in every branch of government, including the Supreme Court.

Atwater died in 1991, and by the end of his life he came to regret what he'd done. But his tactics live on. For example, after Barack Obama was elected president, Republican strategists tapped into white supremacist sentiments to form the Tea Party.[9] On the surface, the Tea Party promoted small government, but their real motivation was opposition to any program that might benefit people of color and challenge white supremacy.[10] This "whitelash," as it has come to be known, continues today in the form of "America First" nationalism and nativism, and in manufactured controversies about the border and critical race theory.

Submit or Starve: Economic Power and Disruption

Neoliberalism was in part a theory that the economy would run better without government regulation. But as the radical theorist David Harvey argues, neoliberalism was also a way for wealthy people to regain the money they felt they deserved. Under New Deal capitalism, corporate leaders were forced to share their profits with workers and pay high taxes. They didn't like it, and once the 1970s recessions hit, they went on the offensive, determined to gain a larger share of the stagnating economic pie.[11]

Perhaps no one exemplifies how ideological and economic power supported each other in these years better than Jack Welch, CEO and chairman of General Electric (GE) for over twenty years. In 1981, Welch became the company's youngest-ever CEO. Not long before, shareholders had been seen as just one type of stakeholder in big companies—workers and the community at large were also taken into account. But to neoliberals, only shareholders mattered. Welch bought into this idea (helped by generous stock options). In his first few years as CEO, he cut GE staff by almost 30 percent—laying off over 100,000 people.[12]

GE had already been moving production to nonunion regions in the U.S. South or overseas, but Welch aggressively expanded offshoring, adding to a growing trend that broke unions and promoted a sense of fear among workers. "Ideally, you'd have every plant you own on a barge to move with currencies and changes in the economy," Welch said.[13]

Welch modeled a transition from industrial to financial capitalism. In 1989 he announced a $10 billion stock buyback, which took money that once would have gone to wages, or to real investment, and transferred it to stockholders (and himself).[14] Today's corporations do the same, buying back a trillion dollars' worth of their own stock by 2018.[15]

Welch also built up GE Capital, a financial services wing of the corporation. He shifted investment money from the company's traditional manufacturing work into banking and credit cards. Within a decade of taking control, GE Capital held $70 billion in assets. Ten years later, GE Capital accounted for 40 percent of the company's profits.[16] This was part of the neoliberal trend that moved power to Wall Street, encouraging speculation rather than productive activity.

Welch later fought the Environmental Protection Agency (EPA) over known dangerous chemicals, such as PCBs, that the company would regularly deposit into the Hudson River in New York. He fought a federally mandated cleanup of the river, and he allowed the company to continue operations that violated state and federal environmental law.[17]

Welch's management style embodies the tenets of neoliberalism: short-term gains at the expense of long-term investment, and profit at the expense of workers and the planet. He also helped usher in an era of CEO and corporate manager extravagance. When he retired, he was given an exit package worth over $400 million, and he continued to charge the company for his family's expenses, down to their toilet paper.[18] (It's worth pointing out that neoliberals insist that having a giant organization take care of all your needs destroys initiative and self-reliance.) Even though GE's stock price rose while Welch was CEO, he had hollowed out the company so that it was unable to weather economic storms ahead. The 2008 economic crisis, for example, bankrupted GE Capital. The company's manufacturing was eventually outpaced by competing companies converting to green energy because Welch had cut the company's research budget.[19]

Imperialism and Incarceration: Military Power

The United States has a long history of using military force both outright and covertly to select or depose foreign leaders. But one example, in particular, demonstrates the way military power contributed to the neoliberal paradigm. When Chileans elected the socialist Salvador Allende as their president in 1970, Henry Kissinger, working as the assistant to the president for national security affairs, warned Nixon that the United States had to take action. Working with the CIA, Kissinger put in place a plan to prevent Allende from taking office. This involved assassinating René Schneider, Chile's top general, because he wouldn't support a coup. The assassination sparked a pro-Allende backlash, but Kissinger got his coup three years later, on September 11, 1973, under Augusto Pinochet (Chile's new top general).[20]

Pinochet abolished the Congress and Constitution and began to implement a new set of economic policies. Working with Chilean economists trained by neoliberals at the University of Chicago, the Pinochet administration implemented reforms to give greater rights to investors and business owners.[21] Nationalized industries were reprivatized. Industries and capital investment were deregulated. Price controls were abolished. This "shock therapy" brought devastation to much of the population. But there was little room for dissent. In the first three years of Pinochet's regime, over 130,000 people were arrested. This reign of terror resulted in over 30,000 people tortured, 2,500 executed, and nearly 200,000 forced into exile.[22]

Kissinger's help was crucial to Pinochet. The United States provided economic and military assistance, diplomatic support, and direct communications with top U.S. leaders. The CIA helped Pinochet build a secret police agency. Even Kissinger's own staff asked that he address Chile's human rights abuses, but Kissinger ignored them. When he met with Chile's foreign minister in 1975, and with Pinochet in 1976, he not only refused to call on them to improve human rights, he actually expressed support. He told Pinochet in 1976: "In the United States, as you know, we are sympathetic with what you are trying to do here. We want to help, not undermine you. You did a great service to the West in overthrowing Allende."[23]

> ### Box 5.1 The Police State and Racial Neoliberalism
>
> U.S. police have played a powerful role in crushing underdog uprisings throughout the country's history. Before the Civil War, only a few large cities had their own police force. But afterward, cities began developing their police to keep control over formerly enslaved people in the South, and over immigrants and labor organizations in the North. Over time the police gained more powers and weapons.
>
> In the early 1970s, Nixon and some state governors launched a "War on Drugs," making it easier for police to arrest people for minor offenses. These arrests were heavily skewed toward Black and Brown people. After decades of relatively low rates of incarceration, the U.S. prison population began to increase in the 1970s, a trend that intensified in the 1980s and 1990s. There are more than 2 million people in prisons today—a 500 percent increase over forty years, even though crime rates began dropping in the 1990s.[24]
>
> In 1973, Nelson Rockefeller, governor of New York, passed the strictest drug laws in the country, including mandatory minimum sentencing. People could now be arrested and sentenced to a minimum of fifteen years in prison, and a maximum of twenty-five years to life, for selling or possessing relatively small amounts of drugs. The impact was extreme. From 1980 to 2007, almost 200,000 people were imprisoned in the state of New York due to drug offenses. Approximately 90 percent of those imprisoned for drug offenses were Black or Latino.[25] Rockefeller had once supported rehabilitation and job-training programs in response to drug use, but instead, the Rockefeller Drug Laws shifted the country to a punishment model.[26]

The War on Drugs was part of the rise of racial neoliberalism. It was purposefully designed to divide and weaken political opponents, and it had an explicitly racist agenda. One of Nixon's advisors, John Ehrlichman, described the effort to a reporter:

The Nixon campaign in 1968, and the Nixon White House after that, had two enemies: the antiwar left and Black people. You understand what I'm saying? We knew we couldn't make it illegal to be either against the war or Black, but by getting the public to associate the hippies with marijuana and Blacks with heroin, and then criminalizing both heavily, we could disrupt those communities. We could arrest their leaders, raid their homes, break up their meetings, and vilify them night after night on the evening news. Did we know we were lying about the drugs? Of course we did.[27]

The War on Drugs was only one part of the ascent of mass incarceration. Policymakers have passed a host of draconian laws in the past several decades. Poverty has been increasingly criminalized, as city after city has passed ordinances making it illegal to panhandle, to sleep on public benches, or to live on the street.[28] As the carceral state grew, the welfare state shrank. It was another, more brutal way to deal with poverty. The carceral state even became a direct cause of poverty. Ferguson, Missouri, is just one example of how cities target poor, Black residents through a host of channels, from traffic stops to late payment on a bill, in order to collect high fees and fines, or worse. Those who can't pay the fees are arrested and jailed in modern-day "debtor's prisons."[29]

Alongside the militarization of police has been the militarization of U.S. borders. The federal government increased funding and staff to patrol the border in this period, which might seem counterintuitive; after all, a free market should

> mean people can move across borders with no restrictions. Indeed, libertarians such as the Cato Institute call for open borders, and many employers prefer to have a large supply of labor. This shows one of the ways in which the neoliberal alliance has been an uneasy one. While forms of power can complement one another, they can also come into conflict (in this case economic and military power). The conservative movement has struggled to determine how to approach immigration into the country. Corporations want and need labor, so they don't want borders closed. But they want immigration on their own terms—such as through guest worker programs that restrict immigrant workers' rights to seek other jobs and make them vulnerable to deportation if they organize.[30] The base of the Republican Party has fought for tighter controls on immigration from poor countries. For now, the base has won the argument, resulting in an unstable compromise. Corporations can move jobs out of the country and bring migrant workers in with restricted rights. This again favors a racialized neoliberal agenda in multiple ways. It forces undocumented people to work with less protection and in fear, and it pits U.S.-born workers against immigrants, dividing and conquering the working class.

The Right Organizes Too: Solidarity Power

This Right-wing racial neoliberal project was contested and complicated. It required building an alliance of people from a range of political traditions and orientations, and that meant finding ways to work together and compromise. In other words, they needed solidarity power.

Conservatives used a variety of avenues to gain allies and build solidarity power, such as forming spaces where overdogs could gather to discuss political analyses, share projections, and develop strategy. The Powell memo wasn't just a document floating around. It was written for an organization, the Chamber of Commerce, that used it to build their membership and power. Overdogs built up other venues to come together. This includes key academic departments, like the University of Chicago economics department and the George Mason School of Law. It includes large global events, business association conferences, and small secret gatherings like the Bilderberg Meeting and Bohemian Grove, which involves work as well as leisure, serving to strengthen social bonds among the elite. While these kinds of spaces have long existed, new ones proliferated in the early 1970s, a time of global political and economic uncertainty.[31]

One of the people who worked relentlessly to build solidarity power for the emerging neoliberal movement was Phyllis Schlafly. Schlafly was an attorney and writer working on conservative causes. She began working at the conservative American Enterprise Institute in the 1940s and then ran for Congress, unsuccessfully, in 1952. In 1964 she wrote *A Choice Not an Echo*, a book in support of Barry Goldwater's presidential run.

Schlafly's work put her in position to build a broad coalition of disparate forces through her signature campaign to defeat the Equal Rights Amendment (ERA). Many believed the ERA was on a sure path to victory—it had the support of two Republican presidents—but Schlafly formed the STOP ERA coalition. She started with her own mailing list built over years, and the organization she founded in 1972, the Eagle Forum. There were Republicans who supported the ERA, so she organized within the National Federation of Republican Women, using extreme case scenarios to peel off supporters. She focused on women in key southern states and built alliances with evangelical churches. She brought new voices into the emerging conservative coalition, organizing rural and suburban white women who feared the ERA could undermine their roles as stay-at-home housewives or force them to join the military.

Schlafly helped the movement harness resentment toward women and LGBTQ+ communities. On the surface, one might think that an ideology so close to libertarianism would celebrate individual rights, including the right for people to control their own bodies and to marry who they want. But as scholar Melinda Cooper shows, neoliberals made an alliance with social conservatives around so-called family values. Neoliberals and social conservatives joined forces in a common effort to privilege the patriarchal family.[32]

Today, the alliance between conservatives in various Christian traditions seems obvious, but it wasn't in the 1970s. Schlafly was one of several organizers who helped cement those ties. The coalition she built disagreed on many things, but Schlafly built solidarity power that was great enough to stop the ERA and then serve as a key foundation for the emerging racial neoliberal order. In particular, Schlafly's work helped activate the fundamentalist churches—even though she herself was Catholic, and those churches had been politically at odds in the prior decades.[33] And while some of the white Republican women had sided with racial justice movements of the time, Schlafly convinced them that they needed to put those views aside to work with the racist wings of the movement "for the sake of the cause" of upholding traditional gender roles.[34]

Shock and Manipulation: Disruptive Power

Overdogs can use disruptive power to great effect, and underdogs would do well to study how they do it.

One of the great disruptors behind racial neoliberalism was Reagan. Reagan had been an actor in his youth, then a spokesperson for GE. He began turning his attention to politics, first attacking communists within his union (the Screen Actors Guild), then making a campaign speech for the conservative presidential candidate Barry Goldwater, and then as governor of California. Reagan was elected president in 1980 and came into office with a bold agenda. He and his team looked to disrupt their own party as well as the status quo. He launched aggressive attacks on a number of fronts. For example, although the EPA had been passed under another Republican, Nixon, Reagan appointed an anti-environmental corporate lawyer to head the agency.[35]

Perhaps his most aggressive act came when thirteen thousand members of the Professional Air Traffic Controllers Organization (PATCO) struck in August 1981, just a few months into Reagan's first term. Reagan immediately declared the PATCO strike illegal and ordered the controllers back to work, despite the fact that the union had endorsed him. Two days later, Reagan fired 11,345 workers who refused to cross the picket line and return to work.

While it was illegal for federal employees to strike, prior unions had struck without penalty. Reagan's actions shocked the nation. Many scholars say it was a turning point for the U.S. labor movement. In the coming decades the number of strikes plummeted. Reagan's action set the tone as corporations made use of a growing union-busting industry, hiring consultants to break up unions. The use of management strategies such as lockouts, outsourcing, and offshoring grew, as did outright labor law violations.[36]

Of course, this was part of building overdogs' economic and political power, but we highlight it also as disruptive power. Disruption is not always about force. It can include emotional manipulation that creates fear, mistrust, and a sense of hopelessness. Employers might hire groups of workers who speak different languages and can't communicate with one another, attempting to disrupt the relationship building necessary to achieve solidarity power.

Racial Neoliberalism Is Not Invincible

Racial neoliberalism did not simply come about via a well-constructed plan crafted out of the Powell memo and put into place by well-resourced corporate and political leaders. While people like Powell, Atwater, Welch, Kissinger, Schlafly, and Reagan were instrumental to neoliberalism's rise, they are only a few of the many people and organizations that worked for the global shift toward conservative politics and economics. The six of them could never have brought about such a change on their own. And it was not a smooth transition. Everyone who worked for this change had to organize, form alliances, test out ideas, and deploy a variety of strategies (summarized in Table 5.1). It required organizing, conflict, and compromise among the various elements that eventually came into coalition. And they had to continually adapt and strategize in response to resistance from the forces against them.

While the Republican Party was the first to fully embrace neoliberalism, some of the initial neoliberal reforms were enacted in the late 1970s under a Democratic president and Congress. By the 1990s, many in the Democratic Party were on board with the neoliberal program. Some of the pivotal laws that ratified racial neoliberalism as the governing consensus were initiated and signed by Bill Clinton, including welfare reform, punitive crime and immigration bills, and the North American Free Trade Agreement. The way that the Democratic Party helped enact a Right-wing program by the 1990s shows how successful the shift to racial neoliberalism was.

Neoliberals' success was decisive and lasting, and in hindsight almost seems inevitable. It can be hard to imagine living in another kind of world. But their victory wasn't inevitable, and it shows signs of faltering. The alliance is tightening up their ranks in some areas but losing support in others. Neoliberal thought is no longer hegemonic within the Democratic Party, university economics departments, or the media. Just as the neoliberal overdogs strategized, built alliances, and organized to achieve victory, so too can underdogs.

Neoliberalism is not invincible. Those hurt by it have power of their own and can resist. Another world is possible.

Table 5.1: Examples of How Overdogs Used the Six Forms of Power to Bring About Racial Neoliberalism

Form of Power	Steps Toward Racial Neoliberalism
Ideological	Creation of new think tanks
	Building conservative media
	Shaping what's taught in schools and universities
Political	Political alliances between employer associations and both parties
	Wide range of laws like welfare "reform," immigration restrictions, crime bills, North American Free Trade Agreement (NAFTA)
	Deregulation and weakening of existing law (like labor law)
	Overdogs collaborate across borders via World Trade Organization, IMF, and World Bank

Form of Power	Steps Toward Racial Neoliberalism
Economic	Corporate restructuring to weaken unions, lower wages, implement just-in-time production, expand trade, expand financial sector, find new areas for profit-making (like schools)
	Financial incentives used as threats and rewards to politicians
	Massive rise in credit/debt to finance the economy
Military and Police	Support coups (e.g., Chile in 1973, Argentina in 1976)
	Repress protests abroad and in the United States
	Rise of mass incarceration in the United States
	"War on Drugs"
	Militarization of border, increased immigration enforcement
Solidarity	Strengthening of U.S. Chamber of Commerce and other industry associations
	Creation of new organizations that unite neoliberal proponents (Business Roundtable, 1972)
	Creation of new spaces that serve as movement hubs and places for strategy development, both nationally and internationally (World Economic Forum, 1971; Trilateral Commission, 1973)
	Formation of the new conservative movement fusing white evangelical churches, Catholics, and the corporate class
Disruption	PATCO and other union busting
	"Volcker Shock" raising of interest rates
	Movement surveillance and infiltration
	Political attacks on Black power organizations

Tools

Tool 3 Conjunctural Analysis
Tool 8 Writing a Powell Memorandum for the Left
Tool 33 Power Analysis

PART II

NOTES OF CHANGE:
SEVEN STRATEGIES UNDERDOGS USE TO WIN

In this section of the book, we look in detail at the seven strategy models for change. No real-world example fits neatly in one category, but the models and case-study examples illuminate important choices, questions, and differences.

The strategy you choose depends on the sources of power available to you. You can't pull off a successful general strike unless you've got masses of people ready to act together (solidarity power) and walk off the job (disruptive power), in a way that hurts employers (economic power) and/or elected officials (political power). If you want to protect your political rights, you're going to need solidarity and political power to make electoral change. In Table 5.2, we summarize how each of the seven strategy models builds from particular forms of power and preview the case studies we feature. We'll show that each of the groups and movements we profile in the cases has a dominant note of strategy, operating from a form of power and theory of change. But their winning melodies use other notes too.

Each strategy model is associated with a set of tactics. A plan to capture control of the government by winning a series of key elections and mobilizing a set of constituencies could be a strategy. Tactics include door-knocking, social media outreach, reforming campaign financing laws, and candidate training. Too often, organizers focus on debates over tactics and forget about strategy, but tactics are not enough to win major change. Dismantling structures of oppression and challenging the deep forms of power held by the overdogs requires more than just tactics, and must be built on a long-term vision and a theory of power. The seven strategy models we profile are underdogs' inheritance and can be their inspiration.

Table 5.2: Strategy Models, Primary Forms of Power, and Examples

Strategy	Form of Power	Chapter Example
Base-Building	Solidarity	Community organization (Make the Road NY)
		Labor union (St. Paul Federation of Educators)
Disruptive Movements	Disruptive	Welfare rights movement
		Workers movements in the 1930s
		Standing Rock
		Civil rights movement: lunch-counter sit-ins, Freedom Rides, Project C in Birmingham
Narrative Shift	Ideological	Occupy Wall Street
		Marriage equality movement
Electoral Change	Political	New Georgia Project
		California Calls
		Working Families Party
		New Virginia Majority
		Democratic Socialists of America
		UNITE HERE
		Community Change Action
Inside-Outside Campaigns	Solidarity	Fight for $15 and a Union in Chicago
	Political	Raising homecare workers' wages in New York State
	Ideological	Health Care for America Now (HCAN)
Momentum	Solidarity	350.org
	Disruptive	Bernie Sanders's presidential campaign
	Ideological	Marriage equality movement
Collective Care	Solidarity	Gay Men's Health Crisis
	Ideological	Movement for Black Lives

Tools
Tool 9 New Grooves **Tool 10** Prompt: Are All Strategies Strategic?

6.1

Base-Building

Community Organizations: Love and Rigor at Make the Road NY

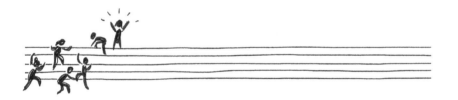

A few days before Easter in 2021, a group of elected officials came to the New York City office of then governor Andrew Cuomo. They weren't there to make a speech or cut a deal. Instead, they got down on their knees to wash the feet of over a dozen undocumented immigrant workers who had been on a hunger strike for weeks. The strikers were calling for undocumented immigrants to get the same pandemic relief other workers had received. Sitting in a wheelchair, waiting for the elected officials to bend before her, Ana Ramirez held up a handwritten cardboard sign that read, "I have not eaten in 17 days, nearly 420 hours. I am an excluded worker, and have served meals to this entire city—the richest and the poorest—for over 15 years. Who feeds us while we feed you?"[1]

Ramirez and other undocumented workers were hailed as "essential" in the early stages of the COVID-19 pandemic, but were denied the relief that flowed from Albany and Washington, DC. A year into the pandemic, many immigrant New Yorkers were without income, had trouble feeding their families, and feared eviction. Ramirez contrasted their situation to "the rich, the most powerful, the thieves that don't pay taxes—they were able to get through the pandemic with comfort and ease."[2] The foot-washing drew on the strikers' cultural and religious traditions: Jesus had washed the feet of his disciples the day before his crucifixion. It symbolized humility and accountability, as powerful people bowed down and showed respect to the people who had kept the city running during its darkest hours.

On day 23, the hunger strikers won. They had beaten the governor and a jaded political class that had dismissed their demands as preposterous. The New York State budget included $2.1 billion for an "Excluded Workers Fund" to provide direct cash payments ($15,600 in almost all cases) to more than 130,000 mostly undocumented workers who had been shut out of all other pandemic relief.[3] Rubiela Correa expressed how she and the other strikers felt when they heard the news: "That is when the joy started . . . triumph that we have done it and we can do everything that we want to do as immigrants in this country even if we do not have any documents."[4]

Deepak heard the news as he prepared to teach a class (appropriately about the cruel exclusions of the U.S. welfare system). He began to cry, in awe and joy that some of the most oppressed people in U.S. society had brought the establishment to heel and delivered real relief for working-class immigrants in the city. He had helped one of his students, Camila Rivandeneyra, get involved as a volunteer. She supported the hunger strikers and translated for them. She conveyed some of the electric energy of the campaign, saying she was moved that it was "led by the people who were being directly impacted" and that they "were treated as the experts."[5]

From Catastrophe to Triumph

The Excluded Workers Fund victory was not just impressive; it was breathtaking. The strikers had broken through a bedrock principle of U.S. social policy that prevented people without legal status from accessing a safety net.

Despite the righteousness of the cause, it's not obvious how such a historic win was accomplished. As Deborah Axt, a key organizer in the campaign, said, "Most of our allies supported us but thought the plan to demand parity to what every other worker got in UI [unemployment insurance] was unrealistic" because of the cost.[6] Undocumented workers can't vote or contribute money to politicians. Yet, they were able to overturn the entrenched political common sense. How? The foundation for the victory was a people-powered organization, built over many decades, that was ready to seize the moment. Ramirez, Correa, Axt, and others were part of Make the Road NY (MRNY), a grassroots community organization with 25,000 members in New York.[7] Axt described how years of patient work led to the victory: "Organizing is a slow build in most years. And I think that's crucial. And in this campaign, we were able to rely on many of the dynamics that we and our allies had made possible over decades of work."[8]

MRNY's deep roots in immigrant New York attuned it to the scale of the crisis and need for a bold solution. The heart of MRNY's base lives in neighborhoods hard hit by COVID-19. Galvanized in a crucible of death and hardship, the organization quickly pivoted to emergency mutual aid to help community members survive the loss of income. And the organization's leaders were determined to win cash assistance for undocumented New Yorkers.

In Chapter 3 we talked about the importance of empathy and imagination in developing strategy—being able to read changes in the conjuncture, sense emergent possibilities, and analyze your opponents' motivations and power. The pandemic created cultural and political openings. People began to see that workers who care for and feed others are more "essential" than stockbrokers. And MRNY leaders saw that Governor Cuomo, a longtime foe, was weakened by scandals of his own making.

The campaign brought together many organizations into an Excluded Workers Coalition and used an array of classic and creative tactics.[9] Activists directed pressure at key legislators on their home turf and launched actions to dramatize the issue. They shut down the Brooklyn and Manhattan Bridges with a march of hundreds of workers and allies under the banner: "Essential Forever. Excluded No More." But even a brilliant campaign and the unusual circumstances of the pandemic can't fully explain the victory, especially against the backdrop of decades of opposition from both

Democratic and Republican parties to providing benefits for undocumented workers. Indeed, no other state provided pandemic relief to undocumented immigrants at the scale that New York has. Social scientists Hahrie Han, Elizabeth McKenna, and Michelle Oyakawa argue that "power is not a function of organizational resources alone." They contend organizations that build constituency bases with "commitment and flexibility, ideology and pragmatism" can seize political opportunities when they arise.[10] Years of deep organizing had set the stage for the victory.

High Touch, High Engagement: Organizing Immigrant New York

There was poetic justice in the organization's 2021 breakthrough. Founded in 1997, MRNY began by working to prevent low-income New Yorkers from losing access to welfare and other public benefits. Democratic president Bill Clinton had just signed the punitive 1996 welfare law, and Republican mayor Rudolph Giuliani followed up by sending notices to terminate cash assistance, food stamps, and other benefits to low-income New Yorkers. The organization's founders decided to focus on building power in immigrant New York and to become a multi-issue organization, developing work in a wide range of areas, including worker rights, housing, environmental justice, health care, immigrant rights, youth power, and LGBTQ+ rights.[11]

Deepak first got to know MRNY during battles about welfare reform. Later, as one of the architects of the March for America in 2010 that brought over 250,000 people to Washington, DC, to push for immigration reform, he saw the organization's muscle in action. March organizers printed signs with the slogan "Change Takes Courage," to demand that Congress act and that President Obama address the crisis of deportations that tore families apart. After months of delays and equivocation from Democrats, immigrant leaders around the country decided to mobilize to change the dynamics. Deepak remembers standing on the stage at the National Mall with lead march organizer Gabe Gonzalez, wondering if anyone was going to show up for this hastily called march. Then, suddenly, they saw a gigantic cloud of dust and hundreds of blue and yellow MRNY shirts in the distance. With less than six weeks' notice, MRNY brought forty-two busloads of people to the march, more than any other organization based outside of Washington, DC.

MRNY's power to mobilize is rooted in its model of organizing, which has four pillars: legal and survival services, transformative education, community organizing, and policy innovation.

Most people initially find the organization when they walk into an office looking for help—with a housing problem or an abusive employer, for example. Before they are connected to services, they meet with an organizer who talks about MRNY's mission and encourages them to join the organization and get involved.[12]

The heart of MRNY's organizing is issue-based committees operating from five community centers—in three boroughs in New York City and in Long Island and Westchester. On any given day, you might walk into one of MRNY's centers and see English classes in the morning, lunch cooked by members midday, and preparation for actions in the afternoon. Typically, between fifty and one hundred people participate in issue-based committee meetings that happen at each borough office every night. More than offices, MRNY's spaces provide a sense of home—with food, services, community, culture, and action.

Deepak attended a meeting of the housing and environmental justice committee in May of 2022 that was typical in its rhythm and structure. The group had adapted to the pandemic by hosting meetings on Zoom. Led by members, the gathering opened with everyone singing the movement anthem, "Venceremos." New people had a chance to introduce themselves, and everyone heard testimony from a longtime leader about the organization's mission and victories. Then, members discussed the organization's priority campaign to pass Good Cause Eviction legislation in Albany, a response to the growing housing crisis in the wake of the expiration of the federal moratorium on evictions. Participants reviewed goals for a petition drive aimed at lawmakers and shared what they heard when they asked people to sign. One member shared a story she'd heard from a person she reached out to about the campaign "who can't sleep at night" for fear of being evicted. The meeting included a push to attend a pivotal rally in Albany, with people making commitments. The group learned about a bill to address climate justice and closed with cumbia, a style of music originating in Colombia.[13]

Representatives from the committees meet in leadership teams that strategize about the campaigns across geography. MRNY's board of directors is composed of a super-majority of community members chosen by active committees. The organization's "high-touch" model emphasizes significant member participation, which means lots of meetings for members to deliberate on campaign goals and strategy. Staff organizers take responsibility for recruiting new people, preparing meetings, and working with members to develop campaign strategy. The organization makes a substantial investment in leadership development, with three levels of leadership training.

"Slow and Respectful Work": Fundamentals of Community Organizing

Historian Charles Payne wrote about the Student Non-Violent Coordinating Committee (SNCC), which laid the groundwork for some of the most famous confrontations of the civil rights era:

> We also have to consider the depth and richness of the personal relationships between organizers and local people, the flexibility of the organizers, their willingness to experiment, their ability to project themselves as men and women of character and the well-honed ability of local people to read character, to recognize "fullness" when it was there. We also have to consider simple persistence. Our collective imagery of the movement does not include George Greene returning to talk to some frightened farmer for the tenth time or a Mary Lane, taking the registration test eleven times before she is allowed to pass, or Donaldson and Cobb [two SNCC organizers] returning at night to a town they were run out of that day. Overemphasizing the movement's more dramatic features, we undervalue the patient and sustained effort, the slow, respectful work, that made the dramatic moments possible.[14]

MRNY exemplifies this slow and respectful work.

The essence of the base-building model is building lasting power through organization. The heart of the model is solidarity power—the power that comes when underdogs unite to confront overdogs—and not in a one-time mobilization. Rather, a community organization is designed so that people can exercise solidarity power over and over again, and so that they can grow that power, and other forms of power, in measurable ways; for example, by increasing membership, expanding geographically, or building more political muscle. The logic of this kind of organizing is as follows:

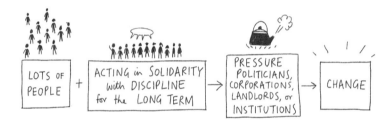

Community groups (and unions) will deploy different sources of power—MRNY made good use of ideological and political power in its campaign to win the Excluded Workers Fund. But the power of organized people is their strategic center of gravity.

In any such organization, there are organizers and members, some of whom become leaders. An organizer is typically a paid staff person responsible for recruiting new members, agitating members to engage on issues they care about, and developing the skills of leaders so that they can understand how power flows in the community, craft strategy, and confront opponents more effectively. Deborah Axt describes the work of an organizer:

> It's mostly spending your time day-by-day in conversation with workers or community members about what's going on in their lives. You surface the shitty stuff that people face, that they're angry or upset about, or inspired to try to change. Then you help them to understand that what they are facing is shared by many other people who are facing the same dynamics, sometimes in

the very same workplace, sometimes more broadly. You connect them to others, invite them to join a committee or a group that is forming, or you help them decide who else might be ready to join them in fighting for change. You invite them to join whatever is emerging in the collective space, to be a part of changing the rules of the game and changing the big picture systems. . . . And you invite people to really picture what it would take for you to go to the boss or the landlord, this time not alone, and say "I want to be treated differently." You help them picture, for once, having enough people with you that you finally have the power to insist. And then you support them in practicing, planning, and acting.[15]

A leader in community organizing is not necessarily someone who is charismatic or has the most radical perspective on an issue—leaders are people with followers, who trust, are moved and mobilized by that leader. Both leaders and organizers will play roles in turning people out for actions and in leading meetings. One measure of a community organization's health is how much responsibility members take for its vision and everyday functioning.

Community organizations come in all kinds of forms: there are institution-based organizations, where groups like churches or schools (rather than individuals) are members, tenant organizations, worker centers, neighborhood organizations, and more. Community organizations are often criticized for being too focused on small, local issues at the expense of national or global issues. But over the last couple of decades there has been a revolution in the field of community organizing in response to a recognition that the issues people face are not only local. Many community organizations have grown in their geographic scope, and most have joined national networks that seek to shape federal and state policy. Key networks and movement hubs in community organizing include the Center for Popular Democracy, Community Change, Faith in Action, the Gamaliel Foundation, the Industrial Areas Foundation, People's Action, Right to the City, and the State Power Caucus. Saul Alinsky famously taught "no permanent friends, no permanent enemies," but today's community organizations usually engage in politics—endorsing and running candidates for office who become long-term allies, like the elected officials who washed the feet of the MRNY hunger strikers. Alinsky, responding to sectarian in-fighting in the Left of his time, argued that community groups should be practical, not ideological. Most base-building community organizations today work on issues community members say are important, but they don't pretend to be ideologically neutral. Many take members through a political education process that helps them connect their lived experience (for example, of unaffordable housing or discrimination) to the way society is structured.

Structured People Power: Common Elements of the Base-Building Model in Community Organizing

For all the changes in the field, some core principles have stood the test of time. These are helpfully laid out by Arnie Graf, a legendary organizer with the Industrial Areas Foundation (IAF) who is known for his mastery of the rules of the craft and for the skill with which he broke them when necessary.[16] Graf contends that any community organization must do the following:

> *Recruit and engage members.* This can happen in a variety of ways: door-to-door, online, or through community institutions like churches. Members often pay dues to support the organization, and with membership come invitations not only to attend protests, but also to come to meetings to learn and strategize about issues. Many community organizers call the process of recruiting new members and collecting dues "base-building." When Deepak started working at the Association of Community Organizations for Reform Now (ACORN), he was handed a copy of a famous talk by farmworker leader Cesar Chavez about base-building. Chavez talked about how this was the lifeblood of organizing, emphasizing the importance of asking even poor people to

finance their own organizations through membership dues because it builds the kind of ownership necessary to overcome fierce opposition.[17]

Identify the self-interest of members. We tend to think of self-interest as something negative. But we all have self-interests, and for oppressed people these are often disregarded. The campaign for the Excluded Workers Fund grew directly out of undocumented workers' urgent need for income. Self-interest doesn't just include material needs—it also speaks to the need for community, recognition, and meaning. Hunger strikers like Ana Ramirez and Rubiela Correa made an extraordinary commitment to the campaign, not only because they would benefit from the fund, but because they felt responsible to their community and found purpose and meaning in a cause larger than themselves. During periods of struggle, people find capacities they didn't know they had, and those moments of self-realization and growth galvanize long-term commitment to a cause and organization.

Build relationships. Racial neoliberalism teaches people to relate to each other transactionally—as consumers, clients, or recipients. The beating heart of a community organization is the network of relationships between its members, which can often cross lines of race, ethnicity, or other forms of identity. These relationships are not personal friendships, though those may develop. Most organizations teach some form of a *one-to-one*, a relational meeting in which two people get to know each other on a deep level, talking about what it means to be a parent, experiences at work, and their values and aspirations for the future. The purpose of these meetings is not instrumental; you're not trying to get someone to do something you want them to do. These relationships are powerful because they expand people's conception of their self-interests. For example, one person may have affordable housing, but when they feel connected to other people who struggle to make the rent, it becomes their issue too, and they will act on it. Relationship building is a force multiplier—it's the glue that holds a group together when things get challenging.

Distinguish problems from issues. Community members encounter many problems—a lack of affordable housing, systemic racism, or the unfair distribution of wealth in society. But a community organization will look for what organizers call an issue—a tangible part of a broader problem that can be addressed through collective action. Examples of issue campaigns include creating a housing trust fund, divesting from policing in favor of community services, or increasing taxes on the rich. Classically, organizers are taught that issues should be "specific, immediate, and winnable." There is value in this formula—oppressed people aren't going to stay involved in organizations that don't address their immediate needs, only work on grandiose, abstract problems, or constantly lose. But it's also true that organizations can choose many different issues to work on—and groups working for transformational change will pick ones that challenge the status quo. MRNY has a set of criteria it uses to assess whether to take on an issue, including whether an issue will attract new members and whether it will build power.[18] And sometimes organizers and leaders must pick an issue that seems unwinnable because it speaks so profoundly to the lived experience of members. Paradoxically, sometimes people who wouldn't have bothered to join a "winnable" campaign are inspired by the boldness of an "unwinnable" one. The genius of the Excluded Workers Fund, for example, was that it expanded everyone's conception of what's possible. (We discuss when it is and when it isn't strategic to make "maximalist" demands in Chapter 14.)

Analyze action and reaction. Some actions, such as many mass protests, provide an opportunity for people to express their outrage but aren't strategic. These protests fail to create change when they lack a target or a power analysis. By contrast, there's a wide repertoire of tactics community organizers use to force an opponent to react—from direct action, in which a group confronts the opponent, to an accountability session, during which a powerful target is invited to answer specific demands from community members publicly. Effective actions are often unexpected. President Obama didn't expect 250,000 people to show up in Washington, DC, in 2010, so he had to hastily arrange negotiations with organizers, including Deepak, in the weeks leading up to the protest. Deepak began the meeting with the president by confronting him about deportations—a topic that was pushed onto the president's agenda by the timely mass mobilization.[19] Similarly, no one expected undocumented immigrant workers to go without food to dramatize the need for the Excluded Workers Fund, or to see elected officials drop to their knees to recognize them. Effective actions are part of a strategy and are informed by a power analysis—they threaten a source of power, money, or legitimacy for overdogs, and compel them to respond. Table 6.1.1 summarizes key components of the base-building model.

Mastering the Craft and Breaking the Rules: Make the Road's Model

MRNY is part of a long tradition of community organizing in the United States that is practiced by groups with varying ideological commitments. There are many lineages, with groups today tracing their roots back to Alinsky, the Black organizing tradition, agrarian populists from the nineteenth century, settlement houses, and others. MRNY exemplifies a modern remix of community organizing principles that emerged in Latino immigrant communities in the 1990s, with other groups like CASA in the mid-Atlantic and the Coalition for Humane Immigrant Rights (CHIRLA) in California developing along similar lines.

MRNY's model incorporates principles of traditional community organizing, but also creatively contradicts them. Staff leaders have had organizing experiences with unions and the IAF and learned from groups like ACORN and the Young Lords. Rather than starting with a ready-made template, one of the co-founders, Andrew Friedman, described the evolution of the organizing approach as "creative reactivity"—being in a constant state of invention and reinvention, sampling from different lineages and responding to community needs.[20] The MRNY model differs from orthodoxy in its emphasis on two things: services and love.

Organizing doctrine usually enjoins against providing services, believing services to be a charitable response that is counter to the aim of changing relations of power. MRNY, however, uses services to recruit people and connect individual struggles to the need for wider social change. This approach has a long history inside and outside the United States, including the work of settlement houses in the early twentieth century and the approach of worker centers today, which organize and engage workers typically not reached by unions.

What distinguishes MRNY's approach from that of other organizations that provide services is their insistence on politicizing the underlying problem that caused someone to reach out for services. Why is rent so unaffordable? Who is responsible? What can we do about it? What MRNY Co-Executive Director Jose Lopez calls an "agitational intake" involves activating the anger people have about injustice and inviting them to join with their neighbors. Rather than adopting a traditional provider–client model, which views the client as a passive recipient, MRNY encourages members to assume responsibility for building power with others facing the same issues. Providing emergency food and services during the pandemic became a springboard into MRNY's campaign to win the Excluded Workers Fund.

When working-class people deal with an abusive landlord, an exploitative employer, or a hostile government bureaucracy as individuals, they learn to submit, evade, or protest ineffectually. To make change, people must learn to be with each other in more cooperative and authentic ways. MRNY's emphasis on culture is not incidental. Simple cultural practices bring alive the organization's motto of "respect and dignity." This kind of nourishment—the spiritual dimension of organizing—is rarely explicitly acknowledged by many community organizers, who talk in terms of power, targets, and metrics. But it's what keeps people coming back. As Javier Valdés, a former co-executive director, put it, when he came to MRNY, it was the "first time I felt I belonged."[21] An internal document explains as follows:

> Creating community means building relationships that go beyond any one narrow issue or campaign, and caring about each person as a vital part of the fabric of our movement. It means creating spaces that are open to all types of activity, where people can teach a music lesson, celebrate the arrival of a new baby, or dress up for Halloween. It means making people laugh, and celebrating our collective achievements on our walls and in

our meetings. . . . The model has the power to create resilient relationships that go beyond narrow self-interest. Outside, in the world, we spend our lives fighting oppression and confronting its daily ugliness. Inside, we gather the strength to continue.[22]

In general, anger is viewed as foundational to community organizing. And anger at injustice provides critical energy to generate momentum for change. But for the long haul, Valdés says, "anger is not enough"; people keep "organizing from love."[23] People see themselves recognized and respected and learn how to relate with each other with reciprocity and care rather than the transactional logic of the market. This way of relating is embedded in the organization's culture. Practices such as singing together and eating together, providing childcare, and introducing new members to the group are not soft "extras"—they create the fabric of the relationship and trust that enable the group to take big risks. Lopez talks about how the organization measures success in terms of not only victories on key issues, but also "whether or not the person who walked into our offices is leaving our organization a better person."[24] A synergistic connection between inner and outer change—change in individuals and how they show up and relate, and changes in policies, systems, and structures—arguably always exists in successful organizations, but rarely is it systematized and emphasized the way it is at MRNY.

The organization also pushes people to expand their conception of who is part of the "we." In 2008, MRNY launched a pathbreaking organizing project with transgender, gender non-conforming, intersex, and queer (TGNCIQ) immigrants who face violence, poverty, and police harassment. As Lopez put it: "As we think about organizing trans Latina women in Jackson Heights, Corona, and Elmhurst, it took a lot of work in the early days of Make the Road to get our members to understand that the issues that affect us are the very same issues that impact our trans brothers and sisters."[25]

One of our former students, Mateo Guerrero, then a lead organizer with MRNY's Trans Immigrant Project, supported trans leaders who campaigned to repeal New York State's notorious "Walking While Trans" law. In June of 2020, a day after fifteen thousand people marched in Brooklyn for

Black trans lives, Guerrero and two of his MRNY colleagues wrote in *City Limits* that the "law is applied as a catch-all to criminalize trans women of color—often just for standing outside their home, walking to the grocery store or walking with friends. Of those targeted, 90 percent of those charged are Black and Brown."[26] MRNY and its coalition partners employed a savvy inside-outside strategy, leveraging new allies elected that fall, and in February of 2021, the New York Assembly voted to repeal the law. On Twitter, Guerrero wrote that the victory was "the result of decades of organizing from Black and Brown Trans communities"—organizing that helped grow MRNY's base and build trans power at the same time.[27]

Key Strategic Decisions: Talent, Structure, and Culture

MRNY was co-founded in 1997 by two law students, Andrew Friedman and Oona Chatterjee, who did not come from the neighborhoods in which they organized. One of the key questions that the organization's leaders faced after the founders left was how to recruit enough organizers with the requisite skills to drive the organization's work as it expanded. According to Valdés, a pivotal decision was to invest in "home-grown talent," developing members to become staff leaders and organizers. Many lead organizers, including Guerrero, Yaritza Mendez, and Julissa Bisono (the latter two are now co-directors of organizing), first became involved through MRNY's youth organizing. The practice of organizer development is not often discussed, but it's one of the most important factors that determines the success or failure of community organizations.

In Chapter 2, we talked about how strategy requires making choices—decisions to do this and not that. For MRNY, a crucial decision was to rarely hire from outside the community—even though they might have found staff people who were able to take the reins of major campaigns more quickly. And it meant investing deeply in organizing training and allowing people to make mistakes and learn from them. It also required delegating power to lead organizers, who have significant autonomy.[28]

Emblematic of this approach is Lopez's trajectory from youth activist to co-executive director. When he was just thirteen years old, hoping to find a summer job, he wandered by MRNY's office in Bushwick. Seeing his cousins inside, he walked in and met Chatterjee, who talked with Lopez and his cousins about the problems they were facing with the lack of youth services and had them watch a film about the Young Lords. Lopez soon became part of a successful citywide campaign to reduce funding for youth jails and increase funding for youth services. He was hooked.[29]

MRNY has also had to make hard decisions about structure and resources. For example, at a pivotal point the organization eliminated a whole department focused on workforce development and invested in legal and compliance strategies to enable it to withstand formidable attacks from political opponents like Governor Cuomo. In its early days MRNY abandoned the "quicksand of the collective"—a consensus-based system that resulted in lengthy deliberation among staff—in favor of a highly participatory and democratic, but also hierarchical, structure to facilitate decision making (Friedman notes that "the collective collectively decided to abandon the collective, so people could have more room to run and move in their areas of work.")[30] And MRNY saw how some large New York unions, constrained by labor law and the need to represent their dues-paying membership, and usually risk-averse in order to protect their power, focused primarily on their own members rather than on the broader working class. MRNY has consciously sought *not* to be parochial. This has led MRNY to make its services available to nonmembers and to support coalitions with groups with fewer resources.

Strengths and Weaknesses of the Community Organizing Model

The MRNY model requires digging in for the long term, to build real bases in specific geographies and then to aggregate those constituencies to wield power in the city, at the state level, and in Washington, DC. The use of solidarity power depends on disciplined action by organized people to overcome the influence of organized money. While the mammoth victory for excluded workers seemingly came quickly, it rested on a foundation of community and political relationships built over decades, and the ability to deliver rewards and punishment to elected officials. It also depended on long-term principled alliances with other organizations.

The model has obvious strengths, including the ability to engage in political trench warfare over long periods, to put forth agendas rooted in the lived experience of community members, and to build power over time. Like other community organizations, MRNY has invested deeply in political action through a separately constituted 501(c)(4) organization that endorses candidates and runs large-scale field operations to turn out voters.[31] It has worked closely with the Working Families Party and other community-based organizations in New York, like NY Communities for Change and Community Voices Heard, to create a "fear factor" among elected officials that has propelled MRNY's issue agenda forward. It's unlikely that the Excluded Workers Fund would have succeeded without a set of political interventions at the state level that elected progressive insurgents and undermined the power first of a group of conservative Democrats and then of Governor Cuomo.

Every organization that acquires real power faces a dilemma: how do you avoid being co-opted by the system you were founded to challenge? Political scientist Robert Michels studied European socialist parties and developed "the iron law of oligarchy." He argued that organizations tend to get more conservative as entrenched leaders prioritize preserving their power and maintaining the organization over social change goals.[32] MRNY wields real political power but has maintained a radical edge, picking fights at or beyond the "left edge of the possible." One key element is leadership that has sustained, rather than suppressed, the organization's culture of organizing and democratic member participation. Lopez defined the organization's "secret sauce" as "bringing everybody along for the ride, from the point of walking in our door to the point of passing public policy."[33]

For all its strengths, the MRNY model depends on conditions that may not be easily replicated. New York has a significant philanthropic sector and well-developed public-funding streams for anti-poverty services. It took twenty-five years in that resource-rich environment to build significant power, and it has been challenging to expand the same synergy between service provision and organizing into states without that kind of resource base. Funding by foundations and donors also creates its own contradictions and tensions that will become pressing as the organization embraces more radical agendas.

Moreover, the "high-touch" model—arguably the heart of MRNY's organizing success—creates dilemmas of its own. The model is staff heavy. Because there is an entrenched issue-based committee structure, the organization can proliferate dozens of campaigns but finds it difficult to focus its power on the most important. This was overcome during the Excluded Workers Fund campaign, but only partially so. And a culture of love can create dilemmas too—how to balance a culture of care with a need for accountability. It's critical to mix love with rigor. An internal document puts it as follows:

> We use goals to challenge ourselves and provide markers against which we measure our progress, and hold each other accountable. Strong organizations get built with rigor, building a little more each day than you had the last. We track our progress on tasks big and small, and pride ourselves on doing the un-sexy work required to make big things possible... We regularly check in on progress, and hold each other accountable.[34]

The Path Is the Destination

The campaign to win the Excluded Workers Fund exhibits many core principles of strategy, including a savvy analysis of the shifting political and cultural currents. It exemplifies the power of vision that is rooted in underdogs' lived experience. MRNY staff and members faced intense grief and suffering as immigrant New York bore the brunt of the pandemic's impact. That pain—and love for each other—became the fuel to imagine and campaign for a bold plan that shattered a long-standing consensus.

The transformation of individuals and their relationships with each other is the magic of organizing, both necessary for victories and a victory in itself. Rubiela Correa said that the campaign to enact the Excluded Workers Fund gave her "the opportunity to do something about my desperation. The doors began to open where I could fight for my dignity, not just for my own but for others."[35] This is the soul of community organizing—achieving tangible, meaningful change in systems and policies by building power and leadership among those experiencing injustice. As organizing has gotten more sophisticated in recent years (making use of technology and communications tools), some of its core principles have gone out of fashion, such as the practice of in-person, relational conversations, and the emphasis on recruiting new people rather than just mobilizing people who are ready to go. At times, the orientation to grassroots, democratic decision making is lost too. But it's hard to imagine a path to lasting social change without much more of the slow and respectful work—the love and rigor—exemplified by MRNY.

Table 6.1.1: Key Components of the Base-Building Model– Community Organizing

Component	Base-Building Model
Form of Power	Solidarity
Theory of Change	Lots of people acting in solidarity with discipline and for the long term → pressure politicians, corporations, landlords, or institutions to make change
Examples of Practitioners and Theorists	Ella Baker, Saul Alinsky, SNCC, Cesar Chavez, IAF, ACORN Charles Payne, Theda Skocpol, Aldon Morris, Hahrie Han
Protagonists and Structure	Organizers, elected leaders, members Representative and usually formally democratic structure
Goals and Methods	Demands are usually specific, immediate, winnable (they can be more ambitious); issues are chosen and defined in terms of member self-interest; recruitment of new people; listening sessions; membership dues; democratic participation; systematic leadership development

Component	Base-Building Model
Tactical Repertoire	Accountability sessions; direct action; strikes; negotiation with targets
	Disciplined and carefully orchestrated, planned actions
What Does Winning Mean?	Demands are wholly or partly achieved; organization is stronger at the end of the campaign than at the beginning and gets "credit" for the win
Time Horizon + When the Model Is Most Effective	Evergreen, but especially useful in slower periods in movement cycles, laying the groundwork for political opportunities or movement upsurges
	"Trench warfare"—change mostly comes in small increments over time
	Seeks to establish permanent institutions
Movement Ecosystem	Works well with electoral change and inside-outside campaigns; relies on disruptive movements for exponential growth and on collective care for sustainability; less history of combining it with narrative shift and momentum
Strengths	Concrete wins that improve people's lives; builds grassroots leadership; can engage in struggle over years
Weaknesses	Can be slow and plodding or focus narrowly on the interests of existing members, and on small local issues to the exclusion of bigger, systemic issues

Tools

Tool 11 Leadership Identification
Tool 12 Collective Care
Tool 33 Power Analysis
Tool 34 Strategy Chart
Tool 35 Leadership Ladder

6.2

Base-Building

Labor Unions: Worker Power, the Common Good, and the St. Paul Federation of Educators

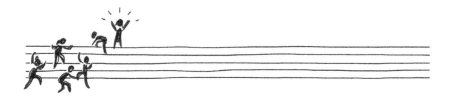

Leah VanDassor grew up in a union town. She saw the power of unions to strike and win higher wages, but when she became a teacher and a member of the teacher's union, she wasn't that interested in it. "I didn't pay attention," she told us in an interview. "Every other year there was a vote for the contract or not, but I didn't know what was going on in the union."[1]

Things began to change when new leaders came in to run the union, the St. Paul Federation of Educators (SPFE) in Minnesota.[2] Suddenly, instead of talking only about wages, union leaders were talking about students and schools. "This really struck a chord with me," says VanDassor. "We were looking at things that would impact our students' lives and therefore impact our working conditions. So that's when I started getting more involved."[3]

A decade later, VanDassor was elected president of SPFE. A year into her term, she found herself leading the union and bargaining for a new contract in the middle of a pandemic. The St. Paul School District called for rollbacks in the contract, claiming that declining school enrollment was creating a $43 million budget shortfall.[4] But along with their colleagues in the Minneapolis Federation of Teachers, St. Paul educators demanded limits on class size, funding and staff for student mental health services, and wage increases, including larger-than-usual pay bumps for low-wage education assistants.

It was going to be a fight. The pandemic was hard on union leaders and members, and everyone was exhausted. Still, when the union came together to discuss their options, "Folks said, 'we might be tired, but we're not stupid. We're fighting back. We're ready to go,'" SPFE organizer Leah Lindeman told us. "And people did the work. The muscle memory was there from the past, they woke it up, they did the organizing work that needed to happen."[5]

When negotiations hit an impasse, almost 80 percent of SPFE members voted in favor of a strike. And just minutes before their deadline on March 7, 2022, the union reached an agreement with the school district. Had they failed to do so, SPFE was prepared to go on strike the next day.

The union didn't win all its demands, but they won a lot, including an average 13.5 percent raise for education assistants, a drop in class sizes, and new funding for school psychologists. Like the slow and methodical work done by Make the Road, SPFE's story shows that persistence can pay off. Lindeman sums it up as follows:

> Because we had done so much work over time and people knew how to organize in their [school] building, they knew what was going on. They trusted each other. Even when you get into those tight moments, that's when that work comes into play. And it was much easier to come together and fight back and win than if we hadn't ever done any of that work.[6]

SPFE celebrated its 100th anniversary in 2019. In the last seventeen years, the union has adopted a number of strategies to advocate on behalf of its members, who number in the thousands. Part of their success has been rooted in their communal and transparent base-building approach.

"Our" Union, Not "the" Union

Unions rely on various forms of power and use many of the strategy models we cover in this book, but we focus on their base-building work because all of their other strategies must be built on a solid foundation of member organization. A strike won't work if members don't stick together. Base-building starts with the theory that union power is predicated on people power. Unions derive strength and influence when the majority of workers are members of the union and when those members participate in union meetings and activities. Power comes from workers' ability to act together.[7]

Stephanie has been a member of, and worked with, unions for decades, particularly with organizers working to make unions more democratic, militant, and inclusive. For several years in the 2000s she helped coordinate national calls of rank-and-file teachers looking to reform their unions and was inspired by the number of educators passionate about making schools work better for teachers as well as for students and parents. Teachers have been transforming their unions around the country, putting them on the frontlines in the fight to save public education. Some of that has been driven by young teachers wanting to bring racial justice into their education work, and much has been driven by veteran teachers who were tired of the growing attacks against public schools.

VanDassor's election—in fact, her candidacy—wouldn't have happened without Mary Cathryn Ricker. Ricker was a teacher who was tired of the way teachers and public schools were being portrayed by politicians and in the media. She decided to run for union president in 2005, and won. Prior to Ricker, the SPFE had a traditional structure—it was run by a president and business agents—Ricker, however, replaced the business agents with organizers who had a history of developing rank-and-file leaders.

The new leadership took several steps to rebuild the union. Ricker explained: "The first step was quite simple: to talk to one another."[8] They established a Contract Action Team (CAT) in each of the sixty schools and cultivated rank-and-file leaders to prepare for the next round of bargaining. "I really honestly think one of the major things we did was start saying 'our union' instead of '*the* union,'" VanDassor says. "Instead of treating our union like a pop machine, we treat it like a gym membership." In other words, you have to work out to get something out of it, and you have to keep working.[9]

VENDING MACHINE   GYM MEMBERSHIP

Next, they knew that changing the culture of the union would require changing the narrative about public schools and teacher unions. The union formed a group to write a mission statement: "A New Narrative for Teachers, Educators, and Public Education." The statement highlighted student success and social justice, emphasizing the strong relationship between student and educator issues and interests.[10]

Most unions bargain with a small team of leaders and lawyers but SPFE used a provision in state law that allowed for "open bargaining," which let all union members, as well as parents and members of the community, attend bargaining sessions. They set bargaining sessions for a regular time on Thursday evenings to make it easier to attend.

Each year the union expanded its efforts to deepen member and community involvement. The St. Paul school district is diverse: over 70 percent of students in public schools are students of color, over 70 percent qualify for free or reduced-cost lunch, and more than one third speak English as a second language.[11] In order to accommodate this wide array of needs and preferences, in 2013, SPFE organizers solicited input from teachers, parents, and community members about how schools could be run better. They wrote up their findings in a report called "The Schools St. Paul Children Deserve," which was subsequently used as the basis for the union's bargaining proposal that year.

The union's membership is predominately white, and SPFE has struggled to address racial equity inside its ranks. Noting strong racial disparities in school discipline, SPFE brought a demand for restorative justice practices into bargaining in 2015. They won an agreement to launch a three-year, $4.5 million pilot program, initially in six schools, and now in twelve. With funding from their parent union, the National Education Association, SPFE created a training curriculum in restorative practice—conflict-resolution methods that attempt to address root causes of behavioral problems and give students new skills, rather than harsh "zero tolerance" disciplinary policies.[12]

The union took on a project to educate themselves and the community about how schools are funded. They created TIGER Teams (Teaching and Inquiring about Greed, Equity, and Racism) to study how "money is being stolen from our school and our community by our state's largest corporations and wealthiest citizens," according to SPFE's website.[13] VanDassor explains that the union is working to change taxes and funding streams in the state, as well as to make corporations pay higher taxes.[14]

The work continues, like any good workout routine. The pandemic has taken a toll, but the hard work of the past decade has helped the union continue and even come out of its recent bargaining with a win.

Labor Union Revitalization

The SPFE story almost makes it sound easy to build a strong union. And, compared to larger unions with entrenched leadership, it was easier to rebuild the SPFE. For instance, when Ricker decided to run for president, the incumbent stepped aside. In Chicago, teachers had to assemble a reform caucus and organize for years in order to win leadership and implement rank-and-file base-building.

While some union leaders see member engagement as a threat to their power, SPFE's story is an example of union leadership that understands member participation as their key focus and source of power. Some unions have always been that way, while others have had to rebuild after years of atrophy. "We were dusty," Ricker said when describing the union.[15]

In Stephanie's work she has heard from workers that in their own workplace, co-workers don't care. People don't have time or are selfish. But as the organization Labor Notes points out in its books and training, apathy isn't real. Everyone cares about something. They might be scared to speak up, or they might believe nothing can change, but they do care. The challenge for organizers is to help turn fear, hopelessness, division, confusion, and inaction into action.[16]

Not all unions see member power as their strength. Some rely on developing strong relations with the employer or policymakers; others focus on legislative gains. But even if a union must rely on legislative action to win union recognition, they still will need to deal with member engagement at some point. And member engagement is the one thing that is 100 percent in a union's control—particularly when workers get active and see themselves as the union.

Some unions have built internal education programs to build solidarity and member participation. The Communications Workers of America (CWA) created a curriculum for members to teach each other about inequality and the ways in which employers, policies, and laws have divided workers by race.[17] Other unions are rethinking what it means to be a leader, challenging the myth that good leaders are charismatic types who lead from above, and instead making space for people who lead by bringing others with them, as well as for more women and people of color. "We need leaders," Lauren Jacobs, the executive director of a network of labor and community groups, told us. "But we need multi-racial leadership, feminist leadership who are committed to their members and to the communities in which they work and live."[18] When leadership reflects the membership, it's better positioned to hear and act on the issues at hand. It can also motivate members to get more involved.

Some renewal has been influenced by **Bargaining for the Common Good** (BCG), an approach that expands bargaining beyond the usual topics of wages and working conditions to broader issues impacting union members and communities.[19] For example, many teachers have come to understand that they can't do their jobs well if they don't also address student issues, like class size and counseling. Shantella Barnes, a special education assistant in the St. Paul schools, works with students with emotional and behavioral disorders. Without adequate support and staffing, she can't do her job well and meet the needs of her students. And without a living wage, her work is stressful: "It makes it difficult for us to come to work and deal with other kids and try to help them when we have to figure out how we're helping our own family."[20]

Structured Worker Power: Common Elements of the Base-Building Model in Labor Organizing

A. Philip Randolph was the founder of the Brotherhood of Sleeping Car Porters, a union of Black workers that led the fight for civil rights, including by anchoring the 1963 March on Washington for Jobs and Freedom. He famously articulated the core of the organizing ethos:

> At the banquet table of nature, there are no reserved seats. You get what you can take and you keep what you can hold. If you cannot take anything, you won't get anything. And if you can't hold anything, you won't keep anything without an organization.[21]

So, how do unions build that organization? Labor organizing includes establishing unions in nonunion workplaces as well as revitalizing existing unions. The nature of base-building plays out somewhat differently in these two scenarios, but there are common core elements in both, as follows:

> *Map the workplace.* How many people work there? What departments or divisions exist? Are there multiple shifts? Part-time or seasonal workers? Even in a unionized workplace you may not have a clear sense of who actually works there. Alongside the workplace, organizers have to map out existing networks of co-workers: Who eats lunch together? Does anyone carpool, or spend time together outside of work hours?[22]

Identify leaders and build a leadership team. Leaders are not necessarily the ones who are most pro-union to start, but the people others look to, those who are good at their job, are trustworthy, and command respect. Leadership teams should be as representative as possible of the workforce.

Develop new leaders. Train members in organizing skills, labor history, strategic thinking, and how to cultivate new leaders themselves. Leadership development can happen through formal and informal training and mentorship.

Identify a key issue. Leadership teams listen to co-workers to understand their concerns in order to figure out what to fight for. Traditional unions fight on workplace issues like wages, health insurance, and scheduling. But workers have interests beyond these traditional issues, like how teachers fight for student issues. Experienced organizers know an effective issue touches workers' sense of respect and dignity. Just like community organizers, union organizers must find the issues that will mobilize members and build power.

Research. Unions study their employer and industry, looking for points of leverage in bargaining, opportunities for new organizing, and potential threats of job loss. Given the enormous power corporations have on almost every aspect of our society, strategists in other traditions and models would do well to learn from unions' expertise in corporate research.[23]

Escalate tactics. The union works backward from the end goal, using tactics that get riskier and more impactful, which could include workers' signing petitions; wearing the same color shirt, sticker, or button; visiting a boss together; holding informational picket lines; building relationships with supporters outside of the workplace; developing bargaining demands with students or patients; and striking. These also serve as "structure tests"—as union organizer Jane McAlevey writes, "How strong is the people's army?"[24] If union leaders call on members to wear a union T-shirt to work, or sign a petition, or show up to a rally, how many will do so? Some organizers have observed that some people don't want to do these types of activities because they don't see how they connect to a larger vision: how does wearing a T-shirt build power? Former union organizer Zack Exley (Chapter 2) found it more effective to involve workers in developing long-term plans as a way to motivate them before asking them to take the small steps.

Build internal structures. Structures such as a shop steward system formalize relationships among members. Shop stewards are workers elected to learn the contract and help co-workers solve problems on the job. In some unions this is a volunteer position, others provide a small stipend. Ideally stewards are trained, attend union meetings, and stay in frequent contact with union leaders, staff, and members. A strong shop steward network may have one steward for every ten or twenty workers.

Internal structures include member committees, such as health and safety, social activities, retirees, international solidarity, diversity, bargaining, and so on. Large unions may also have internal caucuses based around race, ethnicity, or specific interests. Committees and caucuses are ways to build internal solidarity and commitment to the union.

SPFE has found changing the internal structure to be invaluable for building internal participation and strength. Lindeman told us, "We have to trust the members—this is their profession, this is their job, this is their life." Even if it takes extra time to involve members, it has been key to strong member engagement. SPFE members Chong Xiong and Brian Hodge-Rice explained that in the past, stewards would show up and give presentations on the contract, but with their new structure, members are involved in bargaining the whole way and can wrestle with the hard issues as they come up.[25]

Solidarity power is enhanced when elected leaders, member leaders, and union staff can work together creatively as a team, particularly when diverse leaders bring in experience with a range of traditions of struggle and connection to a broad array of networks.[26] (Table 6.2.1 summarizes the key characteristics of the model.)

The theory of change for union strength is similar to what we offered in the prior chapter for community organizations:

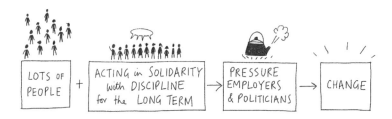

Strengths and Weaknesses of the Union Model

Strong unions have won much for their members and the working class overall. Robust evidence shows that they raise wages, provide job security and benefits, and reduce disparity and discrimination. None of this would have been possible without a base of well-organized members.

Organizing of this kind is labor intensive and time consuming. In the 1990s and 2000s, a group of union leaders took bold steps to bring in new AFL-CIO leadership and push for new organizing, committing 30 percent of their budgets to staff and resources to bring unorganized workers into unions. They hired thousands of young, energetic organizers who traveled the country, living out of hotels and working long days, using the techniques just listed: mapping the workplace, visiting workers at their homes, assessing workers' support for unions, running well-executed campaigns. The efforts sometimes paid off. But for the most part, new organizing could not keep up with the growing labor force, the loss of unionized workplaces when plants shut down, or the loss of members when union workers retired and were not replaced. The victories came at a great cost in terms of union expenditures and burnout among these young organizers.

Most union growth does not happen incrementally, plant by plant, workplace by workplace. As union organizer Mark Meinster writes, "The problem is that even great tactics can't overcome the social, political, and economic forces of capitalism, which combine to make organizing a gigantic challenge.... Employers are under intense competitive pressure to resist workers' demands—there's no generous 'high road' for them to take; they won't willingly give in to a union drive. And employers are compelled to come together as a class to exert power over the government, passing laws and using the courts to challenge unions on all fronts."[27] Instead, union growth comes in "upsurges"—periods where workers rise up more broadly.[28] In the United States, these upsurges took place at the turn of the twentieth century, in the 1930s, and in the late 1960s/early 1970s. There are signs we may be in the beginning of another upsurge as we write this book.[29]

This suggests that the steady, slow work of building unions worker by worker must be paired with other strategies, especially given the added obstacles unions face—intense employer opposition and weak labor laws. Labor organizers have devoted a lot of time and thought to the best ways to bring large numbers of new members into unions. We won't cover that debate here but will note that no one model has had overwhelming success in recent decades.[30]

Town Hall or Army? Tensions in the Union Model

So far, we've explored unions as an example of the base-building model. Now we turn to some of the tensions unique to unions, a product of their unique role in the history of underdog organizing. There are over 14 million union members in the United States as of 2023, and collectively they control almost $30 billion in assets, making them far larger than other underdog organizations.[31] But unlike many underdog organizations that have a self-selected membership, unions represent workers with the full range of political views. This creates tensions unique to the model.

First, a union must represent all workers in the workplace (technically, in a "bargaining unit").[32] In some cases, workers don't have to be members of the union, but under the National Labor Relations Act (NLRA), the union is still legally required to represent all workers. This is different from community organizations, which can establish rules and requirements for who is allowed to be a member. This can be both a strength and a weakness. On the one hand, it means that unions must work hard to unite workers across differences. That might push the union to hire more organizers, build stronger structures of representation, and learn to find common ground among a diverse workforce. On the other hand, it might push the union to focus only on the lowest common denominator, such as a demand for higher wages, and play it safe in terms of bolder demands and decisions, such as supporting a controversial political cause. Regardless, this stipulation affects base-building, as a union that wants to build power may have to appeal to anti-union workers in the process.

Second, unions are democratic organizations. By law, all union officers must be elected, and unions must have constitutions and by-laws.[33] Local elections must take place at least every three years; national elections at least every five years. Leaders can be voted out of office.

In theory this should make union leaders more accountable to members than leaders of organizations without a formal democratic structure. But formal democracy is not always participatory. Participatory democracy requires transparency in union functioning, along with regular membership meetings where members have input on strategy and decision making.

A number of labor scholars have found that true internal democracy augments a union's influence, particularly vis-à-vis powerful employers.[34] For example, sociologist Carolina Bank Muñoz argues that Walmart warehouse workers in Chile were able to win strong contracts in part because internal democracy encouraged creative strategy development and engagement in militant action.[35] Democracy is not just an end, but also a means to building a strong base, she argues.

Not all union leaders agree, which relates to the next tension: unions play a dual role. Labor and peace organizer AJ Muste wrote of the complicated nature of unions in 1928, noting that in addition to serving as "town halls," unions must also function as an army. Town halls are democratic spaces whereas armies are usually top-down, hierarchical operations. This creates tensions within the union: "Imagine the conflict in the soul of a union official who must have the attitude and discharge the functions at one and the same time of both general and a chairman of a debating society," Muste wrote.[36] Indeed, there can be greater struggles within the union, such as between those members who see it primarily as a form of insurance and those who might want the union to play a role in societal transformation. To use VanDassor's analogy, you can see the union as a vending machine where you insert a dollar and get a can of Coke, or you can see the union as a space you attend regularly to work out and get stronger to win big change.

This relates to a larger question: What's the main purpose of unions? Is it to improve wages and working conditions, or to fight for broader demands for members and workers as a whole? Many of the earliest unions were formed as mutual aid for co-workers, who helped fund each other in times of sickness or death, trained one another, and built community (Deepak's father was a member of a union that represented taxi workers—the union paid most of Deepak's tuition for the first year of college). They also worked to keep control over their work by keeping other workers out. Other unions organized all workers in an industry into one union and fought for legislation that would protect all workers and reduce employers' power, such as minimum-wage laws and unemployment insurance. Still, other unions have played a role in overthrowing dictators or apartheid regimes and bringing democracy to countries such as Brazil, South Korea, South Africa, and Indonesia.

This tension reflects different goals. It also reflects different analyses of power and organizing models. We mentioned in Chapter 2 how Exley was trained as a labor organizer in an Alinsky-like model (asking workers to take small steps around least-common-denominator demands), and how he found that many workers were not willing to take or interested in taking the big risk of unionizing for a small goal like a 5 percent raise, but would take risks for a potential big demand. In Exley's approach, labor organizing should tackle larger ideological questions, going beyond the least common denominators of wages and hours. This is likely to require robust political education, including addressing issues that may be divisive, such as structural racism in the labor market and within the union movement.

Finally, it's worth noting that from the beginning, labor unions have confronted powerful opposition. The first legal case against unions in 1806 ruled that the very act of collective worker activity was a criminal conspiracy.[37] Even the landmark NLRA allows unions only insofar as they don't harm business. They have weathered sustained surveillance, sabotage, assassination attempts, and other attacks from corporate opponents and the government itself, far more than most civil society groups, with the exception of Black and Indigenous social justice groups.

Base-Building and Other Strategy Models

SPFE's example shows how the base-building model, built on solidarity power, can interact successfully with the other models of transformational change from below. SPFE used base-building to revitalize its union. It began with teachers talking to one another, but it used other strategies as well—starting with its new mission statement, followed by a narrative shift strategy that built toward disruption.

Unions have used electoral strategies for decades, particularly since the 1930s, when the labor movement developed close ties to the Democratic Party. Unions endorse candidates, they engage in massive get-out-the-vote efforts, and their members voluntarily contribute millions of dollars for their political programs. Unions have prepared members to run for office, and in some cases supported the formation of independent political parties with a stronger labor focus. Electoral politics has yielded limited results on the federal level, where unions have been unable to win favorable labor law reform or other key legislative demands for many decades. Unions have had better success at the city and state levels in certain states, but for the most part they've been taken for granted by the Democratic Party.

Several unions have used an inside-outside strategy to pass legislation that improves conditions for all workers, such as higher minimum wages, paid family leave, and paid sick days. Some have fought for legislation to improve conditions for unionizing workers, such as rules governing government contracting or designating home-care workers as employees with the right to unionize.

Member Power Is Your Biggest Weapon

The SPFE's resurgence is a story of good organizing. It also highlights some strategy fundamentals. When Mary Cathryn Ricker took over the leadership of the union she had to choose: Would she build up the union's capacity to provide better services to members? Or would she take a risk and open the union for members to lead? She chose the latter. In this case, the initial strategic decision was made from the top: the president. But opening up the union ensured that future strategy would be guided by rank-and-file educators. The case shows how strategy may be guided from above, by leaders, in a way that fosters conditions for emergent strategy from below.

Many union leaders find it scary to open the union to greater member leadership, says Leah Lindeman. But by doing so, the SPFE was able to build more power. "Whenever I hear that open bargaining is scary to people I am always baffled," Leah VanDassor explained. "It seems like it's one of our biggest 'weapons' to build our power within SPFE."[38] The union attracted educators, parents, and community members ready to organize for better public schools. They were motivated by winning a better contract, but more than that, they had a vision of schools that worked better for everyone.

Table 6.2.1: Key Components of the Base-Building Model— Labor Unions

Component	Base-Building Model
Form of Power	Solidarity
Theory of Change	Lots of workers acting in solidarity with discipline and for the long term → pressure employers and politicians to make change
Examples of Historical Practitioners and Theorists	A. Philip Randolph, William Z. Foster, Mary Harris "Mother" Jones, Rose Schneiderman, John L. Lewis, Emma Tenayuca, "Big Bill" Haywood, Lucy Parsons, Flint sit-down strikers Most labor unions begin with a base-building model
Protagonists and Structure	Members, shop stewards, elected leaders, organizers Representative and usually formally democratic structure
Goals and Methods	Demands are specific, immediate, winnable (though can be more abstract); issues are chosen and defined in terms of member self-interest; recruitment of new people; membership dues; democratic participation; systematic leadership development

Component	Base-Building Model
Tactical Repertoire	Shop floor direct action, collective bargaining, strikes, lobbying, political engagement
What Does Winning Mean?	Demands are wholly or partly achieved; successful election for union representation; win a collective bargaining agreement; social change for the working class
Time Horizon + When the Model Is Most Effective	Evergreen, but especially useful in slower periods in movement cycles, laying the groundwork for upsurge in worker organizing and action "Trench warfare"—change mostly comes in small increments over time Seeks to establish permanent institutions
How It Works with Other Models/ Movement Ecosystem	Works closely with electoral change and inside-outside campaigns; relies on disruptive movements for exponential growth and on collective care for sustainability; less history of combining it with narrative shift and momentum; some unions were formed out of collective care and some have attempted to revive this
Strengths	Concrete wins that improve people's lives; builds worker leadership; can engage in struggle over years, can build powerful institutions that have great impact on society
Weaknesses	Can be slow and incremental, focused narrowly on the interests of existing members, bureaucratic, undemocratic, and corrupt; at times works to reinforce the status quo against other underdog movements

Tools

Tool 7 Power for Underdogs
Tool 11 Leadership Identification
Tool 13 Bargaining for the Common Good
Tool 34 Strategy Chart

7

Disruptive Movements

Breaking the Rules, Changing the Paradigm: The Welfare Rights Movement

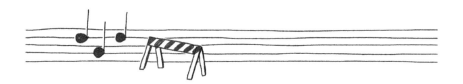

In 1972, Johnnie Tillmon published an article in *Ms.* magazine that criticized the welfare system for being racist, sexist, and degrading by design. She challenged white, middle-class feminists to center the concerns of poor women of color in the women's movement. In "Welfare Is a Women's Issue," she wrote:

> I'm a woman. I'm a Black woman. I'm a poor woman. I'm a fat woman. I'm a middle-aged woman. And I'm on welfare. In this country, if you're any one of those things you count less as a human being. If you're all those things, you don't count at all. Except as a statistic. And that's why welfare is a women's issue. For a lot of middle-class women in this country, Women's Liberation is a matter of concern. For women on welfare, it's a matter of survival.[1]

Tillmon was president of the National Welfare Rights Organization (NWRO), an organization led by Black women who advanced a visionary demand for a guaranteed annual income, a universal income floor that would enable all people to meet their basic needs. "The ladies of NWRO are the frontline troops of women's freedom," Tillmon argued. "Both because we have so few illusions and because our issues are so important to all women—the right to a living wage for women's work, the right to life itself."[2]

The racist provisions of the welfare system established in the New Deal (then called Aid to Families with Dependent Children [AFDC]), had been designed so that few Black women could access aid.[3] But the welfare rights movement in the 1960s and 1970s transformed this. Thousands of poor women across the country, mostly women of color, forced cities and states to open access to cash aid, increase benefit levels, and eliminate restrictive policies. The number of women receiving cash assistance soared from 3.6 million in 1962 to 11.4 million in 1976, a 316 percent increase.[4] This progress happened without Congress acting to expand eligibility or lower barriers to welfare assistance.

How did the welfare revolution come about? Lacking access to typical sources of influence like money, well-heeled advocacy groups, or even public respect, poor women of color had to organize differently. The welfare rights movement exemplifies movements that use disruptive power to stop the functioning of oppressive systems and force concessions from overdogs. Disruptive movements often have a big impact in a short time. If a disruptive movement achieves gains, the settlement can last until either the underdogs or the overdogs decide to challenge its terms.

The first major national campaign Deepak directed, the National Campaign for Jobs and Income Support, focused on undoing the punitive 1996 welfare law.[5] The law had bipartisan support and was the product of racist backlash to the gains achieved by poor women of color decades previously. The campaign brought together dozens of welfare rights groups and other community organizations and elevated the leadership of poor women of color. These women protested and took on senators who pushed punitive policies. In 2002, low-income women dropped waffles on Hillary Clinton's lawn to highlight the then senator's hypocrisy of talking about helping poor children while proposing to expand harsh work requirements.[6] The campaign was unable to undo the 1996 law, but it succeeded in passing expanded cash assistance through a partly refundable child tax credit that delivered $8 billion per year to low-income families.[7] This moved the welfare rights movement a step closer to realizing its vision. Organizing with poor women of color taught Deepak that there was and remains nothing more threatening to the establishment than an uprising of working-class Black women with a radical vision for change.

Fighting for Dignity and Respect

Organizing has been portrayed as something done exclusively by paid, formally trained organizers. But poor women of color began organizing themselves years before the formation of the NWRO. Tillmon was a union shop steward in a laundry in Compton, Los Angeles. She stopped working there after she became ill and decided to stay home to care for her six children. Tillmon was outraged by the treatment she received at the hands of the welfare office, including inspections of her refrigerator, questions about her decision to buy a television, and midnight raids aimed at finding reasons to disqualify her from assistance. She organized a meeting of hundreds of poor women to found Aid to Needy Children Mothers' Anonymous in Los Angeles in 1963.[8]

It was the systematic humiliation of poor women by the welfare system—even more than the paltry benefit levels—that inspired them to organize. As a leaflet distributed outside a Baltimore welfare office put it, "It is time that mothers on welfare stop being treated like dogs."[9] Roxanne Jones, a leader in the Philadelphia Welfare Rights Organization and the first Black woman elected to the Pennsylvania State Senate, talked about her first experience going to the welfare office:

> I went there with the idea I was gonna get help. And I will never forget that day as long as I live. How I was treated, the disrespect... And so, a leaflet came under my door one day, the leaflet said, "If you're on welfare, you have some rights. Would you

like to have money to live on? Would you like to be treated in dignity?" And I kept on readin' and I saw down there the Welfare Rights Organization was holdin' this meeting at Southward Reed. And I went to that meeting that day, it was a community center, and I guess I was so vocal that I became the chairperson that day . . . after a couple of meetings hearing how those other women were treated, we began to, right then, organize to try to change the system. First of all, we wanted to bring about dignity to ourselves because we knew we were somebody. We were mothers, we loved our children just like a working person loved their kids and we wanted to be respected that way. And we began to organize then. That's how I became active, being a welfare mother, being mistreated.[10]

Organized in local groups like Mothers for Adequate Welfare (Boston), Northside Welfare Rights Organization (Milwaukee), Concerned Parents, and Mother Rescuers from Poverty (Baltimore), poor women of color used savvy strategies to win concessions. They showed that oppressed people have leverage—if only in their power to not cooperate with an abusive system.

The nature of the leverage depends on the circumstances. The decentralized nature of the welfare system made it vulnerable to grassroots action. Decisions about who got what were made in local welfare offices. A poor woman facing off against a hostile caseworker had little prospect of winning an argument for increased benefits. But a group of women demanding fair treatment could win.

As another leader, Beulah Sanders, put it, "We went out there and fought for the things that we wanted, which was more clothing, more furniture, and other things that people needed. We had all kinds of demonstrations on welfare and housing. We trained people, taught them just how they go about going in the center demanding what they were entitled to. People came forth with us in big demonstrations at City Hall, and we was quite successful."[11]

Grassroots leaders in the welfare rights movement believed that they would make gains only if elites feared them. A Baltimore welfare rights group promised a "long, hot, angry summer" in 1967 unless their demands were met. The threat resonated with a government focused on how to prevent more urban uprisings.[12] At a welfare office in the Bronx, poor women overturned furniture and ripped telephones off the wall.[13] Tillmon talked explicitly about the role of fear, saying:

> It is true that when we're not heard we have to make people hear us. We do whatever becomes necessary. We're not a violent group . . . even sometimes we might have to throw a rock to get attention. We don't want to throw rocks to hit anybody. But just to make a noise. . . . People don't seem to hear us if we don't demonstrate.[14]

In Chapter 3, we talked about the importance of empathy in developing strategy; getting in the heads of your opponents and potential allies. Welfare rights movement leaders took the measure of their opponents in government—they knew that only when they feared disorder would they make concessions. The *New York Times* described the impact of disruptive actions at welfare offices:

> Whenever the Concerned Parents arrive in any numbers at the Jamaica center—and at least a few of them are there every day until closing time—there seems to be a slight nervousness among the staff, which handles 10,000 cases, a sense of being off-balance. What will come next? Quiet advocacy? A screaming confrontation full of shouted obscenities and charges that a relief client's check is below the right amount? Will they call Dr. McFarland a racist again? Will the police finally be called to make arrests? A picket line? A demonstration for a new campaign?[15]

By throwing officials off balance, welfare rights activists got results. In addition to opening up access to welfare to poor women of color, the movement established a right to a hearing before benefits could be ended, challenged policies requiring sterilization as a condition of assistance, and won repeal of "man in the house" rules that enabled surprise visits to check for men's presence or even clothing at poor women's homes.[16]

In 1966, political scientists Frances Fox Piven and Richard Cloward published "The Weight of the Poor: A Strategy to End Poverty" in *The Nation*. The article called upon women receiving aid to escalate their strategy. Piven and Cloward observed that there was a gap between the number of people eligible for welfare and the number of people who actually received it. And those who did get aid often got less than what they qualified for. This was not an accident. The welfare system was designed to exclude women of color and make the terms of assistance so degrading that many would give up. Piven and Cloward proposed a "massive drive to recruit the poor onto the welfare rolls," arguing that:

> widespread campaigns to register the eligible poor for welfare aid, and to help existing recipients obtain their full benefits, would produce bureaucratic disruption in welfare agencies and fiscal disruption in local and state governments. These disruptions would generate severe political strains, and deepen existing divisions among elements in the big-city Democratic coalition: the remaining white middle class, the white working-class ethnic groups and the growing minority poor.[17]

The theory was that, under pressure, mayors would demand federal intervention, creating the conditions for a national guaranteed income program. The least-powerful people in society could win a national anti-poverty program, not by petitioning their elected officials for policy change, or even by engaging in demonstrations (though they did both of those things); rather, their source of leverage was an organized, mass campaign to sign people up for the benefits they were entitled to by creating mayhem and fear at local welfare offices—a disruption that would reverberate upward and force a response from political elites.[18]

Beyond Protest: Disruption as Strategy

In a discussion Deepak facilitated with Service Employees International Union (SEIU) organizers in the South, longtime union organizer Eliseo Medina reflected on his experience with the United Farm Workers (UFW), Justice for Janitors, and other movements. He argued that to win, working-class people of color need to create a moral crisis, an economic crisis, and a political crisis simultaneously.[19] Making the case to the public about the justice of a cause—the moral crisis—is important, but insufficient (Chapter 8). The welfare rights movement made a moral case, created an economic crisis by putting fiscal pressure on local budgets, and a political crisis by leveraging the growing power of northern Black voters inside the Democratic Party to win concessions. Change wasn't inevitable. The welfare rights movement's genius was to use disruption to mobilize latent economic and political power to achieve immense gains for poor women of color.

When we think of disruption, we often think of protest. But not all disruptions involve protest. W.E.B. DuBois showed how the movement of enslaved people escaping plantations was in fact a general strike that helped defeat the Confederacy. The strike was highly disruptive but also stealthy and quiet. And not all protests are disruptive. Occupy Wall Street (OWS) and the Movement for Black Lives (M4BL), for example, both had a huge impact on public consciousness. But the occupation of public spaces, first at Wall Street and then around the country, did not prevent the 1 percent from making money. And most of the mass protests during the uprising for Black life in 2020 did not directly intervene to stop police violence against Black people. Both relied on other forms of power, especially ideological power. Rallies and marches can be useful tactics to recruit people, strengthen bonds of solidarity, or to dramatize injustice, but they are not usually "disruptive" in the sense we use the word. They lack the "power to wound."[20]

Disruptive movements depend on the use of the strategic leverage that is implicit in every relationship of oppression or exploitation. Underdogs win when they do not cooperate with an unjust system and thus stop it from functioning. Strategists can plan disruptive actions to win concessions. And if they don't have enough power to win on their own, they can try to create the conditions for disruption to spread virally, thereby enhancing their power and chances of success. The theory of change looks like this:

This contrasts with more conventional forms of activism that rely mainly on public demonstrations of grievance:

> People march in streets/hold rallies/use social media → dramatize injustice → create a moral crisis → demands are met

The most familiar disruptive actions happen at the workplace. Workers can shut down production and profits through direct action like strikes or slowdowns. But Stephanie, who has walked many picket lines and engaged in strike support work, has seen efforts fail when workers were not able to disrupt business effectively enough. In the early 1990s, Stephanie was in a student group that provided support to workers at three major companies—Staley, Caterpillar, and Bridgestone/Firestone—in Decatur, Illinois. Despite a massive effort by the workers, the companies were able to lock out the workers, bring in replacement workers, shift production, and outlast the workers' noncooperation. In each case, the companies managed to fire union supporters and push through drastic concessions. In contrast, in 1997, when Stephanie walked the picket lines in solidarity with striking UPS workers, over 185,000 Teamsters effectively shut down the company nationwide for sixteen days. UPS lost millions of dollars as well as public support, and eventually settled a contract with major gains for workers.

But people don't only have the power to disrupt at work. Every system of production requires a system of reproduction. There must be a way to feed, care for, and educate children. In our society, this system is the nuclear family. Because of the gendered division of labor, women take on most of the work involved in raising and caring for children. The total worldwide value of women's unpaid care work is estimated at $10.8 trillion, three times the value of the world's tech industry.[21]

Just as the system of production gives workers the capacity to disrupt, the system of reproduction gives women power. Women's strikes and sex strikes have occurred throughout history. On a day known as "the Long Friday" in 1975, 75,000 women in Iceland (an astonishing 90 percent of women in the country) took part in a general strike called "Women's Day Off" and won an equal pay act the following year.[22]

Against this backdrop, the welfare rights movement's demand to compensate care work can be understood as part of a long lineage of struggle.

Lineages of Disruptive Movements

The techniques of disruption vary widely, but the crucial common element is interrupting the functioning of an oppressive system to force change. Disruptive *actions* involve noncooperation by underdogs that impairs or stops a system such as capitalism, white supremacy, or patriarchy in a specific time and place. A disruptive *movement* involves many actions over time by large numbers of people and many groups aimed at forcing changes in the underlying rules for how the system operates.

The line between these can be blurry because a disruptive action can grow into a movement. Examples include the following:

- Autoworkers at two General Motors plants in Flint, Michigan, and another plant in Cleveland, Ohio, staged a forty-four-day sit-down strike in 1936 and 1937. Workers disrupted production, and by occupying the factory they prevented GM from replacing them. The workers won recognition for the United Auto Workers (UAW), a pay raise, and the right to talk about the union over lunch (which allowed them to sign up more members). These were peak actions in a long arc of disruption by workers that lasted for years.
- During the Great Depression, when millions of people were unemployed, groups of tenants physically prevented landlords from

proceeding with evictions or moved the furniture back into apartments after evictions had happened. In other circumstances, tenants have used rent strikes to force repairs or other concessions.
- In 1960, Black students affiliated with the Student Non-Violent Coordinating Committee (SNCC) launched a campaign to desegregate public facilities in Greensboro, North Carolina. They sought service at "whites only" lunch counters and sat in when they were refused service. The Congress of Racial Equality (CORE) initiated the "Freedom Rides" in 1961 to challenge segregation on buses traveling between states. Mixed groups of whites and Blacks refused to abide by rules requiring separate seating sections and challenged the rules of segregation at bus terminals as they rode south.
- Indigenous people blocked construction of the Dakota Access Pipeline at Standing Rock to defend Indigenous lands and their access to water. Protestors didn't just mount symbolic actions; they nonviolently disrupted access to the construction sites, blocking the project, at least temporarily.

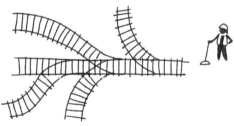

Capitalism, white supremacy, and patriarchy are powerful systems that usually seem impregnable. But these cases show that when people defy the rules of those systems at a large enough scale, they can win. Some people have more capacity to disrupt, such as workers with skills that are hard to replace, or who are at strategically located **chokepoints**. For example, transport workers can bring business to a standstill more easily than can fast-food workers. Disruption is most often used by underdogs, but it can also be used by overdogs, like when employers lock out workers. A dramatic instance of overdog disruption was the insurrection at the U.S. Capitol on January 6, 2021, which halted the counting of Electoral College votes for several hours.

Many of the insurrectionists think of themselves as underdogs, but they were acting at the direction of then President Donald Trump to maintain white supremacy.

Shut It Down: Common Elements of Successful Disruptive Movements

We summarize the key components of the disruptive movements in Table 7.1. The common elements of the model include the following:

> *Breaking rules and norms by stopping work, blocking access to a facility, going where people aren't supposed to go, or breaking the law.* This entails risks—of prosecution, losing a job or a home, being shamed or ridiculed, or violence from law enforcement or opposition groups. Many Freedom Riders were brutally beaten, and a bus was lit on fire by a white mob. Indigenous people at Standing Rock were attacked by police dogs and hosed with water cannons in freezing weather. Poor women of color in the welfare rights movement were shamed for demanding fair treatment by caseworkers and risked their benefits.
>
> *Mass participation.* Individuals break the rules of oppressive systems frequently, but acting alone they have little power to make change. Most of the workers in the Flint factories supported the occupation, and family members and neighbors supplied food to the workers—their solidarity was crucial. Sometimes, small and brave groups will act as vanguards by taking dramatic action that involves huge risks, as was the case with the Greensboro lunch-counter sit-ins or the Freedom Rides. But this vanguard relies on an outpouring of public support, which often comes after the opposition engages in brutal, visually arresting violence, to succeed.
>
> *Mobilizing powerful emotions.* It's not entirely predictable when or how people will rise up—often, horrendous injustices go on for years without much of a coordinated response. But when people do rise up, it's

usually because a potent combination of emotions were unleashed: anger at injustice, together with a sense of hope that things could be better. Sometimes an external event will provide the spark. Often a success will inspire people in a different place, or in another movement, to act. The welfare rights movement arose in conditions of rising expectations thanks to the success of the Black freedom and feminist movements, inspiring both indignation at injustice and a sense that conditions could change.[23]

Preparation for movement moments. Organizers can't manufacture the conditions for mass disruption. But they can do the groundwork that cultivates leaders, gives people a sense of their power, and sharpens their analysis of the vulnerabilities of an oppressive system. Ella Baker and Reverend James Lawson prepared young people in SNCC, and communists organized in the auto plants, developing cadres of leaders, years before the sit-down strikes.

Sustaining a movement once it's begun. Movements are bigger than organizations. Piven argues that in "movement moments," organizations should not focus on signing up new members, collecting dues, or building organizational structures. Instead, they should work to maximize disruption and public support for disruption. Organizations can play an important role in fanning the flames, spreading the action to new areas, and organizing support for people taking risky actions, such as legal help or strike and bail funds. We believe that when possible, organizers should look for opportunities to build organizational strength as part of the settlements won through disruption. For example, the Flint sit-down strikes produced not only gains in wages, but also the recognition of the UAW and provisions that made it easier to sign up members. These organizations can hold, institutionalize, and build on gains for some time after a disruptive movement subsides, ensuring that victories are actually implemented and enforced. But organizers must be careful that the institutional, financial, and legal constraints of their organizing work do not interfere with a movement's growth.

Scaring overdogs. When disruptive movements do succeed, it's because ruling elites decide that making concessions is their best option to quell unrest. A major objective for underdog movements is to instill fear in overdogs—of a loss of profit, of losing legitimacy, of civil disorder, or of a threat to their governing political coalition. Overdogs are more likely to give concessions when the cost of doing so is relatively low. For example, manufacturing employers agreed to labor legislation in the 1930s, but their labor costs were a smaller share of their total costs than in the service sector. Service-sector employers are therefore more resistant to unionization or wage increases, and the level of disruptive power needed to win concessions from them is higher. Similarly, given the central role of policing in maintaining overdog power, it would take an extremely high level of disruptive power to win big reductions in police budgets.

Decentralization with coordination. Disruptive actions such as strikes and campaigns (Project Confrontation in Birmingham [Chapter 3], for example) may be planned and led by organizations, but no one person is in charge of a disruptive movement. Energy spreads from one locale to another, as underdogs hear about victories and successful tactics in other places. The sit-down strikes, for example, actually started in Atlanta, spread to Kansas City, to Cleveland, and then to several plants in Flint—as well as to dozens of other cities.

There are often "hubs"—like the Highlander Center during the civil rights movement, or the NWRO—that provide a home for movement activists to gather, share tactics, and plan actions. Social movement scholars have studied the ways in which organizing can spread and multiply. First is through direct diffusion, when organizations have overlapping memberships or leaders that work together. Indirect diffusion happens when new participants learn about the activity secondhand (e.g., through the media) and it speaks to shared interests or identities. Finally, an intermediary can bring groups together, which is mediated diffusion.[24] Organizers can't plan a disruptive movement, but they can increase the likelihood of diffusion by maintaining relationships with other organizations and building movement infrastructure that fosters effective communication and new connections.

Strategy hubs (Chapter 18) are a way to increase the chances of movement diffusion.

Strengths and Weaknesses of Disruptive Movements

Vibrant disruptive movements can have a huge impact. They can move ideas from the margins to the mainstream and change the common sense. Even after a movement has long faded, the ideas it espouses can circulate. For example, while a guaranteed annual income proposal narrowly failed in the 1970s, in recent years it has gotten new life. Fifty years after the largest welfare rights demonstration in the United States, Congress passed a temporary refundable child tax credit that reduced child poverty by 40 percent in one year (including the lowest levels of Black and Latino poverty on record), realizing a dream that poor women had first articulated generations before.[25] (Unfortunately, as of this writing, it was only for one year.)

Disruptive movements can also have lasting impact by spurring organizational growth and developing leaders. Historically, explosive growth in union membership hasn't come about through shop-by-shop organizing; rather, it has happened in big bursts after waves of disruptive worker movements (Chapter 6.2). Worker movements produce unions more often than unions produce worker movements.[26] And the impact of movements can endure for generations—thousands and sometimes millions of people have their identities and sense of their own agency forever altered through their participation in disruptive movements. Many participants become leaders in social change for their whole lives.[27]

Disruptive movements have weaknesses, too. Most obviously, they only happen at certain times. Periods of worker insurgency or intense action by poor people are the exception in history, not the rule. Underdogs must overcome a formidable range of obstacles to turn the potential for disruption into reality. They have to recognize they have power (which is not easy—thinking that we don't have power can be a self-fulfilling prophecy), coordinate with each other, break rules, and withstand repression. And since disruptive movements can't be summoned into being, the question "What should we do the rest of the time?" is unanswered. Also, disruption is not always well executed. In Chapter 5 we described how air traffic controllers, members of PATCO, went on strike in 1981, hoping to use their disruptive power—the potential for chaos at airports. They had successfully struck in the past, but this time they overestimated their power. Reagan was on a mission to break unions and was willing to use his own disruptive power. The union had alienated union allies when they had endorsed Reagan for president, so other airline unions refused to honor the PATCO picket line. Reagan fired the strikers.

And overdogs don't always make concessions. Sometimes they use violence to crush a strike, or leverage economic or political power, as Reagan did when he brought in replacements for the striking air traffic controllers. Overdogs also use ideological power to delegitimize insurgents, as they did with racist and sexist campaigns to demonize welfare recipients.[28] Overdogs try to shut down disruption through co-optation as well—for example, by giving some striking workers a raise rather than accede to their demands for a union.

Another dilemma is that the vast majority of participants are motivated not by ideological commitment but rather by direct, immediate interests—a bigger welfare grant, preventing mass evictions, or higher wages, for example. A disruptive movement therefore may dissolve if key demands are met. But sometimes disruption can serve a long-term vision—like abolition or a guaranteed annual income. And demands can expand in the course of an upsurge as participants gain confidence and a sense of their own power. Participants in the uprisings to protest the killing of Black people by police developed a compelling critique and program for the transformation of American society.[29]

Most important, disruptive movements sometimes face intense backlash. Overdogs can be forced to make concessions without fundamentally changing their minds, biding their time until unrest subsides to strike back. And disruptive movements can achieve gains without gaining broad public support.

The welfare rights movement won more generous benefits, but it didn't change the common sense about what poor women of color deserved. As a result, parts of the governing coalition defected. Many white workers in the North left the Democratic Party as it responded to demands from movements like the civil rights and welfare rights movements. Reagan capitalized on the stresses inside the Democratic Party's coalition by inventing the myth of "welfare queens." The Right fanned the flames of popular backlash to welfare expansion by demonizing poor women of color. The punitive welfare reform of 1996 which ended the entitlement to cash welfare in the United States was the result. It was supported by both parties and reversed the movement's gains. The problem of backlash is daunting. Addressing it requires complementary strategies, like momentum and narrative shift, to build public will so that a stronger consensus undergirds the gains achieved by disruptive movements.[30]

Disruptive Movements and Other Strategy Models

The profound strengths and limitations of disruptive movements—their ability to achieve big gains and their vulnerability to dissolution and backlash—have generated debate about their role in social change. Some proponents of disruptive movements are contemptuous of organizations, viewing them as slow moving, bureaucratic, cautious, and more focused on self perpetuation than on radical social change. Some proponents of organizations view disruptive movements skeptically, seeing them as incapable of committing to the grind of politics and policy where real change gets institutionalized. We believe there is a profound misunderstanding about the relationship between movements and organizations that casts them as inevitably antagonistic rather than as potentially synergistic.

Organizations and organizers play a key role in laying the groundwork for movement eruptions. Many welfare rights organizations emerged from community organizations.[31] George Wiley, the visionary founder of the NWRO, was a civil rights organizer and was mentored by Rev. Wyatt Tee Walker, architect of Project C, the Birmingham campaign to defeat segregation (Chapter 3).[32] Many of the other organizers in the welfare rights movement came out of the civil rights movement, community organizing, and anti-poverty work. Tillmon was a union shop steward, active in politics and voter registration efforts, and part of the residents' association in her housing project. Other leaders, like Beulah Sanders, had prior experience in tenant and civil rights.

This same dynamic can be seen with other disruptive movements. The first meeting of the legendary activist group ACT UP was co-facilitated by the leader of the Gay Men's Health Crisis, a mutual aid and service organization founded to help gay communities survive the AIDS crisis (Chapter 12). Many ACT UP activists gained skills through their previous participation in women's, peace, and racial justice organizations.[33] The sit-down strike in Flint, Michigan, depended on an organizational infrastructure—the nascent UAW and in-plant organizers connected to Left political parties. The organizers who help lay the groundwork for movements tend to be dissatisfied with the orthodoxies of their craft. But they play a crucial, and often unacknowledged, role in fueling movements.

Organizations often also play a role after movements begin to lose momentum. Leaders in a disruptive movement may have a long-term vision that extends beyond a particular issue. They may build organizations that institutionalize wins and support other movements, as the UAW did with the insurgent civil rights movement in the 1960s, or they may contest for political power. Bayard Rustin, a key organizer in the civil rights movement, proposed that to consolidate and sustain gains, the movement needed to create strategic coalitions with other social forces and move from "protest to politics."[34]

Organizations need disruptive movements too, even though leaders of organizations are sometimes hostile to them. When they are besieged by attacks from overdogs, organizational leaders often succumb to the temptation to protect what they've got, rather than take risks or organize the unorganized. Organizations need the jolts of energy and the creative challenges to habitual ways of operating that movements provide. And organizations rely on movements to generate waves of talent. The community organizing boom of the 1970s, for example, was fueled by people who had experience with the social movements of the 1960s and wanted to continue the work of social change after the upsurges had subsided. Many founding organizers of ACORN, the national low-income organizing group, had formative experiences in the welfare rights movement.

Disruptive movements benefit from and use other models of social change as well. The Flint sit-down strikes might not have succeeded but for a newly elected pro-labor governor who refused to use the National Guard to break them. National politics were important too. The NLRA, passed in 1935, and President Franklin D. Roosevelt's general support of unions created an environment more favorable to labor organizing. Both the welfare rights and workers movements benefited from a sea change in the narrative on racial and economic justice that had been the fruit of decades of organizing. Increasingly, poor people of color and workers came to believe they deserved more, which made them more likely to rebel.

It can be hard to see disruptive movements of the past clearly through the prism of the present. We inevitably tend to look at cash welfare for poor people, for example, through the lens of the backlash against it. Because of the subsequent history, the welfare rights movement doesn't get its due, even in progressive circles. The accomplishments of the movement were considerable, and its impact reverberates in current debates. Dorian Warren of Community Change has led and won fights for progressive guaranteed income plans in recent years. He argues that "the cash payments that most families received after the COVID-19 crisis hit and the temporary refundable child tax credit that dramatically lowered Black, Latino, and Indigenous poverty rates in 2022 were fruits of the seeds planted by the visionary Black women who led the welfare rights movement."[35] With its rallying cry of "mothering is work," the movement laid the foundation for today's reinvigorated debate about care work. The welfare rights movement is an inspiring example of the kind of intersectional movement many of us seek to build.

The welfare rights movement exemplifies the use of strategy as a bridge between the world as it is (conjuncture) and the world as it could be (vision) (Chapters 2 and 3). The movement had a bold vision that was grounded in root ideas about the nature of work, care, and human dignity, and it unfolded in a favorable conjuncture. Leaders correctly assessed the terrain of struggle and seized an opportunity. And poor women of color developed a savvy strategy that won major gains that advanced their vision.

As corporate power and inequality have increased to a level not seen since the Gilded Age, the lineage of practitioners of disruptive power have a lot to teach us. There is more protest than ever, in the United States and around the world, but protests are having less impact in part because most of them are not truly disruptive. In a system as stacked in favor of the overdogs as this one, it's unlikely that underdogs can prevail through the means afforded by conventional politics alone. Entrenched systems of racism have been shaken but not broken by mass protest and narrative shift strategies. The rules are stacked against workers seeking to organize a union. And as the authoritarian threat grows, disruptive power will be an indispensable tool if democratic norms and institutional restraints prove too weak to contain it. The power underdogs have by virtue of their social roles to stop business as usual and make life difficult for the overdogs will be crucial in the years to come.

Table 7.1: Key Components of the Disruptive Movements Model

Component	Disruptive Movements Model
Form of Power	Disruptive
Theory of Change	Underdogs willing to take risks → stop the functioning of an oppressive system → create a moral, economic, and political crisis → demands are met
Examples of Practitioners and Theorists	Rev. Wyatt Tee Walker, Johnnie Tillmon, Frances Fox Piven, Lisa Fithian, Bayard Rustin, SNCC, Communist Party in the 1930s, ACT UP, W.E.B. DuBois, disability rights movement (ADAPT)
Protagonists and Structure	*Disruptive movements:* poor or other marginalized people for whom conventional methods haven't worked; loosely coordinated and under no one's control; organizations may fan the flames *Disruptive campaigns* planned by organizations

Component	Disruptive Movements Model
Goals and Methods	Focus on disrupting an oppressive system and forcing concessions from overdogs who respond out of fear or economic stress; does not require majority popular support to succeed; loose network of activists connected to movement hubs; growth through energy, passion of actions, evidence of success
Tactical Repertoire	Mass unruly protest, occupations of workplaces/public spaces/buildings, workplace strikes, "wildcat" strikes, rent strikes; may be stealthy, as with the general strike of enslaved people; disruptive movements can be wild, unpredictable, and edgy; disruptive actions can be planned and disciplined
What Does Winning Mean?	Mass disruption and civil unrest result in major concessions from elites to restore order
Time Horizon + When the Model Is Most Effective	During "ruptures" when the dominant system is faltering and/or in times of rapid economic, demographic, or technological change Change comes in dramatic, fast bursts of action
How It Works with Other Models/Movement Ecosystem	Depends on organizers who lay groundwork Electoral openings may help them succeed; tension between majoritarian focus of electoral strategies and emphasis on polarization by disruptive movements Can have elements of narrative shift and can shape political agendas Often clashes with inside-outside campaigns Can benefit from collective care work for survival (e.g., strike support or a bail fund) Benefits from other strategies to win popular support to make them less vulnerable to backlash (narrative shift, momentum)
Strengths	Can deliver big changes quickly Can spur rapid growth of organizations and politicization of large numbers of people

Component	Disruptive Movements Model
Weaknesses	Concessions from overdogs are sometimes unstable; gains are often followed by backlash
	Many obstacles have to be overcome for a disruptive movement to succeed, including that people must take great risks
	Some people motivated by immediate needs leave the movement once needs are met

Tools

Tool 15 Disruptive Chokepoints

Tool 16 Prompt: Organizations, Movements, and Times of Upsurge

Tool 17 Tabletop Exercise: The Worker Upsurge

Tool 18 OODA Loops

8

Narrative Shift

Changing the Common Sense:
Occupy Wall Street

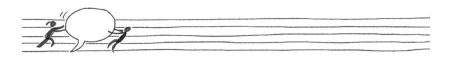

How did racial neoliberalism achieve majority support in the United States and in much of the West during the 1980s, despite the harms it inflicted on working people? In the United States and United Kingdom, Ronald Reagan and Margaret Thatcher swept into office with large majorities, including a significant share of working-class votes. In Chapter 5, we showed how six people organized, strategized, and helped implement the new world order. But a crucial piece of the story lies in how neoliberals were able to shift the narrative in a way that built on the real lived experiences and identities of voters.

Liberal and Left politicians and organizers were confounded when working people voted for politicians who cut vital government programs and taxes on the rich, deregulated businesses, and attacked unions. They assumed people would vote in their economic interests, but to the contrary, the durability of popular support for racial neoliberalism was so strong that eventually the nominal opposition—politicians like Bill Clinton and

Tony Blair—adopted its tenets. Theories that reduce political behavior to economic interest have proved to be of little use in making sense of actual events. White working-class voters shifted to vote Republican in the 1980s and have done so relatively consistently since then, with a few exceptions, such as Barack Obama in 2008.[1]

Thinkers in the Black radical tradition had long articulated a more nuanced view of the relationship between race and class than the views of liberal and Left politicians who discounted the power of white identity. W.E.B. DuBois talked about the "wages of whiteness"—the psychological sense of superiority that even poor whites had access to in America's racial hierarchy.[2] C.L.R. James and Cedric Robinson formulated the framework of racial capitalism to explain how systems of racial domination and capitalism arose together.[3] James and Robinson believed you couldn't make sense of politics without understanding the pivotal role of racism and colonialism in shaping identities and interests.

Stuart Hall (Chapter 2) drew on this Black radical tradition and built on important insights from Antonio Gramsci. He argued that people's lived experience is always complex and contradictory. Workers have other social identities—as parents or tenants or based on their gender or race—that shape their response to the world. Different parts of the working class may have different interests, based on their skill, industry, and location. And individual working-class people may have contradictory interests—for example, their position as workers may incline them to progressive economic ideas, but their negative and even humiliating experience of government bureaucracies may make conservative, populist, anti-government rhetoric appealing.

As Hall put it, "interests are not given but always have to be politically and ideologically constructed."[4] By this he meant that just because a person works in a factory, they may not think of themselves as a worker or see their class interests as relevant. Women don't automatically work together in defense of women's issues: organizers need to do the work to make that identity and those interests politically salient. And to do this, they need a narrative.

Alan Jenkins, former president and co-founder of the Opportunity Agenda, defines *narrative* as "a Big Story, rooted in shared values and common themes, that influences how audiences process information and make decisions."[5] Neoliberalism's triumph was ratified at the polls, but the Right first won popular support for its "big story" by influencing mass culture, media, intellectual life, and civil society.

It's easier to tell a new story when the old story stops making sense. After the 2008 financial crisis, as the world plunged rapidly into a recession, people looked for explanations when they lost their jobs, homes, and savings. Enter Occupy Wall Street.[6]

"We Are the 99%": Occupy Wall Street

In June 2011, some of Stephanie's students occupied a section of downtown Manhattan to protest budget cuts and public-sector layoffs that New York mayor Michael Bloomberg was forcing on the city in the wake of the 2008 crash. For weeks, several dozen protestors stayed in their encampment, "Bloombergville." The protest didn't draw much attention and eventually disbanded.

A few months later, when some of those same activists began talking about occupying Wall Street in September, Stephanie was skeptical. It was hard enough to fight city budget cuts; how could a few dozen people fight something as significant as Wall Street? She didn't voice her pessimism, but she also didn't join the thousand or so people who showed up on September 17, 2011, to Occupy Wall Street (OWS).

The group convened in Zuccotti Park, a few blocks from Wall Street. The police arrived, but for some reason didn't kick out the protestors, so they set up camp and spent the night. They held general assemblies and spontaneous marches through the coming days. A week into their encampment, they joined other groups protesting the execution of Troy Davis (a Black man put to death by the state of Georgia despite strong evidence of his innocence).[7] This time, the police responded by attacking and arresting protestors. Two days later, police attacked another OWS march, pepper-spraying protestors and arresting eighty people. At this point, Stephanie decided to join thousands of other New Yorkers and headed to Zuccotti Park. What she saw astonished her. After years of attending protests, this felt different. It felt liberating. The music, discussions, library, and kitchen made it feel like the seeds of a new community rather than a protest. She was hooked. Over the next several months she spent as much time as she could with OWS, and eventually she and her colleagues Penny Lewis and Ruth Milkman surveyed over eight hundred participants in an Occupy march and interviewed twenty-five central Occupy organizers.[8] Ten years later, they went back to talk to most of those interviewees. All concluded that Occupy had been a success in at least one crucial way: it had changed the narrative about inequality.[9]

Occupy had a lasting impact on changing the common sense about the 2008 economic crash and the economy more broadly. In the years immediately following 2008, progressives failed to organize an effective response, but conservative politicians worked quickly to blame Black homeowners and public-sector workers for the crash. The Tea Party emerged to enable Republicans to capture the House in 2010. Occupy emerged a year later and shifted the blame to the 1 percent and Wall Street.

While the initial gathering date was called by the organization Adbusters, Occupy seemed to emerge from everyone and everywhere. As adrienne maree brown wrote at the time, "I see this as a natural evolution from conversations and gatherings and organizing that has been building for years, call and response across time from the Battle in Seattle [in 1999], the street forums that take analysis beyond the choir."[10]

Occupy made no political demands. They put forward no political platform, supported no candidates or party. There was internal debate about this, with some participants in general assemblies calling for concrete policy proposals or candidate endorsements.[11] Some Occupy activists connected to organizing projects, such as supporting union campaigns.[12] But OWS itself was primarily a project to shift the narrative.

OWS supporters shared stories about inequality, debt, and corporate corruption. A Tumblr account called "We Are the 99 percent" provided a venue for people to share photos and stories. "My mom worked on Wall Street for almost 30 years," one person wrote. "In 2008, when the market crashed, the company she worked for shut down. The CEOs were taken care of, but all the loyal workers were left with nothing. My mom still hasn't found work. I am the 99 percent."[13]

They created a newspaper, *The Occupied Wall Street Journal*. They held daily educational events featuring well-known intellectuals and authors as well as anyone else who wanted to speak. Because they had no permit for a sound system, they used "the people's mic" to amplify voices through the large crowds. A speaker would share a few sentences, and those closest would then repeat the sentence loudly to the next circle of people around them, going back throughout the crowd until everyone heard what was said.

The 99 percent framework lifted up shared values of community, care, empathy, fairness, and morality. The focus on the 1 percent was about anger, justice, morality, and perhaps revenge. These collective values helped shape a "big story" about the economic crisis, rooted in people's experiences. OWS didn't use sophisticated narrative research, such as focus groups or surveys, to develop their message, but the stories spoke to a broader public, and the message spread quickly. Major media outlets flooded the park, giving people a platform to share their views. CNBC created a speaker's corner for protestors, who started to appear on major network news, garnering attention and support.[14]

OWS led to a huge increase in the number of news pieces mentioning income inequality.[15] "Occupy elevated a feeling that capitalism is the crisis, the exploitation and extraction of wealth in service of that top 1 percent," according to Occupy activist Sandy Nurse. "It just falls out of everyone's mouth now." Nurse, now a New York City Council member, adds, "We had a physical home for radical thought and discourse and creativity and experimentation."[16]

Eventually, a coordinated crackdown evicted Occupy camps across the country, leading some to call the protest a failure. But the organizers Stephanie and her colleagues interviewed a decade afterward agree that OWS had a major impact on the political terrain. It opened space to critique the status quo and gave people a taste of what contesting for power might entail. Yotam Marom reflected, "There, during Occupy, standing on that trash can, watching this sea of people, I thought: *We can be powerful. We can be popular. We can win.* It was a defining moment. That feeling, which spread throughout the occupation and across the country, allowed for an unbelievable surge in momentum and energy. I believe it ultimately produced the decade of social movements we've seen since."[17]

While OWS managed to cohere a shared common sense about the reasons for the crash and inequality, there was less coherence around the solutions.[18] The movement grew quickly and gained support from a vast array of people; drawing up a platform would have been contentious and time consuming. But eventually, in order to effect lasting change, OWS needed to find a way to transition into the kind of space where people could debate and discuss and move a critique of the status quo into political action.

At least one OWS working group managed to do that: Strike Debt.[19] Ann Larson explains how she was a student in New York City, worried about student debt, but it wasn't until she participated in OWS that she saw how many others shared her concern.[20] Organizers came together in that space to form the Strike Debt working group, which eventually became the Debt Collective. They put the topic on the political map—so much so that leading Democratic presidential candidates made student debt a key topic in the 2020 elections, and President Joe Biden took a historic first step in 2022 to eliminate debt (the Supreme Court has as of this writing blocked implementation of Biden's proposal). While the measure was far less than what organizers wanted, it was still a significant win and no national politician had acknowledged the student debt crisis before Occupy.

Another solution that Occupy activists pursued was worker organizing. For example, some activists went from Zuccotti to rank-and-file jobs in Walmart warehouses, looking to spark union organizing. In Chapter 10, we describe how OWS contributed to a sense of growing worker power in Chicago, giving momentum to the Chicago Teachers Union Strike and then the Fight for $15 and a Union campaign that would emerge in the fall of 2012.

Other Occupy activists turned to electoral work. New movements operating outside the Democratic Party challenged the corporate centrism of Clinton and Obama Democrats for abetting skyrocketing wealth inequality, bailouts for bankers, and foreclosures that erased working-class wealth. One OWS activist, Charles Lenchner, contacted another, Winnie Wong, about getting Elizabeth Warren to challenge Hillary Clinton in the 2016 primaries, and together they launched Ready for Warren.[21] They were joined by the national progressive political group MoveOn.org, which launched "Run Warren Run" in parallel. Though these efforts didn't entice Warren to run (until 2020), they immediately boosted her power to advance policies.

Former Occupy activists also flocked to the campaign to elect Bernie Sanders for president in 2016, including Lenchner and Wong, who started People for Bernie. And the Democratic Socialists of America (DSA) experienced massive growth when people began to identify capitalism as the source of inequality. All of these efforts blamed the 1 percent, and all pushed for bold policy solutions to address inequality.

Culture and Identity: Narrative Shift as Strategy

There is more than one approach to narrative shift, and organizers have become more sophisticated about it in recent years. Some concepts can emerge and gain popular support quickly, within weeks, as was the case with OWS and Black Lives Matter. But truly shifting a collective set of norms and values can take decades.

Alan Jenkins explains that you can't leave narrative shift up to spontaneous uprisings. Real change takes strategy and organizing. "Narrative change rarely happens on its own, particularly around contested social justice issues," he writes. "It typically results from a sophisticated combination of collaboration, strategic communications tactics, and cultural engagement, all attuned to essential audiences and societal trends. It requires both discipline and investment."[22] Narrative shift strategy rests on the theory that people must develop shared understandings of contradictions and solutions before they can move on to political change.

In the last decade, organizations dedicated to studying and applying narrative shift have emerged, including Reframe, Opportunity Agenda, Narrative Initiative, Pop Culture Collaborative, and Race Forward, to name a few. These organizations start with strategy discussions to identify shared values and goals, research current public opinion and opportunities for shifts, and field-test which new narratives have salience or "stickiness."

Narrative shift also addresses collective identity. Hall's concept of root ideas (Chapter 2) included the notion of a collective "we"—a common identity. A "we" implies a "they." Narrative-shift strategists work to lift up certain dimensions of people's contradictory identities and downplay others; to highlight the heroes of a story, as well as the villains. OWS changed the common sense about inequality but has not yet cohered most of the population around a common identity, in part because they didn't cohere around a common explanation—a "big story" about the *causes* of inequality. Sanders took things much further, but his campaign was not enough to forge a new collective common sense. So when Sanders failed to clinch the presidential nomination in 2016, Donald Trump stepped in, offering his own set of populist explanations and solutions. Whereas Sanders blamed corporate greed for inequality, Trump blamed immigrants, other countries, and globalization. Whereas Sanders proposed regulation, Trump proposed a wall.

Trump and Sanders both spoke to people's identities as underdogs, trampled on by a corrupt and unequal system. But Trump's "we" emphasized white and American identity, and his "they" included a host of enemies. Sanders's "we" emphasized the working and middle classes, and, like OWS, named the 1 percent and greedy corporations as the "they."

As we write, this struggle continues. Which narrative will win?

Values, Heroes, and Solutions: Common Elements of Successful Narrative Shift

We review the characteristics of the narrative shift model in Table 8.1. Common elements include the following:

Listen. Practical radicals must pay close attention to what everyday people are saying and experiencing. It can be in the form of one-on-one conversations, on doorsteps, or in the workplace. Narrative-shift organizations may also rely heavily on polling, focus groups, and "A/B testing," where they see which messages resonate best with potential voters or members. Organizers cannot just push slogans or platforms they want to promote; they have to craft those platforms based on what people need and want.

Empathize. Beyond listening, "empathy is our greatest superpower in narrative change work," Jenkins told us. "Listening without empathy does not provide the insights and understanding necessary to move hearts, minds, and policy."[23]

Find shared values. Several practitioners emphasize the need to create narratives that rest on shared values (Chapter 2). While it may be difficult to get diverse people to agree on a specific policy goal, or to even start a conversation with each other, good organizing can get to the root of shared values, such as community, equality, or democracy.[24]

Name the enemy or target. For OWS, it was the 1 percent. Sometimes there is more than one enemy—for the Right, it was big government and the racial and gender justice movements looking to undermine white supremacy and patriarchy.

Identify the heroes. Who can carry out the solution? Who is the collective "we"? How can we unite to defeat the villains? In OWS, the heroes were the 99 percent.

Identify a solution so practitioners are motivated to work toward change. The campaign to legalize same-sex marriage had a built-in solution: change the law. The fight to abolish slavery had one big solution, but with several smaller steps along the way, such as outlawing the slave trade. OWS activists identified particular solutions, such as eliminating student debt, but there was no easy solution to the larger problems they faced. And because many had no faith in the standard strategies available to them, they saw the Democratic Party as a dead end, unionization as nearly impossible, and policy work as narrow and limiting. And while there was agreement that inequality and the 1 percent were a problem, there was still a wide range of theories about the "why": Was it corporate greed? Was it racial capitalism? Was it a lack of democracy? OWS failed in this domain but did open space for others to take up specific demands and solutions—and win. The media began writing about inequality, and politicians began talking about the 99 percent.[25] Occupy shifted the terrain for the broader movement ecosystem.

Unify large numbers through the new narrative. Some progressives get trapped trying to develop the most sophisticated and complex narrative. But to cohere a historic bloc, in Gramsci's terms, the narrative must be appealing and accessible to masses of people. This doesn't mean the narrative has to appeal to everyone. Many narrative strategists focus on "the moveable middle" or the "persuadables": those who are not hard-core opponents and can, through organizing, be persuaded to join your side. Narrative strategists, including Anat Shenker-Osario, argue that a good narrative actually incites opposition from hard-core opponents, while also winning over persuadables and energizing the base.[26]

Saliency. However, it's possible to use strategic narratives to make a major change with a minority of voters if the issue is a priority. For example, in the case of gun rights, a minority has prevented reforms that most of the population wants. This demonstrates saliency. Gun rights supporters care more (in some cases, only) about this issue, whereas most voters have a variety of interests. While most of the public still opposes assault rifles, the gun rights movement has profoundly shifted the narrative from gun safety to gun rights. Again, narrative shift must be tied to organizing, and the "gun rights" movement has effectively used the electoral system to reward and punish politicians to adopt their agenda. On the brighter side, scholars point out that the civil rights movement won major reforms despite never winning over large segments of the population.[27]

Another concept related to narrative work is the **Overton window**. Developed by the libertarian policy analyst Joseph Overton, it describes the range of policies that are acceptable to the mainstream population.[28] The point is not to take it as a given, but to move it. For example, as late as the year 2000, legalizing same-sex marriage was unpopular; it was outside the Overton window that organizers needed to shift.

The theory of change for narrative shift looks like this:

Narrative Shift Done Well

Deep, lasting narrative shifts must tap into people's lived experiences and help them make sense of the world. Narrative work requires being attuned to cultural currents and openings. It requires good communications work, but at its heart is organizing, particularly among people who don't normally talk to each other. While underdogs don't have the money and access to politicians or corporations that overdogs have, they can tell a new story about their lives and conditions. Everyone can play a part in narrative shift.

Ideological power is also closely connected to vision. Your ability to develop a "story of us"—to create a collective idea of who we are as people and our collective dreams for the future—depends on imagination. Narrative strategists work to draw on and develop shared values, which form the basis of our alternative stories of the past and future.

OWS tapped into the pain and suffering people experienced during the 2008 recession, as well as decades of hostile racial neoliberalism, based on a narrative that blamed individuals for societal problems. OWS flipped that around and demonstrated that the suffering was collective, and that the blame lay not on lazy or weak individuals, but on those who caused the inequality: Wall Street, the banks, neoliberal politicians, the wealthy—the 1 percent.

Organizers face a temptation to craft messages based on what people are comfortable with or believe in at the moment, working with people where they are, rather than engaging on a deeper level. It may seem like the alternative is to alienate the mainstream with radical demands or issues about which only small groups care. Jonathan Smucker, one of the OWS activists Stephanie and her colleagues interviewed, argues that these aren't the only choices. If you think of potential allies along a spectrum, and look to find openings of connection wherever you can, you can tailor your organizing conversations to shift each band in your direction. Smucker argues that the most important priority is to move the passive allies into active allies, and the second is to move those who are neutral into passive allies.[29]

Done correctly, narrative shift both activates the base and persuades the undecided. One such approach is **deep canvassing**, which entails meaningfully engaging with people about their concerns related to a particular issue.[30] After asking questions, an organizer should share their story related to that issue in the hopes of developing a feeling of solidarity. The movement organization People's Action has been a leader in developing this technique. They conducted large-scale experiments with deep canvassing and found remarkable results in shifting voting patterns.[31] The California Nurses Association has been using a version of deep canvassing in their campaign to promote universal health care. Through door knocking, they don't just assess someone's current opinion; they hope to move it.

Narrative Shift Is Hard to Do

Narrative work is challenging for a number of reasons. Common sense is hard to shift. Some narratives are so deeply rooted that they form identities for those who believe them, whether it's "whiteness," "American," "middle class," or "queer."

Rashad Robinson, president of Color of Change, argues that it's easy to have "the wrong narrative about narrative."[32] It's important not to conflate narrative content with narrative power—it's not only about figuring out the right thing to say, but also about how it gets heard at a scale that can lead to change. You might gain popular support from a majority, but winning real change takes more than that. The marriage equality movement was able to highlight the shared value of love and thereby gain empathy from many, but organizers also needed to use other strategies, including electoral change. Deepak asks students in his Social Movements class whether they would rather win the war over the common sense or win a policy goal, if they had to choose—students are generally split, but the exercise underscores the importance of having a strategy that can do both.

Since ideological power is about the power of ideas, it's closely related to the question of who owns and controls the means by which ideas are produced and disseminated. And that, largely, is not underdogs. Having the right story is only part of the solution; having a strategy for the mass dissemination and popularization of that narrative is crucial.

Building a new majority coalition will require engaging people with whom you may disagree and creating space for new people to join a struggle and agree on a common vision.[33] But it also means being strategic about who needs to be present and who doesn't, given an assessment of accessible power and the conditions. Whether from a fear of winning actual power, a desire to be part of a small clique, or a need to be absolutely correct, Leftists often fail to build a new hegemony when they don't focus their organizing and messaging outward.

Smucker argues that Left movements often fail to achieve major impact because they are too internally focused, speaking to one another instead of the larger public.[34] In Smucker's view, OWS fell victim to this problem. While the message "we are the 99 percent" resonated with large swaths of people, the actual practices in Zuccotti Park and other occupation spaces were alienating to some.[35] For example, meetings were frequent and long, and it wasn't clear how to participate without being in the park. And the park was filled with ongoing loud drumming, making it hard to hold conversations.

Another challenge is that narrative shift can be hard to measure. Analysts use public-opinion research, but that involves myriad problems, from sampling errors to poorly worded questions. And opinions can change quickly, particularly in times of political unrest or organizing movement moments.[36] It can also be difficult to measure cause and effect. Did a specific effort lead to narrative shift? There are ways to do this, but it takes time and resources. For example, marriage equality organizers were able to measure narrative shift. They started by listening to people to understand why they resisted the idea of marriage equality, going beyond polls to conduct focus groups, intensive interviews, multiple surveys, and ad development and testing. After much work, they found that a nonpolitical ad had impact. The ad didn't mention same-sex marriage or equal rights. It called for empathy by asking straight people to imagine what it would feel like if they could not marry the person they loved. This shift from a message that led with the differences between queer and straight people to one that emphasized the common ground of "love is love" was not easy. Organizers deployed the ad in one county in California, which ended up being the only Southern California county to reject the anti–marriage-equality measure in 2008.[37]

Narrative shift is strategic only when combined with other models of change from below. In other chapters, we show how narrative shift can play an important role in creating change, such as the way in which environmental organizations in 350.org won climate victories using narrative work as part of the momentum model.

And narrative strategies can support others. In Deepak's experience in the immigrant rights movement, narrative strategies can turbocharge organizing in moments of crisis. He was part of a team at Community Change that led one of the first public campaigns to prevent the deportation of a young immigrant student, Marie Gonzalez, and her parents (Marie won a reprieve, but her parents were deported). The nationwide "We Are Marie" protest campaign attracted media and galvanized the immigrant movement, especially among young people.[38] In 2010, after Arizona's legislature passed its infamous "Show Me Your Papers" law, longtime organizer and leader of Promise Arizona, Petra Falcon, and six young people launched a twenty-four-hour prayer vigil at the state Capitol that drew nearly one thousand people, who surrounded the building, galvanizing press attention nationally. From the courageous public response to a tragedy, an immigrant-led Latino movement to change the politics of the state through civic engagement was born. Many of the leading organizers in the state today were developed in the crucible of the response to that racist law.[39]

More Than Memes:
The Future of Narrative Shift

OWS was effective at capturing the lived reality of people suffering from the economic crisis and identifying a villain (the 1 percent) and a collective identity (the 99 percent). But the narrative shift was incomplete. OWS named the 99 percent as the heroes, but it wasn't clear how this large group of heroes could enact a solution, or even what the overall solution was (with some exceptions, such as the Strike Debt working group).

We've wrestled with narrative shift as a strategy—what we think of it and how to teach and practice it. On the one hand, in an increasingly digital world, with many people receiving information and news online, narrative shift has become all the more important. We're inundated with information, and it's harder to find the time and space to think clearly about it. This makes us more likely to believe information that fits our narrative and reject information that doesn't. The rise in media polarization and disinformation has made the situation even more complicated. That creates serious obstacles for creating a new common sense and constructing a new collective "we."

As narrative-shift strategies have become more and more fashionable, we've been skeptical of some of the shallower approaches that seem to promise that if we say the right words we can bypass the hard work of organizing. But we believe that narrative strategy is crucial. After all, people consume (and create) culture a lot more than they engage with organizing projects. And, as the saying goes: "Culture eats strategy for breakfast."

Narrative shift is more than just a sophisticated communications strategy and the dissemination of the right message. It must be rooted in a deep analysis of cultural, political, and economic conditions. Thinkers like Gramsci and Hall helped explain the ways people develop a host of identities and interests based on their lived experiences, which go far beyond their class identity. Understood this way, narrative strategy is inextricably linked to organizing. Especially in tumultuous times like these, we all need stories to make sense of our lives—and even more, to understand how we can change them.

Table 8.1: Key Components of the Narrative Shift Model

Component	Narrative Shift Model
Form of Power	Ideological
Theory of Change	Storytelling, creative direct actions, and communication strategies grounded in organizing → Make a "far out," unpopular, or politically unfeasible idea part of the new common sense
Examples of Practitioners and Theorists	Occupy activists, Cristina Jimenez, Alan Jenkins, Rashad Robinson, Anat Shenkar Osario, Opportunity Agenda, Race Forward, marriage equality movement, immigrant youth movement
Protagonists and Structure	Movements that emphasize storytelling Activists, cultural workers, media, artists, communications-based organizations, educators, journalists
Goals and Methods	Change the "common sense" about an issue or problem; culture change Storytelling by directly impacted people; pop culture; creative actions; media and communications; organizing; education
Tactical Repertoire	High-visibility actions that capture attention Bold demands/slogans that shift the debate Use of pop culture and media
What Does Winning Mean?	Shifting the common sense and moving the Overton Window of possibility
Time Horizon + When the Model Is Most Effective	When a deep, long-term shift in norms and values is needed May unfold quickly, during a rupture when people are open to an alternative; or slowly, by planting the seeds for a new common sense

Component	Narrative Shift Model
How It Works with Other Models/ Movement Ecosystem	Can be a big part of momentum and collective care models
	Less history of successful integration with base-building or inside-outside campaigns
	Some electoral campaigns (like Sanders's) can shift narrative
Strengths	Can change the popular common sense about an issue in dramatic ways, altering the terrain of struggle
Weaknesses	Can be tactical and focus too much on words rather than action; can win the narrative but lose the policy
	If disconnected from organizing and from a deep analysis of the conjuncture, it can be an alluring but failed shortcut to progress

Tools

Tool 1 Shared Values

Tool 3 Conjunctural Analysis

Tool 19 Resources: Narrative Shift

9

Electoral Change

Politics from the Ground Up: Building Multiracial Coalitions to Take Governing Power

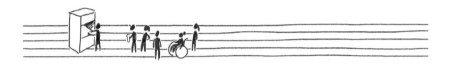

The world woke up on January 6, 2021, to the news that voters in Georgia had elected Democratic Party candidates Raphael Warnock and Jon Ossoff to the U.S. Senate, capping off an incredible, contentious two-month run-off campaign. Democrats and those opposed to Donald Trump breathed a sigh of relief; Democrats would have just enough senators to take the majority.

Nsé Ufot, head of New Georgia Project (NGP), played a major role in turning out voters. A few months before, NGP had turned out voters for Joe Biden, helping him beat Trump by a mere twelve thousand votes in Georgia.

Despite these wins, Ufot held her breath. She'd been working in Georgia politics long enough to know the race wasn't over. She knew the opposition would fight for recounts. She'd seen them play dirty tricks and knew they would again. "I tried to be gracious, and I didn't want to rain on people's parade, because there was just this extraordinary sigh of relief from people who were not steeped in it day to day," she says. "But I knew deep in my bones that they were still trying to steal it. And the election was not over."[1]

It wasn't until inauguration day, January 20, 2021, that Ufot allowed herself to celebrate. "Then I said, 'Okay, we won.' Then I drank a little something and did a little dance," she said.[2]

Ufot and NGP drove the turnout in Georgia that helped the state elect a Democratic candidate for president for the first time since Bill Clinton in 1992. They helped elect the state's first Black senator and first Jewish senator. It was a stunning achievement few thought possible.[3] While Ufot stepped down from her position in 2022, the work she and NGP accomplished in just a short time offers inspiring insights into the potential for electoral change.

Beyond Candidates: Electoral Strategies for Transformational Change

When most people think about creating political change, they think about voting for a candidate they like, or perhaps even running for office. But an individual voter, or even legislator, can't make much of an impact on their own. And the U.S. system has unique electoral obstacles: the Electoral College, the entrenched two-party system, the long history of voter suppression and disenfranchisement, and the outsized role of money in elections. Electoral work requires more than voting.

And for many decades, the Left and community organizations disengaged from electoral work. The Democratic Party left election strategizing to consultants. These consultants received a percentage of the money they spent, win or lose, so the party focused on expensive tactics like TV ads rather than cheaper but more effective ones like base-building. In fact, until the early 2000s, the Democratic Party was more dependent on big-dollar donations than Republicans were.[4]

Overdogs, by contrast, have pursued electoral change with vigor, including efforts to keep underdogs from voting and running for office. This focus demonstrates both the importance of electoral work and overdogs' fear of underdog political power. Despite the odds, the quest for governing power is a key strategy model in transformational change—perhaps now, in the face of rising authoritarianism globally, more than ever.

There are a few dominant strategies for those attempting to win governing power in the United States today. One is trying to influence the existing main political parties. The Justice Democrats and the Democratic Socialists of America (DSA), for example, work to push the Democratic Party to the left by challenging incumbent Democrats in primaries.

A second approach is building independent parties. This has ranged from small, symbolic efforts to promote a platform, to more serious efforts that contest for power, particularly at the city or county level. In the 1990s and 2000s, the Green Party and the New Party each had some success winning local races. Stephanie was a founding member of a New Party chapter in Madison, Wisconsin, called Progressive Dane, that at times held a majority of seats on the city council and school board. The Working Families Party (WFP) grew out of the New Party, and today, operating in twenty states, it is the largest attempt to build an independent party.

Third is to take over the party apparatus in a region or state. This is what a coalition of grassroots groups, including the member-driven political organization Living United for Change in Arizona (LUCHA), are attempting to do in order to push the Democratic Party in a more progressive direction that engages voters and activists of color. In 2021, LUCHA board member Raquel Terán, a leader in the movement that emerged after the state passed harsh anti-immigrant laws, was elected chair of the Arizona State Democratic Party.[5] The Right has deployed a similar party takeover strategy in the Republican Party, with great success.

A fourth approach is changing the rules of the game. For example, making the electoral system more fair and open (in such domains as campaign financing, ballot access, and voter registration). Or deepening democracy by involving citizens and organizations in all aspects of governance. This can happen through inside-outside strategies to change policy, which can use the electoral process to advance issues rather than candidates (Chapter 10).

A final approach is having local and state organizations work to combine voter mobilization with community organization and policy work. Their goal is to elect candidates to city, county, and state office, to deepen political engagement and eventually win governing power. One such group is the New Georgia Project (NGP).

These approaches have won a lot, from electing new people to office to passing important legislation at the city and state levels. But none are close to winning the power needed for transformational change. Even where Democrats control state legislatures, like in New York State, the Left is a small component of the governing coalition. At the local level, many of our working-class students are exasperated by New York's failure to deliver good schools and affordable housing in a city where Democrats control everything. And it isn't clear to what extent the electoral change model—which assumes a functioning democratic system—will continue to work if the Right's assault on democracy succeeds.

We'll discuss a few promising examples of electoral change work and then return to the challenges of the model.

New Georgia Project: Changing the Math

In 2014, Stacey Abrams, then a Georgia state legislator and minority leader, approached Ufot about her plans to shift politics in the state. Abrams pointed out that while the Democrats used to control the state, Republicans were consistently winning most state races by a margin of around 250,000 votes. Abrams calculated that there were five times that many potential Democratic voters—primarily Black people—who were eligible to vote but not registered. Her vision was to build a project to register and engage them. In his book *Brown Is the New White,* Steve Phillips, an early supporter of Abrams, argued that focusing on voters of color would revive progressive fortunes nationwide.[6]

Nsé Ufot was convinced the plan made sense. She left her job as a union organizer to become NGP's first CEO in 2014. Abrams had founded NGP in 2013 with three staff members and a tiny budget. The initial goal was to sign Georgians up for the Affordable Care Act (ACA), but without Medicaid expansion in the state, they soon realized that the Georgians they were working with—mostly low-income Black people—would not benefit from the law. Ufot and Abrams decided that the best way to change policies was to change the people in power who make them. That meant registering people—particularly people of color and young people—to vote, with a goal of one million new voters by 2024.

In 2014, they registered 69,000 people. NGP went to churches, schools, and house to house to find people, have conversations, and help them register. They were diligent about recording contact information so they could follow up later with information about how to vote. Still, they faced challenges; the secretary of state not only refused to add tens of thousands of these new voters to the voter rolls, but also launched a politically motivated investigation into NGP for alleged voter fraud.

NGP persisted. Over the next few years, they trained and deployed over three thousand organizers around the state. They developed creative ways to make politics fun, including using gaming platforms to livestream election activities, like "Twitch the Vote" and designing their own sneakers. Ufot explained how NGP sees culture as central to their project: "We are trying to change the culture of democracy."[7]

Their goal is to build "super voters" who vote in every election. More than that, "we're trying to train and support people who go to city council meetings and are actively engaged in world building."[8] To do this, NGP has engaged people outside of the traditional confines of electoral work to bring joy into organizing and help people feel connected to a national movement. NGP has worked with artists to paint murals on barns in rural areas that illustrate Black and Brown political iconography. "If you live in Mulberry, Georgia, you're going to pass these three barns on your way to school, church, work, or anything that you do. And they often serve as landmarks, like 'make a left at the red barn,'" Ufot told us.[9]

Rather than support a lone candidate, NGP builds sustainable infrastructure to create a culture of organizing. This includes creative new outreach methods as well as old-fashioned grassroots organizing: knocking on doors, making phone calls, and attending events to talk to people. This work is labor intensive, so NGP partners with existing organizations that have members, and people who have followers—like sororities. Ufot says, "If you can run a sorority with 100 Black women—recent college graduates to octogenarians who have very strong opinions about what it means to be a sister and sisterhood—you can lead your community."[10] Once they've made contact with someone, they follow up to make sure people who register actually make it onto the voting rolls. They trained hundreds of people through

NGP's "Peanut Gallery" to monitor boards of elections meetings and report out on any local-level changes. They've trained thousands more to monitor polling sites and protect voters. NGP has the infrastructure for people to check their registration status, correct ballots for errors, get rides to the polls, and help others vote.

NGP conducts year-round organizing and runs issue campaigns alongside their voter registration work. "To the extent that our electoral campaigns are powerful, it's because it's directly connected to our issue-based organizing and our community organizing," says Ufot. "We're constantly thinking about how to electoralize the issues that people tell us they care deeply about, and they're willing to move and take action on."[11] For example, the organization's Black and Green Agenda connects racial and environmental justice work.

Ufot says that NGP is part of a healthy ecosystem of Georgia organizations; it has built deep relationships with other voting rights groups as well as issue-based organizations around the state. So, NGP doesn't need to do it all; each group can focus on what it does best. And like us, Ufot sees strategy and movement work as analogous to making music: "I subscribe to the gospel choir theory of organizing," she says. "We all have notes, and the more we practice together the more in harmony we are. And if an individual vocalist needs to drop out for professional or personal reasons, [we ensure] that the note continues. That the singing continues."[12]

By 2020, NGP had registered over a quarter million voters in the state, in every county. During the 2020 election season they contacted millions of voters—knocking on two million doors, making seven million calls, and sending four million texts.[13] They proved that Abrams was right: registering eligible Black and Brown voters was enough to swing major elections. Not only did Georgia deliver a major win to Biden, but voters also flipped both U.S. Senate seats. Despite massive attacks from the Trump campaign, the Georgia vote held up after multiple recounts. While Democrats' narrow Senate margin was not enough to implement much of the Biden agenda, it did allow for considerable gains, such as implementing taxes on stock buybacks, lowering ACA health care premiums, and funding clean energy production.[14]

Perhaps one indicator of NGP's impact is how hard the opposition is working to retaliate. In 2021, the state made it a crime to pass out food or water to people waiting in line to vote, and restricted the number of drop boxes available to voters, particularly in neighborhoods with higher shares of voters of color. Governor Brian Kemp justified the new law as a response to the work of NGP and others in the 2020 elections: "I was as frustrated as anyone else with the results, especially at the federal level. And we did something about it with Senate Bill 202."[15]

California Calls: A Long-Term Strategy Gets Results

California is considered one of the bluest states in the nation, but it wasn't always that way. The state gave the country Richard Nixon and Ronald Reagan, and voters elected a number of conservative governors and legislators who used the state as a testing ground for Right-wing strategy. For example, in 1978, voters approved Proposition 13, an anti–property tax amendment to the state Constitution that was one of the opening shots in the neoliberal assault on public spending.

In the 1990s, the state passed controversial ballot initiatives that restricted immigrant rights, repealed affirmative action, and tightened criminal sentencing. Anthony Thigpenn, a Los Angeles–based community organizer, decided to fight back. He founded a group called AGENDA aimed at building political power in part by shifting the electorate, focusing on low-income people of color, particularly Black and Brown people inspired by his former experience as a Black Panther. Sabrina Smith, who worked for Thigpenn at the time, explains, "What we realized was that every time we had a defensive fight, we would pull together a coalition, we put together the field operation, we would fight the good fight, and oftentimes, we would lose. And then we'd go back to our policy campaigns, only to have to build that infrastructure for the next defensive fight." AGENDA was created to go on offense.

AGENDA (now known as SCOPE) developed a Power Analysis tool (Tool 33) to systematically look at who holds power in a region.[16] They built the capacity to run citywide campaigns and train organizers, and eventually built enough strength to anchor an alliance of thirty-one grassroots organizations that came together from around the state in 2009, known as California Calls. These organizations realized they could only scale their power and win by working together—particularly given structural barriers in place, such as Proposition 13, which limits public budgets. The alliance began with a year-long intensive program to develop shared values, vision, and strategy among the anchor groups.

California Calls uses sophisticated technology and databases to track and contact voters and potential voters, including registering new voters and engaging low-propensity ones. Organizers stay in contact with voters year-round—not just in election season. They talk about the values of interdependence, racial solidarity, and authentic democracy as well as about candidates. They talk with voters about pressing community issues.

Our former student Lydia Avila, the California Calls statewide field director from Los Angeles' east side, explained that the strategy is "to take the best practices from large-scale campaign electoral work, and the best practices of organizing, to try to do depth and scale at the same time."[17] This means reaching people through petitions, through door-knocking, at events, through social media—and then following up and asking them to join as members and to volunteer with one of the local affiliated organizations or one of the regular civic engagement projects.

Active members are invited to participate in a leadership development program that teaches organizing skills and provides political education. They've trained over 2,500 organizers to date, who serve as the core leaders of their voter outreach program.

Smith, who is now the CEO of California Calls, told us that the alliance is rigorous about testing ideas, evaluating what works and what doesn't, and revising as needed. They do daily reports on calls, contacts, and whatever metrics they've agreed to focus on. They revisit their Power Analysis weekly to see what has changed. They research and field test messages to find the narratives that stick.

California Calls recently worked with the Grassroots Power Project (GPP), an organization that advises many base-building and electoral groups on strategy, to sharpen their vision and strategy. Smith explains, "You start by assessing and being clear on the current fights, then get clear on the forty-year vision. Then, what are the milestone and structural reforms that move you to that long-term agenda? And then what are the stepping-stone fights that move you closer and prepare you to build power to pass the structural reforms?" (Tool 36). For California Calls, the longer vision includes redistribution of wealth, which will entail structural reform to Proposition 13.

The alliance has had remarkable success in building its database and voter contact capacity. It has increased voter turnout, impressively among low-propensity voters who supported key ballot initiatives. Some of those initiatives passed, such as those around school funding, while others aimed at reforming Proposition 13 have yet to pass but have come close.

Working Families Party: Coalitions for Governing Power

WFP formed in 1998 in New York and has since grown into a national party. Maurice Mitchell, the national director of WFP, told us, "We think having an independent political party that is rooted in the interests of working people and organized labor is a strategy to push back on the corporate capture of government, and build greater democracy that would actually be responsive to the multiracial working class."[18]

Because each state has different rules governing things like ballot access, voter registration, and municipal powers, the party takes different forms in each state. For example, in states that allow candidates to run under more than one party ("fusion voting"), like New York and Connecticut, WFP has its own ballot line. Fusion allows WFP to run Democratic candidates on the WFP line, thereby reducing the chance of being a third-party "spoiler." In states without fusion, WFP will run candidates as Democrats in Democratic primaries, or occasionally as WFP candidates in a general election. Mitchell emphasizes that WFP is an independent third party that, "for strategic reasons, aligns in an electoral united front with the Democrats at times in order to fight the far right."[19]

While electoral tactics look different from state to state, the party is held together by core ideas. WFP has made a conscious shift to embrace a racial justice framework in their internal structure, and brought on Mitchell, who had experience in community organizing and the Movement for Black Lives. This orientation informs their strategic decision to center the interests of a multiracial working class. "If we only focus on self-identified progressives and liberals and activists, we will have a lot of people, but the way that those people would overlay on places that are electorally essential to our victory won't add up," Mitchell explains. Getting to majority rule requires organizing "the working class, white people, Black people, Latino people, including people in cities, in suburban communities and rural countries."[20] Mitchell notes that in the past, common wisdom suggested that to build a big coalition you should avoid contentious issues, but WFP has turned that around. "We're doing the opposite; we're leaning into open conversations about race in our work to build a multiracial coalition."[21]

WFP started as a coalition of institutions, such as labor unions, ACORN, and Citizen Action, but over time changed their structure to allow individuals to join as members as well. Both institutions and individuals have a say in internal party decisions. There's a tension in this hybrid model. Institutions bring resources, along with a "long-arc and strategic sensibility," but they also tend to be conservative in terms of risk, according to Mitchell. Individuals bring excitement and energy and push the party to take more risks "in order to advance the party's north star." Furthermore, they are an almost limitless source of potential power. A party needs a "dedicated cadre base" to knock on doors, talk to voters, lobby legislators, and build the organization. The challenge for WFP is to bring the strengths of individuals and institutions together, in a productive tension rather than a destructive one.[22]

Not only does WFP have to find a way to hold its coalition together, but it must also build its capacity to work with its members who are elected officials. "For parties to be coherent—for Nancy Pelosi to deliver all of her members on a vote—it requires a lot of negotiation," explains Mitchell. "Political parties are disciplinary organizations."[23] Typically this is done through sticks—the ability to defeat people in elections or take away their power in other ways—and carrots: benefits of membership. WFP doesn't have many sticks at this point, so they're focused on carrots they can offer elected officials: data infrastructure, donors, and an activist base. WFP identifies and supports their own candidates to run for office. And whereas a community organization sees its job as helping elect candidates and then holding them accountable, the job of a party is to work with members to help them govern.

Relatedly, WFP chooses policy campaigns that help their elected officials govern. Some of that policy work includes efforts to change the rules to expand multiparty democracy through various methods, such as legalizing fusion voting in more states.[24] WFP sees its role as "hacking" the two-party system. The vast majority of candidates they recruit run in Democratic primaries, pushing the party to the Left.

WFP has ambitious goals: to make the Senate work again, build the progressive bloc in the House, and build power in states. And they've developed a federal team to work with progressives in Congress to pursue an inside-outside governing and legislative strategy.

Mitchell has been a popular guest speaker in our classes. Students appreciate his ability to balance a clear-eyed assessment of the challenges of electoral work with the vision of transformational change. He is a true practical radical. He says that despite the challenges of political work, "for folks who sit outside of the traditional limitations of the rigid institutional two-party system, there is a lot to be excited about."[25]

Putting Community Power at the Center: Common Elements of a Strategic Electoral Change Model

WFP, California Calls, and NGP are just three examples of efforts to win power at the city, state, and federal levels. Dozens of other organizations are working to make electoral work more strategic (Table 9.1 describes the characteristics of the model). Some are working in an alliance called the State Power Caucus. Formed in 2017, the caucus has twenty-two organizations from fifteen states.[26] Other groups are forging new paths, building off the best of community and union organizing traditions. They share the following common approaches:

Engaging low-income, multiracial communities. There are many good reasons for Black, Brown, immigrant, and young voters to be cynical about voting and elections. Historically, the system hasn't worked well for them, and mainstream parties and politicians tend to take them for granted. Electoral power organizations take those concerns seriously. For instance, instead of seeing people only as potential voters, they try to bring them into a bigger political project aimed at making structural change. Integrated voter engagement, as practiced by groups like California Calls, works to make potential voters and occasional voters into active participants with a number of campaigns that can provide people with greater agency, as well as help them organize for programs and services. Even the millions of people who are not allowed to vote due to felony convictions or immigrant status can be brought into electoral work as volunteers and leaders.

Taking an organizing approach to electoral politics. UNITE HERE Local 11, a majority-Latino local in southern California, formed a new political organization, Worker Power, that is training union members and allies in using union-organizing approaches to engage voters. Instead of just knocking on a door to tell a voter to show up at the polls, the experience becomes "a miniature house visit"—a way to get to know the voter, listen to their concerns, and have a back-and-forth political conversation. In a break from conventional methods, UNITE HERE canvassers build personal relationships and stay in touch with the same voters over time. This approach engages voters and canvassers, and in the process enriches the democratic practice.[27]

Year-round politics. Political work is more than just marking a ballot every few years, and elections are just one piece of longer movement building. These organizations register voters and get voters to the polls, but they also engage in permanent issue work, like how NGP helped people get access to health care. California Calls helped launch the African American Civic Engagement Project, which links the work of twelve organizations doing a range of projects in Black communities, such as expanding reproductive services and college access, as well as providing services for formerly incarcerated people.

Moving from transactional to transformational organizing.[28] As UNITE HERE organizer Daniel Judt explains, Local 11's Worker Power brings "the thick democratic practices of union membership—sustained political relationships that build solidarity and common ground—into our hollowed-out political sphere."[29]

Improving the electoral infrastructure. These new electoral projects are changing the way politics are done for the better. Organizing at the base is a contribution to, not a distraction from, winning governing power. LUCHA in Arizona has a thirty-year plan for structural change so that ordinary people will have as much power at the state house as lobbyists have.

Political organizations are becoming more sophisticated in their use of data and technology for identifying potential voters, voter issues, voter outreach, and, in some cases, which states or districts to focus on. Steve Phillips describes how NGP, New Virginia Majority (NVM), and a host of other groups are using "detailed, data-driven plans" to build power. They meticulously comb voter registration, turnout, demographics, and trends by county, looking for opportunities to strategically invest in and flip elections. They are building databases and developing new ways to measure voter opinions and engagement. And they are making use of new technologies that make it easier to get up-to-date information from door-knocking and phone-banking.[30]

Community Change Action (CCA) has worked with grassroots organizations to support this approach. CCA has emphasized the importance of rootedness and also of scale. As Deepak Pateriya, formerly chief of staff at CCA, puts it, "We have to build and contest for electoral power at a scale that is commensurate with the degree of societal change we seek. We can't be only marginal players, nor can we solely rely on Left electoral strategies or tactics that only work in a few parts of the country." In Pateriya's view, community-based electoral efforts must grow enough to displace the transactional, consultant-driven approaches that drain rather than build community power.[31]

WFP, state power groups, and their allies identify and train potential candidates to run for office. That includes not only the candidate but also, as Jen Kern, alignment and integration director of WFP, explains, "training the next generation of campaign managers and skilled electoral activist leaders."[32]

DSA also recruits, trains, and works with candidates for city, state, and federal office and is working on developing structures for co-governance. In New York State, DSA has endorsed and helped elect six members of the state legislature and works closely with them in a Socialists in Office Committee. They don't endorse unless they can provide these kinds of resources to support the candidate during and after an election. DSA provided "Albany 101" workshops for the newly elected leaders, focusing on questions such as "How do you actually get a bill through? What is the power dynamic in different situations?" They meet regularly to strategize around goals in the legislature and make sure legislators are working in alignment with DSA issue campaigns.

DSA also works with legislators in their home district offices, where the legislators typically provide assistance to constituents. The strategy is to combine a service-provision model with an organizing model to bring constituents in as more active political participants. For example, a typical legislator's staff might help deal with a bad landlord, whereas DSA members work to build tenant associations in the worst buildings.[33] For DSA, the goal is to work closely with the elected legislators while also constantly organizing the base. "There's no shortcut," explains Sumathy Kumar, co-chair of the NYC DSA chapter. "We have to organize, and we have to build a base in people's districts for them to feel any kind of relationship or accountability to our organization. If we didn't have any members in their districts, why would they listen to us?"[34]

A New Model for Electoral Change

The mainstream formula to win elections focuses on spending massive amounts on media campaigns, TV ads, and mailers, and micro-targeting particular swing-vote constituencies (often with messages that alienate the wider base).

Instead, the organizations we've profiled have adopted a new theory of change:

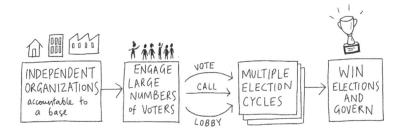

Why It's So Hard to Win Governing Power

The stunning wins from the 2020 Georgia election highlight the potential of the new model. Power-building groups and WFP had a decisive impact in Arizona, Michigan, and Pennsylvania in both 2020 and the 2022 midterms. But there are serious obstacles to winning governing power.

Once elected, legislators face enormous challenges. Policymakers need funds if they hope to run for a second term, and there is pressure to court wealthy donors. Conservatives have resources, research, and lawyers to support their elected people in office; progressive candidates have far less. Stephanie saw dogged activism win at the local level in Madison, Wisconsin, where people power outweighed money. But once you get to the state level, not to mention the federal level, it takes a lot more money to win.

Beyond that, there are structural forces that can limit the work. Electoral power groups have the greatest chance of winning seats at the local level, where it's easier to talk to lots of voters directly, but most state laws limit local governments' ability to create their own economic policies, such as wage rates, taxes, or industrial policy. And corporations and the wealthy threaten to, and do, leave the city, state, or country when faced with higher taxes or new regulations.

And while the model of combining community organizing, policy advocacy, and voter mobilization sounds good in theory, there are tensions between these. Jon Liss of NVM explains that since the organization is focused on building real power, they need to work with candidates they might not align with on the full range of issues that the community wants. For example, if NVM members in the community support greater rights for immigrants, or call to defund police, will they support a candidate for statewide office who doesn't back those issues but is an ally on other demands?[35] These kinds of dilemmas can't be resolved quickly and require a long-term view on organizing, education, and narrative shift, rather than a short-term election-cycle perspective. We talk about strategic alliances and political compromise in Chapter 14.

NVM must also balance the long-term, slow work of community building with the need for fast-moving, large-scale voter mobilization. Election cycles move relatively quickly and require outreach to millions of people. Liss explains that new outreach for base-building rests on one-on-one conversations, and in this model a full-time organizer can reach only about fifteen new people a week given the training, planning, follow-up, and other associated work. The average Virginia state house district has eighty thousand voters, and NVM will attempt to talk to at least twenty thousand of them.[36] Political funding comes in cycles, and often with a sense of panicked urgency. Only brave, somewhat scaled, and lucky organizations can survive the cycle of gambling early enough to be able to build campaign infrastructure, not knowing how much money is coming.

These tensions also raise the question: who is NVM representing? They have 300 active leaders, 2,000 members in chapters, and a voter base of 200,000 people. When it comes time to make political endorsements or develop strategy, these groups—who have different racial and class characteristics—likely have different priorities.

Why We Have to Keep Trying

Progressives often cycle in and out of their interest in electoral politics. Even within community organizing, the role of electoral politics has been contested. In 2004, Community Change convened a national gathering of community organizations to build alignment around a pivot to electoral work. The close 2000 presidential election, the resulting catastrophic war in Iraq, and massive tax cuts for the rich had made it plain that elections have consequences. There was a vibrant debate, with several longtime organizers taking the floor to argue passionately against engagement in electoral politics, viewing it as inevitably leading to co-optation. The conference proved to be a turning point. The debate was resolved in favor of engaging in elections, but only in a way that built organizations and advanced the interests of disenfranchised constituencies.

The 2008 presidential election of Barack Obama created excitement about electoral work, but the following years of economic crisis and austerity brought disillusionment. Obama didn't turn out to be the friend to social movements that he had made himself out to be. Around the same time in Europe, Left parties were on the forefront of cutting social programs and public employment as a way to deal with the recession. As a result, there was a growing turn toward more anarchist-inspired politics, such as using direct action to shut down meetings, and forming alternative institutions like worker cooperatives or urban farms. In Europe and Latin America, large segments of the Left advocated abstaining from voting altogether or voting for "none of the above."

While some of the Left stepped back from electoral work, the Right stepped up. Conservative, anti-immigrant, and racist parties filled the void and grew their numbers. Left forces began to turn their attention back to electoral work, notably via the Bernie Sanders presidential campaigns and the rise of "new municipalist" electoral parties in European cities. The question became: Is there a new way to engage in electoral work that doesn't fall into some of the old traps? Can we elect people to office but continue to organize the base?

The state is not merely a tool for overdogs; it also represents complex relationships between social forces.[37] It uses police, courts, prisons, and judges to repress and discipline workers and citizens. But it also administers social programs and institutions that were won by social movements. States also can include democratic spaces, where citizens are engaged in making decisions and where elected officials must respond to citizens to retain legitimacy. The state is biased in favor of overdogs, but a bias isn't a foregone conclusion. Progressive forces can win reforms that expand the democratic space.[38]

The opposition's aim is to dismantle the state's good features and expand its militaristic and abusive ones. If governing power is left uncontested, they'll succeed. Electoral projects like WFP, California Calls, and NGP demonstrate the viability of another approach.

Electoral Change and Other Strategy Models

Base-building is a key part of strategic electoral work. Ufot refers to the work of "chopping the wood and carrying the water," attending to the fundamentals. Old-fashioned door-knocking and one-on-one conversations are vital. WFP and most state power groups also run inside-outside policy campaigns. The groups must walk a fine line between pushing their base's demands and crafting legislation with their endorsed legislators.

Running candidates and policy campaigns involves narrative work: what messages to use in political ads, how to frame conversations when knocking on doors, and how to talk about elections in a way that appeals to a broad base of voters. In response to widespread cynicism of and alienation from the electoral process, groups like NGP seek to connect politics to people's everyday concerns.

There is a tension between electoral strategies aimed at winning majority support and strategies with bold, visionary demands that don't yet command majority support (like defunding the police). Ideally, these strategies can harmonize, but it requires organizers to be clear about the purpose of each. Bold visionaries should use narrative shift and base-building to push new liberatory ideas, and those ideas shouldn't be used as political litmus tests while public support is being built for them. Since electoral strategies are aimed at winning governing power, it is harder for progressive politicians to present the boldest demands and win in many localities. But they can help socialize new ideas and stay in relationship with movements, working on the left edge of the possible.

The Fight for Governing Power

Organizations working to build governing power must overcome the challenges of the U.S. political system, the role of money, and voter disillusionment and disenfranchisement. The work is hard and filled with heartbreak. And the electoral change model is up against new challenges, as the very foundations of democracy are being undermined.[39] This dysfunction can create a downward spiral: as democracy fades, fewer people participate, causing further erosion. As media sources are co-opted or new sources of disinformation develop, people have less access to accurate information and are less equipped to participate productively in the electoral process. There is good reason for skepticism about the electoral path to power, particularly as we have so few examples of successful progressive governance in the modern era.

But electoral work matters. Though it might not feel like it now, working people have won tremendous electoral victories. Crucially, they've done so by building independent power, not only by electing candidates. Those successes took decades to achieve and likely will again. Some of the biggest changes came alongside party realignment, such as in the 1850s, 1930s, and 1980s, when new parties emerged or large numbers of voters switched party affiliation. We may need to force party realignment to break the current political gridlock.

We can draw inspiration from historical examples of electoral success on the Left, however partial. The Radical Republicans forced a bold agenda for Reconstruction through Congress in the aftermath of the Civil War. And while a backlash eventually ended Reconstruction, the period resulted in some notable and lasting gains, such as forcing Southern states to ratify the Fourteenth and Fifteenth Amendments and founding the South's first public schools. Another example came in the 1980s in Chicago when Harold Washington built a powerful multiracial coalition that won two elections and delivered real benefits to the working-class majority, dramatically reducing poverty and hunger.[40] Biden's surprisingly progressive Build Back Better plan showed the impact of the Left's growing influence in the United States, although the success of Republicans and neoliberal Democrats in blocking the most progressive elements showed how far we have to go.

Despite the challenges, we think there's promise in forging a path for the Left to capture governing power. Even electing a few good candidates to office can have an outsized impact, as we'll see in the next chapter.

Table 9.1: Key Components of the Electoral Change Model

Component	Electoral Change Model
Form of Power	Political
Theory of Change	Independent organizations accountable to a base engage large numbers of voters to participate in multiple ways (vote, call, lobby) over multiple election cycles → Win elections and govern
Examples of Practitioners and Theorists	Anthony Thigpenn, Nsé Ufot, Maurice Mitchell, Democratic Socialists of America (DSA), Bayard Rustin, Community Change Action, UNITE HERE
Protagonists and Structure	Organizations engaged in integrated voter engagement Parties and party-like organizations and coalitions
Goals and Methods	Taking government power through elections to achieve major social change Build a political power base through elections, rather than focus only on electing candidates State or national organizations engaging in year-round organizing and electoral work to connect issues and elections
Tactical Repertoire	Large-scale voter mobilization by a permanent organization that works year-round on issues; running or endorsing candidates for office; changing laws and regulations; ballot initiatives; co-governance
What Does Winning Mean?	Capturing governing power, enactment of a governing agenda, growth in membership of the political alliance
Time Horizon + When the Model Is Most Effective	When the stakes of elections are especially consequential—e.g., to prevent fascist parties from winning Sometimes a slower build Work over multiple election cycles as organizations connect issues to politics, expand their capacity to reach voters, decide elections, and shape policy agendas

Component	Electoral Change Model
How It Works with Other Models/ Movement Ecosystem	Works well with base-building and inside-outside campaign models
	Newer efforts are incorporating elements of collective care
	Tension between majoritarian focus of electoral strategies and minority focus of disruptive movements
	Can be tensions between focus on election outcomes and long-term narrative-shift strategies
Strengths	Building electoral power that is independent of candidates and parties can result in big electoral wins that open space for big policy wins
Weaknesses	Tensions between a radical vision and what it takes to win electoral majorities; potential limits to what can be won through the existing state
	Limited recent examples of successful progressive governance may discourage consistent participation across cycles that this model requires

Tools

Tool 20 Prompt: Electoral Work
Tool 21 Strategic Debate
Tool 36 Long-Term Agenda

10

Inside-Outside Campaigns

Building Coalitions to Seize the Moment: Winning $15 in Chicago

In 2014, Chicago alders (city councilors) voted overwhelmingly to enact the city's first minimum-wage law. The wage would bring an almost 60 percent increase to minimum-wage workers by 2019, when it would reach $13 per hour.

Many observers were surprised Chicago was one of the earliest cities in a movement sweeping the country to adopt higher minimum wages. After all, many of those same alders had voted down a much narrower wage ordinance less than a decade before. And Chicago was run by the anti-union Mayor Rahm Emanuel.

It is difficult for underdogs to win big policy changes. Electing better representatives is part of the solution, but that doesn't mean change has to wait until principled progressives make up 51 percent of a legislature. It's possible to get nonprogressive politicians to support bold ideas, especially if you are starting with a few legislator allies.

That's because most politicians *are* politicians, in the pejorative sense. They respond to pressure and take the path of least resistance. Crucially, they do that whether the pressure is coming from the Right or the Left.

All the tactics we've looked at so far can put pressure on politicians. But "outside" tactics—mobilizing voters, changing people's minds, organizing strikes, marches, and rallies—are usually not enough. The inside approach—understanding the ins and outs of how a legislature works, and what each legislator cares about—is needed as well. This is why it's important to elect even a few progressive politicians. Once insiders are positioned to write legislation that can move the boundaries of what's winnable, then both the insiders and outsiders can pressure the rest of the legislature.

Inside-outside campaigns work best when they take advantage of political openings, such as when there is strong public support for an issue or when elected officials are more vulnerable to public pressure.

Taking on the Political Establishment: Raise Chicago and the Fight for $15

In Chicago, labor and community groups had fought for living wages for workers for decades. They had some victories in the 1990s and early 2000s, but those applied only to workers employed through city service contracts. In 2006, a coalition of union and community organizations in Chicago developed a "Big-Box Ordinance," which would require large retail firms like Walmart to pay workers a living wage. The Chicago City Council passed it, but for the first time in his seventeen years in office, Mayor Richard Daley used his veto power. The City Council attempted to override the veto, but several alders switched their votes, and the veto was upheld.

Five years later, a new mayor came into office. But like Mayor Daley, Rahm Emanuel was no friend of workers. One of his first acts was to limit the right of teacher unions to strike. He had no desire to raise wages either.

Today, though, in 2023, the minimum wage in Chicago is $15.40 per hour. How did organizers finally win?

Part of the answer is solid organizing. In the wake of the Big Box ordinance defeat, Chicago organizers launched successful electoral campaigns to replace several alders who had voted against the living wage, particularly those who had flipped their vote.

And they decided they needed to build power more broadly.[1] They went door-to-door, speaking to Chicago residents to build support for their issue and outrage against the status quo. A group of eighteen labor and community organizations built the Stand UP! Chicago campaign to organize low-wage workers and fight corporate power. In 2011 they held protests at a midwestern corporate summit, shutting down traffic and demanding that corporations receiving tax breaks and bailouts be held accountable for mistreating workers. Sandra Wiekerson, a home-care worker who risked arrest for blocking streets, noted, "This is definitely the beginning of a movement."[2]

Two new labor–community coalitions formed to focus specifically on raising wages: one focused on raising the state minimum wage (Raise Illinois), and one on raising the city minimum wage (Raise Chicago). One of the lead groups was Action Now, a successor organization to ACORN. Action Now worked closely with Service Employees International Union (SEIU) leaders in Chicago and nationally, preparing to build a national labor–community campaign to organize low-wage workers.[3] Alex Han, a labor organizer with SEIU at the time, recalls the groups holding a march on Michigan Avenue in downtown Chicago. They sent groups into retail stores with flyers about the campaign and were met with positive responses from workers. "I think that kind of planted a seed for building some organization with workers in that kind of commercial retail," explained Han.[4] The group increased its efforts to connect with low-wage workers and held worker committee meetings weekly.

But organizers also captured a political moment. The Chicago Teachers Union (CTU) had been undergoing its own change in strategy as a slate of reform leaders took office in 2010 and began a program of deep internal organizing. When Occupy Wall Street (OWS) emerged in the fall of 2011, the CTU—as well as many other city unions and community groups—joined, solidifying connections between large organizations and an activist base.

In September 2012, the CTU held a massive strike that resulted in a major win against Mayor Emanuel. The strike caught the attention of workers around the country. Han says the impact was immediately felt within the worker organizing efforts. "Before the strike, there might be ten workers there one week, or there might be twenty-five. The next week, there might be ten again. But the week after the teachers' strike, there were almost one hundred people in the room."[5]

Just two months after the CTU strike, the national Fight for $15 (FF15) campaign was launched. In Chicago, FF15 focused on organizing workers in workplaces and cooperating with the Raise Chicago and Raise Illinois campaigns. The three groups used a shared narrative about massive inequality and corporate greed.[6]

FF15 organized large marches and events. Raise Chicago organizers knocked on doors and brought community members together in teach-ins to talk about the economy and why it was necessary and possible to raise the minimum wage. "We were able to help people put language and numbers to what they felt," Katelyn Johnson, former executive director of Action Now, told us in an interview. "We made economics more accessible, and we showed people that their feelings were right, and we had the numbers to support what they felt. Affirming lived experiences is more inspiring than any pie chart, especially for workers who felt so undervalued."[7]

Around this time, Stephanie met Han at a labor conference. She had known about the FF15 campaign but wasn't sure how it was unfolding in cities around the country. Han and Mark Meinster, a Chicago-based organizer with the United Electrical Workers Union (UE), told her about how the FF15, along with the teachers' strike, were generating excitement among workers. Meinster explained that the union was even getting cold calls from workers who saw the campaign on the news and wanted to know how they could organize their workplace. He was organizing warehouse workers at the time, and people in that industry were talking about the fast-food strikes. "We actually tied in a few different groups of temp workers in various parts of the McDonald's supply chain to the FF15 work," Meinster told Stephanie later.[8]

The inside strategy involved innovative collaboration with elected officials on legislative work. City leaders began to feel the pressure to address inequality. In early 2013, Emanuel was looking to rebuild his credibility after the teachers' strike, and his administration chose to focus on minimum wage. He proposed a citywide minimum wage of $9.25. The following month, nine alders formed the Chicago Progressive Caucus (CPC) to push progressive legislation. Alder Bob Fioretti, who came into office in 2007 after defeating an incumbent who voted against the 2006 Big Box ordinance, stated, "The city's progressive voices need to stand together to push for policies that create a more just and equitable Chicago."[9]

The alders included many who had been backed by Chicago unions, and some of those same unions were the main contributors to the PAC formed to support the Caucus.[10] CPC alders began to speak out against the mayor's regressive positions on issues like education and worker rights.[11]

Meanwhile, organizers countered by putting a nonbinding referendum on the 2014 ballot, calling for a $15 minimum wage.[12] The referendum passed with 86 percent support, and approval in each of the 103 precincts where it was on the ballot. The CPC followed the results by announcing legislation that would set a city wage phased in to reach $15 an hour by 2019. With twenty-one alders backing the proposal, the pressure on Emanuel was growing, forcing him to convene a working group of alders and stakeholders. The group came back with a proposal for a $13 minimum wage, and it was adopted overwhelmingly by City Council in November 2014.[13]

The bill would phase in a city minimum wage of $13 per hour by 2019, then indexed to rise with inflation. In 2019, the new mayor, Lori Lightfoot, approved legislation to increase the wage to $15 by 2021 for most workers, and to include domestic workers who had been previously excluded.[14] The city estimated this would provide raises to over 400,000 workers.[15]

The national FF15 campaign was a major effort, guided by a unified strategy, that was a risky wager aimed at increasing wages for workers even if they weren't yet in a union. Incredibly, only four years after the campaign began in 2012, dozens of cities and counties, and the two largest states in the country, California and New York, had passed $15 minimum wages. By 2021, eleven states and forty-five cities and counties had passed $15 minimum-wage laws, resulting in raises of $150 billion for over 26 million workers.[16] Not only did the campaign create a national movement, but it also spread internationally, connecting workers from Brazil to Japan to New Zealand.

The fights looked different in every city and state. In some cities the campaign wage was mostly inside, legislative work, and the product of political maneuvering. In other places, the effort resembled Chicago's local organizing among labor and community organizations.

The inside-outside approach worked to establish a $15 minimum wage in Chicago and elsewhere. But FF15 was launched to win $15 *and* a union for McDonald's workers. So far, the union part hasn't happened—in Chicago or elsewhere—but FF15 has changed the national narrative, raised workers' incomes, and laid the groundwork for a new worker upsurge.

Campaigning and Compromises: Common Elements of Inside-Outside

Table 10.1 summarizes key components of the inside-outside campaign model. The campaigns usually involve the following common elements:

> *Build coalitions.* Inside-outside campaigns are almost always run by coalitions because few organizations are powerful enough to win a large policy goal on their own. These could be ambitious federal policies like the Affordable Care Act (ACA) or more targeted city or state campaigns, like the Excluded Workers Fund in New York State, or city rent-control laws. The initial stage of the campaign is bringing partners together to choose appropriate policy goals and legislative targets.
>
> *Research to pick targets.* Using tools such as power-mapping (Tool 33), campaigns determine the appropriate targets. For example, living-wage campaigns targeted city councils. A campaign would list each of the, say, fifteen council members and rate them on a scale in terms of support for the ordinance.
>
> *Craft legislation.* Insiders work with outsiders to develop legislation that is on the left edge of the possible: far reaching, but possible to win.
>
> *Outside pressure.* On the outside, coalition partners gather petitions, sign up voters, run educational programs, call their legislators, and utilize whatever tactics they can to show popular support for the bill.
>
> *The campaigners (the outsiders) make it difficult for the legislators to vote no.* In our example, with fifteen council members, the research would

lead to, essentially, numerous different campaigns, each designed to move any undecided council member. For some, it could mean weekly delegations of voters. For others, an economic impact study could make the difference. The Los Angeles living-wage campaign sent clergy to speak with religious council members; another member switched his vote to "yes" after hearing testimony from the worker who emptied his office wastebasket each night.

Inside organizing. Elected officials build their own coalitions to gain supporters for the bill. They count votes, coordinate lobbying, and communicate with the outside campaigners about negotiations.

Watch for a political opening. The campaign must be constantly organizing, ready to push their legislation forward, waiting for the right moment, such as when a legislator is up for reelection or when there's an economic downturn or even an economic upturn and a tight labor market. It may take multiple cycles to enact the policy. But once the opening is there, the campaign usually moves quickly, in a single legislative or budget cycle.

The theory of change looks like:

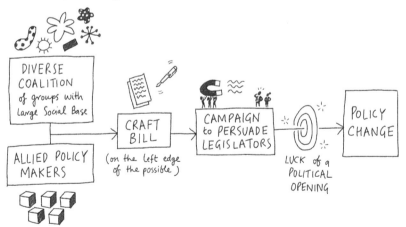

Compromise. Since the main outcome of the inside-outside model is a piece of legislation, it will almost certainly involve compromise. When cities and states began to pass the $15 minimum wage, they phased in the raise, sometimes over many years, and sometimes excluding small businesses. Johnson says that when Emanuel introduced his $13-per-hour proposal, it was a huge compromise because it was phased in over several years and didn't index for inflation or eliminate the tip credit. Supporters debated over whether to accept the compromise or keep fighting. Johnson says, "I was one of the people who said 'let's fight!'" But in the end, she voted in favor of the compromise: "I didn't want the perfect to get in the way of the good. And $13 was a big jump; it was more than my mother was earning at the time."[17]

Johnson says she doesn't regret making the compromise, but it was a difficult agreement to make:

> People were hurting, and I felt it because I know what my family went through. I know what it's like to grow up with working parents and still be on public assistance. But it would have been beautiful if we could have fought more, we just ran out of political time. I feel emotionally complicated about it. I do not know for sure that if we had more people or more time that things would have been different, but I think it could have been possible in a world where political will had a more direct correlation with the needs of the people. It was all so hard and so beautiful, and I deeply hope that there is a world where workers are paid a living wage for their entire working lives.[18]

Similarly, when Seattle first passed a $15 minimum wage, it was phased in over four years, so workers didn't get the full raise for awhile. In some cities, the compromise wage was lower than $15. And while many of the ordinances included indexing for inflation, not all did, guaranteeing that without further raises the wage would drop below a living one. Questions around how to build more power, how to negotiate the best deal possible, and how to know when you've achieved the most you can get, exist in every inside-outside campaign. Some of these tensions arise when people working on other strategies judge the compromises inside-outside campaigns make.

Awareness of this dynamic won't make the tensions go away. But understanding the constraints that campaigners working to bring home a policy win have to work within makes it easier to assess their success or failure on their own terms.

Incremental policy wins can be in tension with long-term vision. We have asked our students to say what they would do when faced with a difficult choice; for example, whether or not to support a legislation that included a path to citizenship for undocumented immigrants but also expanded immigration enforcement. One useful yardstick in assessing a compromise is who will be more and less powerful if a policy is enacted—underdogs or overdogs?

Political compromises can unfortunately mean that legislators agree to some coalition partners' demands but not others'; a coalition with strong solidarity may reject proposals that do this, but powerful coalition partners have been known to make deals for themselves and leave others behind. For example, in 2007, New York City allocated subsidies to a developer who planned to convert the Kingsbridge Armory in the Bronx into a mall. Labor, community, and faith-based groups joined to demand that any retailers in the new space would provide living wages and health benefits. But building trades unions cut their own side deal with the mayor, unionizing only construction workers.[19] Scholars have studied labor–community coalitions and found that certain approaches can improve trust and functioning, such as transparent communication and clear goals. Race and gender lenses are also crucial. Historically, even in progressive movements, women and people of color have had less power, so compromises have often come at their expense. We'll discuss this more in Chapter 14.

Connecting Policy and Power: Strengths and Weaknesses of the Model

When done well, inside-outside organizing can achieve victories that go beyond what any one group could win on their own. Inside-outside campaigns are able to win substantial, concrete gains, and they often create coalitions of groups that may not have worked together before. In fact, they can be a way for groups to overcome past divisions: groups that ordinarily fight one another over small slices can come together to demand a larger pie.

This can strengthen campaigns for further gains. Since the original victory was likely a compromise, organizers must decide whether the next step involves going back to win more of the original demands or using the win to launch into new arenas. For example, some living-wage organizers built off of their success to pass other legislation, like paid sick days and wage-theft laws, and eventually came back to fight for city- or statewide minimum wages. Ideally, this would be driven by a long-term strategy to build power, rather than jumping from one issue campaign to the next.

In addition to potentially painful compromises, another weakness of this model is that passing a law is one thing; enforcing it is another. Meaningful enforcement might require a new inside-outside approach—perhaps with new allies in city or state agencies. Many citywide living-wage ordinances were never enforced or were enforced weakly.[20] To execute and build on a law, organizing must continue after the legislative win.

The inside-outside strategy also runs the risk that legislative wins could demobilize a base rather than invigorate it. A base of members, or workers, is more likely to remain mobilized if they were actively involved in the campaign, and see that the legislative win came from their power, not the goodwill of lawmakers.

Winning Is Good, Actually: Building Power Through Policy Change

Organizers have long debated whether real change can be won through legislative reform. Some schools of thought see any reform as ultimately propping up the system. For example, a higher minimum wage might seem to be a gain for workers, but it increases consumer spending power, thereby sustaining capitalism.

Others, however, point out that legislative reforms can create massive change under certain conditions, such as the New Deal policies of the 1930s, civil rights and voting legislation of the 1960s, and even the ACA of 2010. In fact, reforms can have a contradictory character—for example, a minimum-wage increase can be good for capitalism *and* help build working-class power.[21] Legislative efforts can deliver lasting social change, but they are most likely to do so when connected to organizing and a deliberate strategy to include power-building measures in the legislation.

Lasting change is also more likely when the inside-outside campaign expands a base and develops leaders. Some people aren't moved initially by grand visions of social change. They face poverty wages, abusive landlords, and discrimination. Inside-outside campaigns can be a powerful way to not just mobilize existing members, but also bring new people into the fight. Because these campaigns offer so many opportunities for everyday people to participate—leading actions, negotiating with legislators, or talking to the press—they provide rich opportunities for leadership development. Midwest Academy's Strategy Chart (Tool 34) emphasizes that the goals of a campaign should include increasing an organization's power, membership, and leadership.

Inside-outside strategies can maximize impact with **policy feedback loops**, which allow organizers to win policies that build more power so that they can win bigger changes in the future. Policy feedback loops can also be used to break the opposition's power. We describe policy feedback loops in more detail in Chapter 17, but they are particularly important in inside-outside campaigns because they can have indirect effects beyond the policy win. This is the case with some minimum-wage and living-wage laws, where organizers have won not just a new wage but also new labor offices to implement the laws and monitor compliance. These offices have partnered with community organizations and helped to further organize workers.[22]

We can see that in Chicago's minimum-wage campaign. It won hard-fought gains for low-wage workers and strengthened Chicago labor–community alliances. In 2016, Chicago teachers launched another strike, and this time it took only one day for their demands to be met. And they were joined by other unions and workplaces: daycare center workers, Nabisco workers, university workers, and fast-food workers.[23] Chicago also helped lay the groundwork for a labor upsurge that gained public attention with the improbable victories of Starbucks and Amazon workers in 2022.

> **Box 10.1: Other Examples of Inside-Outside Campaigns**
>
> In New York State, a broad coalition of senior citizens, disability rights groups, workers, and faith-based groups worked together to raise home-care workers' pay through a proposal in the state budget. Organizers worked methodically, contacting people one by one and providing training and support to get involved. Some participated through calling or visiting legislators, while others wrote letters to the editor. There were cultural activities with music and art to build solidarity and a public presence. When it came down to the last two weeks of the legislative budget cycle, coalition members moved into hotels in Albany so they could be in the Capitol every day to pressure the governor.
>
> Insiders—supportive legislators and their staff—helped the coalition engage in this outside pressure at the Capitol. They provided the coalition with meeting spaces in the Capitol. They provided supplies like tape and scissors to post signs around the building (which isn't allowed). They helped the campaigners sneak food for protestors into the Capitol building (also not allowed). When protestors refused to leave the Capitol building, thereby engaging in nonviolent civil disobedience, legislative allies and staff cheered them on and made sure they had adequate press coverage and legal support. In the end, the campaign won the largest investment in home-care worker spending in New York history—$7.7 billion over four years.
>
> The ACA was another example of an inside-outside campaign, and was enacted in a narrow political opening. It barely overcame a filibuster in the Senate and passed by a handful of votes in the House of Representatives. Grassroots community organizations in swing states and congres-

> sional districts ran savvy campaigns to round up the votes, working in partnership with a national progressive coalition called Health Care for America Now (HCAN). HCAN brought together national groups and networks like Community Change, Planned Parenthood, US Action, SEIU, and MoveOn.org, and supported campaigns in target states and congressional districts led by community organizations with local roots. Deepak remembers that members of Congress and Obama's key staff complained about the pressure some of the tactics applied to wavering Democrats—including direct action and civil disobedience—but the ACA would have failed if its fate was decided only in backroom negotiations among insiders. More recently, movement groups and the Congressional Progressive Caucus played a key role in moving Biden's governing agenda in his first two years to the left.[24]

Inside-Outside Campaigns and Other Strategy Models

We call the inside-outside campaign a hybrid strategy model because it relies on multiple forms of power and strategies. A hybrid strategy is a chord rather than a single note.

First, organizations in a coalition use base-building as part of the outside pressure, gaining new members or deepening support of existing ones. The campaign gives the members something to do: sign petitions, lobby, or call their legislator. And a legislative win may open up new ways to build the base. For instance, organizers can knock on doors and talk to people about the opportunities to make use of the win, such as the Excluded Workers Fund (Chapter 6.1).

Inside-outside campaigns are closely tied to electoral strategies, where underdog organizations try to endorse or run like-minded candidates. The goal is to elect some champions so you have someone on the inside—someone to move your legislation and organize within a city council or state house. Also, electoral work changes the playing field for politicians. A politician will pay more attention to, say, Black people in their district if many of them are registered to vote.

Similarly, narrative shifts can move the ground under a politician. This might mean shifting the narrative from "McDonald's workers are low-skill and don't deserve more" to "all work has dignity" and "low-wage work hurts us all." Strong public support can be a factor in forcing reluctant legislators to support the bill. But minimum-wage laws have historically had high levels of public support. Support may be necessary, but it's not sufficient for creating change. That's why both the inside and outside parts of the strategy are necessary.

Truly disruptive strategies can be hard to incorporate into an inside-outside campaign. But Han says some of the early strikes in Chicago did disrupt:

> You had stores just shutting down all over the place. I remember there were four people on staff at a Walgreens in the Loop and they all walked out and locked the door. I remember going to a Subway sandwich shop where all the workers had walked out, and when one of our organizers tried to deliver the strike notice, the manager tried to lock the door on us because he was so angry. There were dozens and dozens of employers that were shut down. It put a real scare into the broader city at the very least.[25]

While the FF15 actions didn't look like this in every city, they did help gain attention, bring in allies, and put some pressure on corporate brands. The disruption campaign may have had an impact on brand image or loyalty. Soon, major corporations announced they were voluntarily raising their starting wage to $15. And in Chicago, the 2012 teachers' strike raised the stakes as the CTU showed that workers could indeed disrupt a city.

"Hard Work, Sweat, and Tears": Using the Power We Have

After the Chicago City Council approved the $15 minimum wage on November 26, 2019, McDonald's employee and FF15 leader Adriana Alvarez said, "Today is the day that fast-food workers like me have fought for with a lot of hard work, sweat, and tears."[26]

Practical radicals can't take shortcuts if they hope to win major gains. They can't ignore base-building, because at the end of the day, organizers' work rests on the idea that legislators can't ignore their constituents. It takes more than social media or TV ads. It takes real people engaging their representatives over and over, and in large numbers. "You cannot just pull the flowers at the end if you haven't been tending the garden," says Ilana Berger of the Fair Pay for Home Care campaign.[27]

The Chicago FF15 campaign demonstrates the strengths and weaknesses of the inside-outside model. Using outside tactics and inside partners can produce big wins for people that change the quality of their lives. But there are limits to how much the system will give. It's about skillfully using the power we have in a particular conjuncture to get as much as we can—and ideally creating more power for underdogs in the process.

Table 10.1: Key Components of the Inside-Outside Campaign Model

Component	Inside-Outside Campaign Model
Forms of Power	Solidarity; Political; Ideological
Theory of Change	Diverse coalition of groups with a large social base + allied policymakers craft a bill "on the left edge of the possible" + campaign to organize legislators + luck of a political opening → policy change
Examples of Practitioners and Theorists	Heather Booth, Pramila Jayapal, Frances Perkins, Health Care for America Now (HCAN), Midwest Academy

Component	Inside-Outside Campaign Model
Protagonists and Structure	Progressive elected and appointed officials working with outside organizations and coalitions to enact major social policy reforms
Goals and Methods	Win a concrete, major policy reform in the medium term, when the balance of forces is nearly equally divided
	Coalition building; development of specific policy goals and targets; orchestration between "insiders" and "outsiders"
Tactical Repertoire	Campaigns to pressure swing legislators, targeting, counting votes, real-time coordination between insiders and outsiders to adjust tactics
What Does Winning Mean?	Win policy campaigns delivering social change
	Ideally also grow the base and shift relations of power through policy feedback loops
Time Horizon + When the Model Is Most Effective	When the balance of forces between overdogs and underdogs is closely divided in governing bodies, so that if underdogs target swing legislators they can pass significant policy changes
How It Works with Other Models/ Movement Ecosystem	Most compatible with base-building and electoral change models
	Doesn't typically incorporate collective care (though there are exceptions)
	Not always compatible with disruptive movements because of focus on winning majorities
	Can conflict with momentum and narrative shift because of its shorter time horizon
Strengths	Can deliver big policy wins, change people's lives, and sometimes alter relations of power

Component	Inside-Outside Campaign Model
Weaknesses	Won't work if the underlying conditions are absent, which they often are
	Compromises can be tough to swallow
	Can deplete rather than build power
	Turns attention toward policy and policymakers, which can divert focus from power-building

Tools

Tool 4 Reverse Engineering
Tool 22 Policy Feedback Loops
Tool 23 Structural Reforms
Tool 33 Power Analysis
Tool 34 Strategy Chart

11

Momentum

Distributed Organizing, Big Results: 350.org and the Divestment Movement

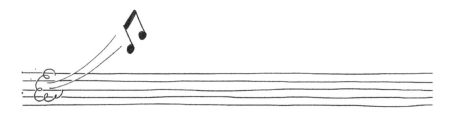

In 2014, the *New York Times* published a "man bites dog" story: "Rockefellers, Heir to an Oil Fortune, Will Divest Charity of Fossil Fuels."[1] John D. Rockefeller was America's first billionaire; his family's wealth was based on oil. At its peak, Rockefeller's company, Standard Oil, controlled 90 percent of the U.S. oil market. Rockefeller was one of the "robber barons" of the Gilded Age, a group of rich industrialists known for their monopolistic and unethical practices, abuse of workers, and outsized political influence.

The Rockefeller Brothers Fund announced their decision a day after the 2014 People's Climate March, which galvanized public focus on climate change. Michael Northrop, program director for its Sustainable Development program, explained to us that the decision to divest came after family members, who were trustees of the foundation, met with ExxonMobil leadership to raise the issue of climate change, and "were rebuffed . . . and not with a great deal of gentility." They concluded that ExxonMobil, the original Rockefeller empire's biggest descendant, was "violating basic principles of morality, endangering the planet."[2] At the time of this book's writing, 1,552 institutions have divested over 40.5 trillion dollars from fossil fuel companies—including ExxonMobil and Chevron, Standard Oil's second-biggest corporate descendant.[3]

These divestments signaled the beginning of a new era in environmental activism. They were a revolt against the broken logic of the mainstream environmental movement, which had spent tens of millions of dollars to pass federal legislation in the Barack Obama years and had come up short.

The basic theory of change for many national environmental groups went something like this:

> Technical expertise + Inside access to policymakers → Policy change

The logic hadn't always been broken. In the 1970s, after social movements raised awareness of environmental issues, the big green groups issued detailed reports and used access to members of Congress and other decisionmakers to persuade them to act. And they got results—the Clean Air Act and the Environmental Protection Agency, for example, and even a prompt, effective international response to the ozone hole (which is now shrinking). A generation of environmentalists mastered these methods.

But in a new century, they risked irrelevance—cavalry in a war of machine guns and tanks. The fossil fuel industry, which played a vanguard role in the neoliberal revolution (Chapter 5), had learned to neutralize the old tactics. In recent decades, oil tycoons David and Charles Koch have funded a suite of Right-wing think tanks, grassroots groups, media groups, and legal groups that narrowed the political space for traditional liberal solutions, such as increased taxation and greater regulation. Fossil fuel dominates politics in states like Texas and West Virginia, and it influences politicians across the country through campaign contributions—just as effectively as Rockefeller's Standard Oil did over a century before. Despite rising public concern about climate change, the fossil fuel industry had the power to brush aside challenges from mainstream environmental groups. "Speaking truth to power," it turns out, can just make you hoarse.

Deepak had seen a similar dynamic play out in a different movement. A generation of anti-poverty advocates had ridden the wave of the 1960s to win improvements in social programs. But neoliberal backlash had resulted in budget cuts in the Reagan era and the evisceration of the social safety net with welfare reform in the 1990s. Deepak and colleagues revisited how they ran national policy campaigns, emphasizing the need to operate from a base of power, with a grassroots constituency of community organizations that could challenge corporate Democrats as well as Republicans, sometimes using confrontational tactics to break through. Such an approach proved essential to passing the Affordable Care Act and winning protection from deportation for young immigrants. Deepak was part of a group of immigrant movement leaders who got arrested at the White House on May 1, 2010, while protesting President Obama's deportation policies.[4] He was surprised and moved to find kindred spirits challenging the broken status quo in the environmental movement. The wave of arrests at the White House over the Keystone XL pipeline began about a year later.

Indigenous Leaders and Youth Climate Activists Spark a Movement

The environmental justice movement began in communities of color experiencing the worst effects of pollution and centered those most impacted. Clayton Thomas-Müller is a longtime Indigenous organizer and a member of Mathias Colomb Cree Nation, also known as Pukatawagan, located in northern Manitoba, Canada. Then working for the Indigenous Environmental Network (IEN), Thomas-Müller supported Indigenous people in Canada fighting the expansion of oil extraction from tar sands, a process that was causing cancer among, and violence against, Indigenous people as white men encroached on Indigenous land.[5]

Indigenous leaders developed a savvy organizing strategy to "bottleneck the [oil companies'] ambitions for expansion" by blocking the construction of pipelines to transport the oil, Thomas-Müller told us. Indigenous leaders developed "a Native rights–based approach utilizing the expectation of self-determination and sovereignty, treaty rights, inherent rights, and other legal instruments that recognize the power of Indigenous people as rights holders in the work."[6] IEN and Indigenous leaders organized Indigenous and non-Indigenous people who would be negatively affected by the pipelines along the routes to great effect.

In 2010, thirteen tribal chiefs and community leaders from the affected areas planned to get arrested at the White House to pressure Obama to cancel the Keystone XL pipeline. If constructed, the pipeline would take oil from the Alberta tar sands all the way to Port Arthur, Texas, potentially polluting the Ogallala aquifer in the process, a source of water for millions of people. May Boeve and Bill McKibben of 350.org called Thomas-Müller and Tom Goldtooth, executive director of IEN, to ask if 350.org could help amplify the action and join the fight.

350.org was founded in 2008 by six Middlebury College students, including Boeve, plus McKibben, a college professor. The organization was named after the safe level of carbon dioxide in the atmosphere, 350 parts per million (we exceeded that level in the 1980s).

It was a tough negotiation between the two organizations, with Thomas-Müller and Goldtooth insisting that Indigenous well-being and leadership be centered in the campaign. The result was the largest civil disobedience action at the White House since the Vietnam War, as well as a model for movement collaboration that, Thomas-Müller told us, really "challenged that dynamic" of white supremacy in the environmental movement "in a beautiful way." He attributes the success of the partnership between 350.org and Indigenous communities, which has endured, to the youth of the 350.org staff, their intersectional analysis, and their willingness to be "accountable to and take direction" from Indigenous leaders. The story vividly illustrates the importance of alliances, a critical element of strategy (Chapter 3). As Thomas-Müller puts it, the fight "could not have been won without a multitude of players."[7]

After the failure of climate legislation early in Obama's first term, 350.org set the goal of building a mass movement to defeat one of the world's most malign, influential industries.[8] As McKibben put it, "We assumed that because scientists had said the world was coming to an end that that would be enough to motivate our political system to act. As it turns out, that's not how politics works. You need to meet power with power."[9]

The Keystone XL fight was a challenge not only to establishment Democrats like Obama, but also to the mainstream green movement. 350.org put forward a new strategy model known as momentum:

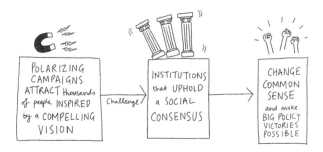

The key ingredients in this new strategy were concerted action by everyday people concerned about climate change (solidarity power), and changing the public understanding of climate change by using dramatic actions that named villains and decisionmakers (ideological power). Rather than plead with politicians to act, 350.org targeted the fossil fuel companies that controlled them. "Calling into question the social license of the fossil fuel industry," its legitimacy, Boeve argued, was the indispensable lever to avert climate catastrophe.[10] Most activists today take it for granted that the climate fight can't be won without a massive, sustained exercise of people power. But that wasn't always so. The Keystone XL fight reverberated through the movement and helped create a new common sense. The struggle had many twists and turns over a decade but the defeat of the pipeline, confirmed in 2021, when Biden took office, was "one of this generation's most monumental environmental victories," as an establishment environmental group put it.[11]

"Camaraderie, Courage, and Risk Taking": A Decentralized Movement Catches Fire

With lessons learned in the Keystone fight, 350.org sought to harness the momentum in a campaign that would give newly energized people something concrete to do and a way to join the movement. The organization led and supported national marches against climate change. And in 2012, 350.org made a crucial strategic choice to focus on divestment, demanding that major institutions sell their shares in fossil fuel companies.

Inspired by the anti-apartheid South African divestment movement of the 1980s, 350.org leaders envisioned a simple, galvanizing campaign that would allow local activists to plug in wherever they were. Instead of pointing everyone toward a centralized target like the White House, the campaign would be unified by a common demand—but with targets close to home for any activist who wanted to get involved. *Rolling Stone* published a landmark article to launch the campaign by McKibben, "Global Warming's Terrible New Math," about what would happen to the planet and humanity if fossil fuel companies burned their existing reserves. The magazine covered the "Do the Math" tour in twenty-two cities that followed, which attracted thousands of young people to concert venues. Prominent activists traveled around the country on a bus like a rock band.[12] 350.org developed a toolkit for local activists who wanted to pressure their universities to act. Staff provided technical assistance on questions like how to recruit people to a campaign, what tactics to use, and how to respond to arguments from the other side.

The campaign soon spread from college campuses to foundations, pension funds, city and state governments, and religious institutions. 350.org leaders believed that to delegitimize the industry, they needed to get major institutions in society to act. Key "pillars" of institutional support held up the social consensus that fossil fuel was a necessary part of a modern economy. Divestment campaigners sought out iconic institutions as targets, like Harvard University and New York City's pension fund.

At its peak, four hundred divestment campaigns were going on at the same time, supported by a lean staff of twenty at 350.org.[13] The campaigners created a "shared DNA"—a core set of demands, cultural norms, and a common story that local activists could adopt. Their logo, an orange X, created a shared brand linking campaigns together in the public imagination. Activists had considerable autonomy to pursue tactics that made sense in their local situation. 350.org built a media operation and a website, Gofossilfree.org, to "show the movement to itself," as Boeve puts it, so activists in any one location could learn from and be inspired by others.[14]

One of the newly energized activists, Varshini Prakash, was a college sophomore at the University of Massachusetts, Amherst (UMass). She had been involved in recycling clubs in high school and sustainable agriculture projects in college, but the Keystone fight made her realize that the fight against climate change couldn't be won by changing consumption habits. It would require a direct challenge to the corporate titans destroying the climate for profit. She learned that "very ordinary people" could exercise power and found the discovery "mind blowing." Prakash decided to bring the fight home and became a leader in the divestment fight on her campus. She describes writing a speech she would deliver at a demonstration and being coached by a 350.org staffer. As "a young woman of color, it was one of the most meaningful moments of my life," Prakash said.[15]

The UMass campaign included a wide range of tactics, including mass petitioning, a "die-in" of one hundred people for Earth Day, civil disobedience leading to dozens of arrests in the administration building, and a 30' x 30' orange divestment banner hanging from the school's parking garage. The students had multi-hour negotiating sessions with the administration. When they were invited to make a brief presentation to the Board of Trustees, the students sang the iconic labor anthem "Which Side Are You On?," which, Prakash said, "freaked the trustees out." Through 350.org, Prakash met activists at other schools who were also struggling against intransigent administrations. Together they brainstormed creative escalation tactics. She describes the campaign as full of "camaraderie, courage, and risk taking."[16] Prakash went on to co-found Sunrise Movement, a vibrant youth-led activist group that has helped push the Green New Deal into the national conversation.

The divestment campaign has had a long tail. Activists have broadened their focus beyond divestment. For example, in Japan, 350.org affiliates are pressuring the country's three largest banks to stop financing fossil fuels. Coalitions are also targeting central banks in South Africa, Europe, the United Kingdom, and the United States.

The campaign has helped change the public's opinion around fossil fuels.[17] For one thing, it shifted consciousness of climate change from something mainly related to individual consumption habits to something that requires challenging corporate power.[18] And it played a role in stigmatizing the fossil fuel industry.[19] Fossil fuel companies are not yet as toxic in the public imagination as tobacco companies. But now, not just the business practices, but also the very legitimacy of the enterprise of oil, gas, and coal extraction, are being questioned, and by powerful institutions and leaders as well.

Two business school professors conducted an analysis of over 42,000 articles about the divestment movement and argued that it made more moderate actions seem more reasonable.[20] This illustrates the radical flank effect, originally conceived by sociologist Herbert Haines, who argued that in the 1960s a growing radical Black wing of the civil rights movement increased popular support for more moderate Black groups.[21] Voices in the financial establishment began talking about "stranded assets" and "unburnable carbon"—translating the moral demands of the movement into a market rationale for divestment.[22]

The divestment campaign was also a hothouse for the growth of movement talent. Leaders not only in 350.org, but also in newer groups like Sunrise Movement and Justice Democrats, got pivotal training and experience in the campaign. Prakash called the divestment movement a "breeding ground for a new generation of climate organizers."[23] Movements are inspired by the desire to win changes in politics or policy, but they often have immense collateral consequences as volunteers become activists for life.

The movement has not yet fundamentally disrupted the industry's business model. But it's had some impact. A study of thirty-three countries found that "increasing oil and gas divestment pledges in a country are associated with lower capital flows to domestic oil and gas companies."[24] And its impact has transcended college campuses and affected national and even global politics. In 2015, Boeve argued that one benchmark for assessing the success of the divestment campaign would be the outcome of climate discussions in Paris among national governments.[25] The Paris Agreement, adopted that year, was a breakthrough—setting a global framework to limit warming to below two degrees Celsius and establishing binding emissions targets for signatories. The victory had many causes, but the demonstration of broad public will for action through the divestment campaign played an important role. And in 2022, President Joe Biden signed the first-ever major legislation in the United States to address climate change, a victory that was made possible by over a decade of work to change the political weather.

Making the Impossible Possible: Common Elements of the Momentum Model

The divestment campaign is an example of the momentum model formalized by Mark and Paul Engler in their book *This Is an Uprising: How Nonviolent Revolt Is Shaping the Twenty-First Century*.[26] The model has been developed further by Momentum, a training institute and movement incubator that works with groups addressing a wide range of issues, including the Sunrise Movement.

Boeve explained to us that the divestment campaign had used principles of the momentum model long before they heard about it. And momentum-driven campaigns have been run for centuries—perhaps originating with the movement to abolish slavery, which exhibits many of its key elements. Giving the approach a name and definition articulates principles that make it easier to consciously plan and initiate a momentum-driven movement.

The momentum model, like inside-outside campaigns, is a chord that brings together several notes of strategy and forms of power (Table 11.1). It's a "hybrid approach that helps movements take the best elements of various organizing traditions based on what serves their goals."[27] Momentum-driven campaigns aim to avoid the pitfall of organization-based models, which can be slow and plodding, and tend to focus on local issues, rather than national or international ones. And unlike some practitioners who emphasize the spontaneity and lack of centralization of social movements, the Englers stress the role of trained organizers and movement hubs.

The momentum model has eight elements:

> *Changing the political weather and the "common sense" on an issue.* Unlike a policy campaign that leverages existing sources of power to pass a bill, a momentum-driven campaign's goal is beyond the horizon of what's possible now. A good example is marriage equality, which was a fringe idea when first proposed and remained so for many years. Con-

gress passed (and President Bill Clinton signed) the Defense of Marriage Act, and LGBTQ+ activists lost in state ballot initiatives an astonishing thirty-two times before they won for the first time in 2012.[28] The marriage equality campaign was ultimately so successful that Karl Rove, who promoted anti-marriage ballot initiatives in 2004 to help George W. Bush get reelected, later denied what he had done.[29]

Organizers in the momentum tradition *establish a Grand Strategic Objective (GSO), something that can be achieved in five years, but not immediately.* A GSO "is lower than the vision" of an ideal society, Lissy Romanow, the former executive director of Momentum, told us, but it's "higher than tactics and higher than campaign strategy.... It's usually crafted to be energizing and simple enough to be memorable."[30] Working at this "meso level" between vision and campaigns, momentum strategists consciously build a bridge between the world as it is and the world as it could be. For 350.org, the long-term vision is to stop climate change, and the GSO was to delegitimize the fossil fuel industry through the divestment campaign.

Polarizing campaigns that expand active and passive support and change public opinion. The core of the momentum model is to create galvanizing fights that attract a passionate minority of intense supporters *and* build passive support for the cause among the mass public.

The internet and social media are crucial tools for momentum-driven campaigns to grow quickly, but traditional media is important too. The news media is drawn to explosive "movement moments"—when thousands or millions of people take action in response to a dramatic injustice, like the killings of unarmed Black people in the United States or the detention and death of Mahsa Amini in 2022 at the hands of Iran's Morality Police. Sometimes these "trigger moments" are unplanned, and other times—as when Rosa Parks refused to give up her seat to a white man, sparking the Montgomery Bus Boycott—they're instigated by trained movement leaders. Momentum organizers seize the moment when unplanned uprisings take place and consciously create movement moments through dramatic escalating actions that force people to pay attention. The Keystone XL pipeline and divestment fights were planned confrontations that forced people to take a side. When successful, momentum campaigns "shift the spectrum of support and isolate the opposition" and "shift the ground under decisionmakers' feet," Romanow says.[31]

Absorbing newly engaged people, investing in their leadership, and giving them tools and support to take action and develop strategy. When there's a lot of energy around an issue—a "whirlwind" of action—momentum campaigners seek to bring people together in mass trainings, to develop concrete organizing skills and instill a shared campaign DNA. Unlike many mass marches, where everybody goes back to life as usual afterward, organizers consciously recruit participants to be part of the campaign for the long haul.

Rather than trying to script or control what local activists do, momentum campaigns frontload a shared set of values, cultural norms, demands, and brands at the beginning of a campaign—and then local activists work with these to develop creative actions of their own. With an emphasis on "distributed action," movement participants initiate actions and strategies without checking in with a national center. The national center amplifies and shares local actions and wins so activists feel that their local campaign is part of the larger movement. A next step in the evolution of the momentum model, Romanow told us, is to invest more deeply in ongoing leadership and strategy development, rather than assume people will self-organize without support.

Weakening the pillars of the dominant consensus on an issue so a new common sense can take hold. In movements against authoritarian regimes, mass movements must win defections from the "pillars" that uphold a ruling government's power—churches, businesses, media, and, crucially, military and law enforcement.[32] When enough pillars begin to wobble, the whole regime may come toppling down quickly. In Chapter 3, we talked about Wyatt Tee Walker's strategy to divide the white power structure in Birmingham in order to defeat segregation. The pillars approach is another method for underdogs to analyze and break apart the overdog coalition.

Sometimes issue-based movements focus on winning defections from key pillars that uphold the dominant consensus. Most of the public opposed marriage equality, and that view was reinforced by institutions like churches that denounced same-sex relationships, businesses that didn't provide benefits to same-sex couples, the entertainment industry that mocked or ignored LGBTQ+ people, and the military, which excluded them from service. In other cases, though, delegitimization rather than defection is the goal. 350.org did not seek to persuade fossil fuel companies to change their behaviors, or recruit employees of these companies to resign or speak out. Instead, 350.org targeted other institutions like banks, universities, and churches with the goal of revoking the social license of the fossil fuel industry, as Boeve put it.[33]

Strengths and Weaknesses of the Momentum Model

The momentum model is a useful complement to other models, such as base-building and inside-outside campaigns, that typically achieve incremental gains and bring home concrete victories. Momentum-driven campaigns can achieve huge gains with surprisingly small bases of active supporters. Political scientist Erica Chenoweth's analysis of nonviolent movements against authoritarian governments worldwide found that if they engage 3.5 percent or more of a population as active and passionate supporters, they're likely to succeed.[34] The specific percentage may not apply to issue-based campaigns, but the core logic that a passionate minority of active supporters can inspire broad public support and change the political weather makes the Momentum approach powerful. Moreover, this model can generate large-scale action on a national or even global scale with relatively few central staff people in the movement hub.

The campaign to elect Bernie Sanders president in 2016 shows the potential of a momentum-style political campaign. The campaign offered a big idea—a political revolution—and over a million people signed up to volunteer and give money. Sanders's small staff quickly developed a distributed organizing infrastructure that allowed volunteers to phone bank, text, fundraise, and more. When done well, the model can help movements grow exponentially rather than linearly. "If you want to be perfect, your reach will be limited by your budget," write Becky Bond and Zack Exley in their book about the Sanders campaign. "To go big you need to hand over control of key work, education, and management processes to volunteers."[35] Allowing volunteers to bring their best skills to the movement expands capacity far beyond what paid staff can provide. The Sanders campaign had many such volunteers, such as a former call center manager from JPMorgan Chase who helped solve a phone-banking challenge for the campaign, or a technology executive at Xerox who became a volunteer lead data manager.[36] And thousands of volunteers formed groups such as Latinos for Bernie, Nurses for Bernie, or Texans for Bernie; they were able to more effectively canvass in their own communities than a paid staff person likely would have.

The momentum model has weaknesses. There is a risk of local groups using the brand of the national movement but engaging in tactics (such as violence) that undermine the credibility of the effort as a whole. Because campaigns are deliberately decentralized, they can be easily infiltrated by opponents. Also, many momentum campaigns focus on a particular issue, like marriage equality or climate change, which can obscure the multi-issue nature of many of the problems we face today. Sometimes momentum-driven campaigns are "heavy on mobilizing but light on organizing," as Prakash put it, meaning they can be better at bringing people out to flashy demonstrations than the slow work of recruiting and training new potential leaders.[37]

Prakash also argues that in the U.S. context, the "come one, come all" ethos of momentum-driven campaigns may work better with middle-class white activists than with working-class communities of color where a high-touch approach (used by Make the Road New York, Chapter 6.1) is more likely to succeed than a mass email. She points out that the Movement for Black Lives (M4BL) worked in the opposite direction of many momentum campaigns, which move from the national to the local. Building off deep organizing and relationships, Black organizers in many cities, from Ferguson, Missouri, to Minneapolis, Minnesota, amplified local police violence to spark a national movement. The immigrant rights movement has similarly been grounded in local organizing, with deep bases in states around the country that strategize together and move nationally on issues like winning a path to citizenship for undocumented people when openings arise. The mass immigrant rights marches in 2006 and 2007 that brought millions of people to the streets were anchored by local groups. The marches in turn spawned exponential growth in the number and geographic reach of immigrant community organizations around the country. This virtuous circle between local base-building and national mobilization may be crucial to the sustainability of momentum campaigns.

Perhaps the greatest weakness of the momentum model is the flip side of its strength: it depends on momentum. Momentum-driven campaigns, as you would expect, often dissolve when the momentum subsides. The Serbian movement Otpor, for example, could not find a way forward after it succeeded in toppling dictator Slobodan Milosevic. Activists were united by that one large goal, but once it was achieved, differences around vision quickly divided them. 350.org appears to have at least partially avoided this problem by building a strong organization. Also, it has kept moving from one momentum-driven campaign to another—from Keystone to divestment to a broader finance focus, and a campaign called "Keep It in the Ground" to block expansion of new fossil fuel infrastructure. Once an issue becomes mainstream, the organization steps back, allowing others to take up the work, while it seeks out the next fight. The next big campaign for the group—a focus on solutions to climate change, such as renewable energy—represents a major departure, since it involves not just saying "no" but also organizing toward a positive vision. The initiative responds to the perspective of activists in the Global South, who have been focused on projects connecting climate change to poverty and energy needs. Achieving synergy between work grounded in local communities and change at national and global levels is the challenging cutting edge for the development of the momentum model.

What's Next? Combining Deep Roots with Broad Reach

The future of the momentum model may depend on how activists working in the tradition integrate other models of social change, and how organizers working in other traditions incorporate momentum principles into their

> **Box 11.1 Bringing Momentum to Politics: The Sanders Presidential Campaign**
>
> Many of our CUNY students worked on the 2016 and 2020 Bernie Sanders campaigns. Jonah Furman was one of them. Furman was an active volunteer on Labor for Bernie in 2019, and in 2020 he was brought onto the national Bernie campaign staff as national labor organizer. One of his first jobs was to organize union members to support Sanders in the Iowa caucus.
>
> Iowa's official caucus system requires people to show up at their neighborhood caucus site at 7 p.m. on caucus day, but this isn't possible for workers who work far from home or on night shifts. The Democratic Party allows groups of people to petition to hold a satellite caucus at alternative times or locations, and in 2020, several unions had signed up for workplace caucuses. When Furman arrived in Iowa, he and campaign staff called through lists of Sanders supporters, looking for people employed in these workplaces. When that didn't yield results, he decided to employ standard union organizing tactics. Furman and other campaign staff would stand outside workplaces, looking for workers coming off their shift at hospitals, factories, and meatpacking plants.
>
> Wearing his Bernie hat and pin, Furman waited outside the JBS Pork plant gates in Ottumwa, Iowa, as a shift ended at 1 a.m. on a cold January evening in 2020. Ottumwa is a small town in rural Iowa. Refugees and immigrants from over fifty countries have ended up there working for JBS. Wendwosen Biftu, a worker from Ethiopia and member of the United Food and Commercial Workers Union, exited the plant and saw Furman's Bernie hat and approached him excitedly with a big hug. Biftu agreed to come into the campaign office to talk about building support for the caucus. He spoke little English, so he brought his ten-year-old daughter

to help translate. The campaign found a Sanders supporter and organizer in Chicago, Adom Getachew, who could speak with Biftu in Amharic and work on a plan to mobilize support from other Ethiopian workers in the plant.[38]

Furman and Biftu continued to use union organizing tactics to get a list of workers in the plant and devise an outreach strategy. Working with other Sanders field organizers, they would show up at shift changes, conduct house visits, and speak with workers from Albania, Liberia, and more. Furman and Biftu were the passionate supporters galvanized by the Sanders insurgency—they and many others helped activate a broad base of millions to participate in the campaign.

On the day of the caucus, Furman realized that national media were all in Iowa, waiting around for the 7 p.m. caucuses to start. But the JBS workplace caucus was scheduled for noon that day. The campaign made sure to get reporters to Ottumwa, where they covered the first contest of the 2020 Democratic primary. The result was an astounding show of support for Sanders from a multiracial, multilingual group of meatpackers. "No one really knew, was Bernie 2020 legit? Did workers want Bernie?" says Furman. The JBS Pork caucus sent a powerful signal that the Sanders 2020 campaign was for real. News spread quickly, likely motivating thousands of tentative Sanders supporters to show up for the 7 p.m. caucuses. Sanders won the Iowa popular vote.

Across the country, our colleague Samir Sonti worked on the Sanders campaign on the East Coast in 2020. He connected with public housing residents in Durham, North Carolina, who had been displaced due to carbon monoxide poisoning in their units, and with workers and patients fighting a hospital closing in Philadelphia. He found volunteers eager to support the campaign and get involved when given an opportunity.

own work. Momentum is perfectly suited for a social media age, when it is possible to gather large numbers of people who care deeply about an issue quickly. But sustainable change will depend on investing in structures that provide for depth of engagement, leadership development, and the kind of "trench warfare" that lasting social change typically requires. Romanow told us that practitioners developing a 2.0 version of the model are asking how they "take responsibility for teeing up the institutionalization of wins."[39]

And movements and campaigns are mixing momentum with other models of change in innovative ways. M4BL and immigrant rights organizers have built locally based community and worker organizations while still taking advantage of movement moments to achieve greater scale. The Sanders story demonstrates how today's people-driven electoral campaigns are making use of social media and massive volunteer organizing to overcome the power of entrenched political establishments and organized money. The Democratic Socialists of America are using methods developed in the Sanders campaign to organize workers,[40] and labor organizer Chris Brooks argues that a new labor upsurge at iconic employers like Amazon and Starbucks is making use of momentum principles.[41] Deepak works with the Union of Southern Service Workers (USSW), which grew out of the Fight for $15 and a Union movement and is supported by SEIU. USSW is organizing low-wage workers across the South and partnered with Momentum, the training institute, to develop an innovative distributed organizing model and train hundreds of worker leaders in the region.

In a world in which the problems we face—from climate change to rising authoritarianism and economic oligarchy—demand people power at a huge and sometimes global scale, the momentum model provides an essential and adaptable framework for social change.

Table 11.1: Key Components of the Momentum Model

Component	Momentum Model
Forms of Power	Solidarity; Disruptive; Ideological
Theory of Change	Polarizing campaigns that attract thousands of people inspired by a compelling vision → challenge institutions that uphold a social consensus → change the common sense and make big policy victories possible
Examples of Practitioners and Theorists	Sunrise Movement, Movement for Black Lives, Gandhi, Momentum.org, Mark and Paul Engler
Protagonists and Structure	A central movement hub that coordinates a broad network of activists engaged in distributed organizing with a shared goal
Goals and Methods	Make a big, overarching policy change that is not winnable in the short term possible in the future
	Harness or create a "whirlwind" of mass action through polarization; create a platform for distributed action to weaken the "pillars" holding up the current social consensus
Tactical Repertoire	Polarizing actions against targets to create energy; cultural DNA and toolkits established by a central hub with wide latitude for local experimentation and creativity; campaigns may target particular "pillars" that uphold the social consensus
What Does Winning Mean?	Often after many years of losses, new social consensus is achieved and gets ratified in public policy through the courts or legislation, or there is significant change in political leadership
Time Horizon + When the Model Is Most Effective	When a fundamental system change is needed that is not possible now
	Unfolds over years when an issue needs to be moved from minority to majority support by deliberate campaigns that engage many passionate volunteers

Component	Momentum Model
How It Works with Other Models/ Movement Ecosystem	Works well with narrative shift
	Strengthened by base-building and collective care
	A momentum campaign can be an electoral campaign
	Can lay the groundwork for inside-outside campaigns, though ambitious goals of momentum-driven campaigns may conflict with more incremental goals of inside-outside campaigns
Strengths	A deliberate movement-building strategy to make the impossible possible, with a strong track record of success
	Ability to recruit large numbers of people quickly
Weaknesses	Tends to work best for single issues; may not work for all constituencies
	Momentum campaigns can dissolve when the goal is achieved
	The breadth of participation momentum enables needs to be balanced with depth so that local ideas, agendas, and leaders can inform movement strategy

Tools

Tool 19 Resources: Narrative Shift
Tool 24 Momentum
Tool 32 Successful Failures

12

Collective Care

Personal Pain to Communal Strength: The Gay Men's Health Crisis Responds to AIDS

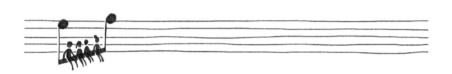

What would you do if your friends were becoming sick with a deadly disease for which there was no vaccine, treatment, or cure? What if the spread of the disease was met with indifference or hostility by the government, media, and even by many family members of the infected? How would you show up?

In 1981, eighty people gathered in an apartment in Greenwich Village in New York City to figure out how to respond to the early stages of the AIDS crisis. Six of them went on to found the Gay Men's Health Crisis (GMHC) to educate the community about what was known about HIV/AIDS, advocate for research on the cause of and cure for AIDS, and to support people who were sick and dying of the disease. GMHC was based in New York City, but its model was quickly replicated around the United States and the world.

Even living through the COVID-19 pandemic, it's difficult to comprehend the extent to which AIDS devastated affected communities. By 1995, one gay man in nine between the ages of twenty-five and forty-four in the

United States had been diagnosed with AIDS, and nearly 7 percent had died. By comparison, COVID-19 has killed 0.3 percent of the U.S. population.[1]

David Hansell was thirty-one years old when he began volunteering at GMHC in 1984. He helped young men write their wills and eventually led the organization's policy and legal work. Hansell described being gay and living in New York City before HIV testing as "a perilous existence. You just felt like you were under threat—your body was a danger to you because you never knew if you were going to wake up one morning and have Kaposi's sarcoma spots [a rare cancer common in people with AIDS] or be sick."[2] Talking to Hansell, Deepak felt echoes in his own body of the fear he knew in the years after the HIV test was developed. Like many other gay men, he would get tested, sometimes at GMHC's offices, and then wait two agonizing weeks to receive the results. Deepak worked through the anxiety by joining a peer sexual education program in college that used information about HIV created by GMHC.

The disease wasn't the only danger. Politicians proposed quarantining or tattooing people who carried HIV, the virus that causes AIDS. President Ronald Reagan didn't even mention the word *AIDS* until four years after the first cases appeared. Senator Jesse Helms proposed a "no promo homo" amendment to prohibit the use of federal funds to "promote or encourage, directly or indirectly, homosexual sexual activities."[3] The amendment passed by 94–2 in the Senate and became law. Employers and landlords fired and evicted people with AIDS with impunity. Media and church leaders blamed gay men for the disease. Right-wing evangelical leader Rev. Jerry Falwell said, "AIDS is not just God's punishment for homosexuals; it is God's punishment for the society that tolerates homosexuals."[4]

The first AIDS cases were reported in 1981 in New York City, but the legendary activist group AIDS Coalition to Unleash Power (ACT UP) did not emerge until 1987. Usually the story told about this time is that there wasn't much activism around AIDS until ACT UP burst onto the scene. Famous for its militant and creative direct actions, ACT UP shut down the Food and Drug Administration (FDA), inflated a giant nylon replica of a condom over Helms's house in a suburb of Washington, DC, and disrupted a mass at St. Patrick's Cathedral in New York City to protest the Catholic Church's opposition to teaching safer sex in schools and condom distribution. Sociologist Deborah Gould argues that the gap from the first AIDS cases to ACT UP's founding can be explained by a pervasive sense of internalized shame in the community—the feeling among gay men that they had brought the disease on themselves because of their sexual practices. Gould argues that many harbored a naïve hope that mainstream society would come to the gay community's rescue.[5]

There's truth in Gould's compelling analysis. But there's another way to understand the arc of AIDS activism, less as a sudden eruption and more as an evolution. GMHC's grassroots community response to the AIDS pandemic had a huge impact on the LGBTQ+ people's sense of themselves and broader public consciousness. GMHC created simple on-ramps for thousands of queer people and their friends and family who were affected to get involved. Volunteering at this scale laid the groundwork for more militant AIDS activism, and for progress on gay equality decades later. The caring work of tens of thousands of volunteers shifted queer people's sense of agency and identity and roused emotions of love, anger, and pride in ways that helped make confrontational strategies possible. By rejecting despair and stepping up to help others, volunteers expanded their sense of what they could accomplish. And they became radicalized by the systemic discrimination and malign neglect the community faced in its time of greatest need. Seen this way, the vibrant AIDS activism of the late 1980s and early 1990s wasn't only a rupture from what came before, but also the result of a process of a change in consciousness, through which LGBTQ+ people remade their identities.[6]

Deepak saw the fruits of this rapid personal and political transformation when he was part of a peer sexual education group in 1988. The group invited a guest speaker, a wealthy white gay man, who spoke about what it was like to live with HIV. The speaker had previously worked on Wall Street. He recounted how being HIV positive and volunteering to help people with AIDS had changed his life—pushing him out of the closet and radicalizing him, which led to his leaving his job to work for Jesse Jackson's presidential campaign. Previously, he had either not voted or voted for Republicans, including for Reagan in 1984. He gave Deepak and the other training attendees blunt advice about safer sex and politics and explained that the drug companies and politicians wouldn't come to the rescue. Queer communities had to save themselves in coalition with other oppressed groups.

GMHC exemplifies the model of social change we call collective care: efforts by an oppressed group to meet its own needs for survival and safety, a vastly underappreciated but essential element in social change movements. When the approach has a consciously political dimension, it works like this:

This contrasts with charity and most philanthropy, which are privatized approaches to care that give little or no thought to social change.

Collective care is deeply undervalued and often rendered invisible in accounts of movements that feature more dramatic movement work. There are many books and documentaries about ACT UP, for example, but hardly any about GMHC.

Building Relationships, Taking Risks: GMHC's Model of Collective Care

GMHC had three core programs: education about HIV and its prevention; supportive care by volunteers for people who were sick; and policy advocacy. The number of volunteers dwarfed the number of staff for many years, and volunteers led and created an astonishing range of programs, from bereavement support groups to peer-to-peer treatment and education work to legal services, most of which were built from the ground up. At its peak, GMHC's "buddy program" placed over ten thousand volunteers a year in the homes of total strangers. Buddies would do whatever needed to be done, from picking up groceries and prescriptions to visiting people at the hospital to providing emotional support.[7]

Many gay men had left their hometowns to find greater freedom in New York City, so the LGBTQ+ community functioned as their support system and family. And because buddies were mostly also gay and at risk, there was little psychological separation between the people providing and receiving help. David Barr, who led treatment and advocacy work at GMHC, talks about how being a volunteer provided "a sort of safe place and a home, and a chance to do something that allowed you to feel like you could respond to the terror." Being a buddy "was not merely, 'I'm here to help this person, I'm doing this charitable service'; it was 'I'm here to help myself, get through this time, by finding a place where I can feel useful and safe.'"[8]

Tim Sweeney, the executive director of GMHC from 1989 to 1993, talks about the buddy program as a radicalizing force in the community, enabling people to "build trusting relationships and take big risks." The experience forced volunteers to confront their own mortality, which led to a "great unmasking . . . [GMHC's volunteers] couldn't avoid very deep self-examination" about their sex lives, who they were "out" to, and how they wanted to live their lives in the face of the threat of death at a young age. Being a buddy required building trust to do "one of the most profound acts in a human's life: caring for someone as they are dying." Volunteers saw injustice up close—like having to find alternatives when a dentist refused to treat the person for whom they were caring. Through being a buddy, volunteers found a way to live their values, challenge norms, and learn by operating out of their comfort zone. And, as Sweeney put it, it was a way to stay "spiritually and mentally healthy."[9]

GMHC prototyped a distributed organizing model by encouraging community members to develop new programs. For example, volunteers proposed and ran an ombudsman program that took complaints from people with AIDS about discrimination by hospitals, employers, or landlords. The organization unleashed creativity among its volunteers and staff and helped develop a generation of talent, serving as a kind of university for advocates who often graduated to key positions in the movement, public health, or government. Sweeney said that when volunteers would ask "what can I do?"

GMHC would tell them "take it home" and organize within the fields in which they worked: business, dance, arts, music, or faith. Broadway Cares, one of the most effective and enduring fundraising appeals, came out of that mobilization.[10]

Early on, the staff of GMHC discovered Joan Tisch, the wife of business leader and co-owner of the New York Giants Robert Tisch, stuffing envelopes in the volunteer office. They enlisted her to use her access and connections to advance the cause. A group of business executives would go to Washington, DC, every year and meet with senators about their economic agenda and include AIDS issues in their discussions. Shocked senators would call Sweeney and say, "Do you know who was in my office? How did you get them to make this a priority?" A group of mothers of people with AIDS had self-organized and came to GMHC for support. Mothers Against AIDS became a ferocious advocacy group that "terrorized" Republican elected officials.[11] GMHC acted as a hub and support for creative and self-organized work that tapped and stretched people's capacities.

GMHC, ACT UP, and Marriage Equality: Collective Care and Other Models of Social Change

GMHC grounded its policy advocacy "in the experience of the people that we were serving," David Hansell told us. "So that if I was sitting in the room with elected officials or whatever, I could tell them that we have one thousand clients who are experiencing this issue who are counting on them to do something."[12] The decision to advocate for AIDS to be classified as a disability, which conferred health and other benefits, came directly out of the experience of working with people who had lost their jobs and their health care. GMHC helped found and lead "so many damned coalitions," as Sweeney put it. With other service organizations, GMHC helped found the AIDS Action Council, the Washington, DC, group that lobbied on AIDS policy. GMHC and AIDS Action played a key role in the enactment of the Ryan White CARE Act, which established an unprecedented role for directly affected communities in deciding how funds should be spent and won inclusion of people with AIDS (PWAs) in the Americans with Disabilities Act.[13]

But those landmark bills weren't passed until 1990. The lack of response from the federal government in the face of escalating deaths, and the infamous 1986 *Bowers v. Hardwick* case, in which the Supreme Court upheld criminal laws against "sodomy," spawned fury in the community.[14] In this climate of rising anger, 250 people gathered at the Gay and Lesbian Community Center in Manhattan on March 10, 1987. Larry Kramer made a speech calling for a militant, direct action response to the crisis. Kramer had co-founded GMHC in 1981 but left after fighting with others about the group's goals. He attacked the organization for not being aggressive enough.

Sweeney spoke at the meeting and made an impassioned and effective call for an end to in-fighting in the community and unity between service and political groups in the movement. He offered GMHC's institutional support. Ironically, when the attendees agreed it was time for more aggressive direct action, Kramer turned to Sweeney to help organize the next meeting, which would end up being the founding meeting of ACT UP. Sweeney and a longtime lesbian organizer, Vivian Shapiro, co-facilitated the first ACT UP meetings for months, and GMHC continued to have a close relationship with ACT UP—many of its staff people were ACT UP leaders. When ACT UP leaders got sick, GMHC was usually the place they turned for support. ACT UP meeting minutes show that GMHC quietly contributed money too.[15] Sweeney believed that being a social movement, not just a service, prevention, and advocacy organization, was crucial to the identity of GMHC. If you "removed yourself from the social movement, you would cut off the roots of the plant, you'd be dead," he told us.[16]

The relationship was not without tension, though it was mostly creative rather than destructive. Although Sweeney had to step back from his public role facilitating ACT UP meetings (since as head of GMHC he often had to negotiate with the people ACT UP targeted), he valued "direct, confrontational advocacy" as "critical and necessary." And he thought that "at some point, there is a pivot when the heat has to turn to light," when the pressure creates an opportunity to negotiate solutions with political and corporate leaders. A vivid example was when Sweeney negotiated with the community's arch-enemy, Catholic cardinal John J. O'Connor, who was serving on the National Commission on AIDS, to win his support for legislation prohibiting discrimination against people with HIV, while at the same time, ACT UP was organizing provocative demonstrations against the church for its opposition to the HIV education needed to save lives.[17]

The complementary relationship between GMHC and ACT UP was nurtured by people who bridged different styles of movement work, such as Barr, who was both on the staff of GMHC and an ACT UP leader. Both Sweeney and Barr brought extensive prior movement experience to their work on AIDS. Sweeney learned community and political organizing in his home state of Montana and was previously the executive director at Lambda Legal Defense and Education Fund when it won the first-ever HIV discrimination case. Barr was a radical lawyer and a child of parents who were active in social movements. Barr told us that

> GMHC and ACT UP were able to work together, not cut each other's throats . . . [because] there were strategists on both sides who appreciated the value of the other and wanted to stay aligned. There's no question that without the public and outside pressure the government would never have put resources in to address the epidemic. But it's also true, I think, that once those doors were open, the dialogue was possible. There was deliberate and conscious coordination—ACT UP will do the action on the outside, and then GMHC would negotiate for what exactly we want and really work on the mechanics of the government's response. It evolved fairly consciously into a pretty effective inside and outside strategy that made a big difference.[18]

Even at its peak, ACT UP organized a small number of deeply committed activists who were willing to engage in highly confrontational actions, which often led to arrests. ACT UP mobilized the intensity, fervor, and appetite for risk-taking of a militant core in the community to take on specific targets like the FDA. In contrast, GMHC reached a broader audience through its volunteer programs and its community-based fundraising. For example, the annual AIDS walk mobilized tens of thousands of people in public demonstrations of mass support for action on AIDS. GMHC gave people who cared many ways to be involved: a "ladder of engagement" that meant volunteers could begin by stuffing envelopes, staffing the hotline, which received thousands of calls a year, or participating in an AIDS walk, and then increase their commitment by becoming a buddy and getting involved in advocacy. Both ends of this spectrum, a radical edge and a broad front that could mobilize whole sectors of society, were necessary for the movement to succeed.

GMHC's wide reach had important mobilizing effects. The largest demonstration demanding a more aggressive and effective government response to AIDS was led not by ACT UP, but by a coalition organized by GMHC around the 1992 Democratic National Convention in New York City. Barr proposed the mobilization to Sweeney as a conscious strategy to get service providers, volunteers, and clients out in the streets to demand political action, something that had never been done before. The coalition sent a letter to each of the presidential candidates requesting a meeting. The only one who met with the coalition was Bill Clinton, who agreed to their demand to give a speech on AIDS. Clinton asked the activists to help him write it. Barr recalls handing Clinton a GMHC condom pack to illustrate the prevention work the group was doing. This was shortly after Clinton was embroiled in an extramarital affairs controversy that threatened his candidacy. Clinton blanched and said, "Oh, imagine if the press saw I had these." Barr retorted, "Well imagine if the press thought you didn't have them."[19]

Jeffrey Levi, a longtime movement leader and director of government affairs at AIDS Action Council in the early 1990s, told us that through the path of mutual aid, the LGBTQ+ movement changed its posture toward government. The movement had first sought to keep government out of queer people's lives, then demanded its intervention to address the AIDS crisis, and ultimately won the state's affirmation of gay relationships through marriage.[20]

Barr argues that activists' work during the AIDS crisis paved the way for future victories. "There would be no gay marriage without the AIDS response. We created infrastructure out of the AIDS crisis all over the world which gave us a sense of 'look what we can do!'"[21] Sweeney says that he and other leaders asked themselves the following question at the beginning of the crisis: "If we're going to go through all this rage and pain and death and suffering, what is going to come out of it at the other end?" They concluded that the end goal was to "dismantle homophobia" and they developed an "extremely conscious" strategy to do so. One major campaign slogan reflecting the strategy was "Cure Hate. Stop AIDS. Homophobia Kills." The seismic, albeit incomplete, shift in culture and policy regarding LGBTQ+ people over the last two decades has its roots in the way the community responded to an apocalyptic tragedy. Sweeney put it this way:

> What is the gift given in a crisis? America at this point was not that far from homosexuality being . . . a mental illness, and we were still criminalized in God knows how many states in the country, so it was pretty hard. America viewed gay men as the most selfish, hedonistic people. The *New York Times* called us "avowed homosexuals." . . . So what we did is we took this crisis and changed how society looked at gay men. People saw that we were doing caretaking of our fellow community members, an unacknowledged role that is normally done by women . . . we just offered it to the world and asked "now what do you think of us? What does it tell you about our humanity, our values, our patience, our connection to God, our love?" . . . We used [the word *love*] because it made it go from just a sexuality connotation to something much deeper and much more shared. And I think that is what really changed people . . . a number of women watched this and were like, well, "I've done it. I've done it for my dad, you know, it's expected of me and my family." The art of leadership is to say "what is the ability to change the framework here?" So, I feel like part of what happened is we owned our own ability to change our destiny.[22]

Despite the tragedy of over 700,000 deaths in the United States (thus far—the AIDS crisis continues), the accomplishments of the AIDS movement and GMHC were astonishing.[23] As Sweeney put it, "We bent the arc of this pandemic. We changed it. We didn't bring an end to it, unfortunately, which is what our goal was, but we definitely saved millions of people."[24] For the first time in U.S. history, the people most affected by a disease led the public health response to it. In so doing, they built organizational infrastructure, narrative, political power, and alliances that paved the way for subsequent changes in policy and culture on LGBTQ+ equality.

Collective Care as Strategy

We were moved to study collective care by a comment from one of our students, Walter Barrientos. Deepak got to know Barrientos in the early 2000s when he was an undocumented immigrant youth activist who was detained by immigration enforcement on his way to a Community Change training. Barrientos is now a leader in the immigrant rights movement and observed in class that our list of (then) six strategy models didn't offer a way to understand the long-term resistance strategies of groups like Indigenous people in Guatemala, who built collective care networks to resist Spanish imperialism and then a series of U.S.-backed authoritarian regimes.

When we share our framework that includes collective care as a distinct strategy model, most of our students and colleagues are excited by it. But some have been skeptical, arguing that collective care is a support to other strategies rather than a model of its own, or questioning whether mutual aid projects amount to transformational change. We are grateful to the skeptics for helping us assess when care is and isn't strategic, how it connects to other models, and under what conditions it should be a more prominent note in strategy (Table 12.1).

We agree that without a consciously political dimension, collective care isn't strategic, because it can't get to scale or address the roots of a problem in structures of oppression. In fact, some activists practice mutual aid or launch cooperatives as a strategy to escape rather than transform systems of oppression. Our view is that if collective care is not embedded in a larger vision for social transformation, it will inevitably be marginalized or captured by the dominant system—as in the case of cooperative living arrangements run by privately owned companies for profit.

Collective care is a powerful platform that can and does support any of the other models of change from below. During the height of the AIDS crisis, GMHC was grounded in collective care, while also skillfully using other strategies, including narrative shift, inside-outside campaigns, and momentum, to leverage sectors of society into action. GMHC also partnered effectively with ACT UP, a disruptive movement.

Care is embedded in the cultures and practices of healthy organizations. It strengthens solidarity by building trust and relationships that can be harnessed for political action, as in the case of Make the Road New York (Chapter 6.1). In our experience, organizations that lack care dimensions are brittle and vulnerable to internal schisms and attacks from opponents. When movements create systems to take care of one another, such as mutual aid, healing justice approaches to deal with past trauma, and community support, they increase the capacity of ordinary people to engage in struggle and of organizers to stay in the movement for the long term. As much as social reproductive labor holds up the economy, collective care is an important but often unacknowledged glue in movement infrastructure. Even ACT UP, known for its militant actions, incorporated elements of care. The ACT UP meetings Deepak attended in Boston began with a check-in question: Who needed help, because of a potential eviction or health crisis, and what were we going to do about it?

Mutual aid organizer Dean Spade notes that people without support are less likely to take risks—the kind of risks needed to build movements for transformative change.[25] Organizing a union in your workplace or taking a public stand on a controversial issue is easier when the community has your back. The bail funds organized at scale by the Movement for Black Lives (M4BL) exemplify this approach.

We also believe that in extremely difficult conjunctures like the AIDS crisis—when there are no short-term political openings and the ruling historic bloc and its ideology seem impregnable—collective care is appropriately a more dominant note in strategy. In her book *Hope in the Dark: Untold Histories, Wild Possibilities*, author and activist Rebecca Solnit talks about how catastrophes can lead to revolutions generations later.[26] Collective care strategies, like disruptive movements, often emerge as a response to crises and tragedies, particularly when governments are failing to meet the moment. When it feels like the world is ending, as it did for queer people in the darkest days of the AIDS crisis, sometimes the only thing you can do is turn toward each other and care for one other. In such circumstances, collective care can be a form of both survival and strategy.

If care infrastructure is built with a political goal in mind, it can seed transformational change. Sweeney told us how he and colleagues were determined to respond to the AIDS crisis in a way that shifted the political horizon, by changing how dominant society understood queer people and how queer people understood themselves. Scholar Erica Chenoweth makes a similar point in a different context, arguing that movements against authoritarian regimes should not over-rely on protests, that a crucial underappreciated ingredient in their success is the creation of "parallel institutions" like mutual-aid groups that "meet community needs that the existing system does not," and "build legitimacy and authority—before they have fully 'won.'"[27]

From Survival to Social Change: Common Elements of the Strategic Collective Care Model

Collective care can be strategic in several ways. It can:

> *Turn emotion into power.* Simple but meaningful actions of collectively alleviating suffering can reverberate over generations by changing consciousness and identity on a mass scale. These strategies mobilize powerful emotions and move people from despair to agency. Both GMHC and ACT UP succeeded in part because of how they turned fear, grief, anger, and love into fuel for action. Barr described to us the profound sense of camaraderie he felt during the AIDS crisis:
>
>> We were all so vulnerable and scared. And then we found this place, GMHC was that place, ACT UP was that place, where you could be together, support one another, work together, and have fun together. And that helped deal with the sense of isolation and fear. You know, it just made us stronger to be together. . . .

I found a home and I found a real sense of community for the first time. So, you know, in addition to the horror, there was all of this joy—*joy* is a really weird word [to use in these circumstances], but not inappropriate. Because I felt sort of protected for the first time.[28]

Create pathways for new participation. Collective care can also provide a wide on-ramp to recruit people to a movement who may not think of themselves as political or be ready for militant direct action, but who are willing to support a bail fund, cook food, or help in other ways. As everyday people take greater responsibility, their leadership and self-confidence blossoms. New recruits can also give the movement a foothold in the institutions and places in which the volunteers are rooted, and help build a wider base of support for a movement's demands.

Increase capacity for political work. Mutual aid directly strengthens people's capacity not only to survive, but also to engage in political struggle. For example, many volunteer ACT UP activists had jobs working at GMHC or received critical help from GMHC when they were sick.

Prepare for movement upsurge. Collective care strengthens the foundation for larger movement upsurges. By fostering networks and relationships in the slow periods, organizers are better prepared for the inevitable tensions and challenges that arise during periods of rapid growth. Care work helps develop skills necessary for organizing and working with others: how to have healthy disagreement and debate, how to develop leaders, and how to work collectively and democratically. Ella Baker grew up in a family with a strong commitment to mutual aid; her grandparents used the land they bought during Reconstruction to house and feed anyone needing help. This shaped Baker's approach to her own organizing work, motivating her to develop a community of leaders and build democratic spaces.[29]

Help organizers stick around for the long haul. Collective care may make organizing more sustainable. Union organizer and author Daisy Pitkin says that the standard model of organizing rests on anger.[30] But a constant war in which activists are angry all the time isn't sustainable. Kyandra Knight, one of our students and an experienced union organizer in the South, says, "Agitation and anger because of injustices are great catalysts for action, but love for ... our communities, our better world, enables us to center our vision for the future and has been a valuable framework for keeping on."[31]

Build ideological power. Collective care can build ideological power by prefiguring a different kind of society and more democratic relationships and organizations. The mutual aid networks that flourished in the wake of disasters like Hurricane Katrina or the COVID-19 pandemic demonstrate the degree to which ordinary people look to help one another in such moments, and how we share a strong tendency toward cooperation and collectivism.[32] MoveOn.org's "Hurricane Housing" effort, in the wake of Hurricane Katrina, was one experiment in mutual aid at significant scale. One hundred thousand people were housed in other MoveOn.org members' homes in the months after the disaster.[33] As scholar Robin D.G. Kelley writes, "collective social movements are incubators of new knowledge."[34] This new knowledge can be generated by any of the organizing work we've discussed in this book, but building systems of collective care and mutual aid can directly and strategically foster what Kelley calls "freedom dreams." The vision of queer liberation forged in the AIDS crisis by people doing care work on the front lines shows how freedom dreams can emerge from nightmares.

Lineages of Collective Care

The collective care model doesn't have one clear or consistent approach. We see strands of it in several different organizing lineages, including parts of the Black radical tradition, mutual aid, feminism, disability justice, labor, environmental, immigrant rights, and Indigenous traditions. Currently, collective care is essential to M4BL, the modern abolition movement, and the solidarity and social economy movement.

Political scientist Deva Woodly argues that M4BL has generated a new model of organizing in which "the politics of care" is a key feature. She explains, "The politics of care practiced in M4BL is characterized by an acknowledgment of trauma and a commitment to healing, an understanding of interdependence, unapologetic Blackness, a defense of Black joy, an insistence on accountability, and an abolitionist perspective favoring restorative justice practices that deal with harm by focusing on accountability and reparation rather than punishment."[35] In this model, care is not just an ethical or moral act but a political one because it asserts that effective democracy is contingent upon first addressing the systems of oppression and working to heal the damage they've caused.

> **Healing justice** is a framework and political strategy to address the impact of systemic violence and oppression and, in particular, widespread generational harm. This framework was generated by Cara Page and the Kindred Southern Healing Collective.[36] It views healing as a collective process, beyond the work any individual could do on their own. For example, decades of racial oppression and police violence impact Black people in deep and systemic ways. Healing justice helps people process trauma and works to alleviate root causes. What this looks like in practice varies, from support groups to social workers at marches, "to provid[ing] de-escalation support for any traumatic incidents or violence with cops or counter-demonstrators."[37]
>
> **Transformative justice** (TJ) is a related approach and offers a way for communities and allies to deal with violence or harm without being reliant on punishment or the carceral state, while working to transform the conditions that make the harm more likely in the first place.[38] We discuss this in Chapter 14, as it relates to processing conflict within organizations and movements. But we note the importance of TJ here because it provides a way for marginalized communities to address destructive behaviors that are caused by oppression under racial capitalism. TJ allows community members to process conflict and remain active in the community, and therefore potentially part of movements. TJ practitioners include Mariame Kaba and Mia Mingus.

Strengths and Weaknesses in the Collective Care Model

We've noted that many forms of collective care are worthy humanitarian responses to suffering, but are not strategic in that they don't build toward transformational change. And when organizers do engage in collective care as a strategy, they encounter dilemmas, as all strategists do with any model. Sometimes groups that emphasize care can suffer from cultural insularity—focusing on how the relatively small number of people who are part of the group are doing and feeling so much so that they lose sight of the wider constituency who may face more dire circumstances. And it is challenging to develop a culture that incorporates both care and organizing practices that emphasize agitation, accountability, and conflict. Because mutual aid is sometimes founded by people in intimate social networks, it can be exclusive. For example, as the demographic profile of the AIDS epidemic changed and AIDS became overwhelmingly a disease of people of color—many of whom did not identify as queer—GMHC sometimes struggled to adapt.[39]

Collective care models also require enormous amounts of time and resources from volunteers, which can be hard to sustain. People engaged in care work face risks of burnout and must contend with the trauma of bearing witness to suffering and sometimes even death.

For all its challenges, we've been inspired by our investigation of collective care. GMHC shows many of the strengths of the model and exemplifies what adrienne maree brown calls emergent strategy—an adaptive response to conditions that unlocks future possibilities, some of which even the protagonists can't foresee. GMHC's collective care work models many of the strategy fundamentals seen in Chapter 3, including the importance of alliances and empathy, and the role of both improvisation and planning in social change. With its emphasis on supporting bottom-up initiatives, collective care relies on the wisdom of groups, not the genius of individual grand strategists. And GMHC was a strategic response to a devastatingly difficult conjuncture, proving that long-term vision can be forged in catastrophe.

We have come to the view that collective care has always been essential to the success and durability of social movements but has been underemphasized in both scholarly and popular accounts, which privilege the more dramatic and militant aspects of movement work. Care work may be even more important today, as compounding crises foster a sense of despair and impotence among people who care deeply, but aren't sure how to get involved or what will have an impact. Stopping climate change, passing major federal legislation, or taking on huge corporations can feel too distant or difficult to animate mass participation. Paradoxically, by giving people confidence in their ability to make change at a more intimate and human level, collective care is a path to unlock the power needed to challenge those seemingly impregnable systems.

Table 12.1: Key Components of the Collective Care Model

Component	Collective Care Model
Forms of Power	Solidarity; Ideological
Theory of Change	Mutual aid/support, healing, meeting urgent needs → allows more people to participate in organizations/movements, take greater risks + changes people's identity and sense of agency + prefigures alternatives → new openings and horizons for social change
Examples of Practitioners and Theorists	Harriet Tubman, Ella Baker, cooperative movement, mutual aid Cara Page, Kindred Southern Justice Healing Collective, Mia Mingus, Dean Spade, Deva Woodly
Protagonists and Structure	Organizations, volunteer networks, and movements that prioritize the physical, economic, and emotional well-being of people affected by injustice and trauma, connected to a larger vision for transformative change
Goals and Methods	Meet immediate needs for survival and well-being; build a network of mutual aid, tapping creativity Participants' sense of agency and identity shifts over time; can be a path to movement recruitment; political and policy solutions emerge organically
Tactical Repertoire	Mutual aid to meet immediate needs; cooperative activity; healing justice to address trauma May support any of the other strategy models (for example, bail funds or strike funds) or function as a dominant note that achieves change by prefiguring alternatives and shifting identities

Component	Collective Care Model
What Does Winning Mean?	The physical and mental health, or economic needs, of the constituency in question are valued, respected, and met
	Creates new possibilities for political or policy change
Time Horizon + When the Model Is Most Effective	When the state is unresponsive to crises facing marginalized groups, when political responses are not effective, or when people are feeling despair about the possibility of change and need to see impact at a smaller, human scale
	When organizations experience internal crises
How It Works with Other Models/ Movement Ecosystem	Fundamental to lasting base-building
	Strike funds and bail funds support disruptive movements
	Can add depth, richness, and wider on-ramps for participation to all other models, though undervalued as a strategy
Strengths	Creates wide on-ramps for large numbers of people to take action, including those who may not be ready to take political action
Weaknesses	Volunteers can experience exhaustion and trauma
	Can be a stopgap that lets policymakers/overdogs off the hook
	If disconnected from a strategy to challenge unjust structures, will have limited impact

Tools

Tool 2 Prompt: Envisioning a Future World
Tool 10 Prompt: Are All Strategies Strategic?
Tool 12 Collective Care
Tool 27 Prompt: Balancing Purpose and Belonging

13

Power from Below: Harmonizing Strategy Models in the Movement for Abolition

When the sun come back,
When the firs' quail call,
Then the time is come
Foller the drinkin' gou'd.

—Lyrics from "Follow the Drinking Gourd"[1]

Harriet Tubman—abolitionist, activist, and formerly enslaved person—used song to communicate with enslaved people close by. Tubman explained, "Slaves must not be seen talking together, and so it came about that their communication was often made by singing, and the words of their familiar hymns, telling of the heavenly journey, and the land of Canaan, while they did not attract the attention of the masters, conveyed to their brethren and sisters in bondage something more than met the ear."[2]

The songs held code, which helped enslaved people share information with one another, including how to escape. One such song was "Follow the Drinking Gourd." The lyrics instruct people to wait until spring (quail season), when the days are longer ("when the sun come back"), to begin their escape. The drinking gourd was the Big Dipper, which points to the north star. The rest of the song points to landmarks to look for. Historians estimate that up to 150,000 people escaped slavery through the Underground Railroad.[3]

The four-hundred-year fight to abolish slavery was filled with advances and retreats, and came in waves.[4] It was fought around the world, on plantations, slave ships, and battlefields, in courtrooms and legislative chambers. In this chapter, we do not provide a comprehensive history of the abolitionist movement. Instead, we selected several elements that highlight how underdog power and strategy played out. Each strategy was relevant in the nineteenth-century abolitionist movement, although not necessarily at the same time. Some strategies worked better under certain conditions, or in new conjunctures. Some forms of power were used to build others.

Solidarity Power, Collective Care, and Base-Building

Enslaved people began building solidarity power and engaging in collective care the moment they were taken from their homes, forming alternative kinship structures on slave ships.[5] People from different ethnicities and tribes were forced to live together, so they had to learn to communicate in new shared languages, thereby developing their capacities for collective resistance. The ability to forge these ties varied by geography. For instance, the very precariousness of life in the rice fields of South Carolina and Georgia, often granted enslaved people some autonomy. Enslavers didn't want to catch malaria or be exposed to the other dangers of rice fields, so enslaved workers had a degree of relative independence and were able to maintain their original languages, religions, and cultural practices in a way that wasn't possible in cotton-producing regions.[6]

And when the Civil War ended, people had to rely heavily on collective care networks to find their lost family members, transition to new housing and work, and build new lives. People gathered by the thousands in what were essentially refugee camps. They formed scores of associations. These local organizing hubs were also key in the political advances made during Reconstruction.[7]

Solidarity power was also used to do base-building work among formerly enslaved people, free Black people, Quakers, and other allies. Numerous organizations were founded in different countries in the late 1700s and early 1800s, such as the Society for the Abolition of the Slave Trade, formed in London in 1787, and the Anti-Man-Hunting League, a secret society formed in 1854 by about five hundred Black and white men in Boston to prevent Black people from being kidnapped and enslaved.

Abolitionists in Britain organized to bring sailors and industrial workers into the fight. During the Civil War, British workers showed up in mass meetings of thousands of people in support of enslaved people, with whom they felt solidarity despite not knowing them. Around 15 percent of Britain's population at the time petitioned Parliament to end the slave trade.[8]

Economic Power and Disruption

Enslaved workers were able to disrupt plantations from producing, through coordinated resistance and revolts. This occurred over decades, wherever slavery was in effect.

We mentioned the general strike in Chapter 7, when approximately half a million people left plantations during the Civil War. But the resistance had gone on for decades prior. The Underground Railroad is an example of disruption rooted in solidarity power. Enslaved and formerly enslaved people helped one another escape and worked closely with white abolitionist allies—an early example of a multiracial alliance. Local communities built communication and support networks that helped enslaved people escape, or protected them once they arrived in a free state.

Hundreds of thousands of people escaped, and took their labor with them. The practice had a psychological impact on plantation owners, larger than any individual act. Overdogs often use tactics to disorient and demoralize the opponent (Chapter 16), but in this case, underdogs used the approach brilliantly. Some Underground Railroad activity was anything but "underground," as abolitionists in the North publicly declared their willingness to break laws and assist escapees, stoking the paranoia of the plantation owners.[9] Disruptive power built political power, as the Underground Railroad also undermined the legitimacy of chattel slavery and forced northern politicians to take sides in legislative battles over federal and state fugitive slave laws. This shows how disruptive power can help movements shift the narrative, building ideological power.

Another attempt to deploy economic disruption was the consumer boycott. Elizabeth Heyrick was born into a wealthy British family in 1769. In adulthood, she converted to Quakerism and became involved in the movement to end slavery. Although the British Parliament ended the slave trade in 1807, it did not end the system itself in the British colonies. Frustrated with the slow political work, Heyrick wrote a pamphlet in 1824 urging consumers to boycott goods made with enslaved labor, in particular sugar from the West Indies. With other women, she organized in her hometown of Leicester, and within a year almost a quarter of the town had joined. The boycott spread throughout the country; estimates suggest over 300,000 people boycotted sugar at the height of the movement.[10] And the boycott allowed an avenue for white women, who lacked formal political rights, to fight for abolition.

We can see the strong link between political power and economic power in the ways politicians used trade policy and tariffs to encourage or discourage the slave trade. And during the Civil War, Abraham Lincoln called on British mills to stop importing Southern cotton. Mill workers in Manchester gave their political support to the Union by voting to support the embargo even though it was against their immediate economic interest. They were willing to endure economic hardship in the short term in order to win a long-term vision.[11]

Enslaved people supported the Union cause directly as well. When permitted, in 1862, almost 200,000 formerly enslaved people joined the Union's army, bolstering its military power. This is an example of bottom-up and top-down forces coming together to advance a struggle: enslaved people left the plantations, crippling the Southern economy and the war effort—the Union victory is inconceivable without that. But Union forces also helped precipitate that flight.

Ideological Power and Narrative Shift

As most movements do, the movement for abolition also waged a war of ideas for the creation of a new common sense. In 1440, Gomes Eanes de Zurara, a member of the Portuguese court, wrote that enslaving Africans would be good for them in the end, as it would "civilize" them and bring them Christianity. Over time, slave traders reified a racial hierarchy, arguing that Black people were less human than white people.[12] This created the ideological power needed to maintain slavery.

Abolitionists had to challenge that ideology and shape a new one, in part by demonstrating the full humanity of enslaved people. Individual fugitive escapes and uprisings may seem like isolated acts, but historian Manisha Sinha argues that they helped influence potential allies and undermine the pro-slavery ideology.[13] Plantation owners had a harder time arguing the enslaved people were happy or treated well given the persistence of uprisings.

Formerly enslaved people and fugitives gave firsthand testimony about the horrors of the system, and some wrote books, such as Olaudah Equiano's autobiography. Abolitionists used visual imagery, such as the drawings of slave ships, music, newspapers, and speaking tours, to spread their message to the public.[14] By 1788, over half of the debating societies in London (a popular spectator sport) hosted debates about slavery.[15] The international context is important. The French Revolution, American Revolution, Haitian Revolution, and colonial independence movements from Spain all occurred within a few decades of each other at the end of the eighteenth century and beginning of the nineteenth, giving new meaning and power to abolitionist arguments.[16]

Organizations of formerly enslaved peoples and some faith-based groups, particularly the Quakers, held public events to share their critiques of the system. They found eyewitnesses, such as sailors on slave ships, to provide testimony to Parliament and public audiences of the cruelty of the system. Abolitionists in the United Kingdom worked to illustrate the harms of slavery as well as expand the public's idea of human rights for all, regardless of race. In 1833, sixty abolitionists from ten states met in Philadelphia to found the Anti-Slavery Society, calling for the immediate, unconditional end to slavery. In just a few years the Society had 1,350 chapters and a quarter of a million members. Formerly enslaved organizers, including Frederick Douglass and William Wells Brown, were members and frequent speakers at Society meetings.[17]

Not all abolitionists shared this moral perspective, however. Many abolitionists were motivated by economic or political aims rather than by an ideological or moral commitment to Black humanity and rights.[18] But language is key to ideological power, and abolition was no exception. One of the key contributions abolitionists made was giving language to this movement. Prior to abolitionism, opponents of slavery did not have the lexicon to name injustices of inequality and slavery. Quakers, known for their pacifism, grounded their argument against the slave trade and slavery in morality and peace. They viewed slavery as inherently violent, describing it as a "state of war." The Quakers provide an inspiring example of the power of vision and the role of faith-based groups in fueling freedom dreams and winning movements.

Narrative shift was also more possible under certain conditions. In his seminal history of the Haitian Revolution, C.L.R. James explains that the French Revolution created a new opening for the abolitionists. After the French legislature passed the Declaration of the Rights of Man in 1789, it became increasingly difficult to justify support for slavery in the French colonies. James writes that French soldiers arrived in Port-au-Prince bringing news that the French Assembly had "declared all men free and equal." Within a few months, enslaved people "were stirring and holding mass meetings in the forests at night. In isolated plantations there were movements. All were bloodily repressed. Revolutionary literature was circulating among them."[19]

The Revolutionary War in the United States created similar contradictions as the colonists fought for "freedom of man" against the British monarchy. But in the end, property rights (embedded in the Constitution) became more of a dominant ideological frame than human rights (embedded in the Declaration of Independence), particularly in the South. While the human rights narrative persisted, the dominant abolitionist sentiment preceding the Civil War focused narrowly on whether slavery should be allowed in new states. Over time, sympathy for Black people and arguments for a more egalitarian economy emerged. The narrative eventually shifted not only because of the words people spoke, but also through sustained, courageous action. DuBois wrote:

> And yet emancipation came not simply to Black folk in 1863; to white Americans came slowly a new vision and a new uplift, a sudden freeing of hateful mental shadows. At last democracy was to be justified by its own children. The nation was to be purged of continual sin not indeed all of its own doing—due partly to its inheritance; and yet a sin, a negation that gave the world the right to sneer at the pretensions of this republic.[20]

Ideological power and narrative shift were crucial elements in the fight to end slavery. The idea that Black people were fully human and deserved to be free was deeply contested. Historian Barbara Fields argued that it was in fact the very claim of "universal liberty" that made racial ideology necessary. Race was constructed as a way to make categories of people that could be excluded.[21] Other historians have built on this work, asserting that the idea of freedom itself was constructed as a part of white identity, and as an elite value.[22] It was only when enslaved people and abolitionists exposed deep contradictions in the status quo that the common sense began to shift.

Political Power, Electoral Change, and Inside-Outside Campaigns

American abolitionists debated various strategies. Some focused on resistance and escape. Others, such as militant abolitionist John Brown, looked to armed struggle. "Political abolitionists" were those who looked to end slavery through court cases, reforms, and laws.

Enslaved people petitioned state courts for their freedom as early as the 1700s, claiming that freedom was a right belonging to all. Those petitions didn't succeed while the colonies were still under British rule, but after the United States established its independence, two enslaved people, Elizabeth Freeman and a man known as Brom, sued plantation owner John Ashley for their freedom, claiming slavery violated the new Massachusetts Constitution. The jury ruled in their favor, and they were freed. Crucially, the case set legal precedent, making slavery essentially illegal in the state.

In 1783 the Quakers launched a grassroots advocacy campaign to petition the U.S. Congress for the abolition of slavery. Similar campaigns took place in England and France, including letter-writing campaigns and political rallies. In England, groups of workers signed petitions and attended mass meetings calling for the end of slavery. They saw connections between slavery and their own fight for workers' rights. In the 1860s, British labor activists organized mass meetings and rallies in support of the U.S. Union Army, expressing their support for abolition.

Political abolitionists debated the best strategy to end the system. Some felt it would most likely happen through small steps, starting with reforms that would be easier to pass, such as outlawing certain parts of the slave trade. Others felt these were weak half-measures that would deflate energy for the movement. But in 1803, Denmark-Norway passed legislation outlawing the importation of slaves in Danish territories. The British Parliament and the United States passed similar measures in 1807. In 1833, the United Kingdom made owning slaves illegal altogether. These campaigns used political power to launch variations of inside-outside campaigns, with elected legislators crafting winnable legislation and working alongside grassroots pressure campaigns. For example, British abolitionist groups produced anti slavery pamphlets that they gave to members of Parliament.

Some pushed anti-slavery reforms through at the state level. For example, New York passed the Gradual Emancipation Law of 1799, which freed children born after July 4, 1799, and women who had reached age twenty-five, and men, twenty-eight. The law was amended and expanded in 1817, but still provided only phased-in freedom. Similar to the inside-outside campaigns of today, wins were difficult political compromises. Still they resulted in the freedom of approximately ten thousand people in New York by 1827.[23] Sojourner Truth was to be freed under the law in 1827, but she escaped with her infant in 1826.

Some political abolitionists formed independent parties to push for full abolition and equality for Black people, such as the Liberty Party, founded in 1840. That party failed, and in 1848 was absorbed into the Free Soil Party, a coalition effort focused solely on keeping new states free of slavery.

In the 1850s, Congress passed a series of laws that favored owners of large Southern plantations, including the 1850 Fugitive Slave Act and the 1854 Kansas–Nebraska Act. Northern politicians saw these acts as a reflection of the consolidating power of the plantation owners. These laws deployed policy feedback loops, using policy not only to entrench slavery but also to increase the political power of slaveholders and weaken the power of their opponents. The two mainstream parties at the time—the Democrats and Whigs—debated the issue, resulting in major splits. The Republican Party was formed in 1854. The Republicans agreed to an anti-slavery position and pulled together a range of people leaving other parties (northern Democrats, Whigs, and Know-Nothings), and eventually displaced the Whigs as the second political party.[24] In 1860, the Republican candidate, Abraham Lincoln, won the presidency.

In the end, the Republican Party was not able to prevent the expansion of slavery into the West with political power alone. Of course, the political battle spilled into the Civil War, which involved military power as well as the other five forms of power. On January 1, 1863, President Lincoln issued the Emancipation Proclamation in a political play to undermine the Confederacy. And then in 1865, U.S. Congress passed the Thirteenth Amendment to the U.S. Constitution to outlaw slavery. These political acts were the culmination of a movement, rather than decrees handed from above by a benevolent president, as some history books might suggest. The Radical Republicans who led the charge in Congress for the abolition of slavery were practical radicals, adjusting their strategy based on the conjuncture and looking for openings to build political power through governance.

Abolitionists were able to use political power to win some gains, including important emancipation laws in northern states. But political power may not be enough to explain those victories. The gains were more likely achieved under particular conditions. Because much of the North's economy was based on manufacturing, trade, and small family farms, there was less need for enslaved labor. However, the southern states were heavily dependent on the lucrative plantation system, and thus fought hard to defend it. To do so, they intensified their race-based justifications, arguing that the white race was naturally superior to people of African descent, and that upending the racial hierarchy would be against the "will of the Almighty Creator."[25]

In the U.S. South, the entire economy, social structure, and racial hierarchy was based on the existence of the slave economy.[26] This raised the stakes for its defenders, who were not willing to compromise. Inside-outside and electoral strategies are more likely to be effective when the opponents are willing to compromise and a political negotiation can bring gains to both sides.

The Momentum Model

The nineteenth-century abolitionist movement was an early example of a campaign that used many of the momentum model features.

Enslaved people opposed slavery from the very beginning, and their resistance soon impacted others. In her groundbreaking work on abolition, Manisha Sinha shows how enslaved people had great influence on the common sense about slavery, and in some cases helped create "defectors." For example, some judges who heard direct testimony from enslaved people suing for their freedom in the United States, England, and France were moved to oppose slavery after hearing about the brutal realities of the system. Other citizens saw the persistence of slave uprisings and the words of fugitive slaves as evidence that the system was unjust. These polarizing fights were crucial to generate passionate support for abolition and to begin to change narratives.

Meanwhile, a few early voices against slavery were found in Christian faiths, among Mennonites, Catholics, Quakers, Puritans, and others. But spreading anti-slavery views within those faiths was not a given: it required organizing, debate, and strategy. Eventually the anti-slavery position became common among Quakers, as the cause was intertwined with other Quaker positions on war and the spread of capitalism. However, pro-slavery attitudes grew within other Christian traditions.

Persuading others to support abolition took place over hundreds of years, but intensified in what Sinha labels the second wave of abolition, or radical abolitionism, which took place from the late 1820s through the Civil War.[27] In this stage, abolition grew into a strong social and political movement that also provoked intensified opposition.

A growing community of free Black intellectuals and organizers led this new wave, grounding it in bold vision: a critique of colonialism and capitalism and a demand for full liberation, connecting with other freedom struggles for Indigenous people and women. They worked with white allies around the world to strategize around demands that could move the struggle forward.

The work had an impact. By the 1840s, popular culture reflected the growing shift in common sense. One of the most popular entertainers of the decade, the Hutchinson Family Singers, began singing abolitionist songs.

With success came internal conflict, and abolitionists split over different visions, strategies, and analyses of the conjuncture. And they sustained constant attack from pro-slavery forces and white militias, who used everything from political maneuvers to harassment and murder to stop them. By the 1850s the abolitionist movement was in disarray. But this could be understood as the outcome of a polarizing struggle. We showed earlier how the fight for marriage equality polarized society, and that proponents lost many times before they started to win. Similarly with the abolitionists, a passionate minority of supporters intensified their commitment to immediate abolition. A growing majority opposed the expansion of slavery, though had not committed to full abolition.

The Role of Military Power

We did not present a military or armed struggle strategy as one of our models in this book, but the story of abolition involves military power. Perhaps the most stunning military victory in modern history happened in the country now known as Haiti. Once a French colony named Saint-Domingue, Haiti was the site of some of the most brutal plantations in the Americas. Enslaved people resisted and fought back from the beginning of the plantation system, but it wasn't until 1791 that the revolts began to cohere into a full revolution.

Within the first ten days of the revolt, enslaved people had taken over large swaths of the colony, and by 1792 they had gained control of one third of the country. Toussaint L'Ouverture and Jean-Jacques Dessalines led much of this movement and built a military force to take on the French army, and then later to ward off the Spanish and British forces. After thirteen years of fighting, Dessalines declared Haiti's independence on January 1, 1804.[28]

By all accounts L'Ouverture was a masterful military strategist. But odds are the Haitian victory would not have been possible at another time in history. The period was unique for at least two reasons: one, as mentioned earlier, the French Revolution of 1789 created an ideological opening—indeed, it exposed ideological contradictions between the French people's fight for rights and the unequal rights in the colonies. Not only were Black people kept in bondage, but free Black people and mixed race people were denied full rights. The second factor was the ongoing battles between France, Britain, and Spain. These battles created numerous opportunities for the Haitian uprising to pit one enemy against the other, forming strategic alliances when necessary. The Haitians also had good fortune when French forces were decimated by yellow fever. Armed struggle resulted in victory in Haiti, but it wasn't a strategy that worked elsewhere.

Even the Haitian uprising required solidarity power to start with. The Black population in Haiti was divided by religion and ethnicity, as well as by race (Black people and mixed race) and status. L'Ouverture helped unite people. The early demands in the movement were for better treatment for free Black people—L'Ouverture himself was emancipated, but he came to see the need for a more inclusive movement calling for freedom—solidarity power was foundational for disruption.

The Haitian Revolution resulted in freedom for approximately 500,000 enslaved people, who then established the first free state for Black people in the Americas. But within a few decades the French government came back and threatened Haiti with war unless it paid "reparations" for what French plantation owners had lost in the war. Haitian leaders decided to avoid war and instead take out loans from French banks, saddling them with massive debt for more than a century. Haiti's story shows that while the revolutionaries built military and political power, it was not enough to ward off French reprisals that later prevented them from building economic power.[29]

The Fight for Liberation

Practical radicals assess what sources of power are available to them, and what strategies are possible given the context. But not all organizing is done because it's the most strategic. Collective care is first and foremost a way to survive. People build organizations out of a need to take action, moral outrage, and community building. But these approaches become strategic when they build power, including other forms of power, and when they create new opportunities.

Abolition was a complex, multi-layered, centuries-long struggle that involved varied goals, multiple actors, and complex alliances. We don't have evidence of many "strategy hubs" that brought together all the forces, particularly the force of the enslaved workers who were prevented from reading, writing, and open communication. But there is evidence that the collective care networks provided some limited opportunities to exchange information, including crucial knowledge for moments of resistance and escape. And Sinha explains, "Fugitive slaves united all factions of the movement and led abolitionists to justify revolutionary resistance to slavery."[30]

The largest uprising in the United States took place in Louisiana in 1811, led by Charles Deslondes. Deslondes was born in Haiti. While young at the time, he witnessed the beginning of the Haitian Revolution before his enslaver fled the country, taking Deslondes with him to the United States. Deslondes was likely inspired in part by the Haitian Revolution when he organized twenty-five enslaved people on his plantation to rise up and attack their enslaver, and proceeded to a local militia warehouse to gather weapons and uniforms. They moved toward New Orleans with plans to capture the city. Dozens of other enslaved people joined them on the way. They were ultimately captured and defeated, and the leaders executed. It was not a successful uprising, but it demonstrates the degree to which enslaved people were likely sharing ideas, information, and resistance strategies—even across nations—despite brutal repression.

There are many examples of how segments of the international abolitionist struggle debated, learned, and strategized together. When the London abolitionists wrote pamphlets and produced visual images of slave ships, they sent copies to allies like Benjamin Franklin in the United States and Jean-Jacques Rousseau in France. U.S. abolitionists Douglass and William Lloyd Garrison were in close contact with British organizer Thomas Clarkson.[31] Sojourner Truth worked for decades to unite the abolitionist cause with women's rights.

We use the abolitionist story to highlight four lessons.

First, *transformational change will likely require multiple forms of power and all seven strategy models*. Base-building is fundamental, but the other models work best under particular conditions. To this end, organizers should consider the ways different strategy models might fit together in a larger long-term struggle.

Second, *underdogs prevail not only by uniting with each other, but by creating or taking advantage of divisions among overdogs*. Overdogs are constantly building their own forms of power and deploying their own strategies. But they are never homogenous. The Haitians exploited the war between the British and French. Enslaved people were able to launch a general strike during the war between the Union Army and the Confederacy. Abolitionists in many countries pushed to deepen the ideological contradictions between the popular struggles for human rights and the slave system.

Third, *struggle involves complex and evolving alliances*. The Haitian Revolution was not just between the plantation owners and the enslaved. It required organizing among free Black people, multiracial people, working-class white people, international sailors, and French legislators. The movement in other countries was equally, if not more, complex. Strategists had to constantly assess the social forces on the ground and their sources of power, as well as the particular conditions in the conjuncture.

Finally, *slavery ended in many countries without war*. The combination of multiple strategies was enough without resorting to military power, even in the United States, where gradual emancipation happened in the North after the American Revolution. It didn't happen in the U.S. South, where overdogs invested in plantation slavery and white supremacy were deeply entrenched and unwilling to compromise. They had built vast wealth and a racial hierarchy for which they were willing to die.

When the Confederacy lost the war, they immediately tried to control the narrative by creating a hypocritical framing that claimed the cause of the war was about states' rights. Before the war, southern legislators pushed the federal government to expand their powers in order to protect southern state rights—slave owners' rights, specifically. For example, the Fugitive Slave Act of 1850 asserted federal power over northern states to protect the rights of slave owners. The Dred Scott decision of 1857 extended this further, ruling that "free state" freedoms were not applicable to Black people, thereby undermining the rights of northern states to set their own laws.

This legacy, both the dismantling of abolition and the racial capitalist roots upon which slavery was founded, is crucial for understanding the current conjuncture. Our hope is that there will be peaceful transitions out of racial neoliberalism, and that by engaging in deep strategy across wide sectors we will be able to avoid war. The abolitionist fight was complicated and messy, and involved alliances of unlikely subjects. Slavery ended in the United States through the actions of people with a wide range of motives and positions. Such unlikely alliances will be necessary today to find a peaceful transition to the next conjuncture. The road ahead is daunting, but as author and activist Mariame Kaba says, "We do this 'til we free us."[32]

Table 13.1: Examples of How Abolitionists Used Strategy Models and Power, 1700s–1800s

Strategy Model and Form of Power	Example
Base-Building and Collective Care Solidarity Power	Mutual aid among enslaved people Underground Railroad (early 1800s–1865) The Society for the Abolition of the Slave Trade (Britain, 1787) British and Foreign Anti-Slavery Society founded; calls the first World Anti-Slavery Convention in London (1840) Anti-Man-Hunting League (Boston, MA, 1854) British workers organize anti-slavery campaigns in support of the U.S. Union Army (Civil War)
Disruptive Movements Economic Power, Military Power, and Disruptive Power	Sugar boycott (late 1700s–1830s) Uprisings on plantations (throughout history) Underground Railroad (networks begin in the early 1800s) General strike (U.S. Civil War, 1860–1865) Haitian Revolution (1791–1804) U.S. Civil War (1860–1865)
Electoral Change and Inside-Outside Political Power	Denmark-Norway outlaws trade of enslaved people (1803) Laws restricting slave trade in England (1807), U.S. (1807) Massachusetts state law nullifying the Fugitive Slave Act (making MA a sanctuary state) (1843) U.S. Congress passes Thirteenth, Fourteenth, and Fifteenth Amendments to the Constitution

Strategy Model and Form of Power	Example
Narrative Shift **Ideological Power**	Popular materials—songs, books, speaking tours, by people such as Olaudah Equiano, Frederick Douglass, and Thomas Clarkson Newspapers and pamphlets Drawings of slave ships, photos of shackles, published and shared widely Quakers assert moral arguments against slavery Public statements by governments
Momentum **Solidarity Power, Ideological Power, and Disruptive Power**	Base-building brings in large numbers of volunteers through various channels Free Black abolitionists push to change the common sense in favor of full freedom for Black people; use injustices to create polarizing fights and build support Pushed prominent figures (judges, clergy, politicians) to "defect"

Tools

Tool 2 Prompt: Envisioning a Future World
Tool 3 Conjunctural Analysis
Tool 7 Power for Underdogs
Tool 33 Power Analysis

PART III

MELODIES FOR MOVEMENTS: UNDERDOG STRATEGY IN THE TWENTY-FIRST CENTURY

In the final section of this book, we explore four dimensions of strategy that are crucial to underdog success: building trust and unity, investing in creativity, learning from our opponents, and mastering the rhythms of social change.

We need trust and unity—components of solidarity power—to collectively develop and practice strategy. Underdog power relies on bringing together large numbers of diverse people, which poses challenges to building unity. In Chapter 14, we discuss common sources of conflict that prevent underdogs from building unity within the Left, and provide tools to address them. We also clarify when and when not to form alliances with forces outside of the Left (including, at times, some overdogs).

Strategists are made, not born, and it takes work to get better at it. In Chapter 15, we provide ways to do this: methods for generating creative thinking, building effective teams, and engaging in regular evaluation and honest assessment of your work.

Another way to get better at strategy is to learn from your opponents. Chapter 16 examines the methods and the "dark arts" used in the military, politics, and Silicon Valley. Underdogs can ethically borrow only some of these techniques, but they need to deeply understand all of the ways in which overdogs strategize.

Strategy is about time and tempo. In Chapter 17, we argue that underdogs need to plan for the long term, and show how it helps to see the ways movement activity ebbs and flows via upsurges and in cycles. Different combinations of strategies make sense in different periods. Strategy should be crafted based on the needs of the movement and on other organizations' actions—it requires an understanding of the movement ecosystem.

Finally, in Chapter 18 we provide our perspectives on the future of the seven models and identify shifts our movements must make to get better at strategy, and also suggest how underdogs can apply the concepts in this book to meet this historical moment.

14

Unity Builds Power: Addressing Conflict in Organizations and Movements

Imagine you live in a town that has been run by Republicans for the last several decades. Since the pandemic, a group of people have been organizing to push the Republican Party further to the right. They have fought mask mandates and absentee voting, and pushed to control the school curriculum. In the upcoming election, they are backing a candidate who claims Donald Trump won the 2020 election.

You are a member of a small labor–community coalition that has generally supported Democrats; a few win, but most don't. A member of your coalition suggests that in the coming election you persuade your members to register as Republican so that they can vote in the primary election for the more moderate candidate as a way to ensure the extreme candidate loses.

What do you do? Immigrant activists confronted a similar challenge in Arizona. They faced a rising tide of racism and nativism that led to the passage of SB 1070, the infamous "show me your papers" law, in 2010. In response, they made the shrewd decision to organize a recall election of Russell K. Pearce, the president of the state senate and leading champion of the law. Pearce was elected from a ruby red Republican district that would never elect a Democrat, so the activists allied with a moderate Republican candidate and encouraged people of color and progressives to vote in the

Republican primary. Deepak remembers being in meetings with immigrant leaders who wrestled with, but ultimately embraced, this brash strategy, rightly in his view. They won a stunning upset, sending a shockwave through national politics by showing there could be a political price to pay for nativism.[1]

Or imagine another daunting challenge: your organization is in the heat of a multiyear campaign to pass legislation that would transform the lives of its low-income members. As the campaign reaches a climax, a number of staff demand that the organization pause its work to address harmful behavior within the organization. As a mid-level leader, what do you recommend to staff, members, and the director?

We pose questions like these to our students to highlight the real-world choices practical radicals have to make regularly. Some of the challenges are about how to build internal unity within your organizations and movements so that you have more power and trust, and can collectively carry out strategy. Others, like the Arizona case, involve creating internal unity about what kinds of external alliances you should build. In particular, are there times when you should work with one set of overdogs to defeat another set? In those cases, underdogs must first have unity among themselves about whether or not to build those alliances, and then they need clarity about how they will work in a broader coalition.

These are not easy questions, and we're always surprised at the spectrum of answers we get. History is filled with difficult choices, and engaging in strategic debate about options, without getting derailed by internal conflicts, is necessary.

Conflict can be productive, and arguments can deepen a sense of unity when handled well. The following are some common themes that have divided underdogs, and ways to address them.

Why We Argue #1: Conflicting Analyses

Conflict can arise from having different analyses of the same political moment. You need to agree on whether you're fighting the right fight. For example, in the 2020 elections, Left organizations had to decide whether to support Joe Biden. Part of that decision involved an assessment of the effectiveness of electoral work, and part was about an analysis of whether a Donald Trump victory and the advance of authoritarianism was an existential threat compared to the potential of a continued neoliberal regime under Biden and the Democratic Party. As it turned out, most organizers were surprised by how far Biden shifted away from a neoliberal agenda when he took office, and some have been surprised at the accelerating radicalization of Republicans since Trump lost.

Too often, debates over strategy happen without grounded conversation about the nature of the moment. Do you differ in your strategic choice because you have a disagreement about the primary threat? A misalignment on ultimate goals? Do you have a different understanding about the sources of power or how much power you actually have? There are organizations and tools to help strategists conduct a sober assessment of the opposition's and potential allies' forms of power. Underdogs can use tools like conjunctural analysis and power analysis and other resources to develop a shared understanding of the balance of forces (Tools 3, 6, and 33).

Why We Argue #2: Conflicting Views About Power

Activists don't necessarily agree that acquiring power is crucial to win transformational change. After witnessing people with power use it for evil or seeing how even the best people can be corrupted by power, many activists want to "Fight the Power," as Public Enemy famously put it. Holding power is a great responsibility and requires making hard decisions and compromises.

As Katey Lauer and Zein Nakhoda, organizers with Training for Change, write:

> Our collective aversion to power has become so great that some activist and organizing cultures have cultivated tendencies that steer us away from having power at all. It shows up in small ways, in our skepticism (or hostility) toward leadership,

including movement leadership. And it shows up in our strategies, for example, when we favor constant mobilization over the work of building more people into our bases.[2]

For some people, this aversion to power also leads to what Maurice Mitchell of the Working Families Party calls maximalism: "considering anything less than the most idealistic position as a betrayal of core values and evidence of corruption, cowardice, lack of commitment, or vision."[3] Maximalism can lead to utopianism (Chapter 2). If you're serious about winning change, you have to build power. Conflict between organizers who aim to build power and activists focused on upholding the most radical stance may not be resolvable, but being honest about differing goals can lower the temperature of the conflict.

Maximalist demands can have their place, however. They can be used strategically to push the left edge of the possible, such as when Representative Alexandria Ocasio-Cortez came into office with demands for free higher education, universal health care, and a Green New Deal.[4] But the key to doing this strategically is to make bold visionary demands with a recognition that education and organizing is necessary to move others, rather than using it as a litmus test to denounce anyone who doesn't share your perspective.

Why We Argue #3: Conflicting Visions and Values

Many historic debates on the Left have come down to a clash in vision. Some socialists want to end capitalism and build an economy based on public ownership, while social democrats favor a mixed economy with a role for private ownership. Liberal feminists are fine with capitalism but want equal access to participate in it; socialist feminists have argued that liberation depends on ending capitalism. Others don't want to get bogged down with debates about long-term plans and would rather focus on concrete reforms to improve people's lives now.

Conflict can arise due to different understandings or interpretations of the larger systems in which we live. For example, segments of the Left have debated whether the primary source of oppression is class exploitation, structural racism, patriarchy, or the interaction of all three. The answer shapes which fights to pick and how to frame them.

These kinds of debates can be healthy and generative, but they often become detached from concrete analyses of power and strategy and lead to unproductive arguments and misunderstandings. That's why we discuss the importance of providing space to talk about vision as a starting point in strategy (Chapter 2 and Tools 1 and 2). You don't have to agree on a vision, but you should understand each other's goals and interests. Even if you don't start with the same vision, you might find you have shared values, overlapping goals and targets, and/or shared material interests. This might be a basis for common action and a way to *build* a shared long-term vision.

Bargaining for the Common Good (Chapter 6.2) is one approach to help groups do just that. Greg Nammacher, president of Service Employees International Union (SEIU) Local 26 in Minnesota, explained to Stephanie how his union got involved in BCG. Nammacher's union represents janitors in large buildings in Minneapolis–St. Paul who are employed by subcontractors rather than the corporations that own the buildings. SEIU knew they needed to target the building owners and did not have enough power to win their demands on their own, but they found environmental organizations that also had targeted the building owners. And while the environmental organization's focus was on pollution (those large buildings were some of the biggest polluters in the city), SEIU 26 was able to work with them to identify common targets and launch a successful campaign that included gains such as eliminating the use of harmful cleaning chemicals. Nammacher explains that this goes beyond getting support; it's about conducting a shared analysis of "who makes the decisions in our communities and then having a long-term vision of common fights against those decisionmakers."[5] Once you're clear on your own vision and values, you need to figure out how to work with others who may not share them, but may share a common target.

Why We Argue #4: Compromise and Alliance Building

At the heart of building alliances is the question of compromise. What are you willing to compromise on in order to work with other groups that don't necessarily share your vision? When is the "enemy of your enemy" a potential ally, and when are they just another enemy? When is it strategic to accept compromises, and when should you hold firm for bigger gains? Should you work in alliance with opponents in order to defeat an even bigger opponent? Progressive strategy often gets derailed by acrimonious debates among activists who share many goals, but differ on whether to pursue or reject reformist, incremental steps. Some on the Left believe that things need to get worse before they can get better, and so making incremental reforms will only legitimize the status quo and derail the possibilities for major transformation.[6]

Deepak uses the analogy of climbing up the stairs of a tall building.[7] Your goal is the top floor, but your allies might only want to go to the tenth floor. On your way, you face enemies blocking your path on the eighth floor. Can you form a tactical alliance at least until you get to the tenth floor?[8]

History is filled with examples of underdogs forming alliances, even with their enemies, in order to defeat a larger enemy. In the 1930s a wide range of organizations fought fascism. But the Left debated which kind of alliance to build. Communists in Europe built a "popular front," combining the efforts of the working class and anti-fascist elements of the middle class in one common formation. But Leon Trotsky argued that a popular front would minimize working-class demands, and that the Left should instead build a "united front": an alliance of working-class elements, independent of the ruling classes, that would still engage the common goal of defeating fascism. The organized political Left doesn't have the power that it held in the 1930s, when the choices of popular and united fronts held immediate and forceful consequences for millions. But to some extent a similar debate is alive today, as progressive groups face at least two serious threats: rising authoritarianism and continued neoliberalism. Most progressive groups chose to ally with neoliberal forces to elect Biden in 2020 because they saw Trump and authoritarianism as the greater threat. Climate activist and scholar Andreas Malm asks whether the Left will need to ally with so-called green capitalists in order to wipe out fossil fuel capitalists because the latter pose an existential threat to humanity.[9]

As we've mentioned, Lenin argued against being dogmatic in short-term approaches—organizers must remain flexible in their tactics while remaining firm in their commitment to follow the north star. That commitment mitigates against certain kinds of flexibility, of course. While most socialists allied with their national governments at the outbreak of World War I, Lenin and others rejected that tactic as directly undermining the international working-class solidarity necessary for a working-class revolution. But there are times when you don't have enough power to win on your own and compromises are necessary to win.

The Amazon Labor Union (ALU) is an example of such an alliance. "The commonality of the issues in the warehouse, that's what brings everybody together," ALU president Chris Smalls says. "If you are on the Left, Right—it doesn't matter. We all have problems in the warehouse that we can agree need to be corrected, and that's what we build off of."[10]

It can be easier to make alliances when your focus is narrow. For example, wide majorities of voters support higher minimum wages, including Republican voters. Living-wage campaigns were able to bring together groups that had never worked together before, such as the Green Party, building trades, and the Catholic Church. There are advantages to building these kinds of alliances; you can bring unlikely partners together to form trust and win common demands. But there is a danger as well. You can end up fighting for a specific policy outcome that may in fact run counter to your deeper agenda, such as accepting a higher minimum wage increase for some workers that comes with greater exemptions of other workers, thereby undermining solidarity within your coalition. Or the issue you most cared about could be sidelined in a final agreement.

This is the kind of risk found in any alliance: Will the groups you partner with come around to support your core values and agenda? Or will they have the power to dominate and institute their own agenda, which could undermine yours? Some organizations fear these risks so much that they choose to avoid any alliances that might lead to "selling out" or being undermined. But this approach most likely means never winning transformational change.[11]

Another form of this risk is making alliances in the wrong direction. Some groups look to partner with others who have power and influence, without considering the implications of who they are excluding. For example, a few days after the disastrous 2016 elections, Deepak was part of a meeting of twelve leaders of major national progressive groups. To his shock, the leader of one of the country's largest unions proposed that we call up Trump's transition team and ask for a meeting to seek areas of common ground. Sure, we had differences with Trump, the union president argued, but we could work together constructively on many things. Fortunately, everyone else understood that we were in the fight of our lives.

And, of course, overdogs build alliances too. Despite having more resources, they usually cannot rule alone. A dictator needs the backing of military generals and financial elites. When the apartheid government of South Africa felt it was losing support in the 1970s and 1980s, President P.W. Botha promoted a "Total Strategy" plan, which tried to solidify support from liberal-leaning white people and Indian and "colored" citizens. The plan also attempted to drive a wedge into the Black population by creating a Black middle class that would support the apartheid regime. The Total Strategy failed, proof that overdogs also face challenges when building alliances.

The trick is to build alliances around common demands and then work on developing a shared analysis and agenda if possible, or at least build more power, which incentivizes allies and opponents to recognize your agenda (see Tools 3 and 33).[12] You need a strategy within a strategy, in a sense, because on one level, your strategy is to win a campaign working within an alliance (such as defeating Trump). On another level, your strategy is to win converts or build enough power to set the direction of the alliance (such as away from neoliberalism).

Why We Argue #5: Organizational Practice and Roles

Another source of conflict stems from having differing views on organizational practices and roles. Our students, whether in management or staff or volunteer positions within their organizations, have shared frustration about their roles in their organization, including differing ideas about the role of leaders. Maurice Mitchell of the Working Families Party spoke to our class a few years ago and shared some ideas about conflict he had been thinking and writing about after observing some destructive trends in progressive movements. Our students were captivated, as Mitchell was clearly naming patterns they were experiencing. We knew Mitchell planned to share his writing with other executive directors, but we saw from our students' reactions that the document would be a valuable contribution to a public audience. Through Stephanie's work at *Convergence* magazine, we urged Mitchell to get his ideas out to the public. The result was an article eventually co-published by three outlets, "Building Resilient Organizations," that has made a huge contribution to our collective conversation about internal conflict.[13]

Maximalism and aversion to power lead some to oppose any leadership at all, but as Mitchell argues, "social change work requires experience, rigor and study," and a host of skills necessary for strategic power-building. Leaders don't have to be paid professionals or hold a college degree. They might be rank-and-file shop stewards or neighborhood block captains. But we should be transparent and unapologetic about the role and need for leaders.

That leaves many questions. Does the organization need to be internally democratic? How much hierarchy is necessary or desirable? How much time should you devote to improving internal structure and processes versus fighting external enemies? There is nothing inherently strategic about one approach over the other, so practical radicals need to figure out how the answers play into and impact their plan.

One of the chief tensions comes from lack of clarity on what an organization is and is not. Leaders, staff, and members have different relationships to the organization, and each should be clear on their own role, as well as the role of the organization in the movement. This may be contested: historically, unionists have fiercely debated what role unions should play (Chapter 6.2). While internal debate about purpose can be healthy, at some point there must be cohesion around a shared understanding in order for an organization to be effective.

Organizational leaders have a responsibility to be clear about their role, and staff have a responsibility to find the organizations that align with their vision and then help build them. The Chinese Progressive Association (CPA) articulates operating values and organizational culture. It is a member-centered mass organization that, the CPA says, does not have a "flat" structure—they are clear about the need for and role of leaders. It also delineates how internal conflicts should be addressed. The CPA asks people to consider, "Are you a critic or an organizer?" and for staff to be organizers, "meaning that they have the ability to hold critique, and the aspiration, patience, compassion and willingness to put in the work to get us to a better place. This means not just identifying and articulating how things are done wrong but taking leadership to make things work better."[14]

This kind of clarity around roles and expectations should be replicated for staff and volunteers working for movement organizations. In fact, it may be even more important for all-volunteer organizations and collectives to have clear roles, as groups without formal structure can become dominated by whomever is loudest, talks the most, or is most eager for power, as Jo Freeman explained in her analysis of feminist consciousness raising groups.[15]

There should also be clarity on what role the organization itself plays in the movement landscape. Some organizations try to be everything to everyone, but this is usually a path to failure. Just as we need a variety of strategies to win, so too do we need a range of organizations playing different roles in a movement ecosystem (Chapter 17).

Why We Argue #6: Balancing Purpose and Belonging

The progressive movement training institute Wildfire writes:

> All groups fighting for justice are both striving to have a concrete impact on the world and create a community where members feel that they belong, amidst a dominant culture that they feel excluded from. When we don't acknowledge these dual goals or bring intention to the ways we navigate them, our groups can fall out of balance, jeopardizing one for the sake of the other. We help groups make intentional choices about how they hold each.[16]

Neglect of internal culture can lead to brittleness, loss of talent and motivation, and conflict that undermines a group's work in the world. On the other hand, focusing only on how those inside an organization are doing and feeling can create insular cultures that are out of touch with or irrelevant to the constituencies they organize.

There is no formula to resolve this tension, but being explicit about the existence of multiple values helps (Tool 27). The CPA's "Operating Values and Culture Document" argues against "falling into the traps of movement martyrdom or a culture of constant urgency and crisis." But it also says that its emphasis on sustainability "does NOT put the individual at the center" because "if overemphasis is placed on simply meeting individual needs for sustainability without the overall community in mind, this may lead to what we call 'selfish-care': a practice of insuring all an individual's needs are met without other consideration. In a capitalist society, we need to constantly manage the tensions of individual and community needs; this is one of the learning edges in the movement."[17]

Why We Argue #7: Personal and Collective Harm and Trauma

Another source of conflict is interpersonal and collective harm and trauma. We've seen that care work can be strategic. The flip side is that efforts to develop strategy may be hindered unless organizations and movements address harm and trauma. This includes things like sexual harassment or violence that members of an organization may inflict upon one another; it also includes trauma that marginalized communities, among whom underdogs are organizing, have endured over generations due to violence, poverty, and oppression.

Transformative justice (Chapter 12) works to create conditions to prevent harm from happening in the first place, and if it does, to center the needs of the person who has been harmed. However, it also considers the needs of the perpetrator, including how they can continue to participate in society (or, in this case, an organization). "Instead of trying to find dangerous people and punish them, we want to stop harm, so we want to ask, 'why was this harm able to happen?'" explains organizer and writer Dean Spade.[18] A transformative justice approach asks: What can we do to change the conditions? What can we do to help the person or people who were harmed to be able to participate in society again? To heal, feel supported, and heard?

When Stephanie heard that the Right to the City (RTC) Alliance was prioritizing transformative justice work, she reached out to RTC staff member Paige Kumm to learn more. Kumm explains that underdogs and their movements have always been vulnerable to conflict and harm, and it's important to confront these to avoid replicating unhealthy patterns. After a specific incident arose within the RTC's staff, the alliance began working with the Bay Area Transformative Justice Collective, led by Mia Mingus, to learn how to process conflict. Staff participated in a six-week course to learn transformative justice skills: how to communicate, how to hold one another accountable, and how to deal with conflict. They underwent a two-year process to address the incident, to repair trust between individuals, and to reconcile with the harm done to the organization.

Drawing on Indigenous practices, everyone sat in a circle and talked until the issue was resolved. "It was definitely intense," says Kumm. "We made requests of the person who committed the hurt, and the harm, to try and address that; to try to repair." The group decided they wanted a formal policy related to the violation; the person who committed the hurt worked with the team to write it. It was difficult and time consuming, but Kumm says, "If we hadn't done that, then I imagine we would have felt more fractured and wouldn't be as strong as a team and therefore as an organization."[19]

Mitchell, however, warns of two related tendencies that can harm movements rather than repair them. One is "the small war": prioritizing internal power dynamics to the detriment of the external fight. We believe that proportionality is an important principle for all actors in movement work—are you devoting your time and resources to the struggles that are most consequential, or are you diverted into squabbles that are less important but close at hand? The second tendency Mitchell warns against is assuming that the collective is responsible for all the care needs of the individuals within it. While organizations should create a supportive, welcoming environment, no group will ever have the resources and capacity to deal with the full range of care needs of members and staff.[20] It can be challenging to balance inward-oriented care work and external power-building.

Why We Argue #8: Racism and Sexism

Racism, sexism, and other forms of bias exist in progressive movements just as they do in dominant society. Discrimination can take many forms. Internally, it can shape who gets to lead, whose opinion is valued, even who gets to speak. It may manifest through organizational cultures that set invisible norms that exclude or oppress. These internal conflicts often revolve around questions of *representation*.

Externally, racism and sexism can show up in the organizing strategies, demands, and alliances that groups make. These are questions of *analysis*—the extent to which the group prioritizes the interests of marginalized groups.

We have been part of both productive and unproductive conflicts about how to address racism and sexism in progressive groups. These issues are charged, and it's not easy to have skillful conversations about them—and even harder in the midst of high-stakes campaigns and opponents that use divide-and-conquer strategies.

Despite the challenges, progressive groups must tackle both representation and shared analysis to make progress. Systems of oppression affect groups differently, and inclusion of their varied perspectives is crucial for progressive agendas to be in touch with the lived experience of communities. Diverse teams (Chapter 17) are better at developing breakthrough strategy. Representation is not enough, though. Groups must struggle toward shared analysis of the role of gender, race, and class so that white leaders, for example, lead with racial justice as their priority. Equity is more than how people treat one another; it leads you to ask questions about organizational and movement strategy: where you organize, what demands you make, and who needs to be part of your coalitions. Race, gender, and class connect to every other source of conflict we identify and should be part of the analysis—for example, who loses in a compromise? (Tools 25 and 26.)

Building diverse coalitions is at the heart of what practical radicals must be able to do. This requires moving past the neoliberal diversity paradigms that have sidelined equity and incorporating equity deeply into your analyses.[21] In our experience, progress also depends on sincere and serious commitment to ongoing dialogue, leading to action and the cultivation of personal and interpersonal skills of self-awareness, empathy, and being able to hold tension.

Why We Argue #9: Infiltration and Intentional Disruption

Finally, internal conflict can be deliberately created by opponents. We mentioned COINTELPRO in Chapter 4: the FBI program used to infiltrate Black liberation organizations to surveil, discredit, and in some cases murder leaders. This is only one example of many (and there are no doubt more we'll never know about). Many core members of Occupy Wall Street attest to the damage police infiltrators caused by disrupting meetings and sowing dissension. There's evidence of police and Right-wing extremist infiltration in the Movement for Black Lives protests of recent years as well.[22]

Social media has created new mechanisms for disruption, particularly in the form of disinformation that causes confusion and mistrust. In 2018, Twitter released a report on a large "troll farm" based in Russia that had nearly four thousand accounts disseminating misinformation about the election and generating support for Trump.[23] The accounts were also used to divide Left movements, such as a coordinated attack on the Women's March in 2017, and on one of the march leaders, Linda Sarsour, who was falsely accused of dangerous political views. The tweets leveraged preexisting internal differences to hinder coalition work.[24]

Organizers should find ways to better inoculate their movements against such infiltration. For example, Stephanie met labor activists in Indonesia who created "guard" organizations of members who were trained to deal with infiltration and provocateurs. They learned de-escalation tactics, formed physical barriers around the perimeters of any march or demonstration, and used song and dance to maintain unity within their demonstration and keep marchers from engaging with disruptors.[25] In this book, we don't address infiltration (including underdog efforts to infiltrate overdog organizations), but it's a challenge for any underdog organization or movement that begins to gain real power.

Toward Cohesion, Alignment, and Generative Conflict

Solidarity is messy, but underdogs don't need to agree on everything to work together. In fact, as political philosopher Rochelle DuFord argues, conflict and disagreement are a part of healthy democracy.[26] There will always be conflict. The question is, how do you develop mechanisms to work through it? How do you build solidarity based not on uniformity but on shared democratic practices?

A defining challenge for Left organizations today is building healthy cultures that encourage real strategic debate *and* building caring communities that people want to join. In our experience, many organizations lean toward one pole or another—either having honest but harsh debates that lead to splits and drive people away or developing a culture of "nice" that prevents engaging differences in ways that are necessary for breakthrough strategy. Reducing harmful and unnecessary conflict can create the conditions for **generative conflict**, which can be healthy for organizations and movements. We're encouraged by the growth of movement infrastructure that is designed to address the inner life of groups, including The Rockwood Institute, Black Organizing for Leadership and Dignity (BOLD),

Generative Somatics, Wildfire, and more. Building trust is fundamental to good strategy.

Dealing with conflict gets easier with practice and training. Generative conflict helps people move beyond binary thinking to see more complexity and a broader range of ideas and identities.[27] This taps into the power of divergent thinking to help us dream bigger and develop breakthrough strategies. As musician David Byrne put it, "You give up a little bit of yourself to synchronize with other people, but you gain something else. You really feel this kind of lifting. . . . It's an ecstatic, wonderful, communal thing."[28]

Tools

Tool 1 Shared Values
Tool 2 Prompt: Envisioning a Future World
Tool 3 Conjunctural Analysis
Tool 6 Resources: Strategy Toolkits and Training Organizations
Tool 14 Resources: Holistic Strategy Development
Tool 21 Strategic Debate
Tool 25 Resources: Principled Struggle, Generative Conflict, and Unity
Tool 26 Prompt: Racial and Gender Equity
Tool 27 Prompt: Balancing Purpose and Belonging
Tool 33 Power Analysis

15

Strategists Are Made, Not Born: The Inner Life of Strategy

Musk. Bezos. Zuckerberg. The popular image of a great strategist is an individual with extraordinary, innate gifts who develops breakthrough innovations on their own. Those three oligarchs look less and less smart as time goes by. And it turns out most of the stories we've been told about great strategists are wrong.

Great strategists are made, not born. Strategy should be developed in teams—by ensembles rather than soloists. And while the popular image of a strategist is almost always a wealthy white man, oppressed people, because they have to strategize simply to survive and have keen insight from the front lines, often make the best strategists. We've talked about how Rev. Wyatt Tee Walker and his colleagues found a way to beat the notorious Bull Connor in one of the most racist cities in the United States, how women of color living in poverty created the welfare rights movement, how LGBTQ+ communities responded to the AIDS crisis through collective care, and how undocumented immigrants won a groundbreaking Excluded Workers Fund.

How did they come up with those breakthroughs? What kinds of deliberations, structures, and practices facilitated innovation? In this chapter we spotlight the "inner life of strategy"—explaining how organizers, campaigners, members, and teams prepared themselves to take on overdogs and win.

Priming the Pump for Breakthroughs: Cultivating Strategic Capacity in Individuals

Business schools teach two kinds of strategies: ones that build on the existing advantages of a company ("exploitation") and ones that identify new ones ("exploration"). Movement groups often use exploitation, scaling existing work or replicating what they've done before. Those situations demand focus, discipline, execution—skills that are important but not the focus of this book. In our view, today's biggest challenges are different from those in the past. Formulas that may have worked well may no longer, or may require adaptation. We need more exploration and innovation. Unionizing Amazon and stopping global climate change are unprecedented challenges and demand new strategies. As Billie Holiday said, "You can't copy anybody and end with anything. If you copy, it means you're working without any real feeling."[1]

The process of innovation can be counterintuitive. Rather than focus solely on familiar paradigms, practical radicals must explore with a spirit of "not knowing" and engage new people, data, and ideas. And even when—especially when—the stakes are high, they need to cultivate an open, adventurous, and playful sensibility. As psychologist Daniel Goleman puts it: innovation requires making a "deliberate cognitive effort to disengage from [the] routine in order to roam widely and pursue fresh paths."[2] As a producer, Brian Eno was renowned for helping the musicians he worked with, like the Talking Heads, U2, and David Bowie, achieve creative breakthroughs. He used note cards called "oblique strategies"—handing musicians cards with random words and phrases like "cut a vital connection," "water," or "gardening, not architecture"—to help them break out of ruts by making new connections and associations.[3]

And innovation takes hard work. Jazz musicians put in countless hours of deliberate practice so that when improvising on stage, they can cultivate a "beginner's mind" and open themselves up to a fresh creative moment. The creative process demands passionate absorption and immersion in the subject, looking at it from a variety of angles, perhaps talking to people inside and outside the field, reading intensely, or visiting people or places to stimulate the senses. Inquiry and creativity are emotional processes that require more than just intellect—passion for the cause is essential fuel for innovation.

In 1991, the president of the Teamsters union, Ron Carey, set out to engage rank-and-file members to revitalize the union. Union stewards are a potential resource to build power, but their responsibilities, such as representing members in grievance procedures, can be exhausting and time consuming. So Carey and the union's education department decided to approach things from another angle—turning the grievance procedure from an individualistic, draining, and service-oriented process into one that was collective, energizing, and organizing-oriented. The union produced a film, *Turn It Around*, teaching members how to do exactly that. Stephanie loves screening the film in classes and seeing how union stewards react. A light bulb goes off as they see a way to flip a tedious aspect of union work into something that can strengthen solidarity power. Looking at a familiar situation with a fresh perspective can open up new possibilities.

At some point, paradoxically, it's often when you deliberately *stop* thinking about the problem and let your unconscious mind do the work that breakthrough insight arrives. That's why people talk about developing great ideas in the shower or when they are dreaming (as Stephanie sometimes did as we wrote this book). The solution itself may not be something wholly new. It may mix different familiar strategies in a novel way, borrow from neighboring disciplines or history, or even be inspired by a metaphor or practice found in art, architecture, science, or spirituality.

So how can individuals nourish their strategic capacity, their ability to develop creative and winning strategies? Organizers and campaigners can incorporate specific practices into their lives that take them out of habitual patterns of thinking. Surprisingly, the key to creativity is to have *routines that break your routines*. One of Deepak's mentors, Industrial Areas Foundation (IAF) organizer Arnie Graf, had the organizers he worked with meet with someone they wouldn't usually talk to every two or three weeks—for example, an architect, a nurse, or an artist. When Arnie proposed this idea, Deepak thought it was ludicrous. Did Arnie understand how much *real* work he had to do? But he found that this process dramatically expanded his repertoire of ways to tackle problems. What might it look like to approach a dialogue with the care, interest, and rigor of a great nurse? What if a campaign were constructed the way an architect might design a building? We provide a list of practices with which practitioners can consciously experiment (Tool 28). No one gets better at strategy except by spending time on it.

Stepping away from the maelstrom of campaigns and the intense demands of organizing is essential to developing good strategy. Unprogrammed time allows the brain to do its work, to put things together in new ways. As Goleman writes: "Sleep deprivation, drinking, stress, and mental overload all interfere with the executive circuitry used to make the cognitive switch [to creative thinking]. To sustain the outward focus that leads to innovation, we need some uninterrupted time in which to reflect and refresh our focus."[4] We've been troubled, though not surprised, to hear from students in leadership positions that they often work to the brink of exhaustion, and past it. Movement work is inevitably demanding, but without breaks and quiet, we can't develop original ideas. Deepak finds that meditation strengthens concentration and cultivates awareness, both of which are valuable supports for creativity. Others find body-based practices, walking, or simply resting or relaxing to be effective.

The saxophonist Sonny Rollins famously stopped recording and doing shows when he was at the top of his field. Instead, for two years, he played for himself on the Williamsburg Bridge, often for fifteen hours a day, in all kinds of weather. "What made me withdraw and go to the bridge was how I felt about my own playing," Rollins said in an interview at age ninety-one. "I knew I was dissatisfied." He reflected on the importance of solitude and space, saying, "I was so close to the sky. It was spiritual."[5] The recording he made when he returned is considered a jazz classic. Organizers may not be able to take two years away from the work, but rather than trying to solve a problem by working harder or doing more of the same, organizers can create space and practices to nourish new modes of seeing, being, and doing.

For some, this may seem self-indulgent or irrelevant to the hard work of movement building. And it's true that the path to victory lies partly in discipline, following a proven formula, and executing it well. But underdogs need to innovate—it's a necessity, not a luxury. Some aspects of movement culture inhibit this kind of creativity: resistance to reflection, anti-intellectualism, narrowing the field of vision to only what's immediately relevant to the exclusion of the larger landscape, and, of course, overwork and burnout. At whatever scale, individual organizers can invest in their own growth and development and encourage their colleagues to do the same.

Organizations can also invest in their members' and staff's growth and development. Big corporations invest in their executives—taking them to retreats, sending them to executive leadership programs, pairing them with mentors, and rotating them through new roles to expose them to people and ideas. Underdogs don't have the same resources, but they too can intentionally develop people's strategic capacity. Our class on Power and Strategy is part of a curriculum at Leadership for Democracy and Social Justice, a new institution focused on training and mentoring for this and future generations of early and mid-career organizers, especially people of color, women, LGBTQ+ folks, and people from working-class backgrounds. Institutions like BOLD, labor centers at universities, Midwest Academy, Momentum, Wildfire, and others offer support for practitioners at various stages of their careers. Groups like the Service Employees International Union (SEIU) have made a major investment in organizers of color by launching programs that focus on advanced campaign strategy.

Socialist and communist organizations have traditionally been a space where organizers learn strategy. These organizations dwindled during the Cold War and even more so in the neoliberal era, but have seen a revival in the past decade. Stephanie has been a member of an organization, LeftRoots, created in 2013, that trains organizers as strategists. In addition to studying theory and international Left movements, members learned a framework to think strategically based on reading the conjuncture and developing hypotheses about cause and effect. Strategy development rests heavily on building trust and unity, and the concepts discussed in the previous chapter. For example, members learn to seek clarity with one another when debating strategy: Do we agree on the same vision for the future? Do we share the same analysis of the conjuncture? Do we understand one another's proposals on which tactics to use and why? Stephanie had been used to a Left culture in which people denounce one another as political traitors of some kind, or a liberal culture that accepts any idea as equally valid, but Left-

Roots trains members in **principled struggle**: a way to engage one another in comradely discussion for the sake of developing better strategy.

Assembling an Exceptional Ensemble: The Qualities of a High-Performing Strategy Team

The best strategy gets done in teams, not by individuals—social change is the work of organized groups, not charismatic leaders.

In his book explaining why the United Farm Workers (UFW) succeeded while other better-resourced efforts failed, Marshall Ganz points to the critical role of teams and strategic capacity in organizations:

> Strategy is the output of a leadership team ... like innovation—it is often a result of interactions among the individuals authorized to strategize on behalf of the organization. Indeed, in complex, changing circumstances, devising strategy requires team members to synthesize skills and information beyond the ken of any one individual, like a good jazz ensemble.[6]

Like assembling an exceptional ensemble, assembling an exceptional strategy team means finding people who are not only masters of their craft, but are also deep and empathetic listeners who have strong emotional intelligence, who understand the necessary background, and who have the flexibility to focus their skills in the creation of something new.

How can you build teams that can generate breakthrough strategies? Ganz identifies five essential factors. First, he highlights the importance of *motivation*, arguing that a person's "commitment to act does not depend on his knowledge of a feasible strategy."[7] Organizers find a breakthrough strategy because they must. The UFW succeeded in organizing farmworkers where the AFL-CIO had failed, in part because the UFW was more motivated.

Second, the team needs people with the *relevant knowledge, skills, and information* to take on the project. This might mean people with previous organizing experience, with deep understanding of the community, and/or with skills in research, communications, or data analysis.

Third, successful organizers *make learning a routine*. Practices such as evaluating actions and events, reflecting on what's working and what's not, analyzing data together, and being able to critique aspects of a strategy are essential. This may seem obvious, but many organizations are spun up in a cycle of doing—moving from one crisis to another with no time set aside to assess how things are going.

Fourth, Ganz emphasizes the importance of *diversity—including divergent ways of thinking and different skills and repertoires*. This kind of diversity can be a source of conflict (e.g., if some people favor large, militant disruption and others favor an inside-outside approach). But it can also be a source of strength, offering the possibility of new syntheses and innovations. Sociologists Kim Voss and Rachel Sherman found that the presence of leaders with experience in other social movements made local labor unions more likely to innovate.[8]

Fifth, Ganz talks about leadership teams' decision-making processes. Teams that have *open, regular deliberations, encourage divergent thinking, and have constructive disagreements* tend to produce better strategy than teams that defer to one person or teams in which members are afraid to disagree with the majority.

We add a sixth factor: *trust*. The extent to which a team can harvest the benefit of diversity and conflict depends on members' trust in one another. Attending to the emotional life of a group—building authentic relationships and trust—is essential to building healthy teams that can have and hold the generative conflict necessary for breakthrough strategy.

In Deepak's experience, there is a profound interplay between the emotional maturity of individual team members and the strategic capacity of teams. He has worked with brilliant strategists who could not tolerate criticism, viewing it as a personal attack. Despite their brilliance, their teams consistently underperformed. Deepak has also worked with people whose individual strategic capacity was initially more limited, but whose presence, groundedness, and open-heartedness were tonics that brought out the best insights from the team. Everyone brings trauma and hurt to movement work. The more that practitioners have attended to their wounds, cultivated awareness of their triggers, and developed compassion for others, the better strategists they'll be, both as individuals and in groups. Groups like the Rockwood Leadership Institute and Generative Somatics that cultivate these skills of self- and other-awareness can play a crucial role.

Developing a high-performing strategy team is a process, not an event.[9] Movement organizations must figure out how to cultivate cultures that can generate innovation over the long term—even, perhaps especially, if things go well. Ganz points out that while David does sometimes beat Goliath, "remaining David can be even more challenging than becoming David in the first place," because success can lead to complacency. "Organizational changes that increase homogeneity, reduce accountability to constituents, suppress deliberative dissent, and disrupt cycles of learning can diminish strategic capacity, even as an organization's resources grow," he writes.[10] Voss and Sherman point to two other factors that enable organizations to engage in innovation and renewal. A political crisis—like the failure of big campaigns—can open local leaders to new ideas or result in leadership changes. And union internationals can force or persuade locals to adopt new practices. Many assume that innovation comes from the bottom up. That is often true, but larger organizations and networks can also spur change from the top down.[11]

Leaders may also change an organization's culture to improve strategy. Sociologist Francesca Polletta argues that culture shapes what strategies are possible for a group. For example, a cultural commitment to nonviolence rules out certain strategies. A culture of democratic participation within an organization could build greater solidarity and therefore be strategic. Deepak has organized and attended a lot of protests. He has, however, been frustrated by organizational cultures that view demonstrations and marches as the *only* way to exercise power. He has tried to get organizations to develop a broader repertoire of tactics that might have a greater impact, but were not seriously considered because they were unfamiliar.[12] No matter how much organizers love a particular song, the quality of their strategy will be better in organizations that culturally value being able to play many tunes in many genres.

Experimentation, Evaluation, and Goal-Setting as Tools for Long-Term Change

Strategy requires regular honest assessments. You should not be afraid to claim failure or victory. Overdogs make use of experiments and evaluation in their strategy work (Chapter 16). Underdogs have fewer resources, and because they are often fighting urgent defensive battles, they don't always have the time to plan their work and evaluate it after. But transformational change requires long-term planning. The plans must include testing new ideas and evaluating what works and what can be improved.

Organizers are relying on more sophisticated data, technology, and research to get smarter about aspects of their work, and in some cases are collaborating with academics. "Big data" and technology are crucial in electoral work. The labor movement has devoted significant resources to accessing better data and experimenting with voter turnout strategies.

Mario Yedidia, national field director for UNITE HERE, told us that the core of the union's approach is to bring an organizing mindset to electoral work. The thousands of paid staff, mainly housekeepers, bartenders, and cooks, who are members of the union and take a leave of absence from their jobs to knock on doors each election cycle have been through tough fights with employers.

The union operates at a remarkable scale, having knocked on 2.7 million doors in the 2022 elections, including 1 million in Nevada, where Democrat Catherine Cortez Masto won reelection to the Senate by a razor-thin margin of under ten thousand votes. UNITE HERE's operation relies on data to figure out where to target resources. The union consciously decided not to outsource data analysis to political consultants. Canvass team leaders use data daily to assess who in their turf needs special focus. Nationally, union staff review data every night and weekly in the run up to the election, and reallocate resources based on what they see. For example, Yedidia told us that the data in Nevada showed that "if we talk to women, especially Latinas, that was where we could win this thing and so we focused as much as we could there." The union also focused on getting "low-propensity voters," who are written off by many political campaigns, to vote early. After the election is over, the union does a rigorous analysis of precinct-level data, comparing turnout to previous elections to evaluate their performance.[13]

Some unions, community organizations, and political groups are becoming disciplined about keeping track of everything, from members' home addresses to voting patterns and participation in activities. Columbia University faculty and staff Alex Hertel-Fernandez, Suresh Naidu, Adam Reich, and Patrick Youngblood founded the Columbia Labor Lab, which collaborates with worker organizations to implement data-driven experiments and evaluation. They worked with a large union local that began attaching QR codes on membership cards, which allowed the union to track participation in union meetings, picket lines, or rallies. The result was a detailed database that could be used to turn out members for phone banking, voting, or a strike. With this data, analysts are better able to predict which types of activities generate participation, and which members use which services. Unions can also use this information to tell field representatives to prioritize talking to members that are predicted to be stewards or strike captains but who have never been previously approached.[14]

All organizers and organizations should cultivate practices of rigorous evaluation at the end of a campaign. (Stephanie learned the importance of evaluation after working on living-wage campaigns, later finding out that many of the laws were passed but never implemented.) Some organizations, like MoveOn.org, even hold "joyful funerals," celebrating the demise of an experiment or campaign and harvesting lessons for the future.

To assess how effective campaigns are in building toward a long-term vision, strategists should set clear benchmarks for building power. Whether a campaign wins or loses, it should succeed in building capacity for the next fight.

In Chapter 4 we described frameworks for levels of power, including one developed by political scientist Archon Fung. Fung's framework asserts that power for liberation includes four levels: everyday power, policy power, structural power, and ethical power. We think these levels provide useful measures of campaign effectiveness. Specifically, organizers should assess the following:

Everyday power: Did the campaign change people's everyday lives for the better? Did they get the raise they fought for? Did they prevent the landlord from evicting them?

Policy power: Did the campaign result in a policy change that improves people's lives? Was the minimum wage increased? Was the policy enforced?

Structural power: Did the campaign change the rules of the game? Are more people allowed to vote? Are immigrants able to naturalize? Can workers form unions?

Ethical power: Did the campaign shift public opinion or collective norms? Does society reject racial discrimination as natural or the norm? Does the public believe that the government can play a positive role in bettering our lives?

Whichever metrics are used, good strategy should include long-term and short-term goals, regular evaluation, and flexibility to adapt based on outcomes. That requires making time and devoting resources to the task.

Beyond the Lightning Strike: Investing in Strategic Capacity

Strategy doesn't descend like a bolt of lightning to select initiates. If that were true, there would be little movement leaders could do except hope to be struck. Moments of inspiration are surely part of the process, but good strategy is not magic—the conditions for it to emerge can be deliberately cultivated in individuals, teams, and organizations. Our colleague Cristina Jimenez told us about "Strategy Idol," a strategy method developed by the New Organizing Institute that United We Dream integrated into their organizing trainings. Based on the iconic TV show *American Idol*, teams would share their proposed strategies in front of a team of judges. The exercise invites creativity and rigor—and fun too!

Yesterday's breakthrough innovation becomes today's conventional wisdom, and underdogs understandably fall back on repertoires that have worked for them in the past. Prioritizing breakthrough strategy in movement organizations will require embracing a paradox. To win, organizers often need to replicate what's worked in the past. But in the face of daunting or new challenges, they will also need to innovate. In these cases, teams charged with strategy must be open to risk-taking, generative conflict, and unfamiliar inputs and ideas. The hallmark of successful twenty-first-century organizations and movements may be the ability to toggle between excellent replication and breakthrough innovation.

> **Tools**
>
> **Tool 9** New Grooves
> **Tool 21** Strategic Debate
> **Tool 28** Prompt: Practices to Support Individual Creativity and Innovation
> **Tool 29** Lean Startup for Social Change
> **Tool 30** Improving the Strategic Capacity of Teams

16

Learning from Our Opponents: How Overdogs Develop Strategy

Deepak looked around nervously as he sat down in a plush chair in an anonymous conference room in a sun-drenched Northern California office building. A staffer stepped to the front of the room and announced: "Welcome to the future of fighting terrorism and crime." When the lights dimmed, he showed an electronic map that lit up, in real time, with reports of terrorist attacks, crimes, and other notable events taking place in the Middle East. He explained that his company had developed an algorithm that predicted with a high degree of accuracy exactly where and when a crime or terrorist attack would occur. The goal, he said, is "to stop them before they started."

Deepak attended this presentation, designed for potential government clients, over a decade ago. It was hosted by Palantir, Inc., one of the world's largest and most sinister big data companies. Founded by Peter Thiel, the iconoclastic PayPal billionaire who helped bankroll Donald Trump, the company thrives on contracts with the Department of Homeland Security and other federal agencies to (among many other things) surveil and monitor immigrants. Deepak was shaken by the presentation, wondering how social justice activists could possibly compete against foes with access to such vast data analysis capabilities. These fears were well founded. Recent exposés have showcased the use of Pegasus spyware by repressive regimes around the world to surveil and stop movement actors.[1]

Underdogs develop strategy because they face overwhelming asymmetries in power, but overdogs innovate and iterate strategy too, often in response to pressure from below. They cannot rely on brute strength alone. The vast literature of counsel to kings and princes over the millennia is rife with paranoia, warning rulers against complacency. Machiavelli's *The Prince* is an iconic strategy manual that enjoins ruthlessness, deception, and cunning in the exercise of power, advising, for example, that "if an injury has to be done to a man, it should be so severe that his vengeance should not be feared."[2]

Today, overdog strategy is developed primarily in three fields: politics, the military, and business. Some strategy is taught formally—instead of advisors writing manuscripts for princes, there are hundreds of business schools, consulting companies like McKinsey, and schools like the Army War College that train overdogs to rule. Some strategic frameworks are passed down in lineages of practitioners; for example, the architects of the modern Republican Party's strategic use of racism (Chapter 5), including figures such as Lee Atwater, Pat Buchanan, Karl Rove, and Steve Bannon.

Why study overdog strategy at all?

Jean Hardisty, a mentor to Deepak who spent her career studying the Right at Political Research Associates and by attending Right-wing gatherings, contended that "to learn from those who are attacking you helps you move beyond a defensive position."[3] If we understand how our opponents think, we're more likely to defeat them.

Underdogs can learn and borrow from overdog strategy too. Overdogs have done this themselves: the Tea Party movement shamelessly used Saul Alinsky's *Rules for Radicals* as a playbook. No one side of the political spectrum has a monopoly on good strategy, and the mark of a good strategist is being open to ideas from all sources.

Because overdogs have controlled the means of sharing information for most of human history, there are vast literatures and histories to explore. Rather than try to cover the history of overdog strategy, we discuss three distinctive strengths of conservative strategy across politics, business, and the military: their mastery of the dark arts, use of experimentation and data, and orientation to long-term planning.[4]

The Dark Arts: Undermining the Opposition, Psych Ops, and Divide-and-Conquer

Overdogs' defining weakness is that they are usually vastly outnumbered by underdogs. Threatened by this imbalance, overdogs develop sophisticated methods to disrupt the opposition. These include measures to weaken institutions that are sources of power for underdogs, psychological operations (psych ops) to confuse people, and, perhaps most famously, divide-and-conquer strategies to set underdogs against one another. Every organizer will confront these methods, frequently in combination.

We saw how conservatives sought to deliberately **weaken underdog strength** in certain spheres of American life, especially universities, which had played a role in the radicalization of young people in the 1960s (Chapter 5). The strategy to undermine the institutional foundations of progressive power grew more sophisticated over the decades. Political scientist Alex Hertel-Fernandez studied how conservative activists, funded by the Koch brothers and others, capitalized on the Republican electoral wave in 2010 to weaken two pillars of progressive strength in America: voting rights and unions. A troika of interlocking organizations led by the American Legislative Exchange Council (ALEC) got state legislators to pass copycat bills to make it hard for people of color, people with disabilities, and young people to vote by using "voter ID" requirements, despite lack of evidence of voter fraud. They also pursued measures to cripple unions, the grassroots muscle for the Democratic Party in many states.[5] The assault on voting rights has continued unabated, and Republicans have upped the ante with laws criminalizing protest to further weaken underdogs.

Jerry Taylor, once a leader at ALEC and an architect of the Right's state-based strategy to weaken progressive institutions, later became a "never Trumper." In a revealing piece, "What Democrats Can Learn from Republicans About Political Power," he writes:

Too many liberals seem to think that good ideas sell themselves, and that the political terrain is far more conducive to their agendas than it actually is. . . . This lack of seriousness about political strategy starkly manifests itself in agenda-setting. Regardless of what the campaign that brought them into office was about, conservatives invariably attend to policy initiatives designed to cripple Democratic power. Right-to-work statutes, public-employee contracts, campaign finance regulation, the promotion of conservative judges: all are top priorities for a right that understands the long-term political advantages that accrue from hobbling muscular Democratic constituencies and the future scope of liberal lawmaking. Democrats, on the other hand, rarely spend political capital on these matters. And when they do, they lack the infrastructure to execute those operations.[6]

Overdogs have paid special attention to **psych ops**: efforts to persuade or confuse hostile populations. The U.S. military has focused on this since its humiliating defeat in Vietnam against an overmatched, but united and committed, opponent. For example, in the Persian Gulf War, the U.S. military set a goal to "dominate the cognitive environment" to gain strategic advantage—by spreading propaganda through leaflets and other means.[7]

One of the pioneers of this approach was the U.S. Air Force pilot John Boyd. He concluded that the military was too preoccupied with the speed and power of aircraft. *Agility* decides who wins a dogfight. In strategy, the question is: who is acting and who is reacting? The "primary objective," he said, is "to break the spirit and the will of the enemy command by creating surprising and dangerous operational or strategic situations."[8] Boyd argued that you should act more quickly than your adversaries in order to keep them off balance.[9]

Boyd's idea that the central objective in warfare is to demoralize your opponent—to prevent them from feeling confident in their command of a situation—is broadly applicable. He developed the **OODA loop**, a framework to design psych ops.

The idea is that the information processing system includes multiple steps:

combatants have to take in information about what's happening, including what the opponents are doing (**o**bserve); they have to make meaning of that action, informed by their training, culture, and what they've previously experienced in combat (**o**rient); then they have to **d**ecide how to respond with an appropriate **a**ction.

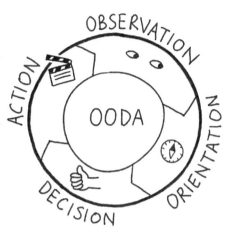

Boyd argued that if a combatant acted unpredictably, introducing information that the opponent didn't know how to make sense of, or if a combatant took many actions in rapid succession, they could freeze the information processing system of their opponent. This is the famous "fog of war"—having to act without understanding what's going on. Boyd argued for **mental warfare**—creating a distorted perception of reality (perhaps a "false flag" attack that is designed to look like it was done by another party). Successful mental warfare lays the groundwork for **moral warfare**—undermining the opponents' will to fight, as they lose confidence in their ability to accurately assess the situation. With the proliferation of online interaction, psych ops has taken on even greater significance, as evidenced by Russian disinformation campaigns that affected the 2016 U.S. election and sowed discord among Women's March leaders in 2020.[10]

Divide-and-conquer is so common that it hardly needs examples. We see it when employers foment racial division and pit workers against each other to avoid unionization. Union organizers have learned to inoculate workers against such efforts, explaining what will happen so they know to expect it. Even so, this strategy continues to succeed, both in the workplace and in society at large.

One throughline of overdog divide-and-conquer strategy is manufactured moral panics—the Right invents threats from "others" that demand a strong, authoritarian response. The enemies identified by the Right have included Muslims, people of Middle Eastern and North African descent, Asian Americans, Black people, Latino immigrants, LGBTQ+ people generally, and trans folks especially. The wave of bills to ban the teaching of critical race theory and targeting trans youth are simply the latest episodes in a revolting history of persecuting vulnerable groups for political gain. Heather McGhee and Ian Haney-Lopez argue that progressives must directly challenge these strategies and that trying to change the subject won't work. They, and others, have developed a race–class narrative that focuses on how overdogs use racism to prevent us from acting on our common interests.[11]

The repertoire of strategies overdogs have developed is daunting. However, underdogs can learn from and adopt some of these strategies. There are some ethical lines—lying and inciting hatred—that we don't advocate crossing, but there are methods for institutional disruption, psych ops, and divide-and-conquer that underdogs can adopt and integrate into their organizing.

For example, underdogs can use **policy feedback loops** (Chapter 17) to deliberately undermine their opposition. Examples might include anti-trust policies to limit the size of corporations, or measures that limit the access of private corporations to government resources—such as ending privatized incarceration, surveillance services, or contracts that allow fossil fuel companies to drill on public land. We've also seen how momentum campaigns can attack the opposition's pillars and undermine them that way.

Underdogs can adopt their own version of psych ops. Deepak received a call when he was onstage during a 2010 march for immigrant rights at the National Mall. It was one of his colleagues, letting him know they had a "mime down." Deepak was flummoxed, asking if we were really talking about "actors in white face paint who don't talk." It turned out that in response to the expected appearance of white supremacists, intent on provoking violence, someone had organized a troupe of mimes to insert themselves between provocateurs and immigrants by making absurd hand gestures and funny faces. When one of the white supremacists was being interviewed by a TV station, the mime blocked the shot, prompting the racist to punch the mime. The mime was fine, but the white supremacist got arrested. The mimes got inside the white supremacists' OODA loop.

The OODA loop can be useful for planning unpredictable and effective tactics like these. What are our opponents expecting us to do? What are they prepared for? What actions might we take that would rattle them? (Tool 18).

Finally, underdogs can disrupt the ruling coalition with divide-and-conquer strategies of their own. The Birmingham campaign known as "Project C" (Chapter 3) won by turning factions of the white power structure against each other. You could apply similar principles to factions of the Right today, often wrongly portrayed as a monolith. In our class, we show how the authoritarian Right is actually a coalition, including privately held corporations (think of the "My Pillow guy"), a gaggle of billionaires like Peter Thiel, small businesses, white evangelicals, avowed racists, and large numbers of ordinary people, including working- and middle-class whites and some people of color. We run an exercise that asks our students how they would drive wedges into this coalition.

Some of our students focus on the alliance between small businesses and large corporations, which is inherently unstable given their different interests. There are also small businesses that could be won over by progressive positions, such as the hundreds of Yemeni corner-store owners who joined the protests against Trump's anti-Muslim travel ban in 2020, or the uncountable small-business owners who would benefit from universal health care. Multinational corporations accommodated themselves to Trump's rule easily enough—he cut their taxes, after all—but public campaigns can force them to stop enabling authoritarianism. The Defend Black Voters campaign in Michigan, led by grassroots groups and supported by Community Change Action, has targeted corporations that contributed to Republicans who supported voter suppression laws. There are always potential divisions in the ruling coalition of overdogs that can be exploited and widened.

Testing Your Theories: Experimentation and the Use of Data

In the summer of 2020, Deepak joined a remarkable cast of characters—from Right-wing "never Trumpers" like Bill Kristol and David Frum to prominent liberals like John Podesta—who came together to . . . play a game.[12] They used a **tabletop exercise** developed by the military in which participants in a scenario have to make decisions in real time, to play out what would happen if Trump tried to hold on to power if he lost the election. Working together in teams, they played different roles—the Democratic Party establishment, Republican leaders in state legislatures, grassroots movements, and state attorney generals. How would each respond to a Trump coup? Each team proposed a move and its impact, and the group would debate to decide if the move was likely to succeed (if we didn't agree, the gamemaster would roll weighted dice). The results of the exercise weren't promising for democracy—the moves taken by Right-wing operatives were ruthless and effective, while the response by the Democratic establishment was legalistic and limp. (The failure of the actual coup attempt may have been due more to the fecklessness of its planners than to the robustness of the response.)

The military has developed a panoply of exercises—including tabletop exercises, war games, live-action drills, and more—to prepare for war.[13] The key to all of these is a commitment to rigorous evaluation. These evaluations, whether of exercises or actual combat, are sometimes called "hot washes"—named after the practice of soldiers' washing their guns in hot water after battle to clean them of residue and grit. These "after-action discussions" should involve everyone who was part of the exercise and require a candid assessment of strengths and weaknesses, often leading to a written post-action report or improvement plan.

Beyond specific events, military strategists consistently evaluate their work to gauge whether they are meeting objectives. This happens during the course of a military campaign and after its completion. In a commander's handbook for the Joint Staff, personnel are advised to ask three assessment questions: "where we are?," "so what and why?," and "what's next?"[14] To do this properly requires extensive data, clear measures, and time. Progressive groups, operating with far fewer resources and in a culture of urgency, often fail to do a thorough assessment of their work, whether they win or lose. And some movement cultures prioritize being agreeable, which prevents hard analysis. We can learn from the way overdogs use experimentation, rigorous evaluation, and data to sharpen strategy (Tool 31).

Silicon Valley has developed a variety of tools to use data both to test assumptions before embarking on a new venture, and to assess the success of an initiative. Given the immense harm that tech companies have wrought, progressives are rightly skeptical of Silicon Valley's claims to being paragons of innovation—they make money by exploiting workers, consumers, and the environment. In the early days, however, Silicon Valley culture developed as a rebellion against the traditional, slow-moving approach of blue-chip corporations, and many of the tools developed in that period are still valuable.

For instance, **lean startup**. The traditional approach in business and in many nonprofits involves coming up with a big new idea, seeking funding for it, waiting for the funding, executing the plan, and then evaluating it. This is known as the "Plan, Fund, Do . . . Repeat" loop. But a lot of time can be wasted waiting for funding that may never materialize, or time and funds can be wasted executing a grand plan that may have been poorly conceived, but is only evaluated after it fails.

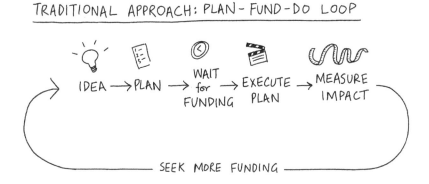

Lean startup, by contrast, proposes "Build, Measure, Learn." Using this approach, a group with an idea builds a "minimum viable product"—the simplest, cheapest prototype of the idea—and tests it with clear measures. In an organizing context, a group might have a hunch that public housing residents are so fed up that they're ready to be organized into a citywide tenant union. Using the lean startup approach, rather than trying to organize the money and talent required for a citywide blitz, a tenant group would develop a simple test—perhaps sending a couple of organizers into two representative buildings to see whether very light recruitment leads to unexpectedly big turnout at a residents' meeting. Leaders of the tenant group could then test their hunch against actual data of turnout at the meeting before proceeding with an ambitious campaign. If their hunch proved correct, they could use that evidence to help attract allies, organizers, and funding support.

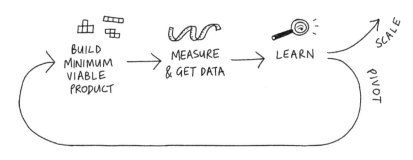

This experimental ethos runs against the culture of many social change organizations. There are obvious and urgent injustices, and organizers want to organize the biggest campaigns they can to address them. They often don't feel they have the "luxury" of running experiments, and in any case, community members are not "customers" or test subjects—they are, ideally, the owners of a people's organization. There is a sordid history of researchers using marginalized people as test subjects without their knowledge and in ways that caused them great harm.[15]

But practical radicals can and should ethically and strategically incorporate this approach into their work. There are innumerable injustices to address, but time, money, and attention are scarce resources. What will you focus on? Rather than going "all in" on something that may or may not deliver the results they seek, people working together for social change owe it to each other to rigorously assess whether a strategy has a chance of success.

And community members can and should be involved in designing and running the experiments so their wisdom about what will work is reflected in the prototype from the beginning. In Silicon Valley terms, this is called **human-centered design**: a process that demands close engagement with potential customers to understand what they actually want, which is often different from what entrepreneurs think they should want.[16]

Finally, whether or not practitioners adopt these specific methods, all organizers and organizations should gather and rigorously evaluate using data. This doesn't have to be complex or daunting; it only requires establishing goals before beginning a campaign or for a particular action, evaluating against those goals, and making meaning of the results. For example: How many people came? Did we hit our goal? If not, why not? Did the action have the intended impact on the target? How do we know? A campaign could assess not only whether a particular issue was won or lost, but also progress in other areas where the group set goals, such as member involvement, growth, alliances, or narrative shifts. Failure can be a good teacher, if groups take time to make meaning of it.

The Long March: A Powell Memo for the Left

In Chapter 5, we discussed the orchestrated rise of racial neoliberalism—how Right-wing leaders and organizations sought to reverse the gains of working people, people of color, and women through a sophisticated, decades-long campaign. There was no single master plan, but the Powell memorandum was emblematic of overdog strategy in this period.

An orientation to the long term is part of the DNA of the American Right. U.S. corporations and the military have historically devoted an extraordinary amount of time and resources to forecasting and planning for the future.[17] They have "futurists" on staff and consulting firms and think tanks on retainer to plan how to maximize profits in an age of climate catastrophe, or how to "protect" the United States from large numbers of climate migrants fleeing extreme heat and drought (caused by greenhouse gas emissions, overwhelmingly from the Global North). This planning is often done for nefarious purposes, and is not always as effective as they wish it would be, but that shouldn't deter underdogs from appreciating its importance.

For the final class of Power and Strategy, we ask our students to read the

Powell memorandum. And then we ask them to write a Powell memo for the Left. It's our students' favorite exercise of the term—they are not confined by the constraints of short-term campaigns and instead have the chance to think across issues and sectors. We ask students who they would write such a memo to (the original was to the Chamber of Commerce), to craft a core vision that they would organize around, and to consider what institutions they might build, weaken, or try to capture to build power.

This exercise always reveals one thing: Almost none of our students have done anything like it before. If there's a distinctive historical weakness of the U.S. Left, it may be its inability to coalesce around, or even come up with, a long-term plan. There are many reasons for this, including funders who encourage fragmentation, the ferocity of the opposition, the lack of a unifying Left party to bring divergent social forces together, and differences in vision. As we've said, some on the Left are even ambivalent about seeking or holding power. Others question the value of long-term plans for some of the reasons discussed in Chapter 2, believing that the best underdogs can do is seize moments and wring the maximum gain possible from those conjunctures.

Practical radicals must build power and create long-term plans in order to translate their vision into reality. And we believe that practical radicals should build plans that span generations, as the Right has done. Even in the absence of a single grand plan, you can come together in key sectors or geographies to strategize for the long term. This is already happening and showing results. We're seeing a rise of movement alliances, often at the state and city levels, where different organizations come together to develop a long-term agenda and a plan to capture governing power. Without the commitment of community leaders in Arizona and Georgia to build power for the long term (Chapter 9), those states would not have gone from red to partly blue in 2020 and 2022.

One useful tool to support long-range thinking in our movements is **transformative scenario planning**, developed by Adam Kahane, who was part of a process that brought white and Black South Africans together before the fall of apartheid to develop a plan for what would come next. It has been applied in cases around the world since then, and versions are used by groups like Social and Economic Justice Leaders to support movements aiming for social change. The idea is to bring movement leaders together, not just to adapt to what the future might bring, but to imagine possible futures and act to transform the system together.[18]

No Doctrines, No Boundaries

Some overdogs advocate a broad-minded approach to strategy. Boyd, the creator of the OODA loop, argued for learning from many traditions—"If you got one doctrine, you're a dinosaur. Period."[19]

As we show throughout this book, underdogs inherit rich and diverse lineages of strategy that are crucial resources in facing today's challenges. Some of underdogs' greatest victories have come from analyzing and dividing the overdog coalition. Studying overdog strategy and adapting some of their methods offers an opportunity for underdogs to learn and innovate. Winning transformational change in the twenty-first century will require mixing and sharing across all these traditions.

Tools

Tool 4 Reverse Engineering
Tool 8 Writing a Powell Memorandum for the Left
Tool 17 Tabletop Exercise: The Worker Upsurge
Tool 18 OODA Loops
Tool 21 Strategic Debate
Tool 29 Lean Startup for Social Change
Tool 31 Resources: Learning from the Opposition

17

Rhythms for Practical Radicals: A Long View

Transformational change can take a long time; the Seneca Falls Declaration demanded women's suffrage in 1848, but the Nineteenth Amendment wasn't ratified until seventy-one years later. And change is rarely linear; there are many ups and downs.[1]

Since the path to get from the world as it is to the world as it could be may take decades, it helps to have a sense of timing; of how the work you do today fits into a long-term plan. This includes ways to think about movements chronologically as well as understanding where your work fits into a larger movement ecosystem at any particular moment. In this chapter, we offer some frameworks that can help ground short-term actions in long-term strategy.

Movement Cycles

In the rhythm of social change, there will be periods of upsurge—intense activity and rapid growth. And there will be lots of slow periods, where nothing seems to work and organizers face defeat after defeat.

One of Stephanie's mentors and a former colleague, Dan Clawson, wrote

The Next Upsurge, detailing how unions grow in spurts.[2] In the United States there was a large growth in union membership from 1897 to 1904 and 1934 to 1939, and in the public sector from 1962 to 1972, periods in which worker organizing coincided with broader social movement activity.[3] There are seeds of another labor upsurge, as made evident with workers at Amazon, Starbucks, and a host of other companies organizing as we write this book in 2023.

Movement upsurges happen—and so often fail to happen—because transformational change can happen only under certain conditions. When the opposition is well resourced and organized, the common sense is strongly aligned against change, and underdogs are with little power, no amount of clever strategy will lead to immediate victory. But there are moments when large numbers of people question the common sense and even elites defect from the status quo.[4] These are moments of potential upsurge.

So, what can you do when the conditions are not yet right for an upsurge? You can prepare for the next one. Social movements should continue building a base and developing leaders so that when an upsurge does happen, they are ready to provide support with skill and informed analysis of the world. This is what Ella Baker and Rev. James Lawson did (Chapter 7).

Seeing movements as part of long cycles can ground activists and help them stay in the fight long-term. Arielle Newton, one of Stephanie's students, helped create a framework called the Movement Cycle. Newton grew up in Far Rockaway, New York, and when Hurricane Sandy devastated the area she got involved in a mutual aid effort to assist neighbors and rebuild the community. Through that, she met activists who had been involved in Occupy Wall Street the year before, and together they helped "Occupy Sandy" grow and succeed. Ultimately, however, the effort subsided as it faced internal challenges and outside pressure. Newton then got involved in Black Lives Matter (BLM), traveling to Ferguson, Missouri, in 2014 and coming back to help form BLM-NYC with others. Newton, along with two other BLM activists and four white allies, decided they needed to study social movements and how they operate. They began meeting regularly to develop tools and frameworks to map out how social movements work.[5] The

Movement Cycle shows movements have six phases. Out of an enduring crisis (such as systemic segregation and poverty in Far Rockaway), people may come together around a trigger point (Hurricane Sandy, for example) leading to an uprising. At some point, due to opposition fightback and/or internal problems, the uprising reaches a peak, and contracts. Eventually there is a period of evolution and then "the new normal." Their framework maps movement change over time, but includes an emotional axis as well. The phases are growing public anger, heroism, honeymoon, disillusionment, learning and reflection, and regrowth. For Newton, the Movement Cycle concept provides comfort when things seem bleak, as she can see that it may be just the downturn of movement activity.[6]

Timing and rhythm are needed to respond to overdog activity as well. Sociologist Beverly Silver shows that autoworker protest and organizing is closely linked to auto company investment. Automakers built factories in the United States, attracting thousands of workers who eventually organized and won higher wages and unions. The companies began to move production to new regions—to Europe, then Asia—and the cycle continued. Investment, industry growth, worker protest, repeat. This suggests that workers are more likely to engage in mass protest when industries are relatively new, growing, and still profitable.[7] Frances Fox Piven and Richard Cloward show that major disruptions in the economy, technology, and demography often create the conditions for disruptive movements. For example, the welfare rights movement arose after technological innovation pushed Black farmworkers off the land and forced them to migrate to northern cities, where they had potentially more political leverage.[8]

None of this means that between upsurges you should only prepare for the next upsurge. The time between upsurges isn't downtime; there is no end of urgent fights. A movement cycle perspective might enable more clear-eyed choices about how to pick and frame campaigns. For example, in peak periods, Left groups might launch a campaign that pushes the boundaries of what's considered possible. In slow times, groups might choose a campaign likely to fail, but that lays the groundwork for the long term or a defensive fight that at least prevents the most severe rollbacks of underdog gains.

Successful Failures

You can't know that conditions aren't right until you've tried and failed. Suffragists tried and failed for seventy years; the masses that responded to Occupy had shown no interest in Bloombergville. You have to fail until you succeed.

But there are different types of failure. Political scientist Eve Weinbaum, another of Stephanie's colleagues at the University of Massachusetts, developed the concept of **successful failure**, a useful way to think about how failures can be building blocks for bigger change. Weinbaum used plant closings in Appalachia in the 1990s to illustrate the difference between failed failures and successful failures. In each plant closing she studied, workers tried to get their jobs back and failed. The failed failures were ones where the workers blamed themselves, their co-workers, or workers in other countries. In the successful failures, workers connected with unions and community organizations and local "strategy hubs" like the Tennessee Industrial Renewal Network. Those campaigns helped workers develop a broader understanding of plant closings, seeing it as part of a bigger process of global capitalism. Appalachian workers traveled to Puerto Rico and Mexico and met with the workers now employed in the outsourced jobs. They built political alliances and campaigns to fight the spread of neoliberal trade policies, and some eventually went on to protest at the World Trade Organization meetings in Seattle in 1999. These workers developed a sense of their agency as political actors, gained leadership skills, and built new organizations and alliances that built power for the next stage of struggle. The workers never got their original jobs back (a successful failure is still a failure), but their organizing became part of a movement and helped change the narrative about the cause of job loss in Appalachia.[9]

Understanding successful failure is even more urgent today, as we are seeing a large increase in the number of protests globally, but they are yielding fewer victories. Sociologist Zeynep Tufekci writes that while the internet and social media have made it easier to get the word out about a movement and to generate large numbers of people in street protests, this rapid and reactive organizing jumps over the skill-building steps that help movements endure. By contrast, for the 1963 March on Washington organizers had to arrange buses, porta-potties, food, water, publicity—details that required people to work together, develop relationships, and negotiate, all of which served the movement later on. While many protests today are failing to win their demands, we need to build skills and capacity along the way even when we lose.[10]

Successful failures build leadership and organization in between upsurges. This is critical because upsurges require involvement and coordinated responses that go beyond the capacity of existing organizations (no organization can pay staff to sit around waiting for the next upsurge). In 2022, far more workers wanted to unionize their workplaces than there were paid staff available to assist them. Existing institutions and leaders must be ready to assist the upsurge, but must not try to control it.

Structural Reforms and Policy Feedback Loops

Some reforms unintentionally support the status quo and reinforce overdogs' power. For example, critics argue that police reforms in response to protests against police brutality, such as body cameras, implicit bias training, civilian review boards, and community policing, tend to increase police funding and legitimacy.

To that end, demands should be evaluated on a few pivotal questions: How does the demand fit into a longer-term vision? Can the campaign be run in a way that builds underdog power and organization? Will the demand, if successful, undermine overdog power? Do the campaign and the demand help to change the common sense about how society works? For example, campaigns to raise the minimum wage could support the current pro-market common sense and argue that higher wages are good for the economy and that hard-working people shouldn't live in poverty. Or, they could argue for a new common sense: that no one should live in poverty at all, and that our economy should be centered around human need rather than economic growth.

There are different names for these kinds of reforms.* We find the framework developed by the Grassroots Power Project (GPP) to be most useful (Tool 36). The goal is to fight for, and win, **structural reforms** (Tool 23) that would transfer power and wealth to underdogs. But since these are big fights and hard to win, you should plan for smaller steps along the way. GPP lists four types of fights: current fights—usually defensive battles to resist overdog attacks; stepping-stone fights; milestone reforms—those that begin to turn to offense and build power to prepare for the last fight; and structural reforms. To win at this stage, you must build alliances and wage a battle for the common sense.

Policy feedback loops are another way to think about building long-term power, similar to structural reforms. The term describes how a small win today can reverberate into larger wins. Policies can be intentionally designed to have secondary effects, but most policies reverberate, sometimes in unexpected ways. Political scientist and policy feedback loop expert Jamila Michener explains there are four kinds of loops:

The first *changes the nature of citizenship*. Overdogs consistently fight to increase their power by restricting citizenship. While voting rights laws or

---

* The French theorist Andre Gorz used the terms "reformist reforms" for those reforms that fought for "what is possible," and "non-reformist reforms" for "what should be." Andre Gorz. 1964. *Strategy for Labor: A Radical Proposal*. Beacon Press.

immigration policy have clear impacts on citizenship, laws around criminalization and incarceration have less obvious but profound impacts. For example, the stringent drug laws of the 1980s not only resulted in greater incarceration, they also reduced the number of voters, because felons are second-class citizens without voting rights in many states. And because punitive policing often makes communities of color suspicious of the state, it is less likely that even the people who can vote will vote.[11] In her research, Michener found that many beneficiaries of the Medicaid program are less likely to participate in politics because the demeaning design of the program makes them feel like less than full citizens.[12] On the other hand, when access to citizenship is expanded, such as with the 1965 Immigration and Nationality Act, the power of underdogs usually expands too.

A second type of loop *changes the nature of the state*.[13] For example, the Homeland Security Act of 2002 not only codified repressive policies, it also included a multi-billion-dollar budget and thousands of state employees in charge of surveilling, arresting, and harassing anyone labeled as a "threat." Vast resources are spent on public employees who work for Homeland Security's divisions, including Customs and Border Protection, Immigration and Customs Enforcement, and the Drug Enforcement Agency. Agencies that enforce wage, safety and health, civil rights, housing, environmental, and financial standards, by contrast, are starved of people and funds.[14] This discrepancy has implications not only for the types of laws enforced, but also the political consciousness of public employees who identify with and are committed to a surveillance and disciplinary state. It also subsidizes corporations that profit from this surveillance and discipline; these corporations then contribute to politicians who promise to safeguard their power.

Underdogs have also used policy feedback loops to change the nature of the state. For example, living-wage advocates in a few cities included provisions that require cities to devote staff and resources to enforce laws. Seattle, Washington, now has an office of labor standards with a full-time staff to monitor workplaces for labor violations. They work with community groups and provide funding so that they can help educate workers about their rights and report violations. In this way, a citywide minimum-wage law not only mandates a higher wage but also expands the capacity of the government to enforce the law and provides a mechanism for informing workers of their rights.

A third kind of loop *changes the power of groups*. The 1935 National Labor Relations Act (NLRA) gave workers more rights in the workplace and laid the groundwork for a union upsurge. Unions then became active political organizations. Over the years, those rights have been whittled away, but even today, almost ninety years after the NLRA was passed, they're not gone. But overdogs realize the power of unions, so they have used policy feedback loops in city and state policies to undermine labor unions where they can, such as right-to-work laws and efforts to defund public schools, which undermines teachers' unions.[15] In contrast, the *Citizens United* Supreme Court decision that allowed more corporate money to flow into campaigns has strengthened the political power of the 1 percent.

Finally, policy feedback loops can *change the political agenda*. The New Deal was filled with policy feedback loops—many of its policies and programs helped reinforce other New Deal values and goals. For example, providing unemployed people with public-sector jobs resulted in more positive opinions about the state. New Deal funding helped build public spaces where people could come together and develop community and solidarity. This all reinforced the New Deal's goals of strengthening democracy and support for a strong government.

The Left is rediscovering the potential of policy feedback loops. Deepak was part of a group of academics who wrote a report on how the Biden administration could create policy feedback loops in five areas: racial justice, health, immigration, labor, and climate. Versions of some of those ideas have been implemented administratively or via legislation. However, Deepak has been disappointed by the resistance of many progressive policy people, on the inside and outside, to the idea of centering power when making choices about priorities. For instance, legislation in the first two years of Biden's term authorized trillions of dollars of new benefits for working-class people, but little money was spent to hire navigators—people who would go door to door to inform people about the new benefits and how they were won.[16] This failure diminished the extent to which the provision of benefits had a lasting impact on recipients' consciousness, or even their willingness to fight for their continuation. The Right, by contrast, understands that governance is a long game contingent less on who offers the best policy and more on who has power.

A Moment in Time: Movement Ecosystems

Since transformational change happens unevenly, in a nonlinear fashion, it can be difficult to coordinate multiple strategies at a particular moment in time. Organizations are often not aligned, with different priorities, roles, strategies, and cultures.

Erik Olin Wright uses the metaphor of a lake to describe changing systems. A lake is an ecosystem of water, soil, fish, and plants.[17] You can introduce a new species of fish into a lake, and it might die right away. But occasionally, the new species will thrive and eventually replace the dominant ones. Wright argues that capitalism can be transformed similarly—it can be eroded by introducing and nurturing healthy and promising alternative forms of economic activity.

Similarly, organizer Lisa Fithian uses complexity science to inform her organizing work. She writes, "Complexity science shows that the greater the variety of inputs, the greater the chances of change. There is not one way, but many. The more strategies we have, the greater our impact."[18] This way of understanding social change has several implications for strategy and the role of organizations.

First, *strategic and organizational diversity is a strength*. One strategy alone is unlikely to work; more strategies will improve chances of success. That doesn't mean any strategy is as good as any other. It is important to be rigorous when choosing where to invest resources. For example, progressive organizations decided to go "all in" to prevent Trump's reelection in 2020. Movement leaders took stock of the situation and concluded that an authoritarian regime would harm vulnerable groups and set back movement building work for years or decades.

Second, *small changes can produce big ones*. Little campaigns can amass into large ones. And even if they lose, if done well, successful failures build leadership and membership and shift common sense.

Third, *no one organization, person, or group can do it all.* Different strands of the movement should play different roles in transformational change. Thinking in this way is useful for organizations to find their place both in the current moment and within a movement cycle. Certain kinds of organizations and strategies have particular roles, and as we saw with the symbiosis between GMHC and ACT UP, they can nourish each other and change over time. As singer and movement leader Harry Belafonte put it, "What makes a movement work are thousands of parts that come together and express itself in favor of a given destination or objective. You have to find men and women who are willing to play the role that each of these things demand."

Fourth, *there should be coordination between organizations and groups.* In the past, cross-movement strategy discussion and alignment happened in organizations like the Communist Party, in training/education spaces and movement hubs, like the Highlander Folk School, through informal alliances between movement leaders, and via bridge builders like Bayard Rustin, who had a foot in more than one movement. Historian and activist Barbara Ransby notes the value of political quilters: organizations that "nurture, sustain, and support base-building organizations while at the same time connecting them through new movement infrastructures, a network of relationships, and a growing movement culture."[19] Ransby names Blackbird, BOLD, and the BlackOUT Collective as three political quilters that have played a crucial role in the growth of the M4BL and the larger Black Lives Matter movement.

Thinking in terms of ecosystems can help you understand and navigate tensions between organizations and strategies at a particular conjuncture. For example, one coalition might push for Medicare for All (a long-term vision), while another coalition might see an opportunity to expand health insurance through an inside-outside campaign focused on Congress (a short-term vision). If the latter seeks expansions through the private insurance industry, it could strengthen insurance companies and undermine the long-term goal of universal public insurance. But, if the two groups understood themselves to be playing different roles, rather than demanding unity in long-term vision, they might agree on a short-term campaign to expand public health insurance framed in a way that points to long-term vision.

Seeking synergy across organizations and strategies is an important way that our movements can have greater impact. In Table 17.1, we list the ways in which each strategy model intersects with other models, and the time and conditions in which it may be most effective.

Building Strategy Across Generations

Dr. Martin Luther King Jr. argued that "the arc of the moral universe is long, but it bends toward justice." Labor organizer Daisy Pitkin reminds us, though, that time can be a weapon of the rich. With more resources and power, they are better equipped to outlast underdogs—all the more reason for them to plan for the long term. As longtime activist and scholar Angela Davis said, "Sometimes we have to do the work even though we don't yet see a glimmer on the horizon that it's actually going to be possible."[20]

We brought together some of our students in fall 2022 to engage in a provocative long-term scenario planning exercise designed by Social and Economic Justice Leaders Group (SEJ), a group that helps movement organizations take the long view. We looked at a potential scenario of climate collapse and authoritarian takeover a decade in the future, and then at a world with a multiracial, feminist, global social democracy three decades from now. Organizers were asked to imagine how we got to those scenarios. The exercise was emotional and eye-opening as participants reflected on what these scenarios would mean for their families and communities. Some brought to mind the ways that their ancestors had survived dark times. Several people reported that this was the first time they'd really seen themselves and their work situated in the long arc of social change. Deepak was moved by some of the shifts that organizers named as necessary to prepare for both scenarios—for example, making deeper investments in collective care, shared vision, popular education, and practices to foster resilience. Shifts in what organizers thought they might do now were only illuminated by looking at change over the span of generations. As Connie Razza, who leads SEJ, put it, "Taking the long view can seem like a luxury with all the urgent crises we confront. But it's an essential practice if we're to break patterns that no longer serve us and find new ways of being and doing that lead to a liberatory future."[21]

Thinking in the long term is liberating and challenging—liberating because it gives you options and agency, and challenging because it forces you to step out of a cycle of reactivity and act as though your choices will reverberate across generations. Today's underdogs are the descendants of generations of organizers who fought bravely for people they would never meet. And they are the ancestors of organizers whose futures depend on today's struggles.

Table 17.1: Seven Strategy Models in Relation to Time and Movement Ecosystem

Strategy	Time Horizon + When the Model Is Most Effective	How It Works with Other Models/Movement Ecosystem
Base-Building	Evergreen, but especially useful in slower periods in movement cycles, laying the groundwork for political opportunities or movement upsurges

"Trench warfare"—change mostly comes in small increments over time

Seeks to establish permanent institutions | Works well with electoral change and inside-outside campaigns

Relies on disruptive movements for exponential growth and on collective care for sustainability

Less history of combining it with narrative shift and momentum |

Strategy	Time Horizon + When the Model Is Most Effective	How It Works with Other Models/Movement Ecosystem
Disruptive Movements	During "ruptures" when the dominant system is faltering and/or in times of rapid economic, demographic, or technological change Change comes in dramatic, fast bursts of action	Depends on organizers who lay groundwork Electoral openings help them succeed; tension between majoritarian focus of electoral strategies and emphasis on polarization by disruptive movements Can have elements of narrative shift and can shape political agendas Often clashes with inside-outside campaigns Can benefit from collective care work for survival (e.g., strike support or a bail fund) Benefits from other strategies to win popular support to make them less vulnerable to backlash (narrative shift, momentum)
Narrative Shift	When a deep, long-term shift in norms and values is needed May unfold quickly, during a rupture when people are open to an alternative; or slowly, by planting the seeds for a new common sense	Can be a big part of momentum and collective care models Less history of successful integration with base-building or inside-outside campaigns Some electoral campaigns (like Sanders's) can shift narrative

Strategy	Time Horizon + When the Model Is Most Effective	How It Works with Other Models/Movement Ecosystem
Electoral Change	When the stakes of elections are especially consequential—e.g., to prevent fascist parties from winning Sometimes a slower build Works over multiple election cycles as organizations connect issues to politics, expand their capacity to reach voters, decide elections, and shape policy agendas	Works well with base-building and inside-outside campaign models Newer efforts are incorporating elements of collective care Tension between majoritarian focus of electoral strategies and minority focus of disruptive movements Can be tensions between focus on election outcomes and long-term narrative-shift strategies
Inside-Outside Campaigns	When the balance of forces between overdogs and underdogs is closely divided in governing bodies, so that if underdogs target swing legislators they can pass significant policy changes	Most compatible with base-building and electoral change models Doesn't typically incorporate collective care (though there are exceptions) Not always compatible with disruptive movements because of focus on winning majorities Can conflict with momentum and narrative shift because of its shorter time horizon

Strategy	Time Horizon + When the Model Is Most Effective	How It Works with Other Models/Movement Ecosystem
Momentum	When a fundamental system change is needed that is not possible now Unfolds over years when an issue needs to be moved from minority to majority support by deliberate campaigns that engage many passionate volunteers	Works well with narrative shift Strengthened by base-building and collective care A momentum campaign can be an electoral campaign Can lay the groundwork for inside-outside campaigns, though ambitious goals of momentum-driven campaigns may conflict with more incremental goals of inside-outside campaigns
Collective Care	When the state is unresponsive to crises facing marginalized groups, when political responses are not effective, or when people are feeling despair about the possibility of change and need to see impact at a smaller, human scale When organizations experience internal crises	Fundamental to lasting base-building Strike funds and bail funds support disruptive movements. Can add depth, richness, and wider on-ramps for participation to all other models, though undervalued as a strategy

Tools

Tool 14 Resource: Holistic Strategy Development

Tool 16 Prompt: Organizations, Movements, and Times of Upsurge

Tool 17 Tabletop Exercise: The Worker Upsurge

Tool 22 Policy Feedback Loops

Tool 23 Structural Reforms

Tool 32 Successful Failures

Tool 36 Long-Term Agenda

18

Learning from Lineages, Harmonizing Our Movements

Most of our thirty-plus years in movement work took place against the challenging backdrop of Right-wing ascendancy. Many of the battles we fought were defensive, swimming against a tide of reaction. But the era of racial neoliberalism may be drawing to a close, and the fight about what should replace it is under way. This is a hugely consequential period in history that will shape the future of our species and our planet. Overdogs are plotting how they stay on top in a world of extreme climate change and spiraling inequality.

How should underdogs respond? Organizers need to learn crucial lessons from our movement ancestors, and adapt timeless principles for this era. But today's movements will have to change—a lot—to rise to this moment in history. Some of these changes will require making unfamiliar and uncomfortable shifts.

So far, we've mostly presented frameworks and stories to illuminate choices organizers made, rather than to argue for "one right way" to do things. In this concluding chapter, we share our perspective on cutting-edge questions for each of the seven strategy models and how they can be harmonized. We explore how movements and organizations can get better at strategy. And we consider this historical conjuncture, particularly the rise of authoritarianism, and use the frameworks developed in this book to sketch how movements might best respond in an era of rupture of familiar paradigms.

The Seven Models Reconsidered

Our journey exploring these seven models and learning about various groups and campaigns has confirmed some views we held previously, but it has also led us to some counterintuitive conclusions.

Our analysis of Make the Road New York and the St. Paul Federation of Educators affirmed our view that deep member engagement and bottom-up strategizing make organizations stronger, and that **base-building** is an indispensable, evergreen strategy for social change. But we also found that robust alliances, expansive social visions, ambitious demands, and practices of collective care—which are not always associated with base-building groups—can add tremendous power to this model and help overcome potential limitations of parochialism.

The field of community organizing as a whole has undergone huge shifts over the last two decades. Most practitioners have embraced the need for vision, political strategies, and work at the state and national, rather than solely local, levels. These shifts have dramatically increased the impact of the field on issues and on elections. But social media and a culture of constant mobilization have eroded fundamental organizing skills, like one-to-one relational meetings, recruitment, and leadership identification, which are the lifeblood of movement work. Sulma Arias, the executive director of People's Action, has rightly called for an "organizing revival" to renew the tradition. A new synthesis, modeled by groups featured in this book, that brings together bold vision, rigorous strategy, and recommitment to the fundamentals of the craft, is emergent.

The labor movement faces a different set of challenges. Despite a record level of public support for unions, workers are blocked from unionizing by a system rigged for employers.[1] The recent upsurge of worker organizing is a hopeful development. There's a vibrant debate about the best path forward, with many promising campaigns under way. History suggests that there will not be a silver bullet solution. Explosive growth will require a sustained worker upsurge (like in the 1930s), and also the use of strategic leverage, political power, disruption, narrative strategies, and movement alliances. The form that worker power takes in this century could be different from familiar union structures, and organizers have to break out of the legal straightjacket that limits what they can do in order to find new vehicles for power. It is almost impossible to contemplate a broader progressive resurgence without a stronger labor movement; building worker power must be a central preoccupation of the entire U.S. Left, not only for union organizers.[2]

Our analysis of the welfare rights movement and other **disruptive movements** shows that when people take actions that stop oppressive systems from functioning, they can win major concessions. In times of social, political, and economic dislocation, underdogs can use disruption to win big gains in a short period of time. We should not confuse protest with disruption; they may not be the same, and they may rely on different sources of power. Even as the speed and scale of protests have increased in recent years, fewer movements have used sustained disruption. The urgency and scale of the problems we face demand a reinvigoration of the lineage of disruptive movements.

Disruption can change everything, but it's even harder to pull off than it seems. The conditions for disruption are not always present, the obstacles to people using their power are significant, and the risk of repression is high. To address the persistent dilemma of backlash (which reversed many of the gains of the welfare rights movement), disruptive movements would benefit from synergies with models that seek to build public will for transformational change. Disruptive movements can win big change *without* changing the common sense about an issue, but their gains will be more durable if reinforced by narrative shifts. Contrary to conventional wisdom, we found that base-building organizations and disruptive movements need each other to succeed—organizers trained in base-building often play a key role in disruptive movements, and disruptive movements create the conditions for explosive organizational growth. A clear-eyed view of this dynamic, fraught with tension as it often is, could accelerate change and make it more lasting. Concretely, we think organizers should be trained in both modes: to lay the groundwork for periods of movement upsurge and to fan the flames when they emerge to maximize gains.

Narrative shift is a booming field in progressive strategy. Occupy Wall Street showed the power of this strategy to change the terms of debate by telling a new story that defines a problem and names heroes and villains. We argue that in our media-saturated world, narrative shift is an essential part of the toolkit. However, shallow versions of this strategy that are disconnected from a social vision, organizing, an analysis of power relations in society, and proposed solutions are likely to fail. There is a big difference between narrative strategies as an alluring shortcut to avoid the hard work of base-building and narrative strategies that are grounded in a power-building agenda.

We identify five ways underdogs use **electoral change** and see value in all of them. In the United States there is distinctive value and promise in an approach that builds independent power through mass-based organizations and coalitions that contest for power across multiple election cycles. Groups like New Georgia Project, California Calls, UNITE HERE, Community Change Action, and the Working Families Party are exemplars of this approach. Given close margins and the stakes of election outcomes in a polarized era, especially for vulnerable people, the importance of electoral strategies cannot be overstated. But the feedback loop between electoral politics and organizing needs attention. Organizations reach exponentially more people at election time, but have yet to convert that scale into membership growth. The most pressing dilemma for this model is that there are precious few examples of successful, lasting progressive governance in the

United States. It is hard to imagine sustaining interest in electoral participation in the multiracial working class if voting does not lead to improved conditions and if the connection between voting and outcomes is not clear. Solving this riddle is of crucial strategic importance.

Under certain conditions, progressives can launch and win **inside-outside campaigns** that deliver major gains and provide opportunities for leadership development on a large scale, as Chicago's Fight for $15 and a Union did. Community-based electoral power, worker and community disruption, and mass engagement in campaign strategy provide some needed edginess that prevent inside-outside campaigns from collapsing into rote advocacy campaigns.

Inside-outside campaigns inevitably involve compromises, which can generate tension with practitioners of other models when there is not a shared vision or shared understandings about movement division of labor. It is essential to have an orientation to long-term vision and power-building rather than just to policy to maximize the potential of these campaigns. An orientation to power allows us to assess painful compromises as practical radicals by making decisions based on whether they build or deplete underdog power, rather than rejecting all compromises because they fall short of our demands. Our movements must emerge from inside-outside campaigns stronger than they started. Good policy wins are not, on their own, enough. **Policy feedback loops** are an essential tool to build underdog power and weaken overdogs. The Right has mastered the nexus of power and policy: a new generation of movement policy folk should be trained to compete more effectively in this terrain.

Momentum-driven campaigns harness the power of big visions, polarizing fights, and social media to generate the scale and speed of people power necessary to tackle the challenges of our time. Distributed organizing gives thousands of everyday people the opportunity to participate in and lead campaigns. Crucially, momentum-driven campaigns can change what's politically possible. 350.org's divestment campaign, for example, has had a long tail, resulting in major breakthroughs in policy and developing a new generation of talent. The Bernie Sanders campaign popularized the Left's vision and developed activists at a large scale. But to reach its potential, the momentum model needs deeper roots in local communities, connection to community struggles, and co-creation by grassroots leaders. Momentum practitioners must also think about how they can take greater responsibility for institutionalizing wins, rather than focusing solely on creating a more favorable narrative environment. Partnerships with practitioners in base-building traditions may be especially fruitful.

We initially planned to write about six models of transformational change. But dialogue with our class and movement colleagues convinced us that **collective care** is a too-often neglected strategy, not just for survival, but also for social change. Our research on the Gay Men's Health Crisis and other movements showed us the potential power of collective care. In a world where so many are afflicted by despair in the face of problems that seem too big to tackle, collective care's emphasis on change at an intimate, human scale can instill the sense of agency and hope needed to power large-scale social change. It can foster powerful new identities and build capacity by giving people more resources, support, and confidence to take risks and join movements. Collective care can easily be marginalized or co-opted if it is disconnected from movements and politics. But, in desperate times, it can be the central strategy to plant the seeds from which radical movements can grow.

These seven strategy models are creatures of historical conditions and political structures. Humans have always come together to organize, but the specific forms that organizing takes depend on circumstances. For example, workers have organized since the beginning of capitalism, but contemporary unions are built according to the rules of the National Labor Relations Act (NLRA) and state public labor laws. A resurgent labor movement will likely need to break the shackles of legal frameworks restricting workers. Many community organizations descend directly or indirectly from Saul Alinsky, who consciously developed the practice of community organizing as a reaction to the sectarian narrowness of the American Left, which had come to be long on radical rhetoric and short on organizing. Many of today's community organizers have in turn reacted to Alinsky's emphasis on self-interest and power by emphasizing vision and ideology. A new synthesis combining broad social vision with renewed rigor in the practice of the craft of community organizing is needed. The methods of contesting for electoral power depend on formally democratic structures that excluded most people for much of U.S. history. As democratic space shrinks, movement practitioners will have to adapt electoral methods and revisit approaches used by our ancestors in other periods.

Historical perspective is important to avoid rote replication of approaches that made sense under past conditions, but aren't relevant anymore. One of Deepak's longtime movement colleagues, Dorian Warren, often asks the question: "Under what conditions" might a proposed strategy work? This materialist view of strategy as a response to concrete historical circumstances gives us the awareness to improvise music that is fresh because of its rootedness in the present moment.

How Movements and Organizations Should Change to Get Better at Strategy

We offer these ideas in the same spirit that we began: not as final words, but to invite dialogue on what seem, to us, to be existentially important questions for our movements.

We need a movement-wide upgrade in power analysis, strategy development, and rigorous evaluation.

Overdogs spend a *lot* of time and resources working on strategy. Deepak studied what business schools, Right-wing leadership institutes, and military officer academies teach their recruits. A good portion of it is stale, mediocre, recycled groupthink. But the best of it orients to power and winning with ruthlessness and rigor. We don't advocate mimicry of overdogs—we have our own profound traditions of struggle from which to draw. But right now, we're not winning enough, and the odds we face are steep. Strategy is too often put off for later or done in a formulaic, rote way. Organizers can and must do better. We need rigorous, carefully grounded strategy development at every step: campaign by campaign; in organizational visioning and design; coalition-building; program development; and funder decision making and resource allocation. Movement groups should make important cultural, structural, and behavioral shifts to upgrade Left strategy.

Our strategy depends on our power. What power do we have, and how can we leverage that for real change? If we don't have the power we need, can we build it? How? What kind of power will overdogs use to gain and stay in control? **Power analysis** and **strategy charts** are fundamental tools. In our experience they are not used frequently enough, and the result can be poorly designed campaigns built on faulty assumptions or wishful thinking. Organizers should learn the art of corporate research, looking for vulnerabilities within the workplaces, supply chains, financial systems, corporate boards, and more. We've emphasized the importance of **conjunctural analysis** too. This tool is even less widely used but is essential to build a shared analysis and to examine shifting power dynamics during a conjunctural shift of the kind we're currently living through.

Underdogs win not only when they are united, but also when overdogs are split. Many of the cases we examine—from Project C in Birmingham to 350.org's divestment campaign—depend on deliberate strategies to break the overdog coalition. In other cases, underdogs capitalize on divisions that are not of their making—as with the Haitian Revolution, whose success depended on war between imperial European powers. Left strategy must increase focus on exploiting and creating fissures in the overdog coalition. The Right and authoritarian forces are growing and developing new methods. Breaking their formidable coalition will require a sophisticated analysis of its component parts and its vulnerabilities.

If we're serious about winning—not just expressing our anger—we must ground our opinions in research. We need to reinvigorate a culture of evaluation, testing, experimentation, and data. We can use methods like **reverse engineering, lean startup, and tabletop exercises** to allow us to interrogate each other's theories of cause and effect. Too many strategy debates unfold with people expressing certainty about the path forward—this, and this only, is the path to victory!—without unpacking the underlying logic, testing ideas, evaluating actions, or using data to measure impact. We need to be scientific in the real sense—that is, we need to learn from trial and error—and we need to bring more rigor to our work.

We need "strategy hubs" that can facilitate a rigorous, ongoing cross-movement dialogue.

Individuals and organizations need to get better at strategy, but we also need discussions across issue, identity, and methodological boundaries. **Strategy hubs** that bring organizers working in different traditions together can turbocharge innovation, sharpen our thinking, and increase our ability to work together even when we disagree.

Sociologist Aldon Morris argued that the civil rights movement was able to achieve breakthroughs because organizers built movement centers—tight alliances of base-building organizations in key cities like Birmingham, Montgomery, and Tallahassee—with enough concentrated leadership and power to consciously steer the course of the struggle. He also points to the importance of "movement halfway houses," like the Highlander Folk School, the American Friends Services Committee, the War Resisters League, and the Fellowship of Reconciliation. These organizations operated outside mainstream society with a goal of radical change. They lacked a mass base but offered critical resources to movements, including training, experienced organizers, and knowledge of movement history, strategy, and tactics.[3]

Today we need a new generation of strategy hubs—formations that bring key movement leaders together to make sense of the conjuncture and develop shared analysis and long-term plans. If we don't devote resources to this work, the urgent and defensive actions will always trump important and offensive ones. Achieving this may require individual organizations to make strategy more explicitly part of people's jobs by creating dedicated positions for long-term strategy. Strategy hubs can allow underdogs to share lessons about the powerful forces that shape and constrain how movement folk go about their work. For example, how do we avoid what scholar Megan Ming Francis calls "movement capture," where established foundations distort or dictate strategy?[4]

Strategy hubs could also help us navigate the complexity of making change, especially organizational roles in different periods of history. We can think of the movement ecosystem as a jazz ensemble, where musicians bring different instruments and skillsets together to create music. At times, they all play together. But there are solos as well: moments where one musician takes center stage and others play a supporting role. In a movement ecosystem, there will be times where a particular strategy will work better than another. The others should not disappear, but rather continue to play harmoniously in the background.

Greater coordination doesn't mean we should aspire to agree all the time. Our movements shouldn't avoid conflict: dialogue and debate can be productive if held in a context of trust and relationships that we commit to build. We need to embrace **generative conflict** and **principled struggle** to make progress. We should start by clarifying our vision, values, assumptions, and analyses, and approach each other with good faith. We should learn from each of the strategy models but be ready to break the rules and innovate. Strategy hubs can provide a valuable forum for this kind of dialogue, as well as movement journals written for and by practitioners, like *Convergence* and *The Forge*.

We must make a much deeper investment to develop the strategic capacity of organizers, leaders, members, and volunteers.

Strategists are made, not born. Groups and movements benefit from wide participation in strategic deliberation. This has not been the default practice in many Left circles—high-level strategy is too often the domain of a small number of people at the top, disproportionately white men. Women and people of color are too often treated as "doers" rather than "thinkers." We have been surprised that some of our students with significant movement responsibilities were never trained in power analysis or strategy fundamentals, including tools used by leaders in their own organizations. These dynamics must be challenged by democratizing access to the wisdom of our lineages.

Repeated experiences have shown us the practical value of expanding who gets to make strategy. When Deepak was at ACORN, two brilliant longtime member leaders, George and LaVerne Butts, suggested a strategy to force NationsBank, the predecessor of Bank of America, back into negotiations. They noticed how alarmed corporate leadership was by public debate about their racist lending record. So they suggested that we release data about racial disparities in mortgage lending every day in a different city and bring community members and local politicians together to excoriate redlining at public demonstrations. The prospect of never-ending and unpredictable firestorms in cities across the bank's service area in the South, at a time of rapid corporate expansion into new markets, eventually brought the CEO back to the table. ACORN won a major settlement leading to more lending in communities of color.[5]

Some of the best ideas we've heard in campaigns didn't come from official leaders, but from people close to the ground, with direct experience as members or organizers. They often have the best ideas because they're willing to take the biggest risks. Good leaders make it possible for everyday people to contribute. Formerly enslaved and free Black people led the strategy and intellectual and moral work of abolition (although white liberals often got the credit).[6] Our movements should invest heavily in developing the strategic capacity of people (our greatest asset) at a mass scale, including paid staff, members, and volunteers.

A lot will need to change in order to make this possible. There is a cultural premium in many organizations on *activity*—getting things done and moving through an often overwhelming task list. This culture inhibits creativity and strategic breakthrough (Chapter 15), and busyness crowds out research, strategic debate, evaluation, and power analysis. The COVID-19 pandemic and the existential threats of authoritarianism and climate crisis have exacerbated this problem. Even senior staff at key organizations spend most of their time in rapid response mode.

We need to consciously develop strategists of a particular kind: **practical radicals**. Many progressives focus on short-term legislative or electoral cycles. We need these pragmatists to be more oriented to a radical vision and long-term strategy so their short-term choices support transformational change rather than undermine it. And while dreaming big and developing long-term visions is great, utopians must be aware of real conditions on the ground, in relationship with bases of organized people, and oriented to strategies to achieve these visions.

We don't have enough practical radicals today, resulting in unnecessary conflict within and between movements. If movement practitioners can't speak a common language of power analysis and strategy, they will devolve into ungrounded accusations of selling out, opportunism, or magical thinking. We must develop leaders who are fluent in the three languages of vision, conjuncture, and strategy.

A distinctive challenge of underdog strategy is bringing together disparate groups into a coalition powerful enough to defeat overdogs. Historian Barbara Ransby invokes legendary civil rights organizer Ella Baker as a model "political quilter":

> She pushed educated college students to see illiterate sharecroppers as "their people," their allies and their political mentors. She pushed Northerners to embrace Southerners in principled solidarity. She organized back and forth across various color and cultural lines, and most importantly, across generational divides. In other words, she was a political quilter. She did not advocate forging coalitions of convenience: short-lived and limited. Instead, she wanted to create a movement and nurture the kind of long-term relationships that would sustain it. She tenaciously stitched together fragments of a progressive community into a patchwork of a movement.[7]

Our task is to build a majority from many minorities, and that requires what longtime movement strategist Gary Delgado calls bridge builders:

> By bridge people I mean people of color, people with disabilities, some gay and lesbian people, and first-generation immigrants—those who, because they don't exactly "fit" in this society, have been forced to carve out their own identities and their own unique perch from which they view the world. The ability of these people to see across and through similarity and difference—to see sideways—and to integrate the knowledge of many cultures can be a valuable asset to developing new multidimensional organizations.[8]

As a contribution to this work, we are part of a team that is building a new national institution, Leadership for Democracy and Social Justice, to train strategists, leaders, and organizers in the early and middle stages of their movement journeys, especially these bridge builders.

We need less methodological sectarianism, more appetite for building majority coalitions, and a more balanced view of the role of leadership.

While moderate Democrats still win in many states, the Left—those looking to upend the systems of oppression that keep underdogs down—hasn't acquired significant power in almost any arena in the United States. That chronic weakness has many historical causes, but a variety of cultural traits have contributed to it. Changing the cultures we create in our organizations and movements can dramatically increase our strategic impact.

First, we should *reject methodological sectarianism*. We both came of age in a period when organizers fiercely defended the "one right way" to do strategy. Many expressed open contempt for the work of others without first seeking to understand it on its own terms. Stephanie felt trapped in harsh debates about "top-down" versus "bottom-up" labor organizing models when in reality many successful campaigns contained some of each. Similarly, she felt pushed to see electoral work in "all or nothing" terms: the path to liberation, or the graveyard of social movements. We think the challenges and complexity we face demand humility and curiosity rather than strident certainty. Working with our students, the research we did, and conversations we had for this book expanded our own appreciation for the astonishing variety of strategies that have produced transformational change.

Learning from movement ancestors and from each other can strengthen our work. We found many connections between strategies; for example, collective care can lay a foundation for disruptive movements, and disruptive movements may create the conditions for the explosive growth of base-building organizations. We're not arguing for an "anything goes" approach, but rather that we keep open minds about strategy. Certain strategies have a larger role to play at certain times. But familiarity with other melodies will strengthen our collective ability to harmonize. As it stands, organizers may be years into their careers before they even become aware that there *are* other traditions and methods.

Second, we must *reject narrow ideological litmus tests* that prevent us from welcoming new people who aren't completely aligned with us. Playing to win means that our organizations and movements must grow exponentially. None of us have fully coherent ideologies or "correct" stances on every issue, especially when we enter a movement. We need to support people to make a journey over time in their political opinions. Longtime movement leader Linda Sarsour uses a striking metaphor here to explain the needed shift:

> Our movements are often extremely self-righteous and very stringent. There's like four doors. It's like when you're going into a prison. You have to go through this door, and then that door closes, and then you go through another door, and then another door closes. And my thing is like, if we're going to do that, it's going to be one person at a time coming into the movement, versus opening the door wide enough, having room to err and not be perfect.[9]

Many of the groups we profile succeeded because they consciously created a *welcoming culture of recruitment*. This did not mean that they allowed racist or sexist behaviors to occur without challenge. Rather, they used political education and agitation to move people over time, viewing awakening as a process, not an event. Evidence suggests that Right-wing movements have successfully recruited partly because they create a culture of belonging that precedes political engagement.[10] We cannot win without power, and we cannot get more powerful without recruitment.

Third, we should *play to win by building majority coalitions that can take governing power.* This will require making alliances and compromises. In Chapter 2, we shared the cautionary tale of the disastrous choices that socialists and communists made in Germany. But the need to participate in broad coalitions to achieve specific objectives doesn't mean we have to give up our radical visions.

We need strategies to win, as well as strategies to navigate within a governing alliance for control. For example, you may need one strategy to defeat authoritarianism, which could involve working in a big-tent coalition with unlikely allies, such as neoliberals. You should have another strategy for how to navigate within your coalition against neoliberalism. In a union, all workers come together to beat the boss; within the union, you might have a strategy to move the union toward an inclusive anti-racist orientation.

Fourth, there's been a broad cultural trend in society toward distrust of leaders and institutions (often justified).[11] That tendency shows up in Left movements and organizations, sometimes resulting in bitter internal conflict. Every situation is different, and there are surely leaders of organizations who merit challenge or replacement. But ultimately, *we need leaders in order to forge and implement winning strategies.* The Right has built and captured institutions over the last few decades. The Left will need to make a similar commitment to the often unglamorous work of institution building to meet this moment.

In a class for Leadership for Democracy and Social Justice fellows, Yotam Marom reflected on his experience in Occupy Wall Street and as a movement facilitator. Marom argued that "when we pretend that we don't have leaders, it makes it impossible to hold them accountable. It makes it impossible for them to train and support other people to become leaders. And it makes leaders go into the shadows to make their decisions there, because that's where they aren't seen."[12]

Often we're presented with a binary, false choice: either a charismatic, individualistic leadership model derived from dominant culture or an absence of leaders at all. But we've met so many leaders who model a better way: committed to inclusion, invested in developing other leaders, oriented to power and winning, and welcoming of accountability and strategic debate.

Finally, practical radicals need to *cultivate temperaments* that are less oriented to enforcing orthodoxies and more *attuned to complexity and nuance*. Hierarchy, compromises, and alliances with forces you disagree with are sometimes necessary and need to be assessed based on context. The best movement strategists we studied and talked to show that it is possible to be radical and practical at the same time.

The Shape of This Conjuncture: Movements in a Time of Rupture

There is a lively debate among movement leaders and in academia about whether we're seeing a break from racial neoliberalism, a paradigm that has defined the terrain of struggle for half a century (Chapter 5). Our view is that this is a moment of rupture, when the old system is faltering. What will replace it is yet to be determined, and will be shaped in part by the choices we make. One of the critical fights of our times is to prevent an authoritarian coalition from seizing power. How might some of the strategy models be useful (or not) in that context?

As authoritarians rewrite laws and stack courts with extremists, we can't rely on lawyers to use the formal rules of democracy to protect us. Organizations with sufficient solidarity power are crucial because they can create and enforce norms even in the absence of legal protections. Frances Fox Piven reminds us that even if authoritarians take control of all branches of government, everyday people still have the ultimate power to shut things down and prevent oppressive systems from functioning. We can build solidarity power and lay groundwork now to create the conditions for people to see and use their disruptive power.

Using electoral strategies to capture governing power in broad coalitions of democratic forces is essential. State legislative races and contests for secretary of state, which receive less attention than races for president or the Senate, have become pivotal. We highlight the challenges of progressive governance, including the rarity of examples at any level of government (Chapter 9). We must solve this problem and show that elections matter not only to prevent the worst from happening, but also as a strategy to build power, make people's lives better, expand democracy, and change the rules of the game. (Those steps are also necessary to address the other existential threat of the climate crisis.)

In the near term, there's likely to be less scope for inside-outside policy campaigns at the federal level, and so resources may be appropriately reallocated to the local and state levels. We must get far better at using inside-outside policy campaigns to alter relationships of power. Base-building is essential, particularly in key geographic regions and with key constituencies. Strategy hubs could take up the question of how to reallocate resources and capacity to specific places where the fight will be won or lost.

A rupture will create big opportunities for momentum and narrative campaigns to reshape mass consciousness. We'll need investments in technological innovation to equip organizers with the tools to fight for hearts and minds in a fast-changing, digitally mediated information landscape. One of the best things that could happen in the fight against authoritarianism would be insurgent mass movements that force issues of racial and gender justice, worker rights, and climate change onto the national agenda. Movements on the offense scramble political battle lines, recruit new people, and make the stakes clear.

There is a moral and strategic imperative to reinvest in collective care as the toll of authoritarian policies, climate disasters, and violence grows. Collective care can be strategic when it sustains movement participants and provides on-ramps to participation for people who may be averse to militant action.

In conditions of authoritarian threat, building an outward-facing "recruitment culture"—one that turns the famous quote that the "Right seeks converts while the Left hunts heretics" on its head—is imperative.[13] We cannot win if we do not grow. The old Left strategy of a "popular front" to bring diverse social forces together will need to be adapted for our times.

And we'll need to borrow some tools from the overdog playbook to disrupt the opposition, for example by strategically dividing the authoritarian coalition and undermining its institutional foundations.

Lastly, we need a broad return toward internationalism on the Left, back to the days when abolitionists fought across continents. In this book, with a few exceptions, we've drawn on examples from the United States. But the forces shaping the world—authoritarianism, climate change, corporate power, mass migration, patriarchy, and white supremacy—are global. Overdogs collaborate across borders to suppress democratic movements. We must overcome ingrained provincialism to build practical working relationships with movements around the world. Given the role that the United States has played in repressing Left movements and governments abroad, U.S.-based organizers have a particular responsibility to maintain an international focus.

There is a long history of fighting authoritarianism in the United States—the genius of the Black freedom struggle has inspired movements throughout the world. Since 1965 and the passage of the Voting Rights Act, however, we've been organizing in systems with formal democratic institutions, a free press, and rights of assembly and protest. Most of us were not trained in the methods of nonviolent resistance to authoritarian regimes and movements forged by earlier generations of organizers. So there will be immediate practical benefits for us to engage with organizers around the world. Though not everything can be translated to a U.S. context, there is so much to learn from the successes, failures, theories, and practices of our movement siblings who have more recent experience with authoritarian threats and regimes in other countries.

Mastery of Tradition and the Role of Improvisation

Scholars like Erica Chenoweth and Zeynep Tufekci have found that protest has been less effective in recent years than in the past, including against authoritarian regimes.[14] This is partly because some newer movements have relied too heavily on rapid mobilizations made possible by social media, and neglected deep organizing, strategic disruption, and collective care. Mastery of the underdog lineages will help organizers better meet the challenges of our time. But looking backward is not enough.

Authoritarian regimes are using "smart repression," including new surveillance technologies and big data, in ways that present fresh obstacles. We live in a fractured, media-saturated information environment that is unprecedented. As longtime progressive organizer Anna Galland puts it:

> Technology has shortened the time horizon of our collective focus and accelerated the pace of collective dreaming. Organizers who work with digital tools and are able to get a very rapid read on a mass base of activists have seen that collective outrage cycles have gotten shorter and shorter. At the same time, the reach of visionaries has exploded. We need to be articulating our visions and dreams, and testing them and spreading them, in the reality of a world drenched in digital content.[15]

So practical radicals must improvise to meet the challenges of our time. Ram Narayan, a renowned Indian classical musician, reflected on how a musician works with a raga, a melodic framework that is the basis for improvisation:

> People talk a lot about improvisation. But it has two aspects.... Our teacher gives us a framework for it or body for it.... The performer's job is to put the soul into the body. Every artist must improvise so as to breathe life or spirit into a rag. It is only the performing artist who can do this. And it is done by improvising.[16]

The lineages of Black freedom movements exemplify this dynamic of mastery and improvisation, and organizers today emphasize a politics of care drawing on the Black feminist tradition.[17] New generations of organizers across fields—in climate justice and labor and community organizing—are both returning to fundamentals and "put[ting] the soul into the body."

We were reminded that organizers need both to be connected to the lineage of struggle and to "breathe life" into inherited traditions when, in November of 2022, we traveled to Columbia, South Carolina. As we were finishing this book, we joined hundreds of workers who founded the Union of Southern Service Workers (USSW), a new union supported by the Service Employees International Union (SEIU) that brings together low-wage workers across industries in the region. Workers reviewed the long history of struggle for worker rights in the South, including key lessons, such as the need for a vibrant multiracial coalition and anti-racist politics, the imperative for "community unionism" that links worker and community issues, and the centrality of worker-led direct action and disruption.

The USSW plans to renew those traditions, but with a lot of improvisation; they understand that traditional methods alone won't work. Cookie Bradley, better known as Mama Cookie, has worked in low-wage jobs in the South for forty years and is a leader with the USSW. She wrote, "We have to define what a union is for ourselves, not let those in power do it for us . . . if the rules that govern union organizing don't work for millions of workers, we must demand a new set of rules." USSW adopted a definition of union that doesn't depend on legal recognition or federal recognition: "workers coming together to use our strength in numbers to get things done we can't get done on our own."[18] Having studied strategy for years, we could find no simple formula to overcome the formidable obstacles these workers face—but we believe that Mama Cookie is right. Workers in struggle, drawing on an inspiring lineage and defying the rules, will find a way forward.

We finished this manuscript in early 2023, with the outcome of the war to shape the future still uncertain. We draw inspiration from our movement ancestors, who fought and sometimes prevailed against far greater obstacles than we face, and from organizers today. The best strategists aren't deterred by the challenges. As practical radical John Lewis put it: "Ours is not the struggle of one day, one week, or one year. Ours is not the struggle of one judicial appointment or presidential term. Ours is the struggle of a lifetime, or maybe even many lifetimes, and each one of us in every generation must do our part."[19]

Afterword

Strategy, we argue in *Practical Radicals*, is a bridge from the world as it is to the world as it could be. Knowing which strategies to prioritize begins with a sober assessment of the world as it is: an analysis of the conjuncture (see pages 28 to 30).

The conjuncture we described in the original edition of this book, though, is already out of date. As we write this, the forces of authoritarianism, white nationalism, and nationalism are ascendant, while neoliberalism—always a tough sell—is faltering. But the authoritarian victory is not assured. We are in a period of dangerous contestation. The story will contain twists and turns, back and forths—it will not be linear, and it may not wind up where we expect.

There are things we know about the conjuncture that can help guide us. Racial neoliberalism has produced immense contradictions. It created tremendous hardship and inequality for most of us, while creating unprecedented wealth for a few. That dynamic continues to drive spiraling economic inequality that undermines democracy and even degrades the quality of information most Americans get through the media. The neoliberal economic model is unstable and unsustainable; its economic growth is based on exploiting people and the planet. The authoritarian turn from neoliberalism won't solve those problems and will in fact exacerbate many.

There is a lot we know about the world as it is, but there's also a lot we don't know. We need to study more. Too many organizers and political operatives looked at the 2024 election results and said, "I was right all along," instead of engaging in honest reflection about strengths and weaknesses and organizing practice. Underdogs need to embrace nuance, curiosity, and listening rather than dogmatism or sectarianism. For instance, there is a lot of work to do to revisit or clarify our basic assumptions and terms we use in organizing. We can't afford to be sloppy or simplistic in how we talk about and understand terms like "working class" and "democracy." The "working class" cannot be reduced to non–college-educated white men, and "democracy" cannot be reduced to the narrow confines of the voting booth. This may seem like mere semantics, but it matters—we use language to understand the world, and that understanding informs our long-term strategy.

Our students remind us that simple answers can't explain voting patterns or political alliances. People are a mix of identities and interests and underdog organizing must be prepared to deal with complexity. It's never *just* about economics, or race, or abortion. President Joe Biden governed as a much more economically progressive president than many, us included, expected. Yet this "post neoliberal" economic agenda—something that might have worked for Clinton or Obama had they tried it—was rejected, suggesting that a narrowly economistic approach to policy and politics won't work anymore. We need deeper analysis.

We also need to learn more about the authoritarian alliance. Their coalition is volatile and many potential fissures exist. For example, the alliance between billionaires and some working-class people is inherently unstable, and that presents an important opportunity. It also raises many questions: Why are so many people drawn to support authoritarians around the world? What role does disinformation play? What about identities and emotions? These are the kinds of questions we need to dig into to understand this moment and its contradictions. One of the key findings in *Practical Radicals* was that major movements win not only when they unite underdogs, but when they divide overdogs. When we understand where the fissures are, we can start to drive wedges into them.

Vision and the World as It Could Be

Many of our movement ancestors were motivated by visions of coherent systems or unifying values, such as democracy, national liberation, socialism, or social democracy. People are now mostly cynical of grand visions, often for good reason: many of those visions collapsed, or became corrupted, or proved impossible to win. But part of overdogs' power is that they always have a big vision, something that Stuart Hall and Antonio Gramsci refer to as a hegemonic project. Such visions may be crude, but they are visions, and overdogs are willing to fight for them.

Underdogs need visions of their own. They may not be grand, one-model-fits-all narratives, but they need to go beyond "win the next campaign." They need to build common ground around how society can be better organized, and how humans should treat one another and the planet. We need to be moving toward forms of governance that are true to their promise of a multi-racial democracy and systems for handling the complex economic, political, and climate challenges ahead. How can we mitigate the worst of the crises to come? How can we be our best selves in hard times? How do we develop mechanisms to deal with crisis and conflict? Crucially, we need a lot more thought about an internationalist world. The crises we face can't be solved in one country alone.

We need to create space for deeper dialogue about shared values, and those conversations need to be rooted in the experience and aspirations of real people.

Strategy as a Bridge

Moving from the world as it is to the world as it could be will take all seven strategies. But not all are equally effective, or available, at all times, and some will be more important than others. Base-building and solidarity power are evergreen, and these times call for a doubling-down on that work.

The administration has deliberately "flooded the zone," attempting to keep its opponents confused and unable to focus (this is a variant of the classic overdog strategy to disrupt underdogs' OODA loops by employing the psychological warfare that we discuss in Chapter 16). Their strategy has created sites of struggle and constituencies ripe for organizing everywhere—government workers, 80 million Medicaid beneficiaries, and millions from communities depending on government services that will be withdrawn: teachers, students, parents, scientists, homecare workers, people with disabilities, and many more. The overdog strategy designed to "shock and awe" can be countered by massive organizing campaigns that engage people—especially those who have not been active before and are impacted by the cuts—in large-scale concrete struggles across a rapidly expanding terrain. The Momentum model is useful in scaling organizing quickly to respond to intensifying harms.

Such organizing should be paired with popular education that draws the connections between what is happening across issues, and points out how divide-and-conquer strategies are being used to distract from the real agenda of concentrating money and power at the top. Creative offensive campaigns—for example, large-scale worker organizing campaigns that expose the contradictions in the ruling coalition—are crucial.

Organizing should also happen inside strategically positioned institutions. For example, immigrants are essential as members of many faith-based organizations and unions, and as workers in many sectors of the economy. Churches, unions, and businesses can be powerful bulwarks against mass deportation. Over time, leaders from different sectors who disagree about many things, but agree about the importance of preserving basic rights and the rule of law, can be organized into a united front of the kind that has brought down authoritarian regimes in countries from Poland to Brazil.

Disruption is another key strategy now, in part because the rules are already being undermined, creating disruption whether we like it or not. The overdogs have become clever about anticipating and co-opting common forms of protest like rallies, marches, and public square occupations.[1] Disruption now requires careful research, creativity, and risk-taking. The United Auto Workers (UAW) engaged in effective disruption during their 2023 strike against the big three automakers. But they know they can't win their bigger demands on pensions and health care on their own, so they have invited unions and community organizations around the country to join them in aligning contracts and campaigns for national coordinated action on May 1, 2028. What the UAW leadership understands is that there is power in numbers, and that underdogs who might not think they have much in common do in fact share similar targets in a bigger fight. Successful disruption, in May 2028 and at other times, will require long-term planning, new relationships, bold leaders, and an engaged membership.

The United States has a long tradition of civil resistance strategies—strikes, boycotts, occupations, and other non-violent means of stopping oppressive systems from functioning. These strategies were critical to the success of the civil rights movement in the 1950s and 60s. But fewer and fewer activists have learned these skills in recent decades. We're heartened that many underdog groups are undertaking mass trainings to renew the lineage of nonviolence and civil resistance, teaching thousands of people about how they can exercise the power they have, and deal with repression and surveillance.

Another strategy that is particularly important now is collective care. As climate crises continue, political violence escalates, inequality grows, public services are destroyed, and deportations and family separations rise, we will need to turn to each other. Mutual aid efforts grew in the pandemic, but they were largely centered around meeting individual needs and petered out as people could not sustain that model. We expect them to revive as things get worse and needs increase again, but collective care has to go beyond charity and good works, helping people develop themselves as political actors and leaders, training them to engage in collective decision-making and action, and helping them take bigger risks along the onramp of political engagement.

Electoral work remains important. Overdogs have intensified their efforts to capture state and local governments, understanding that even limited democratic bodies are powerful checks on their power. Underdogs have to stay engaged in this fight. A "block, bridge, and build" approach can inform electoral work: blocking the advance of authoritarian movements while bridging across divides and building underdog organizations and movements. It will also require underdogs to grapple with difficult questions regarding the role of the Democratic Party, unstable fissures within both parties, and growing voter cynicism.

In order to block the growth of the authoritarian movement—electorally and otherwise—underdogs will need to build alliances with elements of the ruling coalition, peeling off overdogs who willingly defect (or can be forced to defect), creating a united front. United front politics will require underdogs to develop one kind of strategy to block authoritarianism and to be prepared to draw a line in the sand on fundamental democratic concerns: persecution of political opponents, use of military force against protestors, and the use of government to shut down key civil society organizations. Bridging across divides and building underdog organizations and movements will require another kind of strategy, one that takes us beyond racial neoliberalism and is centered on liberatory values.

But even the best strategy won't be enough without power. This historic moment should be a reckoning for progressives and the Left, exposing how much power we have not built and how poor and ineffective most of the "strategy" that most groups pursue has been. It is easy to say (and obviously true) that the dire situation we face is due in large part to the overwhelming money and power of our opponents, and to their investment in serious strategy, and the development of a generations of leaders. But that does not let us off the hook. Some progressives and leftists have made wrong turns in recent decades, away from deep strategy work built on a rigorous and honest analysis of the world as it is and toward magical thinking. Instead of mass organizing and base-building, these leaders have turned to alluring shortcuts of various kinds to try to make social change or performative repetition of tactics that no longer work.

Some have even given up on changing the world, choosing to focus their energy on maintaining fragile organizational bureaucracies or on prosecuting sectarian fights with people and groups who should be allies. Achieving governing power requires a lot of messy work to build big coalitions that inevitably involve hard compromises along the way. This work of coalition-building and tactical compromise is not only not respected—it is actively shunned and condemned in many quarters. These failures are now deeply woven into the culture of many organizations in a way that makes them deeply unattractive to most everyday people. Who wants to be part of groups that don't have a serious plan, aren't committed to winning, and are rife with internal conflict rather than offering welcoming spaces of belonging and community? These tendencies were disabling in the long era of racial neoliberalism. In the era of authoritarianism, they are dangerous. We need a new generation of practical radical leaders who are fearless in building a left with a mass base that is serious about strategy and winning.

Getting More Practical and More Radical

We're thrilled to see the ways readers have been using *Practical Radicals*. We continue to hear from people who are using the book in study groups, in organizer training, in developing long-term strategy, in building electoral projects, and in growing new alliances.

We've also heard great ideas about what we could add to a future edition of the book. Readers want to think more about the role of traditional and social media in narrative shift. Overdogs have been successful in getting their story out widely. What are more effective underdog strategies to reach mass audiences? There has always been corporate-controlled media and underdogs have always struggled to find ways to get their message out. But what may have changed is the combination of the pervasiveness of online engagement (for many people, online is now where they spend time, communicate, and form identities) and the collapse of in-real-life organizations like unions, churches, and even, after the pandemic, workplaces. Also, the democratic promise of online engagement seems to be fading, with more corporate (and authoritarian) consolidation.

Similarly, we need to deepen underdog legal, tech, and research strategy, and we need to address how underdog organizations and movements are financed.

There were several ideas we had hoped to address in the book that we were not able to. For instance, there's a need for a more sophisticated model of human motivation, moving beyond "deliverism" (the idea that if you deliver economic improvements, the impacts will automatically shift political commitments) to understand how people develop a sense of their identities, the role of emotions, and what this means for organizing and social change.[2]

Also, we need a *Practical Radicals* international edition! The crises and contradictions of the conjuncture cross borders; we can't get out of this alone. When underdogs have ignored international analysis and organizing it was to their detriment. We wrote about the international movement to abolish slavery of the eighteenth and nineteenth centuries, and we hope to see a new international struggle unite underdogs.

We are in for difficult times ahead, but we continue to find inspiration in our movement ancestors who fought for the world as it should be. The fight will take many of us playing to our various strengths. As the late Harry Belafonte explained, "What makes a movement work are thousands of parts that come together and express itself in favor of a given destination or objective. You have to find men and women who are willing to play the role that each of these things demand." There is a role for everyone. And as another great musician, Beyoncé, reminds us, "Power is not given to you. You have to take it."

———

Listen to the *Practical Radicals* podcast available on www.practicalradicals.org or wherever you get your podcasts.

AFTERWORD

A *Practical Radicals* Discussion Guide is available at https://thenewpress.com/blog/reading-group-guides/practical-radicals-discussion-guide

Acknowledgments

The origins of this book trace back to a delicious pot of homemade chili. Deepak had left Community Change, his movement home for over two decades, and was exploring what should come next. Frances Fox Piven invited Deepak to her apartment for lunch. He brought the beer, she made the chili. Deepak was delighted and surprised that Frances had invited Stephanie and Penny Lewis, another City University of New York (CUNY) colleague. Stephanie and Penny admitted they had no idea why they were there either, but, like Deepak, never said no to Frances.

Frances, a legendary scholar-activist, argued that Deepak should come teach at CUNY's School of Labor and Urban Studies (SLU), and recruited Penny and Stephanie to help make that happen. Frances said that in her experience academia could be a good platform to do movement work (she would know!).

When Deepak came to SLU, he knew he wanted to digest his movement experiences and explore strategy: what strategy is and how it has been done by the Left and the Right, from both practitioner and academic perspectives. Daunted by the task, he recruited Stephanie and Penny to co-design and co-teach a graduate class on "Power and Strategy" for full-time organizers, mostly from community organizations and unions.

Stephanie had been teaching labor studies for a few decades at SLU, and before that, at the University of Massachusetts, Amherst, all the while being deeply involved in labor and other movements. She knew there was a need for such a course. And she hoped it would establish SLU as a "strategy hub," where organizers from various movements could study, learn from one another, and establish rigorous grounded plans together.

Penny brought deep grounding in theory and practice in the labor movement. She took on a major leadership role at the Professional Staff Congress, the CUNY union, so she had to stop teaching the class with us after that first semester, but her fingerprints are all over the class and book. We're immensely grateful that she pushed us to be clear and rigorous in how we developed key concepts.

This book has been a collective endeavor. We workshopped the content with four classes of students who are accomplished campaigners and strategists. We learned more than we taught as we heard them react to theoretical material and case studies. We interviewed dozens of organizers and were inspired by their work.

We also invited over thirty people—students, other movement leaders, and academics—to review some or all of the manuscript, and two dozen of them participated in three focus groups to critique the book. We're grateful to all of them for their crucial feedback: Lydia Avila, Deborah Axt, Sachaly de Leon, Bill Dempsey, Jennifer Disla, Paul Engler, Alex Hertel-Fernandez, Anna Galland, Hahrie Han, Danny HoSang, Alan Jenkins, Lynn Kanter, Kyandra Knight, Penny Lewis, Jamila Michener, Ruth Milkman, Carolina Bank Munoz, Greg Nammacher, Deepak Pateriya, Lorella Praeli, Connie Razza, Lissy Romanow, Shahrzad Shams, Kevin Simowitz, Samir Sonti, Sarah Stockholm, Kyle Strickland, Joel Suarez, Dominique Thomas, Dorian Warren, and Felicia Wong.

We created and compiled tools for movement groups to develop good strategy. We're grateful to the following for allowing us to include their tools and concepts in this book: Bargaining for the Common Good, Chinese Progressive Association, Grassroots Power Project, SCOPE, Maine People's Alliance, and Midwest Academy.

We'd like to especially thank Olivia Heffernan, a student and accomplished journalist and filmmaker who has reported on activism in the United States and around the world. Olivia was our research assistant on the book from nearly the conception of the project, and brought invaluable editorial skills, insight, and organization to what turned out to be a major undertaking. Her dedication and commitment were astounding. We couldn't have done it without her.

We aren't musicians, so we're grateful to Sam Bardfeld, a gifted jazz violinist who helped us sort out our musical metaphors! Jeff Phillips did extraordinary work with the illustrations that bring concepts in the book to life. Thanks also to the team at The New Press, including our editor, Marc Favreau.

Deepak would like to thank his colleagues at SLU who created such a warm and stimulating environment to explore these ideas, especially his department chair, Steve London, Associate Dean Gladys Palma de Schrynemakers, faculty colleagues Penny Lewis and Ruth Milkman, and his co-instructors Cristina Jimenez and Edwin Robinson. Teaching SLU students who are workers, parents, organizers, and active community members has been a source of joy and inspiration. Deepak is a senior fellow at the Roosevelt Institute, which supported us to do much of the research and writing that led to this book. The outstanding team, including Shahrzad Shams, Kyle Strickland, and Felicia Wong, were hugely helpful and wonderfully supportive. Barbara Picower has supported Deepak in many ventures over the years, and he's deeply grateful for her partnership and friendship. This book draws heavily on Deepak's work at Community Change, and he'd like to thank all his superb colleagues there and at partner grassroots organizations around the country, past and present. Being part of a community of organizers with such resilience, grit, and creativity was a life-transforming gift. While writing the book, Deepak worked with colleagues to build a new institution, Leadership for Democracy and Social Justice, to train organizers and strategists. The incredible team at LDSJ is another organizing family. Together we road tested a lot of the concepts in this book. Thank you Jessica Barba Brown, Ricardo Andres Anez Carrasquel, Nathalie Delpeche, Jennifer Disla, Abigail Feder-Kane, Sasha Graham, Gara LaMarche, Jake Levin, Noelia Morales, Andy Rich, Chris Torres, and Tiffany Traille.

Deepak wouldn't be anywhere without the love of his life, Harry Hanbury, who believed in the importance of this book when he had his doubts, read multiple drafts of it, and provided superb editorial, substantive, and fact-checking help. Deepak's parents, Madhu and Girija Bhargava, lived with the book too and the lessons of kindness, justice, and love they taught him by example shaped his outlook on the world. A key mentor, Pablo Eisenberg, a dear friend and movement colleague Susan Sandler, and a new friend and wise soul Phil Cushman died in 2022—their influence is all over these pages.

You don't get far or last long in movement work without a community of colleagues, mentors, friends, and co-conspirators. Deepak would like to thank his comrades, all of whom had an impact on this book: Akwe Amosu, Sulma Arias, Drew Astolfi, Mehrdad Azemun, Sung E Bai, Oxiris Barbot, Laura Barrett, Ryan Bates, Syd Beane, Lawrence Benito, May Boeve, Ed Booth, Heather Booth, Kevin Borden, Seth Borgos, Dan Cantor, John Carr, Pamela Chiang, Sue Chinn, Corin Coetzee, Larry Cohen, Peter Colavito, DaMareo Cooper, Rob Crawford, Mary Dailey, Gary Delgado, Bill Dempsey, Lisa Donner, Peter Edelman, Don Elmer, Petra Falcon, Dalinda Fermin, Henry Fernandez, Julia Foster, Jane Fox-Johnson, Anna Galland, Anna Garcia-Ashley, Robert Gass, Alisa Glassman, George Goehl, Gabe Gonzalez, Marie Gonzalez, Marissa Graciosa, Arnie Graf, Anton Gunn, Pronita Gupta, Sarita Gupta, Staci Haines, Lee Ann Hall, Jean Hardisty, Jerry Hauser, Connie Cagampang Heller, Jonathan Heller, Wade Henderson, Mary Kay Henry, Alex Hertel-Fernandez, Marielena Hincapié, Arlene Holt-Baker, Zoe Hudson, Maude Hurd, Pramila Jayapal, Alan Jenkins, Cristina Jimenez, Jane Fox Johnson, Jerry Jones, Sabrina Jones, Yolanda Jones, Kate Kahan, Lynn Kanter, Jennifer Kern, Steve Kest, Larry Kleinman, Gara LaMarche, Mary Lassen, Madeline Lee, Grecia Lima, Cristina Lopez, Rudy Lopez, Rebecca Lurie, Kica Matos, Mary Beth Maxwell, Tori O'Neal McElrath, Eliseo Medina, Jamila Michener, Eva Millona, Andy Mott, Cecilia Muñoz, Christine Neuman-Ortiz, Darlene Nipper, Kirk Noden, Ali Noorani, Manuel Pastor, Deepak Pateriya, Mayron Payes, Steve Phillips, Barbara Picower, john powell, Lorella Praeli, Ramon Ramirez, Marvin Randolph, Connie Razza, Betsy Reed, Deirdra Reed, Lenora Bush Reese, Maria Rodriguez, Barbara

Rosenthal, Justin Ruben, Angelica Salas, Gary Sandusky, Steve Savner, Juliet Schor, Charlene Sinclair, TK Somanath, Rich Stolz, Karen Stults, Sean Thomas-Breitfeld, Gustavo Torres, Nsé Ufot, Javier Valdés, Bill Vandenberg, Dorian Warren, Maya Wiley, Ben Wilkins, Jaime Worker, Ryan Young, and Son Ah Yun. He would also like to thank the British wing of his family, the Trenthams—David, Ian, Kamalini, and Neil—for their love and for forcing him to defend his views! Friends Megan Cytron, Christian Perez, and Oscar Perez-Cytron offered a nourishing and happy refuge abroad. Friends Alisa Glassman, Mike Mangiaracina, and Milo Mangiaracina shared joy and insight.

Finally, Deepak was lucky to be mentored in teaching and academia by Stephanie. Working together on the class and the book has been a peak experience of collaboration. The process has been stimulating, joyful, and occasionally madcap (oh, that first test of the technology with organizers from around the country . . . unforgettable!). He's learned so much from her about labor, Left history, and how to weave together a life of ideas and activism in a way that is too rarely done. He's grateful (and surprised) that she said yes to the assortment of wild schemes he proposed.

Stephanie has been lucky to have a number of work and political homes that have helped her integrate theory and practice, from graduate school mentors at the University of Wisconsin, Madison, to colleagues at the University of Massachusetts, Amherst and CUNY, along with comrades in LeftRoots, Convergence, Solidarity, Labor Notes, and her work in labor and living-wage campaigns. In particular she is grateful to some of the practical radicals she has worked with and learned from in political and academic work, as well as friends with whom she has discussed work: Rishi Awatramani, Judy Atkins, Gianpaolo Baiocchi, Rob Baril, Ilana Berger, Johanna Brenner, Mark Brenner, Paula Chakravartty, Dan Clawson, Mary Ann Clawson, Dave Cohen, Max Elbaum, Ellen David Friedman, Becky Givan, Jen Kern, NTanya Lee, Ted Levine, Dan Lutz, Biju Mathew, Faron McLurkin, Mark Meinster, Calvin Miaw, Rick Mines, Carolina Bank Munoz, Max Page, Maria Poblet, Catherine Sameh, Rachel Sherman, Paul Sonn, Alex Tom, Eve Weinbaum, Steve Williams, and Erik Olin Wright. Her LeftRoots cadre circle provided support throughout the pandemic lows: AL, Alex, Farihah, George, Katherine, and Mike; the In It to Win It team helped her sharpen her strategic thinking.

Her colleagues at the CUNY School of Labor and Urban Studies make this work not only possible, but a joy. Ruth Milkman and Penny Lewis in particular have been a constant source of support. Samir Sonti and Joel Suarez gave invaluable feedback on the book draft. Working with the staff and students at the Leadership for Democracy and Social Justice has been inspiring, and she has learned much from co-instructors Cristina Jimenez and Edwin Robinson. And it would be impossible to list all the students from whom she has learned, but they are the audience she writes for first and foremost.

Stephanie is beyond grateful for her partner, Michael Goodwin, who helped her work out ideas and maintain confidence in the project in her most panicked moments. As a professional writer and editor, he was able to provide extensive editing, making the book much better (and shorter!) as a result. Her writing, and life, is better all around with his presence.

Finally, Stephanie is thankful to Deepak for inviting her to teach the course and write the book. She wasn't sure what she was getting into but is overjoyed she agreed to participate. Deepak brought energy, passion, intellectual curiosity, and open-mindedness to the project and is the kind of colleague that makes work fun. Stephanie and Deepak discussed, debated, and worked out complex ideas over several years, learning from one another as well as from the students and materials. She has so much gratitude to Deepak for this opportunity.

Tools, Prompts, and Resources

We have gathered a set of tools for you to better understand and apply the strategy concepts explored in this book. A few are borrowed (with permission), and most we created to fill gaps. Most of the tools are designed for small groups of three to six people. Some of the exercises can be done within thirty minutes, and others will take considerable time to complete.

We encourage assigning a facilitator, notetaker, and timekeeper for each group completing the tool. If you ask groups to report back, provide a template of exactly what to report and a time limit. Facilitator cards are one helpful way to organize report backs (https://www.facilitator.cards/).

This section includes the following:

> **Tools:** Longer exercises that help groups develop strategy
> **Prompts:** Discussion questions or self-reflection exercises to understand the concepts in the book
> **Resources:** Books, websites, articles, and other resources that provide more tools and background reading

1. Shared Values 345
2. Prompt: Envisioning a Future World—Two Reflections 347
3. Conjunctural Analysis................................... 348
4. Reverse Engineering 352
5. Prompt: Strategy Fundamentals 355
6. Resources: Strategy Toolkits and Training Organizations 357
7. Power for Underdogs..................................... 359
8. Writing a Powell Memorandum for the Left 363
9. New Grooves: Application of the Seven Models 364
10. Prompt: Are All Strategies Strategic? 378
11. Leadership Identification 379
12. Collective Care 381
13. Bargaining for the Common Good.......................... 383
14. Resources: Holistic Strategy Development................... 385
15. Disruptive Chokepoints 386
16. Prompt: Organizations, Movements, and Times of Upsurge 389
17. Tabletop Exercise: The Worker Upsurge......................391
18. OODA Loops 395
19. Resources: Narrative Shift................................. 397
20. Prompt: Electoral Work 398
21. Strategic Debate 399
22. Policy Feedback Loops 402
23. Structural Reforms....................................... 405
24. Momentum 406
25. Resources: Principled Struggle, Generative Conflict, and Unity . 407
26. Prompt: Racial and Gender Equity 409
27. Prompt: Balancing Purpose and Belonging...................411
28. Prompt: Practices to Support Individual Creativity and Innovation..413

29. Lean Startup for Social Change 415
30. Prompt: Improving the Strategic Capacity of Teams 417
31. Resources: Learning from the Opposition 419
32. Successful Failures 420
33. Power Analysis 423
34. Strategy Chart.. 426
35. Leadership Ladder 427
36. Long-Term Agenda 430

Tool 1 // Shared Values

Part 1:

1. Start by sharing a definition of *values*, such as the one provided here:

    Values are fundamental beliefs about the world that help guide behaviors and attitudes. Values help make sense of the world and determine what is important.
    Examples: Compassion, integrity, dependability, courage, sustainability, kindness

2. Instruct the group:

    Everyone should take five minutes on their own to think of particular spaces or places that they love and appreciate and in which they feel safe, fully alive, and themselves. What are those spaces like? Have each person translate the description of those spaces into values they believe should guide a future world they want to build, and write five to ten values, each on a sticky note.

3. Ask people to place their sticky notes on a board and group the ones that are the same.

4. Starting with the most common values on the board, groups should draft a one- to two-sentence definition of the value. The definition may involve similar values (for example, democracy and participation). See if you can reach an agreement on a shared definition.

5. Try to find two to five values that the group agrees are fundamental to a shared vision of a future world.

Part 2:

6. In small groups, think about your workplaces, schools, health care systems, and laws, and then do the following:

    - Name the values these institutions rest upon or promote.
    - How do those values compare to the ones your group named in step 5?
    - What are a few things about these institutions, systems, or structures that would need to change to be in alignment with your group's values?

Tool 2 // Prompt: Envisioning a Future World—Two Reflections

1. Reflect on your life experiences. Is there a moment when you felt most free and liberated? Or a scene from a book or movie, some artwork or music, that opened your mind to another world that was more like the one you hope to build?

    What was it about that experience that felt liberating? Did it involve a group of people? If so, were they people you knew, or strangers? Was it something that pushed the boundaries of the familiar? Did the experience change your worldview? What did you learn from that moment about the kind of world you hope to build?

2. What would it look and feel like for everyone to feel cared for?
    - In words or pictures, share that experience.
    - The facilitator should bring a pile of photos of positive things, emotions, interactions of people and nature, and then ask people to pick one to three images and describe why they would include them in the imagined future. Or, time permitting, make a collage.
    - After, the facilitator should ask follow-up questions to call people into more concrete visioning: What would it feel like to live in this world? What would you see when you first step outside in the morning? With whom would you interact?

Tool 3 // Conjunctural Analysis

Use this rubric to begin compiling information that could be used in a conjunctural analysis.

Form of Power	Power from Above (Overdog Power)	Power from Below (Underdog Power)
Ideological	What is the current "common sense" that explains how our society works? How strong or fragile is it? Where are there potential cracks? What is the prevailing "story of us"? (our history as we are taught it)	What is an alternative "common sense"? Is there an alternative "story of us"? Who is the "other" in the story? Is there one that doesn't create an "other"? How popular are alternative stories?
Economic	What are the current major driving forces in the economy? Who controls what we produce? Who holds wealth? Where are there vulnerabilities in the dominant system?	Where do movements have the power to impact the economic interests of those in power? Where are workers strategically placed so that they are difficult to replace? What are the "chokepoints" in economic production and distribution? (Tool 15.) And which of those do we have access to influence?

Form of Power	Power from Above (Overdog Power)	Power from Below (Underdog Power)
Political	Who is in power across the three branches of government? Given that, where can we expect contradictions, stalemates, or conflicts within or across the branches of government? Who is in the current coalition of the political parties? Who's in? Who's left out? What or who is up for grabs or shifting?	What are our sources of power in government? What laws and policies can we use or pass to build more power?
Military (including police and border patrol)	What powers does the military have? What is the state of the relationship between the military and government? How does the military work to keep us down? What powers do police and border patrol have?	How have our movements related to the military in the past? How can we reduce the influence of the military and police? What is our relation to the police? Can we/should we align with them to enforce laws (such as access to voting, prevention of wage theft)? How prepared are we to respond to violence from the state or non-state actors?

Form of Power	Power from Above (Overdog Power)	Power from Below (Underdog Power)
Solidarity	What associations and networks do those in power have? Who are members of the ruling coalition (thinking across economic, political, military and ideological spheres)? What sectors, groups, people? Which ones are key to preventing us from making change? Where are there or could there be divisions in the ruling coalition? How might we disrupt the ruling coalition, drive a wedge, cause layers to peel off?	What organizations do we have? How many members? What resources do they have? How strong is their internal cohesion and member participation? How well do these organizations work together? Are there networks that allow for organizations to operate cohesively as an ecosystem? Who is energized on our issue but has no organization? Who is passively supportive and should be moved to take action? How can we drive a wedge to make it impossible to be neutral, and appealing and meaningful to join our side? Who else across the ecosystem is taking responsibility for organizing those people? Where are there gaps? Given the events in the coming year, what signals will our base and constituencies be getting from the media about what matters? For instance, if it's a general election year, there will be a lot of media coverage around that. How can we build off of that energy to bring people into our organization or urge them to take action? How do we create a majority coalition? Who do we need in our coalition? How many people? Why?

Form of Power	Power from Above (Overdog Power)	Power from Below (Underdog Power)
Disruptive	How are elites causing disruption/chaos?	What are examples of non-economic disruption? Perhaps disrupting the status quo or norms (see Tool 6 for Gene Sharp's 198 methods of nonviolent action)
		Where are the chokepoints? (Tool 15.) Are we located in position to take advantage of those? Do we have enough solidarity power to use disruptive power?

Tool 4 // Reverse Engineering

1. Define the outcome precisely.

   This reverses the way strategy is often done. Usually we start from what we have and ask how we can put it to use. Or, we might start with a problem: workers are underpaid; incomes are too unequal; police brutality in Black communities; the Earth's temperature is rising.

   Instead, start by defining an outcome as clearly as you can. Outcomes are clear and measurable—you will know when it has happened. The outcomes should be grounded in long-term vision and values.

   Examples of outcomes:

   - Ten thousand workers in industry X organized into a union by 2028
   - Reduce homelessness in New York City by 80 percent by 2030

2. Clarify the single shift in the environment that would produce that outcome.

   This is an exercise in radical reductionist thinking. The tendency in most strategy, especially on the Left, is to add multiple parts and subparts to keep people on board a plan. The result is often mush. Instead, in this exercise, we are forcing ourselves to commit fully: what is the *one* cause (A) that would result in outcome (B)?

   This is the central element of reverse engineering. You should go beyond the obvious (for example: to win the election, we need to win more votes). This tool is an invitation to find the deepest causal mechanism.

   It requires blunt, honest critique. Since everything rides on getting this right, everyone, including whoever proposes it, has to welcome interrogating the idea.

   Examples of causes:

   - To win a union of low-wage workers in a conservative southern city, a traditional organizing campaign won't work

because the rules are stacked against workers. We need *sustained disruption by thousands of workers* that scares corporate and political leaders into seeking a settlement.
- To break the authoritarian coalition, we need to peel away support from large multinational corporations by raising the cost of their neutrality or support of far-Right candidates.

3. "Vivid description": What would it look like if this were actually happening?

   Once you've identified the potential shift, you need to imagine living it. What would be going on? Examples? Who is doing what? How are targets responding?

   Example:

   - Thousands of workers in a conservative southern city engage in slowdowns, walkouts, and strikes that disrupt business; workers and allies organize a strike fund to support the workers; the workers' cause becomes a defining fight that is part of popular culture and draws in more workers and community supporters; the movement reshapes the political battle lines in the upcoming election. You should consider *why* the elements of the vivid description are essential to victory. For example, is the strike fund organized to create a sense of broad public support, or is its function to enable workers to sustain a strike that would otherwise be devastating for them?

4. Necessary conditions: What needs to happen?

   All underdog groups operate with scarce resources. Disciplined strategy requires making hard choices about how and where to concentrate time, people, and money.

   With your core team, brainstorm a list of things that need to happen in order to put the cause that will produce the desired effect into motion. For example, for sustained disruption in a conservative southern city to occur, folks might say that there needs to be a core leadership team of workers, organized community support including from clergy, support from elected officials or celebrities, and a massive organizing drive to reach large numbers of workers. You would then ask members of the core team to debate and vote on whether each proposed condition is *necessary* to have or *nice* to have in order to create sustained disruption. For example, the team might decide on the one hand that support from elected officials or celebrities would be nice to have, but is not essential to success. On the other hand, large-scale outreach to workers and worker leadership could be seen as essential. The group might debate what kind or level of community support is necessary at the beginning of the campaign. Once the group settles on "necessary conditions," they can work on the specifics of what it would take to make this happen.

5. Operationalize it.

   Take the resources and people you have and identify what's needed. What new resources and new allies are required to go all in for this big bet? What do you need for the cause (A) to produce the outcome (B)? You may discover that A is impossible—even with more resources—in which case, you begin again with step 1.

   Example:

   - Stop several existing lines of work and redirect X dollars and Y staff to a campaign to organize low-wage workers, build a worker-led organizing committee, and engage in large-scale popular education leading to disruption. Recruit X, Y, and Z allies to help build a national strike fund and establish community/faith coalitions to back the workers. Develop a cultural campaign and invest X resources to reach Y audiences that features workers' voices in popular and social media and recruits artists to shape the narrative.

Tool 5 // Prompt: Strategy Fundamentals

When embarking on a new campaign or organizing drive, here are some questions that a strategy team could ask:

Choices. Are you making choices to commit resources to specific strategies that will have the greatest impact? Or have you built a laundry list of ideas that you won't be able to execute well? What have you decided *not* to do? (See Tool 21: Strategic Debate.)

Empathy. Do you understand the deep motivations of your target (decision makers) and your organized opposition? Can you predict how they will respond to some of your plans? What actions are likely to get targets to move in the direction you want them to? What does the target expect you to do? If you don't know the answers to these questions, what research could you do to better understand the motivations of decision makers and the opposition? (Similar questions could be asked about your own base or persuadable people in the general population.)

Alliances. Who are the key allies you will depend on to build this campaign? Do you understand their motivations? What sources of power do they have that you don't have? (See Tool 33: Power Analysis, Tool 7: Power for Underdogs, and Tool 3: Conjunctural Analysis.)

Cause and Effect. In its simplest form, what action are you proposing that you expect will produce which outcome? What Action A will produce Outcome B? Is that logic compelling and convincing? Are there opportunities to test your hypothesis about cause and effect?

War of Attrition or Annihilation? Are you seeking to get the opponent to the bargaining table to negotiate an agreement? What's the shape of the agreement you can imagine? Or, if you imagine winning outright and being able to dictate terms, what kind of victory will allow you to do that?

Where Does Strategy Come From? Who is on the team making the strategy that will guide the campaign? Who makes decisions to revise the strategy in the heat of battle? How will you meet the need to make fast decisions when necessary? Who is consulted and informed along the way? What processes are necessary to check in with stakeholders to get feedback?

Scripted or Improvisational? How many steps or actions are you scripting at the beginning of this campaign? How long do you expect to follow a scripted plan? As the opponent makes moves of their own, when might you shift to an improvisational response? What freedom do leaders at various levels of the campaign have to experiment? (See Tool 36: Long-Term Agenda.)

Force or Guile? What parts of the campaign, if any, depend on surprise or deception? Are there actions that are designed to confuse, disorient, or demoralize, rather than overpower the opponent? (See Tool 18: OODA Loops.)

Tool 6 // Resources: Strategy Toolkits and Training Organizations

Strategy Development Toolkits and Worksheets

- Assessing Your Organization's Strategic Capacity, by P3 Lab (Jane Booth-Tobin, Kal Munis, Lynsy Smithson-Stanley, Hahrie Han)
- Beautiful Trouble Toolbox, https://beautifultrouble.org/
- The Change Agency Toolkit, https://thechangeagency.org/toolkit/
- Gene Sharp, "198 Methods of Nonviolent Action," https://wri-irg.org/en/resources/2008/gene-sharps-198-methods-nonviolent-action
- Bill Moyers, Movement Action Plan, https://commonslibrary.org/resource-bill-moyers-movement-action-plan/
- Kimberly Bobo, Steve Max, and Jackie Kendall. 2001. *Organizing for Social Change: Midwest Academy Manual for Activists*. Santa Ana, CA: Seven Locks Press.
- Joan Minieri and Paul Getsos. 2007. *Tools for Radical Democracy*. John Wiley and Sons.
- adrienne maree brown. 2017. *Emergent Strategy: Shaping Change, Changing Worlds*. Chico, CA: AK Press.
- Elsa A. Ríos and Surei Quintana, 2021. "Love Notes to Our Social Justice Leaders." Strategies for Social Change, LLC.

Training and Consulting Organizations

- Grassroots Power Project
- Labor Notes
- Leadership for Democracy and Social Justice
- Midwest Academy
- Momentum

- Strategic Corporate Research Summer School, Cornell School of Industrial and Labor Relations, and the AFL-CIO
- Training for Change

Training Organizations with a Focus on Building Healthy and Effective Teams and Organizations

- Black Organizing for Leadership and Dignity (BOLD)
- Generative Somatics
- Management Center
- Rockwood Institute
- Wildfire

Tool 7 // Power for Underdogs

1. For this exercise, assume one of the following options:

   - You are in the leadership of a community organization in a large city; your group joins a coalition to raise taxes on the wealthy in the state.
   - You and your colleagues have just been elected as officers of your union and are looking to improve wages and working conditions (you can choose what kind of workplace/sector it is).
   - You and your neighbors have been dealing with a landlord who won't fix the heat or do basic repairs. They just announced a rent increase.
   - You are part of a climate justice group working to achieve a just transition in your state, both by reducing fossil fuel emissions, and by increasing investments in green sources of energy that benefit low-income communities and communities of color.

2. Using the chart, analyze the following:

   - What forms of power do you currently have? If you don't know, what kind of research would be necessary to figure it out?
   - How might you be able to build more power? Can you use one form of power to build another?

Form of Power	Definition	Factors to Consider
Solidarity	Ability to work collectively (in workplace, organization, sector, or society) Vote as a bloc Take care of one another	Number of members (and the size relative to the number of workers/people in the sector) Resources (money, meeting space, support staff) Internal cohesion, depth of commitment Leadership development and training capacity Strategic capacity Union/organizational democracy Level of militancy Systems of communication and care
Disruptive	Ability to cause disruption and have economic impact, the power to wound (in the workplace and/or in the economy) Ability to block those in control from engaging in racist or sexist practices	Do you have scarce skills? Are you easily replaceable? Location in the workplace, supply chain, economy, and in terms of social reproduction How are white supremacy and patriarchy replicating themselves? Are there ways to disrupt those processes (laws, norms, practices, etc.)?

Form of Power	Definition	Factors to Consider
Ideological	Ability to gain public support/influence "common sense" to shift the narrative in your issue's favor	What is the "common sense" around your issue?
		How much does the public know about your issue/goals, and how might you influence that?
		What groups do your co-workers or organizational members belong to? What groups might support you? What groups will you speak to?
		What tools/resources do you have to influence the "common sense"? (Access to media, ability to engage in actions to get attention, etc.)
Political	The rights people have gained through past struggle (laws, regulations, union contracts)	What are the labor and employment laws, housing laws, voting rights, civil rights—on the federal, state, and city levels?
	The authority to govern	How well are laws enforced?
	The ability to pass laws	What laws are you in a position to change or improve enforcement of?
		Are you or members of your organization in elected office? Or in positions within city/state agencies?
		Do you have a union? How good is your contract?

Form of Power	Definition	Factors to Consider
Economic	The ability to control what is produced, distributed, consumed Ownership/control of wealth, factories, land, machines, labor, and other resources needed to produce goods and services to sustain the economy	What jobs do you hold? Are you able to stop the production, distribution, and transportation of goods and services? Do you have strike funds? Do you have savings? Are you able to run your own production and services?
Military	Control of armed forces Control of police	Knowledge of police infiltration and de-escalation tactics Are you able to defend yourselves and your community; for example, through nonviolence training?

Tool 8 // Writing a Powell Memorandum for the Left

In 1971, Lewis Powell wrote a memo to the U.S. Chamber of Commerce, laying out a thirty-year plan for corporate power. Powell's central concern was restoring the hegemony of the free-market capitalist ideology and weakening its opponents.

1. Have everyone read the Powell memo (available in many places online).
2. Break into small groups of approximately five people. Your task is to begin writing a Powell memo for the Left.
3. Discuss:
   - What is the central thrust of your "Powell memo"—your thirty-year plan for the Left? (Powell was trying to restore the dominance of free market ideology; what is your goal?)
   - Thinking as Powell does about movement infrastructure, what specific institutions might you try to take over, build, or destroy? For example: Delegitimize a major conservative media outlet? Capture the Democratic Party? Take over the state legislature, and if so, where? Recruit churches back to the Left? How? Which ones? How would you engage schools and universities in your plan? Would you try to divide the opposition? For example, break small business from big business?
   - To whom would you write the Powell memo for the Left?
4. Report back to the large group using the following template:

   Our long-term vision is: _____
   Our memo is addressed to: _____
   Three key elements of our thirty-year plan are:

   _____
   _____
   _____

Tool 9 // New Grooves: Application of the Seven Models

The goal of this tool is to open up your thinking to alternative ways of addressing an issue from other traditions of social change. For example, if your default approach is to think in terms of base-building, you would look at one of the other seven models for transformative change (perhaps the one we find most unfamiliar or challenging) and play out what it would look like to approach the situation from that framework.

If the issue we wanted to change was the crisis of affordable housing, displacement, and gentrification in a big city, we might do the following:

1. Look at how to build a mass citywide tenants organization (**base-building**).
2. See how to spark or add fuel to the fire of a rent-strike movement to force landlords into concessions (**disruption**).
3. See how to design a campaign to challenge the dominant story about housing in favor of an alternative story, and to move public opinion in that direction through communication strategies, cultural work, and dramatic action (**narrative shift**).
4. Define a strategy to "electoralize" affordable housing—through a ballot initiative or by getting a candidate to run on a bold housing platform in a primary against an established, high-profile incumbent (**electoral change**).
5. Develop a legislative campaign for affordable housing through the city council that is at the "left edge of the possible" and develop campaign plans to move key swing legislators whose votes are needed to win (**inside-outside campaign**).
6. Develop a bold north star goal, create a polarizing fight to galvanize active supporters, and create training and pathways to support large-scale distributed action to move the "common sense" on the issue and shift support in key pillars of society for the demand (**momentum**).
7. Create a mutual aid network for tenants in which tenants provide

help to each other in addressing the challenges they face as a pathway to recruit and politicize more people (**collective care**).

Using the New Grooves tables as guides, first sketch out how you'd address the issue using the logic of the model most familiar to you. Then, describe how you would develop a strategic response using an unfamiliar model. At the end, note any insight you gained that could apply to your current work.

New Grooves: Key Components of Seven Strategy Models Part 1

Strategy	Form of Power	Theory of Change	Examples of Practitioners and Theorists	Protagonists and Structure	Goals and Methods
Base-Building—Community	Solidarity	Lots of people, acting in solidarity, with discipline and for the long term → pressure politicians, corporations, landlords, or institutions to make change	Ella Baker, Saul Alinsky, SNCC, Cesar Chavez, IAF, ACORN Charles Payne, Theda Skocpol, Aldon Morris, Hahrie Han	Organizers, elected leaders, members Representative and usually formally democratic structure	Demands are usually specific, immediate, winnable (they can be more ambitious); issues are chosen and defined in terms of member self-interest; recruitment of new people; listening sessions; membership dues; democratic participation; systematic leadership development
Base-Building—Labor	Solidarity	Lots of workers, acting in solidarity, with discipline and for the long term → pressure employers and politicians to make change	A. Philip Randolph, William Z. Foster, Mary Harris "Mother" Jones, Rose Schneiderman, John L. Lewis, Emma Tenayuca, "Big Bill" Haywood, Lucy Parsons, Flint sit-down strikers; most labor unions begin with a base-building model	Members, shop stewards, elected leaders, organizers Representative and usually formally democratic structure	Demands are specific, immediate, winnable (though can be more abstract); issues are chosen and defined in terms of member self-interest; recruitment of new people; membership dues; democratic participation; systematic leadership development

Strategy	Form of Power	Theory of Change	Examples of Practitioners and Theorists	Protagonists and Structure	Goals and Methods
Disruption	Disruptive	Underdogs willing to take risks → stop the functioning of an oppressive system → create a moral, economic, and political crisis → demands are met	Rev. Wyatt Tee Walker, Johnnie Tillmon, Frances Fox Piven, Lisa Fithian, Bayard Rustin, SNCC, Communist Party in the 1930s, ACT UP, W.E.B. DuBois, disability rights movement (ADAPT)	Disruptive movements: poor or other marginalized people for whom conventional methods haven't worked; loosely coordinated and under no one's control; organizations may fan the flames Disruptive campaigns: planned by organizations	Focus on disrupting an oppressive system and forcing concessions from overdogs who respond out of fear or economic stress; does not require majority popular support to succeed; loose network of activists connected to movement hubs; growth through energy, passion of actions, evidence of success
Narrative Shift	Ideological	Storytelling, creative direct actions, and communication strategies grounded in organizing → Make a "far out," unpopular, or politically unfeasible idea part of the new common sense	Occupy activists, Cristina Jimenez, Alan Jenkins, Rashad Robinson, Anat Shenkar Osario, Opportunity Agenda, Race Forward, marriage equality movement, immigrant youth movement	Movements that emphasize storytelling Activists, cultural workers, media, artists, communications-based organizations, educators, journalists	Change the "common sense" about an issue or problem; culture change Storytelling by directly impacted people; pop culture; creative actions; media and communications; organizing; education

Strategy	Form of Power	Theory of Change	Examples of Practitioners and Theorists	Protagonists and Structure	Goals and Methods
Electoral Change	Political	Independent organizations accountable to a base engage large numbers of voters to participate in multiple ways (vote, call, lobby) over multiple election cycles → Win elections and govern	Anthony Thigpenn, Nsé Ufot, Maurice Mitchell, Democratic Socialists of America, Bayard Rustin, Community Change Action, UNITE HERE	Organizations engaged in integrated voter engagement Parties and party-like organizations and coalitions	Taking government power through elections to achieve major social change Build a political power base through elections, rather than focus only on electing candidates State or national organizations engaging in year-round organizing and electoral work to connect issues and elections
Inside-Outside Campaigns	Solidarity Political Ideological	Diverse coalition of groups with a large social base + allied policymakers craft a bill "on the left edge of the possible" + campaign to organize legislators + luck of a political opening → policy change	Heather Booth, Pramila Jayapal, Frances Perkins, Health Care for America Now (HCAN), Midwest Academy	Progressive elected and appointed officials working with outside organizations and coalitions to enact major social policy reforms	Win a concrete, major policy reform in the medium term, when the balance of forces is nearly equally divided Coalition building; development of specific policy goals and targets; orchestration between "insiders" and "outsiders"

TOOLS, PROMPTS, AND RESOURCES 369

Strategy	Form of Power	Theory of Change	Examples of Practitioners and Theorists	Protagonists and Structure	Goals and Methods
Momentum	Solidarity Disruptive Ideological	Polarizing campaigns that attract thousands of people inspired by a compelling vision → challenge institutions that uphold a social consensus → charge the common sense and make big policy victories possible	Sunrise Movement, Movement for Black Lives, Gandhi, Momentum.org, Mark and Paul Engler	A central movement hub that coordinates a broad network of activists engaged in distributed organizing with a shared goal	Make a big, overarching policy change that is not winnable in the short term possible in the future Harness or create a "whirlwind" of mass action through polarization—create a platform for distributed action to weaken the "pillars" holding up the current social consensus
Collective Care	Solidarity Ideological	Mutual aid/support, healing, meeting urgent needs → allows more people to participate in organizations/movements, take greater risks + changes people's identity and sense of agency + prefigures alternatives → new openings and horizons for social change	Harriet Tubman, Ella Baker, cooperative movement, mutual aid Cara Page, Kindred Southern Justice Healing Collective, Mia Mingus, Dean Spade, Deva Woodly	Organizations, volunteer networks, and movements that prioritize the physical, economic, and emotional well-being of people affected by injustice and trauma, connected to a larger vision for transformative change	Meet immediate needs for survival and well-being; build a network of mutual aid, tapping creativity Participants' sense of agency and identity shifts over time; can be a path to movement recruitment; political and policy solutions emerge organically

Key Components of Seven Strategy Models Part 2

Strategy	Tactical Repertoire	What Does Winning Mean?	Time Horizon + When the Model Is Most Effective	How It Works with Other Models	Strengths and Weaknesses
Base-Building—Community	Accountability sessions; direct action; strikes; negotiation with targets Discipline and carefully orchestrated, planned actions	Demands are wholly or partly achieved; organization is stronger at the end of the campaign than at the beginning and gets "credit" for the win	Evergreen, but especially useful in slower periods in movement cycles, laying the groundwork for political opportunities or movement upsurges "Trench warfare"—change mostly comes in small increments over time Seeks to establish permanent institutions	Works well with electoral change and inside-outside campaigns Relies on disruptive movements for exponential growth and on collective care for sustainability Less history of combining it with narrative shift and momentum	Concrete wins that improve people's lives; builds grassroots leadership; can engage in struggle over years Can be slow and plodding, or focus narrowly on the interests of existing members, and on small local issues to the exclusion of bigger, systemic issues

Strategy	Tactical Repertoire	What Does Winning Mean?	Time Horizon + When the Model Is Most Effective	How It Works with Other Models	Strengths and Weaknesses
Base-Building—Labor	Shopfloor direct action, collective bargaining, strikes, lobbying, political engagement	Demands are wholly or partly achieved; successful election for union representation; win a collective bargaining agreement; social change for the working class	Evergreen, but especially useful in slower periods in movement cycles, laying the groundwork for upsurge in worker organizing and action "Trench warfare"—change mostly comes in small increments over time Seeks to establish permanent institutions	Works closely with electoral change and inside-outside campaigns; relies on disruptive movements for exponential growth and on collective care for sustainability; less history of combining it with narrative shift and momentum. Some unions were formed out of collective care and some have attempted to revive this	Concrete wins that improve people's lives; builds worker leadership; can engage in struggle over years, can build powerful institutions that have great impact on society Can be slow and incremental, focused narrowly on the interests of existing members, bureaucratic, undemocratic and corrupt; at times works to reinforce the status quo against other underdog movements

Strategy	Tactical Repertoire	What Does Winning Mean?	Time Horizon + When the Model Is Most Effective	How It Works with Other Models	Strengths and Weaknesses
Disruption	Mass unruly protest, occupations of workplaces/public spaces/buildings, workplace strikes, "wildcat" strikes, rent strikes; may be stealthy, as with the general strike of enslaved people; disruptive movements can be wild, unpredictable, and edgy; disruptive actions can be planned and disciplined	Mass disruption and civil unrest result in major concessions from elites to restore order	During "ruptures" when the dominant system is faltering and/or in times of rapid economic, demographic or technological change Change comes in dramatic, fast bursts of action	Depends on organizers who lay groundwork Electoral openings may help them succeed. Tension between majoritarian focus of electoral strategies and emphasis on polarization of disruptive movements Can have elements of narrative shift and can shape political agendas Often clashes with inside-outside campaigns Can benefit from collective care work for survival (e.g., strike support or a bail fund) Benefits from other strategies to win popular support to make them less vulnerable to backlash (narrative shift, momentum)	Can deliver big changes quickly Can demand people take great risks Concessions from overdogs are unstable; gains often followed by backlash Some people motivated by immediate needs leave the movement once needs are met

Strategy	Tactical Repertoire	What Does Winning Mean?	Time Horizon + When the Model Is Most Effective	How It Works with Other Models	Strengths and Weaknesses
Narrative Shift	High-visibility actions that capture attention Bold demands/slogans that shift the debate Use of pop culture and media	Shifting the common sense and moving the Overton Window of possibility	When a deep, long-term shift in norms and values is needed May unfold quickly, during a rupture when people are open to an alternative; or slowly, by planting the seeds for a new common sense	Can be a big part of momentum and collective care models Less history of successful integration with base-building or inside-outside campaigns Some electoral campaigns (like Sanders's) can shift narrative	Can change the popular common sense about an issue in dramatic ways, altering the terrain of struggle Can be tactical and focus too much on words rather than action; can win the narrative but lose the policy If disconnected from organizing and from a deep analysis of the conjuncture, it can be an alluring but failed shortcut to progress

Strategy	Tactical Repertoire	What Does Winning Mean?	Time Horizon + When the Model Is Most Effective	How It Works with Other Models	Strengths and Weaknesses
Electoral Change	Large-scale voter mobilization by a permanent organization that works year-round on issues; running or endorsing candidates for office; changing laws and regulations; ballot initiatives; co-governance	Capturing governing power, enactment of a governing agenda, growth in membership of the political alliance	When the stakes of elections are especially consequential—e.g., to prevent fascist parties from winning

Sometimes a slower build

Works over multiple election cycles as organizations connect issues to politics, expand their capacity to reach voters, decide elections, and shape policy agendas | Works well with base-building and inside-outside campaign models

Newer efforts are incorporating elements of collective care

Tension between majoritarian focus of electoral strategies and emphasis on polarization by disruptive movements

Can be tension between focus on election outcomes and long-term narrative shift strategies | Building electoral power that is independent of candidates and parties can result in big electoral wins that open space for big policy wins

Tensions between a radical vision and what it takes to win electoral majorities; potential limits to what can be won through the existing state

Limited recent examples of successful progressive governance may discourage consistent participation across cycles that this model requires |

Strategy	Tactical Repertoire	What Does Winning Mean?	Time Horizon + When the Model Is Most Effective	How It Works with Other Models	Strengths and Weaknesses
Inside-Outside Campaigns	Campaigns to pressure swing legislators, targeting, counting votes, real-time coordination between insiders and outsiders to adjust tactics	Win policy campaigns delivering social change Ideally also grow the base and shift relations of power through policy feedback loops	When the balance of forces between overdogs and underdogs is closely divided in governing bodies, so that if underdogs target swing legislators they can pass significant policy changes	Most compatible with base-building and electoral change models Doesn't typically incorporate collective care (though there are exceptions) Not always compatible with disruptive movements because of focus on winning majorities Can conflict with momentum and narrative shift because of its shorter time horizon	Can deliver big policy wins, change people's lives, and sometimes alter relations of power Won't work if the underlying conditions are absent, which they often are Compromises can be tough to swallow Can deplete rather than build power Turns attention toward policy and policymakers, which can divert focus from powerbuilding

Strategy	Tactical Repertoire	What Does Winning Mean?	Time Horizon + When the Model Is Most Effective	How It Works with Other Models	Strengths and Weaknesses
Momentum	Polarizing actions against targets to create energy Cultural DNA and toolkits established by a central hub with wide latitude for local experimentation and creativity Campaigns may target particular "pillars" that uphold the social consensus	Often after many years of losses, new social consensus is achieved and gets ratified in public policy through the courts or legislation, or there is significant change in political leadership	When a fundamental system change is needed that is not possible now Unfolds over years when an issue needs to be moved from minority to majority support by deliberate campaigns that engage many passionate volunteers	Works well with narrative shift Strengthened by basebuilding and collective care A momentum campaign can be an electoral campaign Can lay the groundwork for inside-outside campaigns, though ambitious goals of momentum-driven campaigns may conflict with more incremental goals of inside-outside campaigns	A deliberate movement building strategy to make the impossible possible, with a strong track record of success Momentum campaigns can dissolve when the goal is achieved Tends to work best for single issues; may not work for all constituencies The breadth of participation momentum enables needs to be balanced with depth so that local ideas, agendas, and leaders can inform movement strategy

Strategy	Tactical Repertoire	What Does Winning Mean?	Time Horizon + When the Model Is Most Effective	How It Works with Other Models	Strengths and Weaknesses
Collective Care	Mutual aid to meet immediate needs; cooperative activity; healing justice to address trauma May support any of the other strategy models (for example, bail funds or strike funds) or function as a dominant note that achieves change by prefiguring alternatives and shifting identities	The physical and mental health, or economic needs, of the constituency in question are valued, respected, and met Creates new possibilities for political or policy change	When the state is unresponsive to crises facing marginalized groups, when political responses are not effective, or when people are feeling despair about the possibility of change and need to see impact at a smaller, human scale When organizations experience internal crisis	Fundamental to lasting base-building Strike funds and bail funds support disruptive movements Can add depth, richness, and wider on-ramps for participation to all other models, though undervalued as a strategy	Creates wide on-ramps for large numbers of people to take action, including those who may not be ready to take political action Can change identities, build self-confidence, and combat despair Volunteers can experience exhaustion and trauma Can be a stopgap that lets policymakers/overdogs off the hook If disconnected from a strategy to challenge unjust structures, will have limited impact

Tool 10 // Prompt: Are All Strategies Strategic?

We've argued that each of the seven models can be strategic depending on time, place, and conditions. But you might disagree! We invite you to make your case as to why any of the models are not strategic and can instead distract or derail movements for transformative change. Or, you may want to add a new model.

After using the New Grooves tool (Tool 9) to explore the various models, use the Strategic Debate tool (Tool 21) to prepare your case as to why a particular model is not, in fact, strategic, or why an additional one should be added.

Tool 11 // Leadership Identification

The Leadership ID tool can be used to help develop members as leaders, or junior staff to take on larger roles.

1. Name the **explicit and implicit criteria** you use to identify who you invest in. Organizers should look for people who are influential in their communities or workplace, rather than for the loudest activists who may not have many followers.
2. Do you see any **unconscious biases** in these criteria? (gender, race, class, disability, sexuality, or certain personality types or forms of self-presentation to which you react negatively)
3. Bring to mind **someone you are consciously investing in** or might invest in. Also consider who is reaching out to you for time, ideas, and feedback—is this a sign of potential or a result of privilege?
4. **Understanding the whole person**: stick figure exercise (see following section).
5. What **specific behaviors** do they exhibit that speak to our Leadership ID criteria?
6. What **small tests** might you design to check for leadership capacity? (for example, do they meet their commitments to bring new people to a meeting?)
7. What are the potential leaders' **learning edges**, and what experiences or training might support their growth?

Understanding the Whole Person: Stick Figure

8. Who are they? On the left of the figure, list the variety of roles that the person plays—at work, family, volunteer, civic. What made them? On the right of the figure, list the experiences and implicit and explicit motivations that drive them. *Artwork by Deepak Bhargava.*

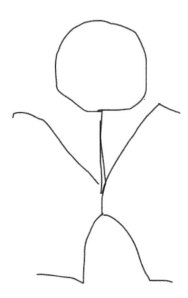

Tool 12 // Collective Care

Oppressed groups often undertake projects of mutual aid or collective care when the state fails to respond to urgent human needs—for example, some of the initiatives during the COVID-19 pandemic. In other cases, people may take on projects to support people taking risks in social movements—for example, the bail funds that were established during the uprising for Black lives in 2020. In this exercise, you will imagine a collective care initiative and explore how it connects to other strategies for social change.

Steps:

1. Define a particular group that you are part of or working with that shares common interests, identities, or needs.
2. Identify the urgent needs in the community that are not being met by the state (such as food, care, or connection). A dialogue with community members is an effective way to generate examples.
3. Brainstorm ways that people in the community who are experiencing these issues could support one another to get those needs met. What community, faith-based, or neighborhood groups already exist that might be worth connecting with? Are there existing institutions that could be utilized, such as a public library, the post office, or public schools?
4. Co-design a collective care effort—what support or training do people need in order to provide or receive help? What technology or other means can you use to coordinate the work and connect people to support each other? What individual resources do you bring to the group?
5. Pilot a collective care program on a small scale. Create simple ways for people giving and receiving help to give feedback.
6. Decide together whether to change, expand, or end the program.

Questions to ask:

1. Can this collective care strategy deepen or expand participation and engage community members who might not participate in other forms of action?
2. Will the work transform how people providing and receiving support see themselves, their capacity, or their identity? How could the work be designed to shift individual and community consciousness? For example, what venues are created for people to co-design the work and try out new ideas? Will people have a chance to discuss how immediate crises are rooted in systemic problems? What rituals are established to evaluate, make meaning, celebrate, or mourn together?
3. How can collective care connect with other strategies for social change? For example, does it allow people to take greater risks when they take action, including disruptive action? Can the information gathered help inform a policy or advocacy agenda? Can the distributed network be used for organizing or electoral mobilization? How could attention to the work change the narrative about the issue or the people involved in addressing it?

Tool 13 // Bargaining for the Common Good

Bargaining for the Common Good (BCG) is an approach to collective bargaining that brings multiple stakeholders into negotiations to fight for broad demands that can have a positive impact on workers and community members. (See Chapter 6.2 on how the St. Paul Federation of Educators used a BCG approach to raise standards for students, teachers, and parents.)

In practice, the BCG process takes several years, and should start by defining common values (Tool 1). The tool we offer here can be used in a classroom or workshop setting to help participants learn about the concept. This tool would also work well with Tools 30 and 33 (Improving the Strategic Capacity of Teams and Power Analysis).

1. Have each participant review the Concrete Examples of Bargaining for the Common Good for background (www.bargainingforthecommongood.org).

2. Set up small groups so that there are representatives from each stakeholder group (for example, each small group should have one or two members from the union, student groups, environmental groups, housing groups, or whoever is in the room).

3. Assign one group member to facilitate and another to take notes.

4. Each member of the small group should share the following information:

    - What are one to three demands your group is working on?
    - Who is your main target?
    - Do you have indirect targets?
    - What is the main form of power you bring to the campaign?
    - What is the timeline for your campaign?

5. Once each member has shared, discuss the following in your small group:
   - Can you find overlapping demands?
   - Can you find common targets (direct or indirect)?
   - Can you align your campaign timelines?

6. Reconvene in a large group and share ideas to see if you can come up with two or three collective demands, a common target, and a tentative campaign timeline.

Tool 14 // Resources: Holistic Strategy Development

- Emergent Strategy Ideation Institute, https://esii.org/
- U-School for Transformation, "Theory U," https://www.u-school.org/aboutus/theory-u
- Deepa Iyer. 2022. "Social Change Ecosystem Map." Building Movement Project. https://buildingmovement.org/wp-content/uploads/2022/04/Ecosystem-Guide-April-2022.pdf.

Tool 15 // Disruptive Chokepoints

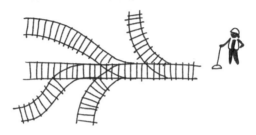

All systems have vulnerabilities—chokepoints—places where a disruption would slow, wound, stop, or threaten the functioning of the whole system.

Disruptive power includes the following:

- Identifying the vulnerabilities in a system or opponent (chokepoints or bottlenecks)
- Assessing who has access to those vulnerabilities
- Developing a plan to shut down the chokepoint

Steps for disruption:

1. Start with your campaign or issue and think about the people, systems, and structures that enable the status quo to function.
2. Create research teams to research each of the following, looking for chokepoints.
- Production and distribution:
    - How is the product or service created? What is the flow of inputs and outputs? (think of factories, warehouses, distribution centers)
    - How and where are products shipped to sell?
    - How and where are services created and provided?
    - Who are the suppliers and distributors that buy or sell related products or services?

- What are the rules and regulations that govern the industry and the distribution of its output? (for example, environmental laws that dictate how it can operate, trade regulations that determine where it can get its inputs)

- Flow of money:
  - Who invests or loans money? What debts are owed?
  - How are people paid? (employees, suppliers, creditors)
  - What are the rules and regulations governing the debt?

- Flow of information:
  - Where do people find out necessary information? (Consider everything from word of mouth to independent media and culture to corporate media and culture.)
  - Who controls the production of information?
  - Are there rules and regulations that govern production or distribution of information?

- Reproduction:
  - What are the social reproductive systems that allow the system to function? Who takes care of children? Who feeds people and provides housing and care?
  - How and where is health care provided?
  - What emotional labor is needed to keep the system running?

- Social norms and customs:
  - Are there social norms and expectations that keep the system running?
  - Are there unwritten rules that most people tend to abide by?
  - Are there cultural practices that are considered subversive?

3. Once you have identified chokepoints, identify who has access to those chokepoints.

   For example: We know that several of the world's largest ports are in

China; that most banks need their transactions to go through a single organization in Belgium; and that the digital cloud is not dispersed but located in a few key storage facilities. Disruptive power requires identifying not only the chokepoint, but the people who have access to those chokepoints (workers, investors, coders, etc.).
4. The general rule is that the more people required to shut down or close off a chokepoint, the harder it is to disrupt. Strategically, we have more power with chokepoints that can be shut down with fewer people, particularly if those people are not easily replaceable.
5. Go through your list of chokepoints and determine who has access. Is it someone in your coalition? Is it someone you can build an alliance with?
6. Develop a plan. For the chokepoints to which your group or coalition has access, discuss the steps it would take to shut or slow down the system. How would you actually disrupt?

Tool 16 // Prompt: Organizations, Movements, and Times of Upsurge

There are periods of history when large numbers of people are moved to take action to address injustice—think of the uprising for Black life in 2020, the immigrant rights marches of 2006, or the movements of workers and tenants in the 1930s.

How should organizations with membership respond in such periods? Activist-scholar Frances Fox Piven argues that a classic mistake is to think organizationally rather than in terms of movement during upsurges. She argues that community organizations and unions should not try to capture the energy of movement upsurges; for example, by signing up members. Instead, she says, they should do everything they can to amplify, support, and spread the activity. That might involve setting up strike funds or bail funds to provide support for people taking big risks, encouraging members to show up in support at big actions, or offering training in basic leadership skills, like how to run large meetings. It can also mean helping to spread the disruption to other cities or constituencies. Others argue that it's important to have a strategy to consolidate organizational power gains in times of upsurge to implement gains (for example, by winning unions at peak times in worker insurgencies) to defend against backlash to continue work in the slow times between movement upsurges.

Discussion questions:

- Think of a recent crisis or period of upsurge (for example: the COVID-19 pandemic, popular mobilization in response to police violence, Trump's effort to reverse the outcome of the 2020 elections). How did your organization respond? Is there something it could have done differently? Why did it respond the way it did, and what political and power factors were/are at play in the organization?
- What crises can we imagine could happen in the coming five years? (Wars, recessions, climate disasters, police violence, another pandemic?)

- When the next crisis hits, where will people turn for help? Is your organization in a position to help? Does your organization have allied groups that can step in? What would it take to get your organization ready to respond?
- When people want to act, who will give them something to do other than donate?
- To whom will the media turn to make meaning of the moment? Do you want them to turn to your organization? Why/why not? If you do want them to turn to your organization, how will you put yourself in that position, and what will your message be?
- Will your organization's posture be to spread and support the disruption or to try to institutionalize gains?

Tool 17 // Tabletop Exercise: The Worker Upsurge

This is a discussion-based exercise in which key people in power adopt roles and practice responding to a specific scenario. It is often used in disaster preparedness—for example, to help a team of first responders imagine what could happen and what they would do. It can also be used to test how a group responds under pressure, including its creativity. In some versions of tabletop exercises, a group leader (or "game master") will ask a team to work together to come up with responses to a given situation. In other cases, like the following example, different team members are assigned different roles—including allies and opponents—to illuminate the different ways that other actors could respond to a situation. The spirit of the exercise should be collaborative learning rather than competition—a "no fault" approach encourages people to propose creative or risky ideas. An evaluation of the exercise, sometimes called a "hot wash," is critical. It may produce an after-action assessment of the team's performance and strengths and weaknesses in the response, a "lessons learned" document, and an improvement plan.

You can use this tool with a real-life case for a campaign your organization is planning. The scenario below illustrates how it could work.

Scenario Example

Thousands of low-wage, service-sector and fast-food workers, overwhelmingly people of color, take militant action to demand a union in a mid-size southern city. The city has a conservative corporate establishment, a Democratic city government, and an increasingly far Right Republican state government. The spark for the upsurge is unclear. Many factors have contributed to lay the groundwork, including the following:

- Worker leadership has been cultivated by unions and community groups, including through the Fight for $15.
- Police killings of Black people have put thousands of people in the streets, giving people experience with direct action.
- Widespread reports of health and safety violations during the

pandemic have galvanized workers to take action in specific worksites.
- A tight labor market has given workers a greater sense of power.

International unions and local community groups are supporting the workers' actions, but they are not in control of the situation. Thousands of workers have now engaged in rolling strikes, moving across different sectors of the low-wage economy. Workers are not showing up for days at a time, creating a meaningful disruption for employers, though the strikes are not yet sustained. The story is on the front page of local newspapers and has begun to inspire similar action nationwide.

Like Justice for Janitors in Los Angeles or the Hormel strike, the worker upsurge has inspired widespread public sympathy for the workers as their stories are shared in the media. People, especially young activists around the country, begin to travel to the city to volunteer. A national strike fund to support the workers is organized. Faith, racial justice, and other civil society groups begin to rally around the cause. The workers are demanding not only better pay and working conditions, but also a union and collective bargaining agreements. The intensity of the worker action catches local overdogs off guard. After a couple of months of sustained disruption, you're at a tipping point.

How the following players respond to the upsurge will play a critical role in determining its future.

Groups

1. The corporate leadership of the mid-size southern city.
2. National companies with operations in the city. Examples of possible responses of Groups 1 and 2:
   - Try to defuse the protest with a wage increase
   - Hire replacement workers, fire people
   - Ask the police to repress
3. The Democratic political leadership in the city. Examples of possible responses:

- Try to broker peace
- Pass policy in city council
- Tell the workers and unions to cool it

4. The far Right Republican governor and state legislature. Examples of possible responses:

   - Racialize the debate and try to divide workers
   - Preempt local policy
   - Threaten corporations that want to settle
   - Bring in the National Guard

5. Local union and community organizing group leadership. Examples of possible responses:

   - Sign up members
   - Turn out members to actions, organize support
   - Help spread the action to other worksites and in the community

6. National unions, community organizing, racial justice, and other progressive infrastructures. Examples of possible responses:

   - Organize a strike fund
   - Spread the uprising to other cities
   - Send volunteers

7. Workers organizing committee of striking low-wage workers

   - They've gotten notice—what do they do next?

Some of these groups are broad categories, and you might take note of tensions within the group.

Your Task: In your small group, identify two to three options for how your actor (far Right Republican governor, corporate leadership, etc.) could respond. Then choose one "play"—a specific action you will take in response to the workers' upsurge and be prepared to explain why you chose the play and what impact you expect it to have.

(The Workers Organizing Committee has a slightly different task, since they will have already made their "play" with the upsurge. Not knowing what the institutional leaders are planning, their task is to plan the next round of escalation.)

You don't need to know labor law technicalities: these are situations in which the law is less relevant.

You should designate a reporter, and each group should come back and present its play, why they chose it, what impact it will have, and why that play is going to work.

Next Step in the Game: Each team will present its "play" to the full group. The other teams will weigh in. If need be, the facilitator should roll dice to decide whether the play has the desired impact. After all the groups have had a turn, the facilitator resets the game with a new scenario, taking into account the impact of all the previous actions.

Time permitting, you can do a second scenario and a second round of plays.

Hot Wash: Evaluate the exercise. What did everyone learn? What surprised them? What lessons can they carry forward? For example, what mistakes might they avoid, and what ideas show promise?

Tool 18 // OODA Loops

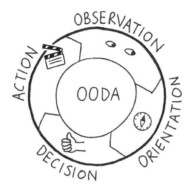

Answer the following questions with respect to a specific opponent.

1. What are the implicit filters your opponent is bringing to the situation—including ones that may be unconscious? For example, do they operate from a sense of overwhelming confidence in their dominance, or are they insecure, or even paranoid?
2. What past experiences might shape how they see current events? For example, how have they defeated previous opponents?
3. What information might they NOT see now that you do? For example, about discontent within the ruling coalition or rising anger among underdogs?
4. What actions, based on prior experience, are they expecting from you? For example, do they expect protests or demonstrations? Have they prepared extensively for a certain kind of critique?
5. What actions would disrupt their OODA loop because they won't be able to make sense of the action using past experience as a guide? Or because they will misinterpret the action, resulting in a poor decision? For example, would a new constituency joining your coalition or a defection from the ruling bloc to support your position rattle them? What about a fresh tactic?

6. Speed: What three things could you do in fast succession that would freeze or distort their decision making or prompt a ham-handed response that would itself create opportunity? For example, perhaps instead of just a typical protest, what if there was a protest, followed by a disruptive action, followed by an announcement of support for your position by an unexpected ally, followed by release of a critical investigation by a friendly reporter?
7. What actions could you take that would demoralize your opponent? For example, how could you use humor and mockery to throw them off balance?
8. What implicit filters are you bringing to the situation that may be blinding you to opportunities? For example, do you assume the ruling coalition can't be divided, so that all of your energy is focused on building the base? Or, do you assume that negative press coverage will have an impact on the target despite evidence that they have ignored it in the past?
9. What research about your opponent could you do to deepen your analysis?

John Boyd Quote

Demoralization: "to break the spirit and the will of the enemy command by creating surprising and dangerous operational and strategic situations."

Tool 19 // Resources: Narrative Shift

Several organizations offer training, consulting, and toolkits for narrative shift work. We list a few to start with.

Opportunity Agenda

- "Vision, Values, and Voice: A Communications Toolkit," https://www.opportunityagenda.org/explore/communications-toolkit

Narrative Initiative

- Four Baskets Self Assessment
https://www.narrativeinitiative.org/resource/four-baskets-self-assessment

Race Forward

- https://www.raceforward.org/practice/tools/butterfly-lab-narative-design-toolkit

Tool 20 // Prompt: Electoral Work

In small groups, discuss the following:

1. Can you share an example of when you used electoral work well?
2. Is there an example of when it was used poorly?
3. What makes electoral work more or less strategic?

Discuss as a group. Consult the following table and discuss it as well. Do you agree with the chart? Is there anything you would change or add? How does it compare with the electoral work you have done or seen?

Some Guidelines for Using Electoral Work More Strategically

Less Strategic	More Strategic
Focus on a candidate	Focus on broad social change goals
Raises money, builds infrastructure for one candidate	Builds independent organizations and movements
Get-out-the-vote is the main priority	Deep canvassing; conversations about worldview; connects people to organizations
Focus on likely voters	Includes nonvoters, infrequent voters, and involves people who can't vote (because of immigration status, convictions, or age)
Goal: elect a candidate	Goal: build governing power
Effort ends on election day	Plans for continued work on accountability, support for progressive electeds

Tool 21 // Strategic Debate

This tool is intended to help develop the skills of formulating an argument for a strategy and engaging in productive debate. In this exercise, you won't have access to all the information you would need in real life to create a grounded proposal, so the emphasis is more on learning to present a position and discuss it, as well as on learning to push others in your group to refine their thinking.

You can use this tool in a variety of ways. For example, we've used it to have groups debate strategies to organize workers into unions, assuming they are in the organizing department for a major union. Here, we present a scenario related to elections.

For this exercise, assume you are in the leadership of a large community organization based in a swing state. You have won gains at the local level but face barriers on what you can win without winning more at the state level, and you know your members are at risk of harm due to federal policy.

Your organization wants to build a ten-year plan for its electoral strategy.

1. Divide into five small groups. Assign each group one of the following strategies:

    - **Influence the existing main political parties** (e.g., push the Democratic Party to the left by challenging incumbent Democrats in primaries).
    - **Build an independent party** (e.g., a fully independent Green Party or the fusion model represented by the Working Families Party).
    - **Promote issues rather than candidates** (e.g., a ballot initiative or state law to raise the state minimum wage or change electoral process rules like campaign financing).
    - **Take over the Democratic Party apparatus** in a region or state.
    - **Build state power** through year-round voter mobilization,

community organization, expansion to new areas in the state, and policy work (e.g., California Calls, New Georgia Project).

Your task is to develop a case as to why this is the *best* strategy. Discuss the factors that are relevant in choosing a strategy. How will you accomplish your strategy? If you need information that you don't have, you might consider how you would get that information.

2. Choose someone to present to the group: What strategy does your group propose, and why? Consider the following factors:

   - Vision: What is the end goal?
   - Power from above: Who is the target, and what are their sources of power?
   - Power from below: What sources of power do you have? What sources could you gain if you build alliances?
   - "The moment": What is the balance of forces? What are the current conditions and potential openings? With whom can you make compromises, and should you?
   - Your theory of cause and effect: If you do X, what will happen?

3. The format of the exercise is as follows:

   - Your group will have twenty-five minutes to prepare its case.
   - When you reconvene, ask a spokesperson from each group to present their case in two to three minutes. Then, open the floor for others to ask questions.
   - Ask a small group of people to develop hard questions for the presenting group, playing the role of skeptic. Those questions should focus on: 1) Is the goal clearly articulated? Will you know if it's achieved or not? 2) Is the power analysis correct? Has the presenting group misjudged the power of opponents or allies, or assumed a political opening that doesn't actually exist? 3) Is the theory of cause and effect sound? Are the proposed actions likely to have the intended impact? 4) Is the plan realistic? Can it be accomplished in the timeframe specified, and was

the group clear about what resources (people, money, alliances) are required?

Good strategy means making hard choices! The success of this tool depends on everyone's welcoming rigorous debate and challenge in the spirit of developing a winning strategy.

4. Debrief the exercise. What did the group learn? What courses of action seem more or less promising? What research, testing, or experimentation is needed?

Tool 22 // Policy Feedback Loops

Policy feedback loops durably reshape the distribution of power in society. They strengthen or weaken opposing social groups, alter people's relationship to government and their social identities, and create new openings for further reform. Common examples are policies that expand or restrict voting rights, or laws that make it easier or harder for workers to form unions.

Policy feedback loops work by changing:
- The resources, identities, and behaviors of individuals in the public (e.g., citizenship); or
- The capacities and resources of government agencies/the state; or
- The power, strategies, and goals of interest groups, social movements, and private-sector businesses; or
- The political agenda: what issues are front and center for the public and policymakers?

Steps:
1. Pick a specific area of policy; for example, labor, housing, policing, immigration, income support, racial justice, reproductive justice. Then, pick a specific arena for contestation: city, state, or federal.

2. Identify current policy proposals that you support.
3. Identify ways that policy proposal could be modified to create feedback loops and do one or more of the following:

   - Strengthen or weaken the power of particular social groups
   - Change people's consciousness or identity
   - Change the capacity and resources of the government
   - Redefine a political agenda

   It may help to think about how you would measure these outcomes. For example, how will you know if the power of a particular group has grown? How will you measure a change in consciousness? What kind of resources would you hope to grow within the government?

Goal	Policy Components to Meet This Goal	Measures of Success
Increase power of your constituency, organization, or coalition		
Decrease the power of your opponents		
Change people's consciousness or identity		
Increase the capacity or resources of government to do X		
Change the political agenda		

4. If you were to win and have the policy and the feedback loop in effect, what additional policy shifts might be possible that are not possible now?
5. How would you sell the policy proposal to elected officials, other stakeholders, and your own social base? Would you talk about the power-shifting impact of the proposals explicitly because it would make certain groups more likely to support it? Or would you downplay that impact to avoid antagonizing certain groups, and emphasize its merits on other grounds?

Tool 23 // Structural Reforms

Identify a specific issue area (such as income, wages, housing, health care, childcare, education, immigration, policing, or racial justice) or a corporate or worker rights campaign that you are part of now or are thinking about.

Pick a demand that is getting attention in the public discourse or being considered by policymakers (like "cancel rent," refundable child tax credits, higher minimum wages, the Green New Deal, the PRO Act, reparations, legalization of undocumented immigrants, universal childcare, or Medicare for All). Keep in mind that you are *not* evaluating the demand from the perspective of whether it's substantively the most radical demand you can make. Rather, you are assessing it based on the current state of discourse and social forces and asking the following questions:

1. How does the reform demand fit into a longer-term vision? (Tool 36: Long-Term Agenda.)
2. Would the demand, if achieved, prefigure an alternative to the existing system? How?
3. Does it challenge the prevailing "common sense" about the issue, how it is best addressed, and by whom? How?
4. Does making the demand or achieving the demand help working-class or racial or gender justice movements build power? How?
5. Would the demand take power away from your opponents? How?
6. Would the demand shift the role of the state? How?
7. Are there contradictory aspects to the demand? (They may in some respects affirm the existing system and in other ways undermine it. For example, a higher minimum wage both challenges profits and increases the legitimacy of capitalism.)
8. If you answer "no" to questions 2–7, you can conclude that the demand is *not* a structural reform. How might you modify it to be a structural reform demand?

Tool 24 // Momentum

1. Pick a big, long-term goal that can't be achieved immediately, but could be won in a five-year time horizon. This could be a big policy idea, like Medicare for All or a guaranteed annual income policy. In other countries, the momentum model has been applied to campaigns to topple a dictator.
2. What diverse social forces could be galvanized to fight for that goal? This would include identifying the potential hard-core volunteer activists who would devote substantial time to the campaign over many years.
3. What big polarizing fight might you create or build from that gathers potential activists together in large numbers? Momentum practitioners call this the "whirlwind": when lots of people gather for a major rally or demonstration because they are passionate about a cause. You seek to capture the energy for long-term organizing by training a portion of the people mobilized in the big moment.
4. What shared story, strategy, structure, and cultural norms do you want to "frontload" at the beginning of a campaign through mass training, materials, and social media?
5. How can you amplify the work of local activists and share creative actions across the network to inspire them and make them feel part of something bigger?
6. What "pillars" uphold the current social consensus? What can you do to topple them so that your demand eventually becomes mainstream? For example, LGBTQ+ activists worked to change policies and practices in a variety of sectors: business, the entertainment industry, the military, and churches. When enough of those pillars fell, the social consensus against gay marriage collapsed. Or, how might your campaign help delegitimize a powerful actor, as the divestment campaign sought to do with the fossil fuel industry?
7. What happens if you win? Can you imagine how a victory might lead to an even more ambitious goal?

Tool 25 // Resources: Principled Struggle, Generative Conflict, and Unity

Generative Conflict

The Wildfire Project describes generative conflict as follows:

> Engag[ing] conflict in ways that generate more possibilities, greater connection, and fuller expression, instead of shutting those things down. This includes both moving past conflict avoidance and unhealthy attachment to conflict.

Resources:

- Wildfire Project, "Six Elements," http://wildfireproject.org/six-elements/
- Yotam Marom, "Moving Toward Conflict for the Sake of Good Strategy," *Medium*. January 13, 2020.
- Mediators Beyond Borders International, "Dialogue and Facilitation," module created by Ken Cloke, Wendy Wood, and Scott Martin.
- Tess Walshe, "The Art of Argument: How to Have a Generative Conflict," *Slick*. November 17, 2021.

Principled Struggle

NTanya Lee explains principled struggle in the following way:

1. We struggle for the sake of building deeper unity.
2. We are honest and direct while holding compassion.
3. We each take responsibility for our own feelings and actions.
4. We seek deeper understanding by asking questions and reading a

text (such as an article or proposal) before we launch our counter argument.
5. We look for the right time and place to engage one another (such as in a dedicated session rather than in the middle of a coalition meeting).

See adrienne maree brown, "A Call to Attention Liberation: To Build Abundant Justice, Let's Focus on What Matters," *Truthout*. March 16, 2018.

Building Unity

Resources:
>Maurice Mitchell, "Building Resilient Organizations: Toward Joy and Durable Power in a Time of Crisis," https://convergencemag.com/articles/building-resilient-organizations-toward-joy-and-durable-power-in-a-time-of-crisis/
>
>Plus Discussion Guide, https://convergencemag.com/articles/building-resilient-organizations-discussion-guide/

Tool 26 // Prompt: Racial and Gender Equity

No one tool is adequate to address conflict related to race and gender in organizations and movements. Equity is an enormous topic that demands sustained engagement. The following are some questions for your group to unpack sources of conflict and to identify potential paths forward.

1. **Are we operating from a shared analysis of structures of oppression and exploitation, such as gender, race, and class?** For example, in this book we've been using the historical and conceptual framework of racial capitalism to understand the way inequality arose and persists. There are many frameworks available—for example, a "diversity" paradigm that focuses on whether or not a group's staff or leadership is sufficiently inclusive, or "intersectionality," which holds that multiple systems of oppression must be considered simultaneously. If your group doesn't have a common framework, does everyone agree you need one, and if so, what process would you use to develop one?
2. **What's the relationship between our shared analysis and our work in the world?** For example, if we believe racism is a wedge that drives working-class people apart, is the right response to downplay race in our campaign work or to tackle it head-on? Is political education of members needed? New certain strategic alliances?
3. **What's the relationship between our shared analysis and our internal work?** If we hold feminist and anti-racist principles, is it important that leadership and staff are representative of women and people of color? Why? Might there be legitimate exceptions to this principle, such as a white anti-racist group? Is shared analysis as important as representation? For example, how important is it that white leaders who represent the organization hold an anti-racist analysis? How do our organizational systems, cultures, and practices support full participation by diverse groups?
4. **What's the current reality? Is there a gap between our analysis and**

our practice? What is the nature and extent of the gap, and what are the causes? Are there differing perceptions among different stakeholders and, if so, how might the group come to an agreement on a common assessment of the current reality?

5. **What steps might we take to close the gap?** For example, do we need to build deeper alignment around the shared analysis? Do we need to clarify roles and responsibilities—for example, for elected leaders, boards, staff (including staff unions), and staff leadership? Are structural or cultural shifts required?[*]

---

[*] This prompt draws on an internal report by Community Change, "A Vision for Racial and Gender Justice," March 2020, and an exchange with Kate Kahan, who was one of the principal authors of that report.

Tool 27 // Prompt: Balancing Purpose and Belonging

The movement training institute Wildfire points out that most progressive groups are trying both to instill a sense of belonging among members *and* to fulfill their purpose of challenging oppressive systems in society. Sometimes these goals can be synergistic. For example, members of a union or community organization who feel heard, seen, and cared for by each other are far more likely to take risks and stick together than those who don't. However, purpose and belonging can also come into contradiction. For example, if an emphasis on caring prevents a group from having tough conversations about accountability or performance that could generate conflict.

Group members may have different views about whether a group is too inwardly focused ("navel-gazing") or too outwardly focused (ignoring "toxic internal culture"). This prompt is meant to surface those differences in a way that can be constructively engaged with. In a group, discuss the following:

1. Define your "community"—are we talking about paid staff, members, or others?
2. Do we agree that purpose and belonging are both important values? Can we each identify occasions in which they have supported one another and times when they have come into conflict? Share some examples in the group.
3. Ask people to spread out in a room, with people on one side believing that the group has focused too much on belonging, and people on the other side who believe the group has focused too much on purpose. Those in the middle can place themselves between the two sides, with some closer to one side than the other. Ask people to share why they placed themselves where they did on the spectrum. What organizational practices or dynamics are they thinking of?
4. Ask people from both sides of the spectrum to engage in respectful conversation (see the principled struggle resources). How would they respond to the points made by the other? Do the differences represent differences in value, priority, or perceptions of reality and current

practice? Ask participants to state the other perspective fairly and to note what points they think are legitimate or could be addressed.
5. Debrief as a group. Where are the ongoing disagreements that will have to be managed, and how can the group hold the tension? Is there anything noteworthy about who is on what side of the debate, by virtue of position, role or gender, race, or class, and if so, what meaning do we make of that? Are there places where the group could move toward greater alignment and cohesion? What are some next steps?

Tool 28 // Prompt: Practices to Support Individual Creativity and Innovation

You can identify, test, and evaluate practices that "prime the pump" for your best creative thinking. Choose practices that are pleasurable, fit into your schedule, and open you up to new ways of thinking. You can explore with colleagues what has worked for them and how they have integrated the practices into their routines. You might pick one new practice from the following list, try it for a few months, and assess what impact it's had on your creative thinking.

Deep listening. How can you practice deep listening—nonjudgmental, complete attention—with community members, allies, or even opponents?

Journaling. Some people spend fifteen or twenty minutes in the morning writing down whatever comes up as a way to routinely open the channel to what lies below their conscious mind.

Encounters with the unfamiliar. Everyone risks getting in a rut, talking to the same people in the same circles over and over again. You can establish a practice to introduce unfamiliar material into your mindstream. This might involve setting a meeting every two or three weeks with someone outside your usual network who you find interesting. It could be an architect, a nurse, a neighbor, or a poet. You aren't trying to "get anywhere," but rather to understand how they think, work, and create as an end in itself.

Encounters with practitioners in neighboring disciplines. If you're a community organizer, you might talk with a labor or environmental organizer about a campaign you are working on. Or perhaps you seek out an activist in a different state or even in another country. People who work in a field similar to but also different from yours often have useful and provocative insights because they speak your language but approach problems from another angle.

Unprogrammed time for no activity and radical quiet. A mind that is always checking off tasks and ruminating about immediate problems is unlikely to come up with breakthrough ideas. Allowing for unprogrammed time—to rest, to meditate, to be still—allows your brain to process information below the level of the thinking mind.

Working with the unconscious. Some people work deliberately with the unconscious by analyzing their dreams or engaging in creative right-brained activity, like drawing or playing that generates new patterns.

"A room behind the shop." French philosopher Michel de Montaigne advised keeping a "private room behind the shop." This might be a physical place separate from work or home, but what de Montaigne was trying to emphasize is the value of having an activity unrelated to your work—a sport, music, art, craft—that allows you to express your creativity in different ways. There are unpredictable and delightful insights that can come from your hobbies.

Nature and art are touchstones. For many people, being in nature is relaxing and regrounding, and as adrienne maree brown says, "the natural world is a great teacher if we are fully present in it." Others find inspiration in art, music, or dance, finding that it changes how they look at the world and opens up possibilities when they return to tackle hard problems.

Reading inside and outside your field of practice. It's obvious that reading about other campaigns, new developments, and history in your field can help you see things in new ways, but many of us don't make this a priority. We can also be stimulated by things unrelated to what we're working on. Many creative breakthroughs come through thinking in analogies, so seemingly unrelated material can be fuel. The proliferation of podcasts, videos, and lectures means that we can take in ideas in ways other than reading.

What matters most is that you adopt a routine that breaks your routines by introducing new material, ideas, and perspectives into your mindstream. Such practices are not luxuries, but essential to become a good strategist.

Tool 29 // Lean Startup for Social Change

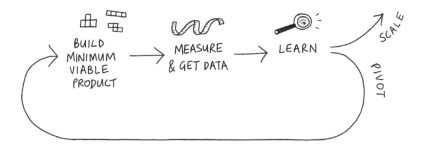

1. **Identify a hypothesis you want to test.**

   Examples might include: public housing residents in New York City are ready to build a citywide tenant organization to fight for better conditions; or, if we build a clinic providing immigration services now, we'll be able to grow our membership rapidly; or, if we ally with small businesses we'll be able to change the mind of key legislators on a piece of legislation about gentrification. **Build a minimum viable product (MVP) to test your hypothesis.**

   Rather than build a whole program to fully implement your idea, design the cheapest possible test to see if your hunch is correct. For example, you might take small-business people to visit with two or three legislators—does their attendance have an impact? Or, you might advertise a temporary immigration services clinic providing limited services and see what the response is from the community, and whether people can be converted into members.

2. **Measure the results.**

   It's essential to collect data to assess whether your hypothesis is correct. You may find that your hypothesis is wrong, correct, or, most likely, that there's an element of it that is worth building on. For example, you might do an organizing drive in a public housing development or two, and measure turnout to a public meeting, comparing it to previous turnout. Or, you might see whether including small businesses in a campaign to sway a few target legislators has an impact on their support for the legislation you propose, compared to meetings without small businesses with similarly positioned legislators.

3. **Declare failure, move to full-scale implementation, or build a new MVP.**

Lean startup encourages "failing fast." We want to rule out unworkable ideas quickly, so we can spend scarce money and time to investigate other ideas. Alternatively, if the hypothesis shows great results, you might move to full implementation. Or, if the results are mixed, you could build a new MVP based on a revised hypothesis. For example, if you find that there is a weak response to your organizing drive in one public housing development, but a strong response in another, you might look for factors that make the difference—presence of a pre-existing tenants' organization? Conditions in the development?—and develop a new hypothesis to test.

Tool 30 // Prompt: Improving the Strategic Capacity of Teams

Strategy is the work of teams. Marshall Ganz identifies five factors that make for a team that is capable of achieving breakthroughs (below). We've added a sixth. By yourself, or with others, assess the current reality of the team in which you do most of your social change work. As you consider the list of factors, consider the following prompts:

What are the strengths of your team? What could be improved? What cultural habits, practices, or structures enable or inhibit strategic breakthroughs?

Motivation. As Ganz puts it, "commitment to act does not depend on his knowledge of a feasible strategy." Motivation *precedes* strategy. When people are deeply committed, they bring more focus, enthusiasm, and persistence. Motivated teams will seek out new ways of doing things and have a greater appetite for risk.

Salient knowledge on the team. A successful team will bring together people with the right knowledge and skills to contribute to solving a problem. Depending on the situation, this might mean people who know a community or constituency well, or people with specialized skills like communications or policy.

Learning practices. High-functioning teams have a reflective practice—they regularly conduct evaluations of their work and learn from successes and failures. They are capable of looking honestly at a situation and learning from divergent perspectives.

Diversity. Teams where everyone comes from the same background, thinks the same way, or knows how to do the same things are not likely to innovate. Groups tend to lose diversity over time, especially in ways of thinking.

Decision-making processes. Open, regular, deliberations that encourage divergent thinking support creativity and good strategy.

Trust. A team where people believe in each other's commitment to the cause, competence, sincerity, and good faith is more able to hold disagreements and make new strategies out of different perspectives.

The P3 Lab at Johns Hopkins University has developed a facilitation guide for assessing the strategic capacity of teams: https://www.p3researchlab.org/strategic_capacity_blog.

Tool 31 // Resources: Learning from the Opposition

These are tools developed in business or the military to support good strategy:

Transformative Scenario Planning: Adam Kahane, 2012. *Transformative Scenario Planning: Working Together to Change the Future*. Berrett-Koehler.

Human Centered Design: Ideo.com and Ideo.org

Reverse Engineering (Tool 4)

OODA Loops (Tool 18)

Lean Startup (Tool 29)

Tabletop Exercise (Tool 17)

Tool 32 // Successful Failures

This tool helps develop clarity about campaign goals and outcomes, whether you win or lose. "Successful failures" build for the long term even if we don't win our campaign (Chapter 17). This tool pairs well with Tool 4: Reverse Engineering and Tool 9: New Grooves.

Think about a campaign you are working on and come up with measures that would determine whether the campaign was a successful success, failed success, successful failure, or failed failure.

We first provide an example:

Outcome	Living-Wage Campaigns
Successful Success You win your campaign, build new leaders, shift the common sense, create new capacity for the next fight	A new coalition is built between labor, community, faith, and student organizations to fight for a living wage The coalition brings together groups that have not worked together before; leaders and members develop trust and relationships Workers are brought in to help design campaign demands and strategy; workers and community members are given training in political economy, local politics, and organizing The coalition wins their demand for a $20 wage There is broader public support for worker issues The coalition has included strong enforcement language and a mechanism for the city to involve worker representatives in enforcing the higher wage Workers in a few workplaces unionize

Outcome	Living-Wage Campaigns
Failed Success You win your campaign but the win is never enforced, or is watered down to the point that there is no change, you don't build capacity or new leaders, or there is no impact on the common sense	A few union and community leaders lobby the mayor to pass a living-wage ordinance The ordinance passes The city has assigned no staff to enforce the law No workers know about the new law and therefore don't realize they are not being paid their new wage
Successful Failure You lose your campaign, but in the process still manage to build new leaders, shift the common sense, and create new capacity for the next fight	A new coalition is built between labor, community, faith, and student organizations to fight for a living wage The coalition brings together groups that have not worked together before; leaders and members develop trust and relationships Workers are brought in to help design campaign demands and strategy; workers and community members are given training in political economy, local politics, and organizing The city passes a $20 wage, but the law is overturned by the state Workers in a few workplaces unionize
Failed Failure You lose your campaign; the campaign does not build new leaders, influence the common sense, or build capacity	A new city council member promises to raise wages to $20 There is no meaningful campaign or base-building, no change in public consciousness, and no increase in underdog power The council member introduces the bill but it is stalled in committee

Now, fill out the rubric using potential outcomes for your campaign.

Outcome	Your Campaign
Successful Success	
Failed Success	
Successful Failure	
Failed Failure	

Tool 33 // Power Analysis

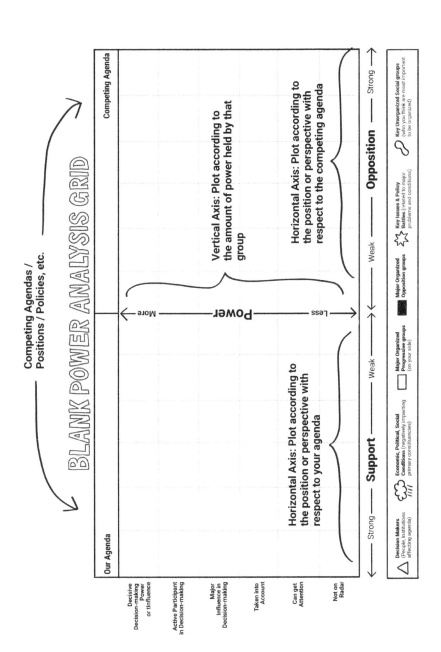

Permission from SCOPE granted.

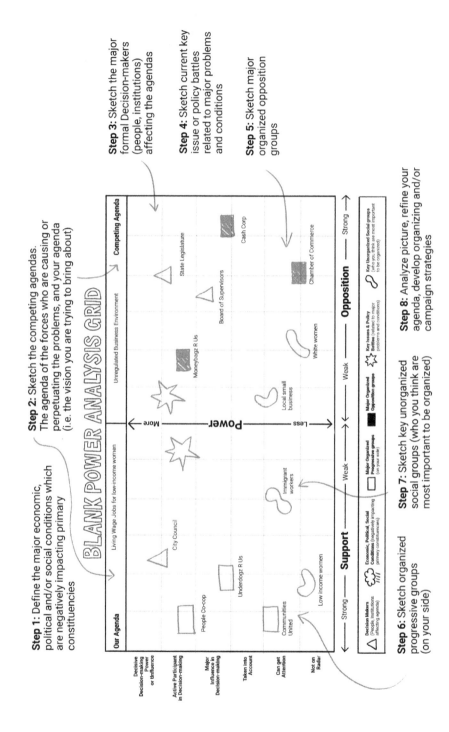

TOOLS, PROMPTS, AND RESOURCES 425

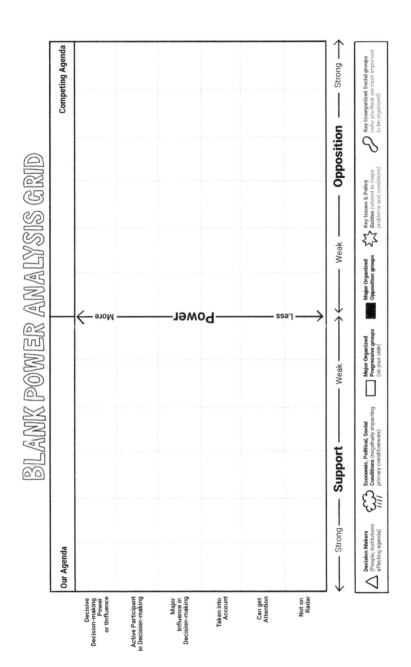

Tool 34 // Strategy Chart

The Midwest Academy Strategy Chart

Goals	Organizational Considerations	Constituency People Power	Decision-Maker	Tactics
Long-Term What you really want. Example: Fair and liveable wages for all workers in state! **Intermediate** What you are trying to win now. Example: $15 state minimum wage law. **Short-Term** A step to the Intermediate Goal. Example: Get Rep. Smith to vote yes. *Goals are always concrete improvements in people's lives!*	**What resources can you put in now?** • Number of people? • Social media lists? • How much time? • Meeting space, copiers, etc. • Money? *Be Specific! Use numbers!* **How will you build your organization?** • How many new members? • Money to raise? • New leaders? • Public recognition *How much? How many? Be specific!* **Internal problems?** • How to solve/reduce.	**Who cares about the issue?** • Whose problem is it most directly? • What do they gain if they win? • Who else will be an ally on this issue? • What power do they have over the Decision-Maker? • How are they organized; where can you find them? • What risks are they taking? *How many? Be specific!* **Opponents?** Can you neutralize or divide any opponents?	The person who has the power to give you what you want! • Elected or appointed or corporate? • Do you have electoral or consumer power? • Analyze your potential power over them very concretely so that you can use it strategically! *Always a person with a name, not an institution!*	How you will show power to the D-M so they will say yes to the goals? **1. Show power directly to the Decision-Maker** • Letter writing • Petitions • Phone calling • Social Media Tactics • Group Visits to Decision Makers • Media Events • Rallies, Actions • Public Forums • Strategic Civil Disobedience • Etc, etc. – be creative! **2. Public Education and Organization Building** • Teach-Ins • Media events, etc. • Social Media • Rallies/Banners

Permission from Midwest Academy granted.

Tool 35 // Leadership Ladder

MPA Leadership Development Ladder

I.D #		Definition	Example of Activity
5	*Member*	☑ Sends MPA a check	Not active
4	*Volunteer*	☑ On our contact and turnout lists ☑ Have attended at least one event or taken one action ☑ If they have done no activity *after repeated personal invitations* over a year, they become a 5 again	Attends a rally or MPA event, gives public testimony, writes a letter to the editor, usually calls their senator/representative when asked, volunteers every year on Election Day, etc. ***People off MPA member lists that came to a public hearing for our lead environmental campaign ***Members who visited their local hospital for our health care research ***A resident of downtown Lewiston who came to one of the community events organized to raise awareness about City destruction of affordable housing
4+		☑ Have had a 1-on-1 relational meeting done with organizer or top-tier leader	The key to moving these folks is that as soon as someone shows some interest and comes to an event, a one on one meeting is scheduled.
3	*MPA Activist*	☑ Attends chapter meetings, trainings, or issue committee meetings ☑ Begin to take ownership, see MPA as a shared responsibility, says "we" not "you" when talking about MPA ☑ Have had an initial LD meeting with an organizer where we get to know them more, ask them to take responsibility for some project, talk about MPA worldview ☑ LD plan is started: organizer talks with them about the skills they have, those they want to learn, and the role in MPA they want to work towards	***Threes were the leaders in building our small business coalition by visiting local businesses face to face and asking them to sign up. More that 1500 small businesses were signed up in support of universal single payer in more than 130 towns in Maine. ***Threes help solicit food donations and advertising sales for our annual fundraising dinners ***Threes speak at press events, attend big organizational events like lobby day and retreats, and usually go to chapter meetings ***Threes can always be counted on to generate phone calls/emails from 4s and 5s

---

Permission from Maine People's Alliance granted.

3+ ready to move to a 2!		☑ Dependable and accountable—identify with MPA ☑ Have a drive to more and are curious about other parts of MPA ☑ Attendance and participation are regular ☑ Work closely with an organizer or advanced leader on leading a project ☑ Share our worldview—they understand all our issues in the broader context of work for social change ☑ A *second* LD meeting has been done, including some self-assessment and the plan is updated and adjusted	***They take personal responsibility for making sure that all the things listed above are done and done well ***They begin to consistently and strategically think about the importance of developing other leaders ***They are willing to commit to learning the skill of engaging new members in 1-on-1 relational meetings
2	*Member Organizer*	☑ Identify as an MPA leader ☑ Take specific responsibility, make specific commitments, are dependable ☑ Do turn-out, know organizer's math, build the base ☑ Have been through training on how to do one:one meetings, other specific trainings ☑ Train 3s and 4s	***Train 3s and 4s on how to collect DirigoChoice enrollee stories, write letters to the editor, prepare public testimony, understand a power analysis, etc. ***Serve on statewide issue committees and are part of strategic planning for our campaigns ***Represent MPA at coalition meetings **Plan and carry out MPA events like Lobby Day, the annual dinners and running specific projects that directly involve organizing (such as taking a list of 3s and 4s, recruiting and training them for a project)
2+ ready to move!		☑ Training on organizing skills ☑ Aware of their own development ☑ A third LD meeting is done including self-assessment, worldview check-in and discussion, member-organizer plan, and MPA strategy ☑ Their LD plan is revised	***Have done above types of activities successfully and begin to take personal responsibility for making sure that all the things listed above are done and done well. ***Very aware of their own development: they know what that are good at and can train others to do and they know what they want to work on improving
1	*Lead Organizer*	☑ Potential statewide board member ☑ Written into organizing plan—MPA can count on the fruits of their labor ☑ Do 1-on-1s regularly ☑ Undergone leadership trainings ☑ Lead spokesperson ☑ Part of strategic planning of organization	In addition to all the activities listed above, they now understand the process that has brought them to this level and **start working to help develop other members in the same way. They take on the role of "member organizer"**. Some may step back from some of the roles they have previously filled in order to develop other leaders to fill those roles. Other 1s might decide to run for office and become an MPA organizer inside the capitol. Others may become long-term Board members.

MAINE PEOPLE'S ALLIANCE LEADERSHIP DEVELOPMENT LADDER

1 – LEAD ORGANIZER
- Spokesperson/board member
- Written into organizing plan
- Does 1:1s regularly

2 – MEMBER ORGANIZER
- Identifies as an MPA Leader
- Dependable, responsible, accountable
- Believes in MPA's worldview
- Trains others

3 – ACTIVIST
- Attends Chapter Meetings
- Has had a 1:1 meeting with a leader
- Says "we" not "you"

4 – VOLUNTEER
- Has participated in <u>one</u> event or action in the last year

5 – MEMBER
- Contributes $
- Not Active

Healthy Organizations look like this:

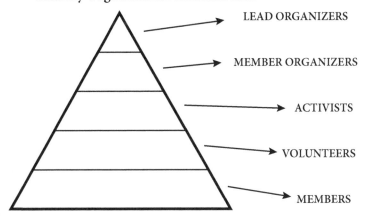

Permission from Maine People's Alliance granted.

430 TOOLS, PROMPTS, AND RESOURCES

Tool 36 // Long-Term Agenda

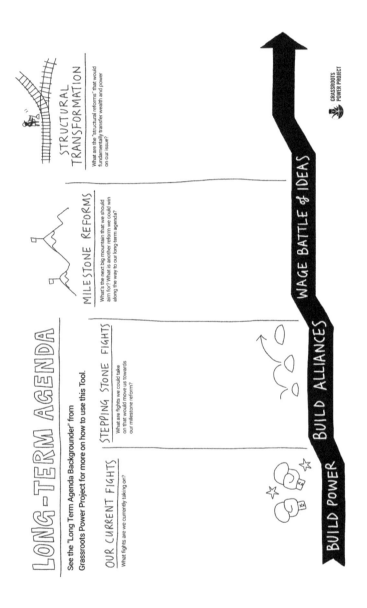

Permission granted from Grassroots Power Project.

Notes

Preface

1. Beverly Silver, Sahan Savas Karatasli, and Sefika Kumral. 2018. "A New Global Tide of Rising Social Protest? The Early Twenty-First Century in World Historical Perspective." Johns Hopkins University.

2. Bayard Rustin. 1965. "From Protest to Politics: The Future of the Civil Rights Movement." *Commentary*, February. https://www.commentary.org/articles/bayard-rustin-2/from-protest-to-politics-the-future-of-the-civil-rights-movement/.

1. Lineages of Change

1. Cate Lineberry. 2017. "The Thrilling Tale of How Robert Smalls Seized a Confederate Ship and Sailed It to Freedom." *The Smithsonian Magazine*, June 13. https://www.smithsonianmag.com/history/thrilling-tale-how-robert-smalls-heroically-sailed-stolen-confederate-ship-freedom-180963689/.

2. W.E.B. Du Bois. 1935. *Black Reconstruction in America*: 1860–1880. New York; London; Toronto; etc.: Simon & Schuster.

3. Manisha Sinha. 2016. *The Slave's Cause: A History of Abolition*. New Haven: Yale University Press; Adam Hochschild. 2005. *Bury the Chains: The British Struggle to Abolish Slavery*. New York: Houghton Mifflin Harcourt; C.L.R. James, 1938. *The Black Jacobins*. London: Secker & Warburg.

4. Frederick Douglass. 1857. "West India Emancipation," delivered on August 3. https://www.blackpast.org/african-american-history/1857-frederick-douglass-if-there-no-struggle-there-no-progress/.

5. We use overdog instead of enemy in part because it isn't always clear who the enemy really is, and because the overdog coalition may contain segments of people we want or need to peel off as allies, such as white working-class voters or small-business owners.

6. Saul Alinsky. 1972. *Rules for Radicals*. New York: Random House.

7. Charles M. Payne. 2007. *I've Got the Light of Freedom: The Organizing Tradition and the Mississippi Freedom Struggle*. Berkeley: University of California Press, 264.

8. Social justice organizations and unions often compete with one another for members and resources, intensifying the desire to say "our way is best" and discount other approaches.

9. We build on the important work of Mark Engler and Paul Engler, who identify three models: organization (what they call structure), disruptive movements, and momentum. See Mark Engler and Paul Engler. 2016. *This Is an Uprising: How Nonviolent Revolt Is Shaping the Twenty-First Century*. New York: Nation Books.

10. Luca Perrone, cited in John Womack Jr. Edited by Peter Olney and Glenn Perušek. 2023. *Labor Power and Strategy*. Oakland: PM Press.

11. Marianne Garneau describes a variety of forms of worker disruption, from sabotage to marches on the boss. Marianne Garneau. 2020. "Big Strikes and the Sabotage of the Labor Movement." *Organizing Work*. November 12. https://organizing.work/2020/11/big-strikes-and-the-sabotage-of-the-labor-movement/.

12. Alan Jenkins. 2018. "Shifting the Narrative." Othering and Belonging Institute. April 18. https://belonging.berkeley.edu/shifting-narrative.

13. *ENJ Jazz In Europe Magazine*. "20/Fifth." p. 3. https://www.europejazz.net/Documents/dl/magazine25th_print.pdf.

14. See, for example, Claus Offe and Helmut Weisenthal. 1980. "Two Logics of Collective Action: Theoretical Notes on Social Class and Organizational Form," *Political Power and Social Theory* 1: 67–115.

15. Kyle Strickland and Felicia Wong. 2021. "A New Paradigm for Justice and Democracy: Moving Beyond the Twin Failures of Neoliberalism and Racial Liberalism." The Roosevelt Institute. https://rooseveltinstitute.org/wp-content/uploads/2021/11/RI_A-New-Paradigm-for-Justice-and-Democracy_Report_202111-1.pdf.

16. In one experiment, when some players of the board game Monopoly were given two rolls of the dice each turn, they credited their own skill rather than their starting advantages for their success when they won. Paul Piff. 2013. "Does Money Make You Mean?" Presented at the TEDx Marin, October. https://www.ted.com/talks/paul_piff_does_money_make_you_mean/transcript?language=en. There is also considerable evidence that wealth makes people less compassionate and more entitled. See: Paul K. Piff, Daniel M. Stancato, Stéphane Côté, Rodolfo Mendoza-Denton, and Dacher Keltner. 2012. "Higher Social Class Predicts Increased Unethical Behavior." *Proceedings of the National Academy of Sciences* 109 (11): 4086–91. https://doi.org/10.1073/pnas.1118373109.

17. Isaiah Berlin. 2013. *The Hedgehog and the Fox: An Essay on Tolstoy's View of History*. 2nd ed. Princeton: Princeton University Press.

2. You Can't Build What You Can't Imagine

1. Deepak Bhargava. 2020. "From Resistance to Governing." *The Nation*, March 12. https://www.thenation.com/article/politics/resistance-governing-obama-administration/.

2. Rosa Leviné-Meyer. 1977. *Inside German Communism: Memoirs of Party Life in the Weimar Republic*. London: Pluto Press, 177.

3. As we finished writing this book, we came across scholar Michael Dawson's formulation of "pragmatic utopians," which is similar to our concept of pragmatic radicals. He writes: "We need a pragmatic utopianism—one that starts where we are, but imagines where we want to be. . . . Pragmatic utopianism demands not just the critically important step of beginning to imagine a just and good society but action. Movements must be organized to build that society, test competing visions, and fight off the forces of reaction and privilege that profit from the degradation of the great majority of humanity and the very earth itself." Michael C. Dawson. 2013. *Blacks In and Out of the Left*. Cambridge: Harvard University. Excerpts of the book found at: Michael Dawson. 2013. "What's Next for the Black Left?" *Salon*, July 7.

4. We treat pragmatists, utopians, and pragmatic radicals here as entirely different groups of people. In fact, many of us have experiences with all three orientations to social change, with one being more dominant at different stages of life or when we occupy different roles.

5. Stuart Hall. 1988. *The Hard Road to Renewal: Thatcherism and the Crisis of the Left*. London: Verso.

6. See, for example: Aldon D. Morris. 1984. *The Origins of the Civil Rights Movement: Black Communities Organizing for Change*. New York; London: Free Press; Collier Macmillan; and Charles M. Payne. 1995. *I've Got the Light of Freedom: The Organizing Tradition and the Mississippi Freedom Struggle*. Berkeley: University of California Press.

7. Writer adrienne maree brown explains how reading the science fiction author Octavia Butler, who featured the visionary leadership of a young Black girl in her *Parable* series, opened her mind to new possibilities. brown realized that she had been living in other people's imaginations, ones constrained by scarcity. She sees visionary fiction, and organizing, as a way to build alternatives and to engage in "an imagination battle." She asks, "What does it look like to imagine a future where we all get to be there, and not causing harm to one another, and experiencing abundance?" Krista Tippett. "On Being with Krista Tippett: adrienne maree brown: We Are in a Time of New Suns." On Being. https://onbeing.org/programs/adrienne-maree-brown-we-are-in-a-time-of-new-suns/.

8. Robin D.G. Kelley. 2002. *Freedom Dreams the Black Radical Imagination*. Boston: Beacon Press, 17.

9. Black Panther Party. 1966. "Ten Point Program." Black Past. https://www.blackpast.org/african-american-history/primary-documents-african-american-history/black-panther-party-ten-point-program-1966/.

10. Mariame Kaba. 2018. "A Jailbreak of the Imagination: Seeing Prisons for What They Are and Demanding Transformation." *Truthout*, May 3.

11. Eduardo Gudynas, director of the Latin American Centre for Social Ecology, has helped develop the concept as an alternative vision to neoliberalism and colonialism.

12. As historian Robin D.G. Kelley puts it: "The most powerful, visionary dreams of a

new society don't come from little think tanks of smart people or out of the atomized, individualistic world of consumer capitalism where raging against the status quo is simply the hip thing to do. Revolutionary dreams erupt out of political engagement; collective social movements are incubators of new knowledge." Kelley, *Freedom Dreams*, 8.

13. Reverend Edwin Robinson. 2023. "Power and Strategy" class lecture, City University of New York. February 7.

14. Though speculative fiction like *Woman on the Edge of Time* by Marge Piercy can provide stimulating ideas that motivate us to dream big and keep organizing.

15. The Haudenosaunee Confederacy, called the Iroquois by the French, is an alliance of six Native American Nations (Mohawk, Oneida, Onondaga, Cayuga, Seneca, and Tuscarora).

16. Rutger Bregman's book *Utopia for Realists* is an example of scholarship showing just how easy it would be to implement some of these big ideas.

17. Michael Dawson develops the idea of "linked fate" as a way to explain enduring political solidarity among African Americans across class lines. Michael C. Dawson. 1995. *Behind the Mule: Race and Class in African-American Politics*. Princeton: Princeton University Press.

18. SEIU. 2020. "Equity and Justice for All Nursing Home Workers and Residents." June 17. https://www.seiu.org/blog/2020/6/equity-and-justice-for-all-nursing-home-workers-and-residents.

19. Becky Bond and Zack Exley. 2016. *Rules for Revolutionaries: How Big Organizing Can Change Everything*. White River Junction: Chelsea Green Publishing, 42.

20. Interview with Ilana Berger, May 31, 2022.

21. Steve Williams. 2015. "Organizing Transformation: Best Practices in the Transformative Organizing Model." New York: Rosa Luxemburg Stiftung. https://leftroots.net/wp-content/uploads/2016/03/Steve-Williams-Organizing-Transformation-Rosa-Luxemburg-Foundation.pdf, 18.

22. There have been many versions of this quote, including one version attributed to Dolly Parton. Garson O'Toole. Quote Investigator. https://quoteinvestigator.com/2017/06/25/adjust-sails.

23. Deepak Pateriya and Patricia Castellanos. 2003. *Power Tools: A Manual for Organizations Fighting for Justice*. Los Angeles: Strategic Concepts in Organizing and Policy Education; Bill Moyer. 2001. *Doing Democracy: The MAP Model for Organizing Social Movements*. Gabriola Island: New Society Publishers.

24. V.I. Lenin. 1917. "On Compromises." *Rabochy Put* 3 (September).

3. How Underdogs Win

1. Lawrence Freedman. 2013. *Strategy: A History*. New York: Oxford University Press, xii.

2. Psychologist Daniel Goleman writes that people with little power "sense the feelings of those who hold power." It is a form of survival strategy, to learn to read nonverbal cues, likes and dislikes, and patterns of those who hold power over you. Daniel Goleman. 2006. *Working with Emotional Intelligence*. New York: Bantam Books.

3. Niccolo Machiavelli. 1532. *The Prince*. Edited and translated by David Wootton. Indianapolis/Cambridge: Hackett Publishing, 1995, 54.

4. Helmuth von Moltke, quoted in Freedman, *Strategy*, 104.

5. Richard K. Betts. 2022. "Is Strategy an Illusion?" *International Security* 25 (2): 5–50.

6. Jean Hardisty and Deepak Bhargava. 2005. "Wrong About the Right." *The Nation*, October 20.

7. Sun Tzu. *The Art of War*, as cited in Lawrence Freedman. 2013. *Strategy: A History*. New York: Oxford University Press, 193.

8. Andrew Boyd and Dave Oswald Mitchell, eds. 2012. *Beautiful Trouble: A Toolbox for Revolution*. New York: OR Books, 112–13.

9. Midwest Academy. "Organizing for Social Change." https://organizingforsocialchange.com/.

10. Taylor McNeilly. 2019. "Wyatt Tee Walker: Chief Strategist for Martin Luther King Jr. in the Struggle for Civil Rights." *The Conversation*, February 25. https://theconversation.com/wyatt-tee-walker-chief-strategist-for-martin-luther-king-jr-in-the-struggle-for-civil-rights-109493.

11. Aldon D. Morris. 1984. *The Origins of the Civil Rights Movement: Black Communities Organizing for Change*. New York; London: Free Press; Collier Macmillan, 260. There are differing accounts of the Birmingham campaign. We rely here primarily on Morris.

12. "African American Legends: Rev. Wyatt T. Walker on the Civil Rights Movement." 2016. CUNY TV. https://www.youtube.com/watch?v=ynaxw4brpMI.

13. Yotam Marom. 2020. "Moving Toward Conflict for the Sake of Good Strategy." *Medium*. January 13. https://medium.com/@YotamMarom/moving-toward-conflict-for-the-sake-of-good-strategy-9ad0aa28b529.

14. Richard Rumelt. 2011. *Good Strategy, Bad Strategy: The Difference and Why It Matters*. 1st ed. New York: Crown Business, 20.

15. Peter Dizikes. 2020. "When the Butterfly Effect Took Flight." *MIT Technology Review*. https://www.technologyreview.com/2011/02/22/196987/when-the-butterfly-effect-took-flight/.

16. adrienne maree brown. 2017. *Emergent Strategy: Shaping Change, Changing Worlds*. Chico: AK Press.

17. Claus Otto Scharmer. 2007. *Theory U: Leading from the Future as It Emerges: The Social Technology of Presencing*. Cambridge: Society for Organizational Learning.

18. brown, *Emergent Strategy*, 155–56.

19. Winnifred Lewis. 2021. "Failure Leads Protest Movements to Support More Radical Tactics." *Social Psychological and Personality Science* 13 (3). https://doi.org/10.1177/19485506211037296.

20. Alexander Hertel-Fernandez, Suresh Naidu, and Adam Reich. 2021. "Schooled by Strikes? The Effects of Large-Scale Labor Unrest on Mass Attitudes Toward the Labor Movement." *Perspectives on Politics* 19 (1): 73–91. https://doi.org/10.1017/S1537592720001279.

21. Email communication to the authors, September 12, 2022.

22. Black Music Scholar. "Nina Simone: 'Putting a Spell' on the Jazz Era." https://blackmusicscholar.com/nina-simone-putting-a-spell-on-the-jazz-era/.

23. Gary Delgado. 2018. "The Last Stop Sign." *Shelterforce*. https://shelterforce.org/1998/11/01/the-last-stop-sign/.

24. Krista Tippett. "On Being with Krista Tippett: adrienne maree brown: We Are in a Time of New Suns." *On Being*. https://onbeing.org/programs/adrienne-maree-brown-we-are-in-a-time-of-new-suns/.

4. The Change Ensemble

1. Rev. Martin Luther King Jr. "Where Do We Go from Here?" August 16, 1967. https://kinginstitute.stanford.edu/where-do-we-go-here.

2. Michael Mann analyzed the first four forms of power as foundational to understanding the history of any society, and Erik Olin Wright and Beverly Silver developed the ideas of "associational" and "structural" power. We've adapted the terms for organizers, and we use solidarity power in place of associational power, and disruptive power in place of structural power. Erik Olin Wright. 2000. "Working-Class Power, Capitalist-Class Interests, and Class Compromise." *American Journal of Sociology* 105 (4): 957–1002; Michael Mann. 2012. *The Sources of Social Power*. New York: Cambridge University Press; Beverly J. Silver. 2003. *Forces of Labor: Workers' Movements and Globalization since 1870*. Cambridge Studies in Comparative Politics. Cambridge; New York: Cambridge University Press.

3. Sabeel Rahman. 2020. "Realizing Democracy." *Stanford Social Innovation Review*, Winter. https://stanford.ebookhost.net/ssir/digital/66/ebook/1/index.php?e=66&user_id=241847&flash=0.

4. Edward S. Herman and Noam Chomsky. 1988. *Manufacturing Consent: The Political Economy of the Mass Media*. 1st ed. New York: Pantheon Books.

5. Terry Eagleton. 1991. *Ideology: An Introduction*. London: Verso, viii.

6. Derek Bok. 1998. "The Great Health Care Debate of 1993–94." Public talk, Harvard University. https://www.upenn.edu/static/pnc/ptbok.html.

7. Lisa Fithian. 2019. *Shut It Down: Stories from a Fierce, Loving Resistance*. White River Junction: Chelsea Green Publishing; Nick Estes. 2019. *Our History Is the Future*. New York: Verso Books.

8. Justin McCarthy. 2022. "Same-Sex Marriage Support Inches Up to New High of 71%." *Gallup News*, June 1.

9. "'Love Is Love' and Other Stories: The Role of Narrative in Winning the Freedom to Marry." 2020. *The Forge*, July 17. https://forgeorganizing.org/article/love-love-and-other-stories-role-narrative-winning-freedom-marry.

10. There is a rich debate within the social sciences about the nature of the state: is the state a neutral playing field, an instrument of capitalists, or something else? For background on this debate, an excellent resource is Erik Olin Wright's course syllabus, "Sociology 924: Theories of the State," University of Wisconsin, Madison (https://www.ssc.wisc.edu/~wright/924%20readings%202005/session%201%20comments.pdf), and Chapter 5 of his book *How to Be an Anti-Capitalist in the 21st Century*. New York: Verso.

11. More than one thousand socialists were elected to office in the United States between 1900 and 1920, according to Socialist Party records. This included "two members of Congress, dozens of state legislators, and more than 130 mayors." See Jack Ross, "Socialist Party Elected Officials 1901–1960," Mapping American Social Movements Project. https://depts.washington.edu/moves/SP_map-elected.shtml.

12. David Rolf. 2018. *A Roadmap to Rebuilding Worker Power*. New York: The Century Foundation. https://tcf.org/content/book/roadmap-rebuilding-worker-power-2/.

13. Joe Pinsker. 2015. "How 14,000 Workers Managed to Slow Down the Entire Economy." *The Atlantic*, February 24.

14. Micah Uetricht. 2012. "Strike Supporters Shut Down Illinois Walmart Warehouse." *Labor Notes*, October 2. https://labornotes.org/2012/10/strike-supporters-shut-down-illinois-walmart-warehouse.

15. Philippe Delacote. 2009. "On the Sources of Consumer Boycotts Ineffectiveness." *Journal of Environment & Development* 18 (3); Matthew Garcia. 2012. *From the Jaws of Victory: The Triumph and Tragedy of Cesar Chavez and the Farm Worker Movement*. Berkeley: UC Press.

16. On May 4, 1970, the National Guard opened fire on a group of anti-war demonstrators at Kent State University, killing four students and injuring eight. COINTELPRO was a counter-intelligence program designed by the FBI to surveil and discredit American political organizations from 1956 to 1971. They had agents infiltrate organizations, spy on them, and use information to break up groups. The FBI also used the information to arrest and murder activists. Though COINTELPRO was disbanded, the FBI continues to use some of the tactics today. See, for example, Michael German. 2020. "The FBI Targets a New Generation of Black Activists," Brennan Center for Justice. June 26.

17. Erica Chenoweth. 2021. *Civil Resistance: What Everyone Needs to Know*. Oxford: Oxford University Press, 13.

18. Carolina Bank Munoz. 2017. *Building Power from Below: Chilean Workers Take on Walmart*. Ithaca: ILR Press; Mike Parker and Martha Gruelle. 1999. *Democracy Is Power: Rebuilding Unions from the Bottom Up*. Detroit: Labor Notes.

19. Deva R. Woodly. 2022. *Reckoning: Black Lives Matter and the Democratic Necessity of Social Movements*. New York: Oxford University Press.

20. John Womack Jr. Edited by Peter Olney and Glenn Perušek. 2021. *Labor Power and Strategy*. Binghamton: PM Press.

21. Frances Fox Piven. 2011. "The Nature of Disruptive Power," in *Who's Afraid of Frances Fox Piven?* New York: The New Press.

22. David E. Sanger and Nicole Perlroth. 2021. "F.B.I. Identifies Group Behind Pipeline Hack." *New York Times*, May 10.

23. Large symbolic protests that don't result in change can also be deeply demoralizing and reduce participants' confidence in the efficacy of collective action.

24. C. Wright Mills. 1956. *The Power Elite*. New York: Oxford University Press; William G. Domhoff. 1967. *Who Rules America?* Englewood Cliffs: Prentice Hall.

25. Stefan Schmalz, Carmen Ludwig, and Edward Webster. 2018. "The Power Resources Approach: Developments and Challenges." *Global Labour Journal* 9 (2): 113–34.

26. Patricia Hill Collins. 2000. *Black Feminist Thought: Knowledge, Consciousness, and the Politics of Empowerment*. New York: Psychology Press.

27. Archon Fung. 2020. "Four Levels of Power: A Conception to Enable Liberation." *Journal of Political Philosophy* 28 (2): 131–57. https://doi.org/10.1111/jopp.12196.

28. Richard Healey. 2015. "Organizing for Governing Power." Grassroots Policy Project. https://funderscommittee.org/wp-content/uploads/2018/06/Healey-Organizing-for-Governing-Power-Dec2015.pdf.

5. Setting the Stage

1. James McGill Buchanan, a lesser-known yet extremely important figure in disseminating the new ideology, said: "Conspiratorial secrecy is at all times essential to mask efforts to protect the wealthy elite from the will of the majority." Nancy Maclean. 2017. *Democracy in Chains: The Deep History of the Radical Right's Stealth Plan for America*. New York: Viking.

2. Lewis Powell. 1971. "Attack on American Free Enterprise System" (The Powell Memo). August.

3. Anders Walker. 2015. "A Lawyer Looks at Civil Disobedience: How Lewis F. Powell, Jr. Reframed the Civil Rights Revolution." *University of Colorado Law Review* 86 (4).

4. Jane Mayer. 2021. "The Secret Papers of Lee Atwater, Who Invented the Scurrilous Tactics That Trump Normalized." *New Yorker*, May 6.

5. In 1973, Atwater designed Karl Rove's campaign for chairman of the College Republicans. Although Rove lost, Atwater contested the victory and filed an appeal—the contest was eventually decided by then Republican National Committee chairman George H.W. Bush, who overturned the results and gave the victory to Rove.

6. Ian Haney-López. 2014. *Dog Whistle Politics: How Coded Racial Appeals Have Reinvented Racism and Wrecked the Middle Class*. Oxford; New York: Oxford University Press.

7. Rick Perlstein. 2012. "Exclusive: Lee Atwater's Infamous 1981 Interview on the Southern Strategy." *The Nation*, November 13.

8. Jane Mayer, "The Secret Papers of Lee Atwater."

9. Theda Skocpol and Vanessa Williamson. 2012. *The Tea Party and the Remaking of Republican Conservatism*. Oxford; New York: Oxford University Press.

10. Lawrence Glickman and John S. Huntington. 2021. "America's Most Destructive Habit." *The Atlantic*, November 7.

11. David Harvey. 2007. *A Brief History of Neoliberalism*. Oxford: Oxford University Press.

12. Ryan Hogg. 2022. "'Neutron Jack' Fired Thousands of GE Workers and Helped the Rise of 'Trumpism.' A New Book Explains Why He Was Wrong." *Business Insider*, June 5.

13. Steve Lohr. 2020. "Jack Welch, G.E. Chief Who Became a Business Superstar, Dies at 84." *New York Times*, March 2.

14. Harold Meyerson. 2011. "Business Is Booming." *American Prospect*, January 27. Stock buybacks were essentially illegal until the SEC, during the Reagan administration, adopted a new rule to legalize the practice.

15. Matt Egan. 2018. "Corporate America Gives Out a Record $1 Trillion in Stock

Buybacks," *CNN Business*. https://www.cnn.com/2018/12/17/investing/stock-buybacks-trillion-dollars/index.html.

16. Stephen Maher. 2020. "Jack Welch Is Dead. Neoliberalism Lives On." *Jacobin*, March 6.

17. Brenda Lyons. 2014. "Dredging Up the Truth." *Times Union*, March 8; "General Electric to Pay $2.25 Million for Violating Federal and State Environmental Laws in Waterford, New York." 2015. Department of Justice. https://www.justice.gov/opa/pr/general-electric-pay-225-million-violating-federal-and-state-environmental-laws-waterford-new.

18. John Cassidy. 2020. "How Jack Welch Helped Create Bernie Sanders." *New Yorker*, March 3.

19. David Gelles. 2022. *The Man Who Broke Capitalism*. New York: Simon & Schuster.

20. The National Security Archive. 2013. "Kissinger and Chile: The Declassified Record." September 11. https://nsarchive2.gwu.edu/NSAEBB/NSAEBB437/.

21. Orlando Letelier. 2016. "The 'Chicago Boys' in Chile: Economic Freedom's Awful Toll." *The Nation*, September 21.

22. "Commission of Inquiry: Chile 03." 2003. National Commission on Political Imprisonment and Torture.

23. Peter Kornbluh. 1999. "Kissinger and Pinochet." *The Nation*, March 11.

24. Michelle Alexander. 2010. *The New Jim Crow: Mass Incarceration in the Age of Colorblindness*. New York: The New Press.

25. NYCLU. 2009. "The Rockefeller Drug Laws: Unjust, Irrational, Ineffective." March. https://www.nyclu.org/sites/default/files/publications/nyclu_pub_rockefeller.pdf; Human Rights Watch. 1997. "Human Rights Violations in the United States." https://www.hrw.org/legacy/summaries/s.us973.html.

26. Brian Mann. 2013. "The Drug Laws That Changed How We Punish." *NPR* and *Prime Time Media Project*.

27. Dan Baum. 2016. "Legalize It All: How to Win the War on Drugs." *Harper's*, April.

28. Harvard Criminal Justice Policy Program and Human Rights Watch. 2017. "Criminalization of Poverty as a Driver of Poverty in the United States." October 4. https://www.hrw.org/news/2017/10/04/criminalization-poverty-driver-poverty-united-states.

29. The Department of Justice found that over 16,000 people in the city of 21,000 had outstanding arrest warrants. U.S. Department of Justice, Civil Rights Division. 2015. "Investigation of the Ferguson Police Department," 5. https://www.justice.gov/sites/default/files/opa/press-releases/attachments/2015/03/04/ferguson_police_department_report.pdf.

30. For a compelling account of the abuses of guest worker programs, and an inspiring story of how workers in one instance fought back, see Saket Soni. 2023. *The Great Escape: A True Story of Forced Labor and Immigrant Dreams in America*. Chapel Hill: Algonquin.

31. For example, the World Economic Forum was founded in 1971 to bring together global elites—funded by major corporations—to "improve the state of the world." In 1973, David Rockefeller of the Rockefeller family founded the Trilateral Commission, a small elite international nongovernmental organization created to strengthen ties between global leaders.

32. Melinda Cooper. 2017. *Family Values: Between Neoliberalism and the New Social Conservatism*. Princeton: Princeton University Press.

33. Jane J. Mansbridge. 1986. *Why We Lost the ERA*. Chicago: University of Chicago Press; Lesley Kennedy. 2021. "How Phyllis Schlafly Derailed the Equal Rights Amendment." *History*. https://www.history.com/news/equal-rights-amendment-failure-phyllis-schlafly.

34. Ilyse Hogue. 2020. "How Phyllis Schlafly Found the Right Balance of Racism and Misogyny and Charted the Future of the Radical Right." *The Forge*, July 24. https://forgeorganizing.org/article/how-phyllis-schlafly-found-right-balance-racism-and-misogyny-and-charted-future-radical-0.

35. Leif Fredrickson et al. 2018. "History of US Presidential Assaults on Modern Environmental Health Protection." *American Journal of Public Health* 108 (S2): S95–S103. https://doi.org/10.2105/AJPH.2018.304396.

36. Jon Schwarz. 2021. "The Murder of the U.S. Middle Class Began 40 Years Ago This Week." *The Intercept*, August 6.

6.1. Base-Building: Community Organizations

1. The group of elected officials were Brad Lander, then a City Council member and currently New York City comptroller, council members Antonio Reynoso, Steve Levin, and Van Bramer, Senator Jessica Ramos, and assembly member Carmen De La Rosa. Dean Moses. 2021. "Striking, Starving Workers Have Feet Washed by Pols Outside Cuomo's Manhattan Office on Holy Thursday." *AM New York*, April 1. https://www.amny.com/news/pols-wash-feet-of-striking-starving-workers-in-manhattan/.

2. New York Communities for Change [@nychange]. 2021. Twitter. https://twitter.com/nychange/status/1375562441468342281.

3. "The Case for Continuing New York's History-Making Excluded Workers Fund." The Century Foundation. March 14, 2022. https://tcf.org/content/commentary/the-case-for-continuing-new-yorks-history-making-excluded-workers-fund/.

4. "2021 Four Freedom Awards: Freedom from Want & Freedom from Fear Awards Ceremony." (video recording). The Roosevelt Institute. https://vimeo.com/639215987.

5. Email communication from Camila Rivandeneyra, July 13, 2022.

6. Comments by Deborah Axt to a class at the CUNY School of Labor and Urban Studies, October 20, 2021.

7. MRNY has expanded to other states, including Connecticut, Nevada, New Jersey, and Pennsylvania.

8. Comments by Deborah Axt to a class at the CUNY School of Labor and Urban Studies, October 20, 2021.

9. Other key organizations in the campaign included New York Communities for Change (a grassroots organizing group that is a descendant of ACORN), the New York Immigration Coalition, National Day Laborer Organizing Network (NDLON), and dozens of other immigrant rights groups and worker centers throughout the state.

10. Hahrie Han, Elizabeth McKenna, and Michelle Oyakawa. 2021. *Prisms of the People: Power and Organizing in Twenty-First-Century America*. Chicago Studies in American Politics. Chicago; London: The University of Chicago Press, 9.

11. The Excluded Workers Fund victory followed a series of other remarkable accomplishments. In 2018, as part of a coalition, MRNY helped to win the statewide DREAM Act, drivers licenses for undocumented immigrants, and unprecedented tenant protections in the state legislature. After undocumented MRNY youth members watched the 2016 presidential election returns in horror, the organization decided to anchor the resistance to Trump. They helped organize mobilizations at airports to protest the Muslim ban and led major marches to protest policies against family separation.

12. Nearly 80 percent of people who participated in an organizing activity at MRNY first encountered the organization through services. Ryan Schutt and Sonia Sarkar. 2021. "Organizational Profile: Make the Road New York." The P3 Lab, December 15.

13. Observation of MRNY's housing and environmental justice committee, May 3, 2022.

14. Charles Payne. 2007. *I've Got the Light of Freedom: The Organizing Tradition and the Mississippi Freedom Struggle*. Berkeley: University of California Press, 264.

15. Interview with Deborah Axt, April 6, 2022.

16. Arnie Graf. 2020. *Lessons Learned: Stories from a Lifetime of Organizing*. Chicago: ACTA Publications.

17. Cesar Chavez. 1971. "Cesar Chavez on Money and Organizing." https://libraries.ucsd.edu/farmworkermovement/essays/essays/MillerArchive/041%20On%20Money%20and%20Organizing.pdf.

18. Interview with Jose Lopez, May 10, 2022.

19. Peter Wallsten. 2012. "President Obama Bristles When He Is the Target of Activist Tactics He Once Used." *Washington Post*, June 10.

20. Interview with Andrew Friedman, June 1, 2022.

21. Interview with Javier Valdés, May 13, 2022.

22. *Make the Road: The Recipe for the Franchise*, undated working draft, provided and reviewed June 2022.

23. Jane McAlevey. 2013. "Make the Road New York: Success Through 'Love and Agitation.'" *The Nation*, May 22.

24. Interview with Jose Lopez, May 10, 2022.

25. Ibid.

26. Eliana Fernandez, Mateo Guerrero, and Adilka Pimentel. 2020. "Opinion: Albany Must Do More to Stop the Criminalization of Our Communities." *City Limits*, July 17. https://citylimits.org/2020/07/17/opinion-albany-must-do-more-to-stop-the-criminalization-of-our-communities/.

27. Make the Road, Twitter, March 16, 2021.

28. Interview with Javier Valdés, May 13, 2022.

29. This chapter focuses on MRNY's adult organizing work. Another part of the organization focuses on multiracial youth organizing.

30. Interview with Andrew Friedman, June 1, 2022; email communication from Friedman, July 18, 2022.

31. Under U.S. tax law, a 501(c)(4) organization can engage in unlimited lobbying and grassroots lobbying, whereas there are limits on how much a 501(c)(3) organization can

do. A 501(c)(4) organization can also undertake political activity that is explicitly partisan, which a 501(c)(3) organization cannot do.

32. Robert Michels. 2016. *Political Parties: A Sociological Study of the Oligarchical Tendencies of Modern Democracy*. Eastford: Martino Fine Books.

33. Interview with Jose Lopez, May 10, 2022.

34. *Make the Road: The Recipe for the Franchise*.

35. "2021 Four Freedom Awards."

6.2. Base-Building: Labor Unions

1. Interview with Leah VanDassor, May 13, 2022.

2. In 2019, the union changed its name from St. Paul Federation of Teachers to St. Paul Federation of Educators to be more inclusive of its full membership.

3. Interview with Leah VanDassor, May 13, 2022.

4. *MPR News*. 2022. "Educators in St. Paul, Minneapolis Public Schools Vote in Favor of Strike." February 18.

5. Interview with Leah Lindeman, May 13, 2022.

6. Ibid.

7. Katy Fox-Hodess found that even though dockworkers are in strategic places in global supply chains, it is difficult for unions to win gains for members before building the capacity to strike. Only some unions, such as in Chile and Portugal, were successful in turning that strategic position into union strength. Those were the unions that took the time to build strong organization within the union first. These unions also need strong public support to protect them should they face threats such as brutal state repression or privatization. Katy Fox-Hodess. 2022. "Global Solidarity on the Docks." *New Labor Forum* 31 (1): 50–58. https://newlaborforum.cuny.edu/2022/06/10/global-solidarity-on-the-docks/.

8. Mary Cathryn Ricker. 2015. "Teacher-Community Unionism: A Lesson from St. Paul." *Dissent*, Summer.

9. Interview with Leah VanDassor, May 13, 2022.

10. Steven Greenhouse. 2019. *Beaten Down, Worked Up: The Past, Present, and Future of American Labor*. New York: Alfred A. Knopf.

11. Ricker, "Teacher-Community Unionism."

12. Josh Verges. 2017. "Instead of Suspensions, Six St. Paul Schools Try Restorative Circles." *Twin Cities Pioneer Press*, June 9. https://www.twincities.com/2017/06/09/instead-of-suspensions-six-st-paul-schools-try-restorative-circles/.

13. "Fight for Public School Funding (TIGER)." SPFE Website. https://www.spfe28.org/get-involved/fund-our-public-schools/.

14. Interview with Leah VanDassor, May 13, 2022.

15. Greenhouse, *Beaten Down, Worked Up*.

16. Alexandra Bradbury, Mark Brenner, and Jane Slaughter. 2016. *Secrets of a Successful Organizer*. Detroit: Labor Notes.

17. Sarah Ngu. 2018. "Shared Foundations." *Jacobin*, February 2.

18. Stephanie Luce. 2021. "Unions Take Up the Fight for Racial Justice." *Convergence*, May 19. https://convergencemag.com/articles/unions-take-up-the-fight-for-racial-justice/.

19. Joseph A. McCartin and Marilyn Sneiderman. 2020. "Collective Action and the Common Good," in *Strike for the Common Good: Fighting Back for the Future of Public Education*, Rebecca Kolins Givan and Amy Schrager Lang, eds. Ann Arbor: University of Michigan Press.

20. Becky Z. Dernbach and Sahan Journal. 2022. "Why Minneapolis and St. Paul Educational Assistants Are Ready to Strike." *MPR News*, February 28. https://www.mprnews.org/story/2022/02/28/why-minneapolis-and-st-paul-educational-assistants-are-ready-to-strike.

21. Andrew E. Kersten and Clarence Lang. 2015. *Reframing Randolph: Labor, Black Freedom, and the Legacies of A. Philip Randolph*. New York: NYU Press, xii.

22. Bradbury, Brenner, and Slaughter, "Secrets of a Successful Organizer."

23. "Strategic Corporate Research Summer School." The ILR School.

24. Jane McAlevey. 2019. "Jane McAlevey on How to Organize for Power." *Current Affairs*, April 21. https://www.currentaffairs.org/2019/04/jane-mcalevey-on-how-to-organize-for-power.

25. "Building a Contract Action Team." 2022. Presentation at Labor Notes Conference, Chicago, June 17.

26. Marshall Ganz. 2009. *Why David Sometimes Wins: Leadership, Organization, and Strategy in the California Farm Worker Movement*. Oxford: Oxford University Press.

27. Mark Meinster. 2020. "How Unions Can Lay the Ground for the Next Upsurge." *Labor Notes*. October 15. https://labornotes.org/2020/10/how-unions-can-lay-ground-next-upsurge.

28. Dan Clawson. 2003. *The Next Upsurge*. Ithaca: Cornell University Press.

29. Marilyn Sneiderman and Stephen Lerner. 2022. "Making Hope and History Rhyme: A New Worker Movement from the Shell of the Old." *New Labor Forum*. https://newlaborforum.cuny.edu/2022/12/13/making-hope-and-history-rhyme-a-new-worker-movement-from-the-shell-of-the-old/.

30. See, for example, Bill Fletcher Jr. and Fernando Gapasin. 2009. *Solidarity Divided: The Crisis in Organized Labor and a New Path Toward Social Justice*. Berkeley: University of California Press; Carola Frege and John Kelly, eds., 2004. *Varieties of Unionism: Strategies for Union Revitalization in a Globalizing Economy*. Oxford and New York: Oxford University Press; Sarita Gupta, Stephen Lerner, and Joseph A. McCartin. 2019. "Why the Labor Movement Has Failed—and How to Fix It." *Boston Review*; Rob Hill and Stuart Eimer. 2022. "Winning Against the Odds: The 32BJ Organizing Model." *New Labor Forum* 31 (1); Chris Brooks. 2022. "How Amazon and Starbucks Workers Are Upending the Organizing Rules." *In These Times*, May 31.

31. Chris Bohner. 2022. "Now Is the Time for Unions to Go on the Offensive," *Jacobin*, June 5.

32. This is not necessarily the case everywhere. In some countries, there can be more

than one union in a workplace, and unions represent only the workers that choose to join that particular union.

33. The Labor-Management Reporting and Disclosure Act created strict guidelines for internal union elections.

34. Mike Parker and Martha Gruelle. 1999. *Democracy Is Power*. Detroit: Labor Notes; Judith Stepan-Norris and Maurice Zeitlin. 2002. *Left Out: Reds and America's Industrial Unions*. Cambridge: Cambridge University Press; Francesca Polletta argues that participatory democracy may seem unwieldy but is in fact worth the investment. It is strategic because it can build leaders, expand capacity, and encourage tactical creativity. Francesca Polletta. 2002. *Freedom Is an Endless Meeting*. Chicago: University of Chicago Press.

35. Carolina Bank Munoz. 2017. *Building Power from Below: Chilean Workers Take on Walmart*. Ithaca: Cornell University Press; Parker and Gruelle, *Democracy Is Power*.

36. A.J. Muste. 1928. "Factional Fights in Trade Unions: A View of Human Relations in the Labor Movement," in *American Labor Dynamics in the Light of Post-War Developments: An Inquiry by Thirty-Two Labor Men, Teachers, Editors and Technicians*. J.B.S. Hardman, ed. New York: Harcourt Brace Jovanovich, 332–48.

37. *Commonwealth v. Pullis*, 3 Doc. Hist. 59. 1806.

38. Interview with Leah VanDassor, May 13, 2022.

7. Disruptive Movements

1. Johnnie Tillmon. 1972. "Welfare Is a Woman's Issue." *Ms.*, Spring.

2. Ibid.

3. Ira Katznelson. 2006. *When Affirmative Action Was White: An Untold History of Racial Inequality in Twentieth-Century America*. New York: Norton.

4. "Trends in the AFDC Caseload Since 1962." Assistant Secretary for Planning and Evaluation (U.S. Department of Health and Human Services). https://aspe.hhs.gov/sites/default/files/private/pdf/167036/2caseload.pdf.

5. Harry Hanbury, dir. 2002. *Fired Up! The National Campaign for Jobs and Income Support*. Documentary. https://youtu.be/L-jHcNZeVGY.

6. Raymond Hernandez. 2002. "With a Step Right, Senator Clinton Agitates the Left." *New York Times*, May 22.

7. Robert Greenstein. 2001. "The Changes the Next Tax Law Makes in Refundable Tax Credits for Low-Income Working Families." Washington, DC: Center on Budget and Policy Priorities.

8. Premilla Nadasen. 2012. *Rethinking the Welfare Rights Movement*. American Social and Political Movements of the Twentieth Century. New York: Routledge.

9. Rhonda Williams. 2001. "'We're Tired of Being Treated like Dogs': Poor Women and Power Politics in Black Baltimore." *Journal of Black Studies and Research* 31 (3–4): 31–41.

10. Interview with Senator Roxanne H. Jones from Washington University, St. Louis archives. 1968. http://repository.wustl.edu/concern/videos/j9602449d.

11. The People's Forum NYC. 2019. "Beulah Sanders Way: Organizing for Welfare Rights." March 18. https://www.youtube.com/watch?v=cvMQz7CcBnM.

12. Williams, "'We're Tired of Being Treated like Dogs.'"

13. Nadasen, *Rethinking the Welfare Rights Movement*, 55.

14. Ibid.

15. Richard Rogin. 1970. "Now It's Welfare Lib." *New York Times*, September 27.

16. Wilson Sherwin. 2019. "Rich in Needs: The Forgotten Radical Politics of the Welfare Rights Movement." New York: The Graduate Center, City University of New York.

17. Frances Fox Piven and Richard Cloward. 1966. "The Weight of the Poor: A Strategy to End Poverty." *The Nation*, March 8.

18. Martha F. Davis. 1993. *Brutal Need: Lawyers and the Welfare Rights Movement, 1960–1973*. New Haven: Yale University Press.

19. Discussion between Eliseo Medina and SEIU organizers in Raise Up the South, October 4, 2022.

20. John Womack, Jr. Edited by Peter Olney and Glenn Perušek. 2023. *Labor Power and Strategy*. Oakland: PM Press.

21. Max Lawson, Anam Parvez Butt, Rowan Harvey, Diana Sarosi, Clare Coffey, Kim Piaget, and Julie Thekkudan. 2022. "Time to Care: Unpaid and Underpaid Care Work and the Global Inequality Crisis." Oxfam International. https://www.oxfam.org/en/research/time-care.

22. Sally Howard. 2021."How Can Women Get Equality? Strike!" *The Guardian*, March 14.

23. See Deborah B. Gould. 2009. *Moving Politics: Emotion and ACT UP's Fight Against AIDS*. Chicago: University of Chicago Press. https://www.degruyter.com/isbn/9780226305318; and Jeff Goodwin, James M. Jasper, and Francesca Polletta, eds. 2001. *Passionate Politics: Emotions and Social Movements*. Chicago: University of Chicago Press, for case studies on the role of emotion in social movements.

24. Rebecca Givan, Kenneth Roberts Kolins, and Sarah Soule. 2010. "Introduction: The Diffusion of Social Movements," in *The Diffusion of Social Movements*. Cambridge: Cambridge University Press, 1–15.

25. Elise Gould. 2022. "Child Tax Credit Expansions Were Instrumental in Reducing Poverty Rates to Historic Lows in 2021." Economic Policy Institute. https://www.epi.org/blog/child-tax-credit-expansions-were-instrumental-in-reducing-poverty-to-historic-lows-in-2021/.

26. Dan Clawson. 2003. *The Next Upsurge: Labor and the New Social Movements*. Ithaca: Cornell University Press.

27. Paul Almeida. 2019. *Social Movements: The Structure of Collective Mobilization*. Oakland: University of California Press.

28. Lucy Williams and Jean Hardisty. 2015. "The Right's Campaign Against Welfare." https://jeanhardisty.com/essay_therightscampaignagainstwelfare.html.

29. M4BL. "Policy Platforms." https://m4bl.org/policy-platforms/.

30. For more on the backlash, see Hardisty and Williams, "The Right's Campaign Against Welfare"; and for a history of the evolution of ideas about welfare and welfare

policy, see Linda Gordon. 1999. *Pitied but Not Entitled: Single Mothers and the History of Welfare, 1890-1935*. Cambridge: Harvard University Press.

31. Nadasen, *Rethinking the Welfare Rights Movement*, 15–16.

32. Nick Kotz and Mary Lynn Kotz. 1977. *A Passion for Equality: George Wiley and the Movement*. New York: W.W. Norton and Company, 59–62, 119.

33. Sarah Schulman. 2021. *Let the Record Show: A Political History of ACT UP New York, 1987–1993*. 1st ed. New York: Farrar, Straus and Giroux.

34. Bayard Rustin. 1965. "From Protest to Politics: The Future of the Civil Rights Movement." *Commentary Magazine*, February 1. https://www.commentary.org/articles/bayard-rustin-2/from-protest-to-politics-the-future-of-the-civil-rights-movement/.

35. Email communication from Dorian Warren, November 21, 2022.

8. Narrative Shift

1. It is difficult to measure class in polling data. Some scholars use income level as a proxy; others use college education—neither is ideal. The 2016 and 2020 elections show a growing gap between college-educated and non-college-educated voters, particularly white voters. Nicholas Carnes and Noam Lupu. 2021. "The White Working Class and the 2016 Election." *Perspectives on Politics* 19 (1): 55–72.

2. W.E.B. Du Bois. 1935. *Black Reconstruction in America: 1860–1880*. New York: The Free Press.

3. Arun Kundnani. 2020. "What Is Racial Capitalism?" October 23. https://www.kundnani.org/what-is-racial-capitalism/.

4. Stuart Hall. 1988. *The Hard Road to Renewal: Thatcherism and the Crisis of the Left*. London; New York: Verso, 167.

5. Alan Jenkins. 2018. "Shifting the Narrative." Othering and Belonging Institute. https://belonging.berkeley.edu/shifting-narrative.

6. Occupy Wall Street was not the first large protest in the post-2008 recession era. It came on the heels of the Arab Spring, which began in December 2010, and large protests and State House occupation in Wisconsin against Governor Scott Walker's anti-union budget, starting in February 2011.

7. Ed Pilkington. 2011. "Troy Davis Execution Goes Ahead Despite Serious Doubts About His Guilt." *The Guardian*, September 22.

8. Ruth Milkman, Stephanie Luce, and Penny Lewis. 2013. "Changing the Subject: A Bottom-Up Account of Occupy Wall Street in New York City." January. Russell Sage Foundation. https://www.russellsage.org/research/reports/occupy-wall-street-movement.

9. Ruth Milkman, Stephanie Luce, and Penny Lewis. 2021. "Did Occupy Wall Street Make a Difference?" *The Nation*, September 17.

10. adrienne maree brown. 2011. "From Liberty Plaza." October 9. http://adriennemareebrown.net/2011/10/09/from-liberty-plaza/.

11. Doug Henwood. 2011. "The Occupy Wall Street Non-Agenda." *LBO News from*

Doug Henwood. September 29. https://lbo-news.com/2011/09/29/the-occupy-wall-street-non-agenda/.

12. Peter Wallsten. 2011. "Occupy Wall Street and Labor Movement Forming Uneasy Alliance." *Washington Post*, October 20.

13. Henwood, "The Occupy Wall Street Non-Agenda."

14. CNBC. 2011. "Occupy Wall Street Speaker's Corner." October 24. https://www.cnbc.com/2011/10/24/occupy-wall-street-speakers-corner-october-24-2011.html.

15. Milkman et al., "Changing the Subject: A Bottom-Up Account of Occupy Wall Street in New York City"; Milkman et al., "Did Occupy Wall Street Make a Difference?"

16. *The Nation*. 2021. "What Occupy Wall Street Organizers Would Do Differently." September 17.

17. Yotam Marom. 2021. "Reflections on Occupy: Revolutions Are Made by Those Who Intend to Be Powerful." *Convergence*, September 28. https://convergencemag.com/articles/reflections-on-occupy-revolutions-are-made-by-those-who-intend-to-be-powerful/.

18. Stephanie Luce. 2011. "Some Concerns About Pushing Demands at Occupy Wall Street." *Solidarity*, October 23. https://solidarity-us.org/some_concerns_about_pushing_demands/.

19. Hannah Levintova. 2022. "The Fight for Student Debt Relief Started a Decade Ago—at Occupy Wall Street." *Mother Jones*, July.

20. Tammy Kim. 2022. "How We Won on Student Debt, with Ann Larson and Eleni Schirmer of the Debt Collective." *Time to Say Goodbye*. https://goodbye.substack.com/p/how-we-won-on-student-debt-with-ann#details.

21. David Dayen. 2021. "Occupy Ten Years On: An Interview with Winnie Wong." *American Prospect*, September 17.

22. Jenkins, "Shifting the Narrative."

23. Alan Jenkins. Email communication with the authors. September 10, 2022.

24. The Opportunity Agenda. 2019. "Vision, Values, and Voice: A Communications Toolkit."

25. Milkman et al., "Changing the Subject: A Bottom-Up Account of Occupy Wall Street in New York City."

26. Anat Shenker-Osorio. 2018. "Messaging This Moment Handbook." Center for Community Change. https://communitychange.org/wp-content/uploads/2017/08/C3-Messaging-This-Moment-Handbook.pdf.

27. Andrew Kohut. 2020. "From the Archives: 50 Years Ago, Mixed Views About Civil Rights but Support for Selma Demonstrators." Pew Research Center. https://www.pewresearch.org/fact-tank/2020/01/16/50-years-ago-mixed-views-about-civil-rights-but-support-for-selma-demonstrators/.

28. Derek Robertson. 2018. "How an Obscure Conservative Theory Became the Trump Era's Go-to Nerd Phrase." *Politico*, February 25.

29. Jonathan Smucker. 2017. *Hegemony How-To: A Roadmap for Radicals*. Chico: AK Press.

30. David Fleischer, Brandyn Keating, Kelly Beadle, Justin Klecha, Aimee Martin, Virginia Escobar-Millacci, Josh Nussbaum, David Broockman, and Joshua Kalla, "Deep Canvassing Primer," https://bernalillodems.org/wp-content/uploads/DeepCanvassingPrimer.docx.pdf.

31. People's Action. 2021. "How to Defeat Trump and Heal America." https://peoplesaction.org/wp-content/uploads/2020/09/PA-ReportDeepCanvassingResults09.14-FINAL.pdf.

32. Rashad Robinson. 2020. "Changing Our Narrative About Narrative: The Infrastructure Required for Building Narrative Power." *Non Profit News*, July 17. https://nonprofitquarterly.org/changing-our-narrative-about-narrative-the-infrastructure-required-for-building-narrative-power-2/.

33. Antonio Gramsci used the term *historic bloc* to describe the alliance of social groups that come together around a new common sense and world order.

34. See also: Anand Giridharadas. 2022. *The Persuaders: At the Frontlines of the Fight for Hearts, Minds, and Democracy*. 1st ed. New York: Alfred A. Knopf.

35. Smucker, *Hegemony How-To: A Roadmap for Radicals*.

36. ORS Impact. 2019. "Measuring Narrative Change." https://www.orsimpact.com/DirectoryAttachments/7182019_123705_659_Measuring_narrative_Change_FINAL_rev_17July2019.pdf.

37. Proteus Fund. 2019. "Hearts and Minds." https://www.proteusfund.org/wp-content/uploads/2018/09/Hearts-and-Minds-CMC-Publication.pdf.

38. Laura Wides-Munoz. 2018. "A Family in Missouri Had a Life for 15 Years. Then They Were Torn Apart." *The Guardian*, January 30.

39. Peter O'Dowd. 2010. "Ariz. Churches Mobilize Against Immigration Law." NPR, August 1. https://www.npr.org/templates/story/story.php?storyId=128907091; and website of PromizeAZ, the organization that sponsored the vigil. https://www.promiseaz.org/the_vigil.

9. Electoral Change

1. Interview with Nsé Ufot, May 6, 2022.

2. Ibid.

3. Biden said in a post-election interview that his campaign made little effort to win Georgia because they did not think they could win. Steve Phillips. 2022. *How We Win the Civil War*. New York: The New Press, 197.

4. Jerome Armstrong and Markos Moulitsas Zuniga. 2006. *Crashing the Gate*. White River Junction: Chelsea Green Publishing.

5. Hahrie Han and Liz McKenna. 2021. "To Learn About the Democratic Party's Future, Look at What Latino Organizers Did in Arizona." *Washington Post*, February 9; Lisa Magana and César S. Silva. 2021. *Empowered!: Latinos Transforming Arizona Politics*. Tucson: University of Arizona Press.

6. Steve Phillips. 2016. *Brown Is the New White: How the Demographic Revolution Has Created a New American Majority*. New York: The New Press.

7. Interview with Nsé Ufot, May 6, 2022.

8. Ibid.

9. Ibid.

10. Ibid.

11. Ibid.

12. Ibid.

13. Georgia passed an automatic voter registration law that went into effect in 2016. And although the state has not been consistent in administering it, and there were ways that voters could fall through the cracks, NGP voter registration work was still necessary. *The Great Battlefield Podcast*. 2020. "Transforming Georgia with Nsé Ufot of The New Georgia Project." Episode 527. November 13.

14. John A. Yarmuth. 2022. *H.R.5376—117th Congress (2021–2022): Inflation Reduction Act of 2022*.

15. Democratic Party of Georgia. 2022. "Kemp Admits SB 202 Was Result of Frustration with 2020 Election Results." May 2. https://www.georgiademocrat.org/kemp-admits-sb-202-was-result-of-frustration-with-2020-election-results/.

16. Deepak Pateriya and Patricia Castellanos. 2003. "Power Tools: A Manual for Organizations Fighting for Justice." Los Angeles: Strategic Concepts in Organizing and Policy Education (SCOPE).

17. Interview with Lydia Avila and Sabrina Smith, October 28, 2022.

18. Interview with Maurice Mitchell, November 16, 2022.

19. Ibid.

20. Ibid.

21. Maurice Mitchell, presentation to Power and Strategy course, CUNY School of Labor and Urban Studies. November 22, 2021.

22. Interview with Maurice Mitchell, November 16, 2022.

23. Ibid.

24. Fusion voting allows more than one party to endorse a candidate on their ballot line. For example, Joe Biden can run for president under both the Democratic Party and Working Families Party ballot lines in New York State. This allows voters to vote for a candidate on either line, expressing their alignment with a particular party. Fusion used to be a common practice in the country but many states have repealed these rights. A Supreme Court decision in 1998 left this power in the hands of the states.

25. Steven Pitts. 2021. "Maurice Mitchell." *Black Work Talk*. Season 1, Episode 13. May 5.

26. Maria Poblet. 2022. "States of Solidarity: How State Alignment Builds Multiracial Working-Class Power." In *Power Concedes Nothing: How Grassroots Organizing Wins Elections*. Linda Burnham, Max Elbaum, and Maria Poblet, eds. New York: OR Books.

27. Daniel Judt. 2022. "Building Worker Power." *The Forge*, September 28. https://forgeorganizing.org/article/building-worker-power.

28. Poblet, "States of Solidarity."

29. Judt, "Building Worker Power."

30. Phillips, *How We Win the Civil War*.

31. Deepak Pateriya. 2022. "Win Justice and Beyond: Winning Elections While Building Power for the Long Term." In *Power Concedes Nothing: How Grassroots Organizing Wins Elections*. Linda Burnham, Max Elbaum, and Maria Poblet, eds. New York: OR Books.

32. Interview with Jen Kern, July 28, 2022.

33. Liza Featherstone. 2022. "New York's Democratic Socialists Are Playing the Long Game." *Jacobin*, January 11.

34. Stephanie Luce. 2021. "DSA's Sumathy Kumar & the Socialists in Office Committee." *Convergence Magazine*, August 20. https://convergencemag.com/articles/dsas-sumathy-kumar-the-socialists-in-office-committee/.

35. Jon Liss. 2022. "New Virginia Majority: We Win by Expanding Democracy." In *Power Concedes Nothing: How Grassroots Organizing Wins Elections*. Linda Burnham, Max Elbaum and Maria Poblet, eds. New York: OR Books.

36. Ibid.

37. The scholar Bob Jessop calls this a "strategic-relational" theory of the state. Bob Jessop and Jamie Morgan. 2022. "The Strategic-Relational Approach, Realism and the State: From Regulation Theory to Neoliberalism via Marx and Poulantzas, an Interview with Bob Jessop." *Journal of Critical Realism* 21 (1): 83–118. https://doi.org/10.1080/14767430.2021.1995685.

38. Erik Olin Wright. 2021. *How to Be an Anticapitalist in the Twenty-First Century*. New York: Verso Books.

39. Sarah Repucci. 2021. "Reversing the Decline of Democracy in the United States." Freedom House. https://freedomhouse.org/report/freedom-world/2022/global-expansion-authoritarian-rule/reversing-decline-democracy-united-states.

40. Pierre Clavel. 2013. *Activists in City Hall*. Ithaca: Cornell University Press.

10. Inside-Outside Campaigns

1. Marc Doussard and Jacob Lesniewski. 2017. "Fortune Favors the Organized: How Chicago Activists Won Equity Goals Under Austerity." *Journal of Urban Affairs* 39 (5): 618–34. https://doi.org/10.1080/07352166.2016.1262684.

2. Deana Rutherford. 2011. "Thousands Rally to Demand Greedy Banks and Corporations Pay Their Fair Share." SEIU Healthcare. June 30. https://seiuhcilin.org/2011/06/thousands-rally-to-demand-greedy-banks-and-corporations-pay-their-fair-share/.

3. Madeline Talbot. 2020. "The Origins of Fight for $15 in Chicago." *The Forge*, April 14. https://forgeorganizing.org/article/origins-fight-15-chicago.

4. Interview with Alex Han, April 13, 2022.

5. Ibid.

6. Interview with Katelyn Johnson, June 14, 2022.

7. Ibid.

8. Email communication with Mark Meinster, July 24, 2002.

9. Ted Cox. 2013. "Progressive Aldermen Unite, Vow to End 'Business as Usual.'"

DNAinfo, March 12. https://web.archive.org/web/20151123140732/http://www.dnainfo.com/chicago/20130312/chicago/progressive-aldermen-unite-vow-end-business-as-usual.

10. Carol Felsenthal. 2011. "Garrido Decides Against Recount in the 45th, but Is 'Contemplating' Suing SEIU." *Chicago Magazine*, April 11. https://www.chicagomag.com/Chicago-Magazine/Felsenthal-Files/April-2011/Garrido-Decides-Against-Recount-in-the-45th-Ward-Against-Arena-but-is-Contemplating-Suing-SEIU/.

11. Ethan Corey. 2014. "Chicago Aldermen Want a $15 Minimum Wage in Their City, Too." *In These Times*, June 17.

12. The referendum called for establishing a minimum wage for firms with revenue for "companies that perform work within the city of Chicago where the employing company had annual gross revenues in excess of $50 million in the last tax year."

13. Bill Chappell. 2014. "Chicago Council Strongly Approves $13 Minimum Wage." NPR, December 2. https://www.npr.org/sections/thetwo-way/2014/12/02/368026116/chicago-council-strongly-approves-13-minimum-wage.

14. Office of the Mayor of Chicago. 2021. "Mayor Lightfoot Celebrates Historic $15 Minimum Wage in Chicago." https://www.chicago.gov/content/city/en/depts/mayor/press_room/press_releases/2021/june/15DollarMinimumWage.html.

15. City of Chicago. 2019. "Chicago's Minimum Wage Increased to $13 an Hour." https://www.chicago.gov/content/city/en/depts/bacp/provdrs/enforce/news/2019/july/minumumwage.html.

16. Many of the new laws phased in the wage increases, so not all had reached $15 by 2021. Yannet Lathrop, T. William Lester, and Matthew Wilson. 2021. "Fight for $15 Movement Has Won $150B in Wage Raises for 26M Workers in Less Than a Decade." National Employment Law Project. https://www.nelp.org/news-releases/fight-for-15-movement-has-won-150b-in-wage-raises-for-26m-workers-in-less-than-a-decade/.

17. Interview with Katelyn Johnson, June 14, 2022.

18. Ibid.

19. *The Real Deal*. "Building Trade Group Throws Support Behind Kingsbridge Armory." October 23. https://therealdeal.com/2009/10/23/building-trade-group-throws-support-behind-kingsbridge-armory-including-the-building-and-construction-trades-council-of-greater-new-york/.

20. Stephanie Luce. 2004. *Fighting for a Living Wage*. Ithaca: Cornell University Press.

21. Erik Olin Wright. 2018. *How to Be an Anticapitalist in the 21st Century*. New York; London: Verso.

22. Luce, *Fighting for a Living Wage*.

23. Chicago teachers held another successful strike in 2019.

24. Paul Windman. 2023. "How Progressives Found Their Way to Real Power in Biden's Washington." *Washington Post*, January 12.

25. Interview with Alex Han, April 13, 2022.

26. Sam Heller. 2021. "McDonald's Workers Celebrate City's New $15 Minimum Hourly Wage." *Chicago Sun-Times*, July 1.

27. Interview with Ilana Berger, May 31, 2022.

11. Momentum

1. John Schwartz. 2014. "Rockefellers, Heirs to an Oil Fortune, Will Divest Charity of Fossil Fuels." *New York Times*, September 22.

2. Interview with Michael Northrop, July 5, 2022.

3. "Global Fossil Fuel Commitments Database." https://divestmentdatabase.org/.

4. Peter Wallsten. 2012. "President Obama Bristles When He Is the Target of Activist Tactics He Once Used." *Washington Post*, June 10; Julia Preston. 2010. "Immigration Advocates Rally for Change." *New York Times*, May 1.

5. Interview with Clayton Thomas-Müller, July 11, 2022.

6. Ibid.

7. Ibid.

8. Deepak joined the board of 350.org in 2020, becoming its board chair in 2022.

9. Matthew Nisbet. 2013. "How Bill McKibben Changed Environmental Politics and Took on the Oil Patch." *Policy Options*, May 1. https://policyoptions.irpp.org/magazines/arctic-visions/how-bill-mckibben-changed-environmental-politics-and-took-on-the-oil-patch/.

10. Karl Mathiesen. 2015. "May Boeve: The New Face of the Climate Change Movement." *The Guardian*, April 8.

11. Melissa Denchak and Courtney Lindwall. 2022. "What Is the Keystone XL Pipeline?" NRDC. https://www.nrdc.org/stories/what-keystone-pipeline.

12. Bill McKibben. 2012. "Global Warming's Terrifying New Math." *Rolling Stone Magazine*, July 19.

13. Interview with May Boeve, April 5, 2022.

14. Ibid.

15. Interview with Varshini Prakash, May 11, 2022.

16. Ibid.

17. David Roberts. 2015. "College Students Are Making Global Warming a Moral Issue. Here's Why That Scares People." *Vox*, April 19.

18. Brinda Sarathy and Jessica Grady-Benson. 2015. "Fossil Fuel Divestment in US Higher Education: Student-Led Organising for Climate Justice." *International Journal of Justice and Sustainability* 21 (6): 661–81.

19. Roberts, "College Students Are Making Global Warming a Moral Issue."

20. Todd Schifeling and Andrew J. Hoffman. 2019. "Bill McKibben's Influence on U.S. Climate Change Discourse: Shifting Field-Level Debates Through Radical Flank Effects." *Organization & Environment* 32 (3): 213–33. https://doi.org/10.1177/1086026617744278.

21. Herbert H. Haines. 1984. "Black Radicalization and the Funding of Civil Rights, 1957–1970," *Social Problems* 32 (1). http://irasilver.org/wp-content/uploads/2011/08/Reading-Movement-funding-Haines.pdf.

22. David Roberts. 2017. "The McKibben Effect: A Case Study in How Radical Environmentalism Can Work." *Vox*, November 17.

23. Interview with Varshini Prakash, May 11, 2022.

24. Theodor F. Cojoianu, Francisco Ascui, Gordon L. Clark, Andreas G.F. Hoepner,

and Dariusz Wójcik. 2021. "Does the Fossil Fuel Divestment Movement Impact New Oil and Gas Fundraising?" *Journal of Economic Geography* 21 (1): 141–64. https://doi.org/10.1093/jeg/lbaa027.

25. Mathiesen, "May Boeve: The New Face of the Climate Change Movement."

26. Mark Engler and Paul Engler. 2017. *This Is an Uprising: How Nonviolent Revolt Is Shaping the Twenty-First Century*. New York: Bold Type Books.

27. Internal Momentum document authored by Dani Moscovitch and Vera Parra. 2022.

28. William Saletan. 2012. "Gay Marriage Ballot Measures 2012: Why Did Same-Sex Marriage Opponents Lose All Four Referenda?" *Slate*, November 19.

29. Wayne Slater. 2010. "Karl Rove Says He Didn't Engineer Anti-Gay Marriage Amendments. He Did." *Dallas News*, August 26. https://www.dallasnews.com/news/politics/2010/08/26/karl-rove-says-he-didn-t-engineer-anti-gay-marriage-amendments-he-did/.

30. Interview with Lissy Romanow, September 27, 2022.

31. Ibid.

32. For more on the pillars concept see Srdja Popovic, Slobodan Djinovic, Andrej Milivojevic, Hardy Merriman, and Ivan Marovic. 2007. "Pillars of Support," from *Canvas Core Curriculum: A Guide to Effective Nonviolent Struggle*, Centre for Applied Nonviolent Actions and Strategies. Translation: Giorgi Meladze, September 2017. https://www.nonviolent-conflict.org/wp-content/uploads/2019/02/Pillars-of-Support-PDF-English.pdf.

33. Interview with May Boeve, April 5, 2022.

34. Maria Stephan and Erica Chenoweth. 2012. *Why Civil Resistance Works*. New York: Columbia University Press; Erica Chenoweth, Andrew Hocking, and Zoe Marks. 2022. "A Dynamic Model of Nonviolent Resistance Strategy." *PLoS ONE* 7 (17). https://doi.org/10.1371/journal.pone.0269976.

35. Becky Bond and Zack Exley. 2016. *Rules for Revolutionaries: How Big Organizing Can Change Everything*. White River Junction: Chelsea Green Publishing, 184.

36. Ibid.

37. Interview with Varshini Prakash, May 11, 2022.

38. Megan Day. 2020. "How Bernie's Iowa Campaign Organized Immigrant Workers at the Factory Gates," *Jacobin*, February 4.

39. Interview with Lissy Romanow, September 27, 2022.

40. Jonah Furman. 2020. "Bringing Bernie 2020 Organizing Tools to the Workplace." *The Forge*, August 4. https://forgeorganizing.org/article/bringing-bernie-2020-organizing-tools-workplace.

41. Chris Brooks. 2022. "How Amazon and Starbucks Workers Are Upending the Organizing Rules." *In These Times*, May 31.

12. Collective Care

1. Dana Rosenfeld. 2018. "The AIDS Epidemic's Lasting Impact on Gay Men." The British Academy. https://www.thebritishacademy.ac.uk/blog/aids-epidemic-lasting

-impact-gay-men/; "Mortality Analyses." Johns Hopkins University & Medicine. https://coronavirus.jhu.edu/data/mortality.

2. Interview with David Hansell, June 1, 2022.

3. Peter L. Allen. 2002. *The Wages of Sin: Sex and Disease, Past and Present*. Chicago: University of Chicago Press.

4. Christopher Reed. 2007. "The Rev Jerry Falwell." *The Guardian*, May 17.

5. Deborah Gould. 2009. *Moving Politics: Emotion and ACT UP's Fight Against AIDS*. Chicago: University of Chicago Press. For more on ACT UP, two essential (and contrasting) accounts are *Let the Record Show: A Political History of ACT UP New York, 1987–1993* by Sarah Schulman, and *How to Survive a Plague: The Inside Story of How Citizens and Science Tamed AIDS* by David France.

6. As scholars Morris and Braine put it, "open challenge [to a dominant system] usually follows the internal development of a community of resistance that includes a maturing oppositional consciousness, collective identity, and organizational infrastructure." Aldon Morris and Naomi Braine. 2001. "Social Movements and Oppositional Consciousness." In *Oppositional Consciousness: The Subjective Roots of Social Protest*. Jane J. Mansbridge and Aldon Morris, eds. Chicago: University of Chicago Press.

7. Philip M. Kayal. 1993. *Bearing Witness: Gay Men's Health Crisis and the Politics of AIDS*. New York: Routledge.

8. Interview with David Barr, May 31, 2022.

9. Interviews with Tim Sweeney, May 12, 2022 and June 10, 2022.

10. Ibid.

11. Ibid.

12. Interview with David Hansell, June 1, 2022.

13. Interviews with Tim Sweeney, May 12, 2022 and June 10, 2022; interview with Jeffrey Levi, May 27, 2022.

14. Gould, *Moving Politics: Emotion and ACT UP's Fight Against AIDS*.

15. Ibid.

16. Interviews with Tim Sweeney, May 12, 2022 and June 10, 2022.

17. Ibid.

18. Interview with David Barr, May 31, 2022.

19. Ibid.

20. Interview with Jeffrey Levi, May 27, 2022.

21. Interview with David Barr, May 31, 2022.

22. Interviews with Tim Sweeney, May 12, 2022 and June 10, 2022.

23. For more on the ongoing toll of the epidemic, see: Walt Odets. 2019. *Out of the Shadows: Reimagining Gay Men's Lives*. New York: MacMillan.

24. Interviews with Tim Sweeney, May 12, 2022 and June 10, 2022.

25. Dean Spade. 2020. *Mutual Aid: Building Solidarity During This Crisis (and the Next)*. London; New York: Verso.

26. Rebecca Solnit. 2006. *Hope in the Dark: Untold Histories, Wild Possibilities*. New, Expanded ed. New York: Nation Books.

27. Erica Chenoweth. 2021. *Civil Resistance: What Everyone Needs to Know*. New York: Oxford University Press, 47.

28. Interview with David Barr, May 31, 2022.

29. Barbara Ransby. 2003. *Ella Baker and the Black Freedom Movement*. Chapel Hill: University of North Carolina Press.

30. Daisy Pitkin. 2022. *On the Line: A Story of Class, Solidarity, and Two Women's Epic Fight to Build a Union*. 1st ed. Chapel Hill: Algonquin Books of Chapel Hill.

31. Kyandra Knight, email communication, October 12, 2022.

32. For example, see Solnit, *Hope in the Dark*; and Spade, *Mutual Aid*.

33. Laura Dawn, ed. 2006. *It Takes a Nation: How Strangers Became Family in the Wake of Hurricane Katrina: The Story of MoveOn.Org Civic Action's HurricaneHousing.Org*. San Rafael: Earth Aware.

34. Robin D.G. Kelley. 2002. *Freedom Dreams: The Black Radical Imagination*. Boston: Beacon Press, 6.

35. Deva R. Woodly. 2022. *Reckoning: Black Lives Matter and the Democratic Necessity of Social Movements*. New York: Oxford University Press, 90.

36. Cara Page and Erica Woodland. 2023. *Healing Justice Lineages: Dreaming at the Crossroads of Liberation, Collective Care, and Safety*. Berkeley: North Atlantic Books.

37. Dean Spade and Andrea Ritchie. 2020. "Study and Struggle: Abolition, Intersectionality, and Care." Haymarket Books Teach-in, September 29.

38. Restorative justice looks to heal harm in a damaged world, while transformative justice looks to heal and go deeper to examine why the world is damaged in the first place and how it might be made better. See work from Mariame Kaba at http://mariamekaba.com/ and Mia Mingus at LeavingEvidence.wordpress.com.

39. GMHC provided services to gay and other people of color, and had many people of color on its staff. However, it was not positioned to be the lead support agency in Black and Latino New York. GMHC participated in coalitions where it advocated for funding of organizations with roots in those communities.

13. Power from Below

1. A song used by enslaved people to communicate instructions for the Underground Railroad. H.B. Park version, "Follow the Drinking Gourd."

2. Sarah H Bradford. 1886. *Harriet: The Moses of Her People*. New York: Geo. R. Lockwood and Sons.

3. Eric Foner. 2016. *Gateway to Freedom: The Hidden History of the Underground Railroad*. New York: W.W. Norton.

4. Manisha Sinha. 2016. *The Slave's Cause: A History of Abolition*. New Haven: Yale University Press.

5. Marcus Rediker. 2008. *The Slave Ship: A Human History*. New York: Penguin Books.

6. Eric Foner. 1983. *Nothing but Freedom: Emancipation and Slavery*. Baton Rouge: Louisiana State University Press.

7. Thulani Davis. 2022. *The Emancipation Circuit: Black Activism Forging a Culture of Freedom*. Durham: Duke University Press.

8. Alfred W. McCoy. 2021. *To Govern the Globe: World Orders and Catastrophic Change*. Chicago: Haymarket Books, 145.

9. Foner, *Gateway to Freedom*.

10. Heyrick was not the first to call for a sugar boycott; others had also done so in support of anti-slavery in several countries in the 1790s. Adam Hochschild. 2005. *Bury the Chains: The British Struggle to Abolish Slavery*. New York: Houghton Mifflin Harcourt.

11. Hochschild, *Bury the Chains*.

12. Ibram X. Kendi. 2017. *Stamped from the Beginning: The Definitive History of Racist Ideas in America*. New York: Random House.

13. Sinha, *The Slave's Cause*.

14. Brian Gabrial. 2016. *The Press and Slavery in America, 1791–1859: The Melancholy Effect of Popular Excitement*. Columbia: University of South Carolina Press.

15. Hochschild, *Bury the Chains*.

16. Robin Blackburn. 2013. *American Crucible: Slavery, Emancipation and Human Rights*. New York; London: Verso Books.

17. Louis Ruchames, ed. 1963. *The Abolitionists*. New York: G.P. Putnam's and Sons.

18. Eric Williams. 1944. *Capitalism and Slavery*. Durham: University of North Carolina Press.

19. C.L.R. James. 1938. *The Black Jacobins*. London: Secker & Warburg Ltd., 182.

20. W.E.B. Du Bois. 1935. *Black Reconstruction in America: An Essay Toward a History of the Part Which Black Folk Played in the Attempt to Reconstruct Democracy in America, 1860–1880*. New York: The Free Press, 125.

21. Barbara Jeanne Fields. 1990. "Slavery, Race and Ideology in the United States of America." *New Left Review*, June.

22. Edmund Morgan. 1976. *American Slavery, American Freedom*; Tyler Stovall. 2021. *White Freedom: The Racial History of an Idea*. Princeton: Princeton University Press; Alex Gourevitch. 2014. *From Slavery to the Cooperative Commonwealth*. Cambridge: Cambridge University Press.

23. Peter Eisenstadt, ed. 2005. *The Encyclopedia of New York State*. Syracuse: Syracuse University Press.

24. Adam Rothman. 2016. "The Truth About Abolition." *The Atlantic*, April.

25. "The Declaration of Causes of Seceding States." 1861. https://www.battlefields.org/learn/primary-sources/declaration-causes-seceding-states.

26. Blackburn, *American Crucible*.

27. Sinha, *The Slave's Cause*.

28. James, *The Black Jacobins*.

29. Selam Gebrekidan, Matt Apuzzo, Catherine Porter, and Constant Méheut. 2022. "The Root of Haiti's Misery: Reparations to Enslavers." *New York Times*, May 26.

30. Sinha, *The Slave's Cause*, 2.

31. Hochschild, *Bury the Chains*, 356.

32. Mariame Kaba. 2021. *We Do This 'Til We Free Us: Abolitionist Organizing and Transformative Justice*. Chicago: Haymarket Books.

14. Unity Builds Power

1. Randy Parraz. 2021. *Dignity by Fire: Dismantling Arizona's Anti-Immigrant Machine*. Phoenix: Organizing Institute for Democracy.

2. Katey Lauer and Zein Nakhoda. 2022. "Report from the Training Room: Overcoming Aversion to Power." *Convergence*, October 18. https://convergencemag.com/articles/report-from-the-training-room-overcoming-aversion-to-power/.

3. Maurice Mitchell. 2022. "Building Resilient Organizations: Towards Joy, and Durable Power in a Time of Crisis." *Convergence*, November 29. https://convergencemag.com/articles/building-resilient-organizations-toward-joy-and-durable-power-in-a-time-of-crisis/.

4. Anand Giridharadas. 2022. *The Persuaders: At the Frontlines of the Fight for Hearts, Minds, and Democracy*. 1st ed. New York: Alfred A. Knopf, 156.

5. Interview with Greg Nammacher, September 11, 2020.

6. This is known as accelerationism, a theory that is not supported by evidence. Versions of this theory can be found among the Right-wing as well, such as in the White Nationalist movement.

7. Deepak Bhargava. 2021. "Social Democracy or Fortress Democracy? A Twenty-First Century Immigration Plan." *New Labor Forum*, August 26. https://newlaborforum.cuny.edu/2021/08/26/social-democracy-or-fortress-democracy-a-twenty-first-century-immigration-plan/.

8. Some argue that going along the same route with allies is not actually moving together but instead taking a dangerous detour that will hinder your chances of making it to the top floor. This is the view that achieving some reforms within capitalism will only strengthen capitalism, making it harder to overthrow.

9. Andreas Malm. 2021. *How to Blow Up a Pipeline*. London: Verso; Nancy Fraser and Andreas Malm. 2021. "Dialogue: Nancy Fraser with Andreas Malm on the Politics of Change," webinar, Lund University, Centre for Sustainable Studies, June 8.

10. Chris Smalls. 2022. "Black Labor Struggles over Time: An Intergenerational Panel." Panel at Labor Notes, Chicago, June 17.

11. Alicia Garza. 2021. *The Purpose of Power: How We Come Together When We Fall Apart*. New York: One World.

12. For more on building powerful, lasting coalitions, see Amanda Tattersall. 2011. *Power in Coalition: Strategies for Strong Unions and Social Change*. Ithaca: Cornell University Press; Fred Rose. 1999. *Coalitions Across the Class Divide*. Ithaca: Cornell University Press.

13. Mitchell, "Building Resilient Organizations."

14. "The Chinese Progressive Association Leadership Team's Operating Values and Culture Document" (Revised). January 2018.

15. Jo Freeman. "The Tyranny of Structureless." https://www.jofreeman.com/joreen/tyranny.htm.

16. *The Wildfire Project*. "How We Do It." http://wildfireproject.org/how-we-do-it/.

17. "The Chinese Progressive Association Leadership Team's Operating Values and Culture Document."

18. Dean Spade, Victoria Law, Pauline Rogers, and Andrea Ritchie. 2020. "Abolition,

Intersectionality, and Care." Chicago: Haymarket Books. https://www.higheredinprison.org/events/abolition-intersectionality-and-care.

19. Interview with Paige Kumm, June 14, 2022.

20. Mitchell, "Building Resilient Organizations."

21. Olúfẹ́mi O. Táíwò. 2022. *Elite Capture. How the Powerful Took Over Identity Politics (and Everything Else)*. Chicago: Haymarket Books.

22. Sahil Singhvi. 2020. "Police Infiltration of Protests Undermines the First Amendment." Brennan Center for Justice. August 4. https://www.brennancenter.org/our-work/analysis-opinion/police-infiltration-protests-undermines-first-amendment; Lois Beckett. 2020. "'Boogaloo Boi' Charged in Fire of Minneapolis Police Precinct During George Floyd Protest." *The Guardian*, October 23.

23. Aja Romano. 2018. "Twitter Released 9 Million Russian Troll Tweets. Here's What We Know." *Vox News*, October 19.

24. Ellen Barry. 2022. "How Russian Trolls Helped Keep the Women's March Out of Lock Step." *New York Times*, September 26.

25. The first of these kinds of guards, the Garda Metal, was formed by Baris Silitonga from the metal workers union. Interview with Baris Silitonga, February 7, 2017.

26. Rochelle DuFord. 2022. *Solidarity in Conflict: A Democratic Theory*. Stanford: Stanford University Press.

27. Amanda Ripley. 2021. *High Conflict: Why We Get Trapped and How We Get Out*. New York: Simon & Schuster; Peter T. Coleman. 2021. *The Way Out: How to Overcome Toxic Polarization*. New York: Columbia University Press.

28. "The Theater of David Byrne's Mind." 2022. *Radiolab*. December 7. https://www.radiolab.org/episodes/the-theater-of-david-byrnes-mind.

15. Strategists Are Made, Not Born

1. Billie Holiday and William Duffy. 2011. *Lady Sings the Blues: The 50th-Anniversary Edition with a Revised Discography*. New York: Crown, 53.

2. Daniel Goleman. 2013. "The Focused Leader." *Harvard Business Review*, December 1.

3. David Byrne as interviewed in *The Mind Explained: Creativity*, Netflix series. 2021. Producers: Ezra Klein, Joe Posner, Chad Mumm, and Claire Gordon.

4. Goleman, "The Focused Leader."

5. John Fordham. 2022. "'I Was So Close to the Sky. It Was Spiritual': Sonny Rollins on Jazz Landmark The Bridge at 60." *The Guardian*, January 21.

6. Marshall Ganz. 2009. *Why David Sometimes Wins: Leadership, Organization, and Strategy in the California Farm Worker Movement*. Oxford; New York: Oxford University Press, 10.

7. Ibid., 12.

8. Kim Voss and Rachel Sherman. 2000. "Breaking the Iron Law of Oligarchy: Union Revitalization in the American Labor Movement." *American Journal of Sociology* 106 (2): 303–49. https://doi.org/10.1086/316963.

9. A useful framework from business schools is the "six conditions" for team effec-

tiveness: right people, real team, compelling purpose, sound structure, team coaching, and supportive context. https://6teamconditions.com/.

10. Ganz, *Why David Sometimes Wins*, 19.

11. Reshaping organizational structures can enable better strategy. For more on this, see Melanie Brazzell. 2021. "Building Structure Shapes." P3 Lab at Johns Hopkins. https://www.p3researchlab.org/building_structure_shapes.

12. Francesca Polletta. 2012. "Three Mechanisms by Which Culture Shapes Movement Strategy: Repertoires, Institutional Norms, and Metonymy," in *Strategies for Social Change*, Gregory M. Maney, Rachel V. Kutz-Flamenbaum, Deana A. Rohlinger, and Jeff Goodwin, eds. Minneapolis: University of Minnesota Press.

13. Interview with Mario Yededia, November 21, 2022.

14. Alexander Hertel-Fernandez, Suresh Naidu, Adam Reich, and Patrick Youngblood. 2021. "Quantitative Data Tools for Service Sector Organizing." *New Labor Forum* 30 (1): 42–50. https://doi.org/10.1177/1095796020982999.

16. Learning from Our Opponents

1. Dana Priest, Craig Timberg, and Souad Mekhennet. 2021. "Private Israeli Spyware Used to Hack Cellphones of Journalists, Activists, Worldwide. *Washington Post*, July 18.

2. Niccolo Machiavelli. 1532. *The Prince*. Edited and translated by David Wootton. Indianapolis/Cambridge: Hackett Publishing, 1995.

3. Jean Hardisty. 2000. *Mobilizing Resentment: Conservative Resurgence from the John Birch Society to the Promise Keepers*. Boston: Beacon Press, 189–90.

4. For a good history of overdog strategy in the military and business, we recommend Lawrence Freedman's *Strategy: A History*. 2013. Oxford: Oxford University Press.

5. Alexander Hertel-Fernandez. 2021. *State Capture: How Conservative Activists, Big Businesses, and Wealthy Donors Reshaped the American States—and the Nation*. Oxford: Oxford University Press.

6. Jerry Taylor. 2020. "What Democrats Can Learn from the Republicans About Political Power." Niskanen Center. August 10. https://www.niskanencenter.org/what-democrats-can-learn-from-the-republicans-about-political-power/.

7. Bruce R. Pirnie and Samuel Gardiner. 1996. "An Objectives-Based Approach to Military Campaign Analysis." RAND Corporation. https://www.rand.org/pubs/monograph_reports/MR656.html.

8. David S. Fadok. 1995. "John Boyd and John Warden: Air Power's Quest for Strategic Paralysis." Maxwell Air Force Base: School of Advanced Airpower Studies.

9. Fadok, "John Boyd and John Warden: Air Power's Quest for Strategic Paralysis," 14.

10. Ellen Barry. 2022. "How Russian Trolls Helped Keep the Women's March Out of Lock Step." *New York Times*, September 26.

11. Heather C. McGhee. 2021. *The Sum of Us: What Racism Costs Everyone and How We Can Prosper Together*. New York: One World; Ian Haney-López. 2014. *Dog Whistle Politics: How Coded Racial Appeals Have Reinvented Racism and Wrecked the Middle Class*. Oxford; New York: Oxford University Press. Another useful framework is "othering" and "belonging," developed by john powell: http://www.otheringandbelonging.org/the-problem-of-othering/.

12. Jess Bidgood. 2020. "A Bipartisan Group Secretly Gathered to Game Out a Contested Trump-Biden Election. It Wasn't Pretty." *Boston Globe*, July 26.

13. The British Labour Party used war game techniques to plan how it would approach governance and a backlash from corporations in 2017. George Eaton. 2017. "Why Labour Is Wise to Use 'War Game' Planning for Government." *New Statesman*, September 26.

14. "Commander's Handbook for Assessment Planning and Execution." 2011. Suffolk: Joint Staff, J-7 Joint and Coalition Warfighting. https://www.jcs.mil/Portals/36/Documents/Doctrine/pams_hands/assessment_hbk.pdf.

15. See, for example, Donna M. Mertens and Pauline E. Ginsberg, eds. 2009. *The Handbook of Social Research Ethics*. Thousand Oaks: SAGE Publications.

16. For more on human-centered design, see Ideo.com and Ideo.org.

17. Most economists acknowledge that a negative byproduct of neoliberalism was a turn to short-termism, focusing on immediate profits rather than long-term growth. In the beginning of the neoliberal period many capitalists still organized with one another as a class (Chapter 5). Economist Doug Henwood argues that in the last few decades, even this kind of capitalist organization has broken down, leading to a disjointed ruling class run by wealth-seeking individuals. Doug Henwood. 2021. "Take Me to Your Leader: The Rot of the American Ruling Class." *Jacobin*, April 27.

18. Adam Kahane. 2012. *Transformative Scenario Planning: Working Together to Change the Future*. San Francisco: Berrett-Koehler Publishers.

19. As cited in Richard Bookstaber. 2017. *The End of Theory: Financial Crises, the Failure of Economics, and the Sweep of Human Interaction*. Princeton: Princeton University Press, 173.

17. Rhythms for Practical Radicals

1. Bernadette Cahill. 2015. *Alice Paul, the National Woman's Party and the Vote: The First Civil Rights Struggle of the 20th Century*. Jefferson: McFarland.

2. Movement activity can spread exponentially and geographically, such as in 1848, 1968, or 2011, when Left movements in many countries engaged in similar protests. It can happen for overdogs as well, such as the current wave of authoritarian electoral victories.

3. Dan Clawson. 2003. *The Next Upsurge: Labor and the New Social Movements*. Ithaca: ILR Press; Mark Meinster. 2020. "How Unions Can Lay the Ground for the Next Upsurge." *Labor Notes*, October 15. https://labornotes.org/2020/10/how-unions-can-lay-ground-next-upsurge.

4. Sidney Tarrow, Charles Tilly, and Douglas McAdam. 2001. *The Dynamics of Contention*. New York; London: Cambridge University Press.

5. Tool available on Beautiful Trouble's website. Several people in the group went on to form Movement NetLab, which develops tools to help social movements. Some refer to the tool as The Movement Compass. Bill Moyer has another variation of social movement cycles.

6. Interview with the Arielle Newton, November 1, 2022.

7. Beverly J. Silver. 2003. *Forces of Labor: Workers' Movements and Globalization Since 1870*. Cambridge; New York: Cambridge University Press.

8. Frances Fox Piven and Richard A. Cloward. 1993. *Regulating the Poor: The Functions of Public Welfare.* New York: Vintage Books.

9. Eve S. Weinbaum. 2004. *To Move a Mountain: Fighting the Global Economy in Appalachia.* New York: The New Press.

10. Zeynep Tufekci. 2017. *Twitter and Teargas: The Power and Fragility of Networked Protest.* New Haven: Yale University Press.

11. Amy E. Lerman and Vesla M. Weaver. 2014. *Arresting Citizenship: The Democratic Consequences of American Crime Control.* Chicago Studies in American Politics. Chicago; London: University of Chicago Press.

12. Jamila Michener. 2018. *Fragmented Democracy: Medicaid, Federalism, and Unequal Politics.* Cambridge; New York: Cambridge University Press.

13. The French sociologist Pierre Bourdieu wrote of the "left hand of the state": the public-sector and welfare state that supports citizens, and "right hand of the state": finance and courts that support corporations. Overdogs work to undermine the left hand but enhance the right hand. R.P. Droit and T. Ferenczi. 1992. "The Left Hand and the Right Hand of the State." *Variant* 32.

14. In contrast, before the tech crash of the early 2000s, only one federal lawyer kept watch on investment fraud in Silicon Valley—he had to do his own copying, when a single case could reach half a million pages. David Callahan. 2014. *The Cheating Culture: Why More Americans Are Doing Wrong to Get Ahead.* Boston: Mariner Books, 203. For a comparison of the shocking disparity in spending on enforcement on behalf of overdogs compared to spending on behalf of underdogs see: Alex Hertel-Fernandez and Deepak Bhargava. 2020. "Looking Ahead: Enforcement for the Many, Not the Few." *Democracy: A Journal of Ideas* 60 (Fall). https://democracyjournal.org/magazine/special-symposium/overview-enforcement-for-the-many-not-the-few/.

15. Alexander Hertel-Fernandez. 2021. *State Capture: How Conservative Activists, Big Businesses, and Wealthy Donors Reshaped the American States and the Nation.* Oxford: Oxford University Press.

16. Howard Gleckman. 2021. "Pandemic Bill Would Cut Taxes by an Average of $3,000, with Most Relief Going to Low- and Middle-Income Households." Tax Policy Center. https://www.taxpolicycenter.org/taxvox/pandemic-bill-would-cut-taxes-average-3000-most-relief-going-low-and-middle-income-households.

17. Erik Olin Wright. 2021. *How to Be an Anticapitalist in the Twenty-First Century.* New York: Verso Books.

18. Lisa Fithian. 2019. *Shut It Down: Stories from a Fierce, Loving Resistance.* White River Junction: Chelsea Green Publishing.

19. Barbara Ransby. 2018. *Making All Black Lives Matter: Reimagining Freedom in the Twenty-First Century.* Oakland: University of California Press, 7.

20. Angela Y. Davis. Edited by Frank Barat. 2016. *Freedom Is a Constant Struggle: Ferguson, Palestine, and the Foundations of a Movement.* Chicago: Haymarket Books, 29.

21. Email communication from Connie Razza, November 7, 2022.

18. Learning from Lineages, Harmonizing Our Movements

1. Justin McCarthy. 2022. "U.S. Approval of Labor Unions at Highest Point Since 1965." Gallup. https://news.gallup.com/poll/398303/approval-labor-unions-highest

-point-1965.aspx; Celine McNicholas, Margaret Poydock, Juila Wolfe, Ben Zipperer, Gordon Lafer, and Lola Loustaunau. 2019. "Unlawful: U.S. Employers Are Charged with Violating Federal Law in 41.5% of All Union Election Campaigns." https://www.epi.org/publication/unlawful-employer-opposition-to-union-election-campaigns/.

2. Jake Grumbach and Ruth Berins Collier. 2022. "The Deep Structure of the Democratic Crisis." *Boston Review*. The authors argue for the crucial role of unions in sustaining multiracial democracy.

3. Aldon Morris. 1984. *The Origins of the Civil Rights Movement*. New York: The Free Press.

4. Megan Ming Francis's research shows how philanthropy changed the agendas and strategies of Black freedom struggles in the twentieth century; for example, by encouraging the NAACP to emphasize school integration rather than the fight against racial terror and violence, which was a higher priority for many movement participants. Megan Ming Francis. 2019. "The Price of Civil Rights: Black Lives, White Funding, and Movement Capture." *Law and Society Review* 53 (1): 275–309. https://doi.org/10.1111/lasr.12384.

5. Leslie Wayne. 1992. "Fading Red Line; A Special Report; New Hope in Inner Cities: Banks Offering Mortgages." *New York Times*, March 14.

6. Manisha Sinha. 2016. *The Slave's Cause: A History of Abolition*. New Haven: Yale University Press.

7. Barbara Ransby. 2011. "Quilting a Movement." *In These Times*, April 4.

8. Gary Delgado. 1998. "The Last Stop Sign." *Shelterforce*. November 1. https://shelterforce.org/1998/11/01/the-last-stop-sign/.

9. Anand Giridharadas. 2022. *The Persuaders: At the Frontlines of the Fight for Hearts, Minds, and Democracy*. New York: Alfred A. Knopf, 39.

10. Ziad W. Munson 2010. *The Making of Pro-Life Activists: How Social Movement Mobilization Works*. Chicago: University of Chicago Press. For a vivid portrayal of the recruitment strategies of the anti-abortion movement, see https://battlegroundfilm.org.

11. Maurice Mitchell. 2022. "Building Resilient Organizations: Toward Joy and Durable Power in a Time of Crisis." *Convergence* and *The Forge*, November 29.

12. Presentation by Yotam Marom, November 2, 2022. This is an old and recurring theme in movements. See the classic text by Jo Freeman from the feminist movement, "The Tyranny of Structurelessness." https://www.jofreeman.com/joreen/tyranny.htm.

13. John Leo. 1990. "Wit Is the Opiate of the Masses." *U.S. News & World Report*, November 26.

14. Erica Chenoweth. 2020. "The Future of Nonviolent Resistance." *Journal of Democracy* 31 (3): 69–84; Zeynep Tufekci. 2017. *Twitter and Tear Gas: The Power and Fragility of Networked Protest*. New Haven; London: Yale University Press.

15. Email communication from Anna Galland, September 2022.

16. *Derek Bailey's on the Edge: Improvisation in Music*. Documentary. 1992.

17. Deva Woodly. 2021. *Reckoning: Black Lives Matter and the Democratic Necessity of Social Movements*. Oxford: Oxford University Press.

18. Cookie Bradley. 2022. "The South's Racist Past Is Harming Workers Today. Unions Can Help Us Build a New Future." *USA Today*, November 26.

19. John Lewis. 2017. *Across That Bridge: A Vision for Change and the Future of America*. New York: Legacy Lit, 56.

Afterword

1. Vincent Bevins, 2023. *If We Burn: The Mass Protest Decade and the Missing Revolution*. New York: PublicAffairs.

2. Deepak Bhargava, Sharzad Shams and Harry Hanbury, June 23, 2023. "The Death of 'Deliverism'," *Democracy Journal of Ideas*, https://democracyjournal.org/arguments/the-death-of-deliverism.

Index

abolitionist movement
  and coded song, 228–229
  disruption by the, 120, 230–231
  Douglass on the, 5
  four lessons of the, 241–242
  ideological power of the, 232–233
  military power of the, 238–240
  momentum of the, 237–238
  narrative shift of the, 233–234
  political power of the, 234–237
  Smalls' work in the, 3–4, 12
  solidarity of the, 229–230
  strategies and power use by, 243*t*–244*t*
Abrams, Stacy, 155, 157
ACORN, 131, 315
ACT UP, 130, 210–211, 215–217, 220, 221–222
action and reaction analysis, 88–89
Action Now, 175, 176
Affordable Care Act (ACA), 184–185
African American Civic Engagement Project, 163
AGENDA, 158–159
Aid to Families with Dependent Children (AFDC), 115
Aid to Needy Children Mothers' Anonymous, 116
AIDS Action Council, 214, 217

AIDS Coalition to Unleash Power. *See* ACT UP
AIDS crisis
  arc of activism during, 209–212
  collective care during the, 11–12, 219–222, 225
  disruption and the, 130
  Gay Men's Health Crisis and ACT UP, 214–219
air traffic control strike, 69–70, 128
Alinsky, Saul, 6, 85–86, 278, 310
Allende, Salvador, 64
alliances
  in abolitionist movement, 241
  AIDS crisis, 215–217
  building majority coalitions through, 317, 319
  compromise and, 254–256
  cross-movement strategy and, 299
  economic power and, 49
  electoral change and, 157, 159
  as element of strategy, 32
  in the environmental movement, 193
  in inside-outside campaigns, 10–11, 175–178, 181, 184–185
  labor-community coalitions, 175, 181, 183
  with Make the Road NY, 91–92, 94

alliances (*continued*)
  of political quilters, 316
  shared values and, 25–26
  solidarity power and, 52–53
Alvarez, Adriana, 187
Amazon Labor Union (ALU), 255
American Legislative Exchange Council (ALEC), 279
anger activation, 90, 91, 222–223
Anti-Man-Hunting League, 230
Anti-Slavery Society, 13, 232–233
apartheid government of South Africa, 256
Appalachian plant closings, 293
Arias, Sulma, 306–307
Arizona, 44–45, 148, 154, 249–250
Ashley, John, 234–235
Association of Community Organizations for Reform Now. *See* ACORN
"Attack on the American Free Enterprise System" (Powell Memo). *See* Powell memo
Atwater, Lee, 61–62
authoritarianism, fighting, 200, 201, 221, 320–323
auto workers, 292. *See also* General Motors strike
Avila, Lydia, 159
Axt, Deborah, 79–80, 84

Baker, Ella, 7, 125, 222, 316
Bargaining for the Common Good, 103–104, 253
Baril, Rob, 25–26
Barnes, Shantella, 103–104
Barr, David, 213, 216, 217, 221
Barrientos, Walter, 219
base-building, 9
  in the abolitionist movement, 230
  in the civil rights movement, 7
  with disruption, 308
  for electoral change, 167, 169
  and the Excluded Workers Fund, 78–80, 87
  in the immigrant rights movement, 192
  in inside-outside campaigns, 185
  key components of, 96t–97t, 112t–113t
  in labor organizing, 104–110
  lessons learned in, 306–307
  by Make the Road New York, 80–86, 88, 89–96, 220

  and momentum, 203, 310
  in right-wing movements, 13–14
  in slow cycles, 291
  by St. Paul Federation of Educators, 98–104, 111–112
  and strategy hubs, 321
Bay Area Transformative Justice Collective, 260
Belafonte, Harry, 299
Berger, Ilana, 27, 187
Biden, Joe
  Build Back Better plan of, 170
  climate change legislation of, 197–198
  decision to support, 29, 250–251, 255
  and elimination of student debt, 140
  Georgia win of, 152, 157
  and policy feedback loops, 297
  role of progressives in agenda of, 185
Biftu, Wendwosen, 204–205
Big Box Ordinance, 174, 177
Birmingham campaign, 35–37
Bisono, Julissa, 92
Black and Brown people
  and electoral change, 155, 156, 157, 158, 163
  union demands of, 26
  and the "Walking While Trans" law, 91–92
  and the War on Drugs, 65
Black liberation, 22–23
Black Lives Matter (BLM) movement, 291
Blair, Tony, 136
Bloombergville protest, 137
Boeve, May, 193, 194, 195, 197, 198, 201
Bolivia, 22–23
Bond, Becky, 26, 202
border control, 66–67. *See also* immigrant rights movement
Botha, P.W., 256
Bowers v. Hardwick, 215
boycotts, 35–36, 49, 54, 231
Boyd, John, 280, 281, 289
Bradley, Cookie, 324
breakthrough strategy, 261–262, 263, 265, 266–270, 275–276
bridge builders, 299, 317
British abolitionists, 230, 232, 235
Brom, 234–235
Brooks, Chris, 206
Brotherhood of Sleeping Car Porters, 104

brown, adrienne maree, 38–39, 42, 138
Brown, William Wells, 233
Buen vivir, 21–23
Build Back Better plan, 170
"Building Resilient Organizations" (Mitchell), 257
burnout and collective care, 225
business and the Powell memo, 59–60, 67–68
Butler, Judith, 56
butterfly effect, 38
Butts, George and LaVerne, 315

California, electoral change in, 158–160
California Calls, 158–160, 163
California Nurses Association, 146
Campaign for Community Values, 25
capitalism
  abolitionism and, 237, 238
  conflicting views on, 252
  disruption and, 123
  green, 255
  and higher minimum wages, 182, 183
  industrial to financial, 63
  managed, 14, 58, 61, 62
  and the Occupy Wall Street movement, 139, 141
  racial, 14, 136, 242
care, collective. *See* collective care
care work, unpaid, 121–122
Carey, Ron, 267
cause and effect, in strategy, 32, 37–39, 147–148
Chatterjee, Oona, 92, 93
Chenoweth, Erica, 51, 201, 221, 322
Chicago $15 minimum wage campaign, 173, 174–178, 179–180, 183, 186–187
Chicago Progressive Caucus (CPC), 177
Chicago Teachers Union (CTU), 175–176, 183, 186
Chile, 109
Chinese Progressive Association (CPA), 258, 259
choice, in strategy, 32, 37–38, 42–43
Christian-neoliberal alliance, 69
CIA, 64
citizenship, nature of, 295–296
civil rights movement
  community organizing in the, 83

  disruptive power of, 54, 123
  multiple strategy use in the, 7
  radical flank effect of, 197
  and school history textbooks, 21
  strategy hubs within the, 126, 313
  tactics used in the, 35–37, 41
  welfare rights movement's emergence from, 129–130
Civil War, U.S., 3–4, 12, 230, 231, 236
Clarkson, Thomas, 241
Clawson, Dan, 290–291
Clinton, Bill, 71, 81, 135, 217
Clinton, Hillary, 20, 115–116
Cloward, Richard, 119, 292
coalitions. *See* alliances
coded song, 228–229
collective care, 11–12
  in the abolition movement, 240
  among former slaves, 229
  common elements of, 221–223
  and fighting authoritarianism, 321
  and the Gay Men's Health Crisis, 209–220
  key components of, 226*t*–227*t*
  lesson learned from, 310
  lineages of, 223–224
  as a response to catastrophe, 220–221
  and solidarity power, 53
  strengths and weaknesses of, 224–226
  vision and, 22, 27
collective harm and trauma, conflict over, 259–261
collective identity and narrative shift, 142
Collins, Patricia Hill, 57
Columbia Labor Lab, 274
Commander's Intent, 34
common sense
  ideological power and, 46, 59–60
  momentum model and, 198–199, 200, 237
  movement upsurges and, 291
  narrative shift and, 135, 138, 140, 142, 146–147, 149
  structural reforms and, 294
Communications Workers of America (CWA), 103
communist "popular front," 254
Community Change, 25, 148, 167
Community Change Action (CCA), 164, 283
community organizing. *See* base-building

community unionism. *See* labor-community coalitions
compromise, 179–181, 182, 254–256, 309
conflict within movements
　over analyses, 250–251
　compromise and, 254–256
　cultivating temperaments to handle, 320
　healthy handling of, 263–264
　opponent-fueled, 262–263
　over organizational practice and roles, 257–258
　over personal and collective harm and trauma, 259–261
　over power, 251–252
　over purpose/belonging balance, 258–259
　over sexism and racism, 261–262
　strategy hubs and, 314
　successful team-building and, 271
　over visions and values, 252–253
Congress of Racial Equality (CORE), 123
conjunctural analysis, 28–30, 40, 41–42, 131–132, 242, 312
corporate executive compensation, 63
corporate political power, 45–46
Correa, Rubiela, 79, 87, 95–96
COVID-19 pandemic, 25–26, 78–79, 80, 131, 209–210
cross-movement strategy, 299, 313–314
cultural identity, 142, 225
cultural practices, and community organizations, 90
culture, organizational, 258, 259, 261, 272
Cuomo, Andrew, 78, 80, 93, 94
cyclical nature of movements, 290–292

Dakota Access Pipeline, 47, 123
Daley, Richard, 174
dark arts, 279–283
data use. *See* technology and data use
Davis, Angela, 300
Davis, Troy, 137
Debt Collective, 140
decentralization, 126, 202
decision-making processes, 271
deep canvassing, 146
defections from dominant institutions, 200–201
Defense of Marriage Act, 199

delegitimization of dominant institutions, 201
Delgado, Gary, 42, 317
democracy, in labor unions, 109
Democratic National Convention, 1992, 217
Democratic Party
　electoral change and the, 154, 155
　Iowa primary of 2020, 204–205
　labor unions' ties to, 111
　neoliberalism in the, 70–71
　and Occupy Wall Street, 140–141, 143
　policy details vs. vision of, 20
　Republican tactics against, 279–280
　support of New Deal programs by, 61
　and the U.S. Senate elections in Georgia, 152–153, 157
　welfare rights movement and the, 120, 129
　Working Families Party candidates and the, 160, 162
Democratic Socialists of America (DSA), 141, 154, 165, 206
Deslondes, Charles, 240
Dessalines, Jean-Jacques, 239
diffusion, disruptive movement, 126–127
disruption
　abolitionist movement's use of, 230–231
　AIDS crisis and, 210–211, 220
　common elements of successes in, 124–127
　inside-outside campaigns' use of, 186
　key components of, 132t–134t
　lessons learned in, 307–308
　lineages of, 122–124
　of movements by opponents, 262–263
　organizations and, 129–131
　power of, 53–55
　of racial neoliberalism, 69–70
　strategic use of, 7, 9–10, 11, 120–122
　strengths and weaknesses of, 127–129
　welfare rights movement's use of, 114–119, 131–132
distributed action and the momentum model, 200
diversity in movements, 261–262, 271
diversity of strategies, 298
divestment movement, 190–191, 195–200, 203
divide-and-conquer strategy, 61–62, 281–282, 283
dog whistle politics, 61
Douglass, Frederick, 5, 233, 241

drug laws, 65–66
Du Bois, W.E.B., 120, 136, 234

Eagle Forum, 68
economic inequality. *See* Occupy Wall Street (OWS) movement
economic power
　abolitionists' use of, 230–231
　of corporations, 45
　disruption and, 54, 55
　in Marxist theory, 56
　of neoliberalism, 62–64
　of the southern plantation system, 236–237
　underdogs' use of, 49–50
　and welfare rights, 120
　and worker rights, 121
ecosystems, movement, 157, 298–300, 301*t*–304*t*, 314
Ecuador, 22
Ehrlichman, John, 66
electoral change, 10
　abolitionist movement and, 235–236
　approaches to, 153–155
　in California, 159–160
　common elements of strategy, 162–165
　fighting authoritarianism through, 321
　in Georgia, 152–153, 155–158
　governing power through, 166–170
　and inside-outside campaigns, 185–186
　key components of, 171*t*–172*t*
　labor union use of, 111
　lessons learned in, 308–309
　and Occupy Wall Street, 140–141
　and other strategy models, 169
　overdogs' strategy for, 279
　technology and data use for, 273–274
　and the Working Families Party, 160–162
　See also political power
elites and power, theory of, 56–57
Emancipation Proclamation, 236
Emanuel, Rahm, 173, 174, 175, 176–177, 180
emergent strategy, 38–39, 225
emotional elements, 124–125, 221–222, 292
empathy, 32, 143, 148
enemies, naming, 143
enforcement after legislative wins, 182
engagement. *See* member engagement
Engler, Mark and Paul, 198

Eno, Brian, 266
environmental activism, 63, 190–200, 201, 203, 253
Equal Rights Amendment (ERA), 68–69
Equiano, Olaudah, 232
ethical power, 275
evaluation of strategy
　data use in, 273–274, 283–284, 287
　establishing routine for, 271
　by lean startups, 285
　rigor in, 159, 312
　specific areas of, 274–275
everyday power, 275
Excluded Workers Fund, 78–80, 87, 88, 89, 90, 95–96
Exley, Zack, 26, 110, 202
experimentation, 273, 274, 283–287
ExxonMobil, 190–191

failure, failed vs. successful, 293
Falcon, Petra, 148
Falwell, Jerry, 210
family values, 68
fast-food workers, 176, 178, 186, 187
FBI COINTELPRO program, 262
fear and disruption, 118, 125–126
Ferguson, Missouri, 66
Fields, Barbara, 234
Fight for $15 (FF15) and a Union campaign, 176, 177–178, 186–187
financial crisis of 2008, 28–29, 138–139, 145
Fioretti, Bob, 177
Fithian, Lisa, 298
Flint sit-down strikes, 122, 124, 125, 126, 130, 131
force, in strategy, 33–34
fossil fuel industry. *See* environmental activism
Foucault, Michel, 56
Francis, Megan Ming, 314
Franklin, Benjamin, 241
freedom dreams, 22, 23–25
Freedom Rides, 123
Freeman, Elizabeth, 234–235
Freeman, Jo, 258
French Revolution, 233, 239
Friedman, Andrew, 89, 92, 93
frozen power, 48

Fugitive Slave Act, 236, 242
Fung, Archon, 57, 274
Furman, Jonah, 204, 205

Ganz, Marshall, 270, 271, 272
Garrison, William Lloyd, 241
Gay and Lesbian Community Center, 215
Gay Men's Health Crisis (GMHC), 11–12, 130, 209–220, 221–222, 225
GE Capital, 63
General Electric (GE), 62–63
General Motors strike, 122, 124, 125, 126, 130, 131
generative conflict, 263–264, 314
Georgia elections, 152–153, 155–158
German Communism Party (KPD), 18–19, 41
Getachew, Adom, 205
Giuliani, Rudolph, 81
Goldtooth, Tom, 193
Goleman, Daniel, 266, 268
Gonzalez, Gabe, 81
Gonzalez, Marie, 148
Gould, Deborah, 211
Gradual Emancipation Law (New York), 235
Graf, Arnie, 86, 267
Gramsci, Antonio, 46, 47, 136, 144, 149
grand strategic objectives (GSOs), 199
Grassroots Power Project (GPP), 57, 159, 295
Great Depression, 122–123
Green Party, 154
Guerrero, Mateo, 91–92
guile, in strategy, 39
gun rights movement, 144

Haines, Herbert, 197
Haitian Revolution, 238–240, 241
Hall, Stuart, 19, 21, 28, 136, 149
Han, Alex, 175–176, 186
Haney-Lopez, Ian, 282
Hansell, David, 210, 214
Hardisty, Jean, 278
Harvey, David, 62
Healey, Richard, 57
healing justice framework, 224
hegemony, 46
Helms, Jesse, 210
heroes, identifying, 143, 149
Hertel-Fernandez, Alex, 274, 279

Heyrick, Elizabeth, 231
high-touch organizational model, 83, 95, 202
higher education, 24
Hinson, Sandra, 57
historical narrative, 21
Holiday, Billie, 266
home-care workers, 27, 184
Homeland Security Act, 296
hope, motivation through, 26
housing issues, 82, 123–124, 223
human-centered design, 287
Hurricane Katrina, 223

Iceland, 122
ideological litmus tests, 318–319
ideological power, 46–47
 abolitionists' use of, 232–233, 234
 and collective care, 223
 and narrative shift, 145, 147
 overdogs' use of, 59–60
 racial neoliberalism's use of, 71t
immigrant rights movement
 alliance of, with moderate Republicans, 249–250
 base-building by, 192
 collective care in the, 219
 March for America for, 81–82, 88–89
 and the momentum model, 202–203
 and narrative shift, 148
 psych ops used by, 282
 See also border control
improvisation, 34–35, 323–324
incarceration rates, 65
independent political parties, 154, 160–162, 235–236
Indigenous Environmental Network (IEN), 192, 193
Indigenous people, 47, 123, 192–193, 194
inequality, economic. *See* Occupy Wall Street (OWS) movement
infiltration of movements, 262–263
information processing systems, 280–281
innovation. *See* breakthrough strategy
inside-outside campaigns, 10–11
 of the abolitionist movement, 235
 Affordable Care Act, 184–185
 Chicago $15 minimum wage campaign, 173, 174–178

common elements of, 178–181
and fighting authoritarianism, 321
home-care workers' pay raise campaign, 184
key components of, 187*t*–189*t*
labor union use of, 111
lasting change and results of, 182–183
lessons learned from, 309
Make the Road NY's use of, 92
strengths and weaknesses of, 181–182
use of other strategy models in, 185–186
intergenerational strategy, 24, 288, 300–301
internal care work, 261
international agreements, 197
International Day of Protest against the Iraq War, 54
International Longshore Workers Union (ILWU), 49
internationalism, 322
interpersonal harm and trauma, conflict over, 259–261
Iraq War, 54
issue identification, in labor organizations, 105
issues vs. problems in community organizing, 87–88

Jacobs, Lauren, 103
James, C.L.R., 136, 233
January 6th insurrection, 50, 123–124
JBS Pork workplace caucus, 204, 205
Jenkins, Alan, 136–137, 141, 143
Jimenez, Cristina, 275
Johnson, Katelyn, 176, 180
Jones, Roxanne, 116
Justice Democrats, 154

Kaba, Mariame, 22, 224, 242
Kahane, Adam, 288
Kansas-Nebraska Act, 236
Kelley, Robin D.G., 22, 223
Kemp, Brian, 158
Kern, Jen, 165
Keystone XL pipeline, 192–193, 194, 196, 199–200, 203
King, Martin Luther, Jr., 45, 60, 300
Kissinger, Henry, 64–65
Knight, Kyandra, 222–223
Koch, David and Charles, 191

Kramer, Larry, 215
Kumar, Sumathy, 165
Kumm, Paige, 260

labor-community coalitions, 175–176, 181, 183, 253, 293, 324
labor unions
base-building by, 98–112, 112*t*–113*t*
cyclical nature of, 291, 292
disruption by, 121, 122
and electoral change, 163
and group power, 297
upsurges in, 294
use of technology and data by, 273–274
vision and, 26
See also strikes; workers
Labour Party (United Kingdom), 19, 21, 28
Lambda Legal Defense and Education Fund, 216
Lauer, Katey, 251
Lawson, James, 125
leaders and organizers
in community organizing, 85
and conflict over roles, 257, 258
in divestment campaigns, 197
and electoral change, 159
in labor unions, 104, 109
need for, 319–320
training of, 269–270
work of, 84–85
Leadership for Democracy and Social Justice (training institute), 269
lean startups, 285–286
"Left-Wing Communism" (Lenin), 17
LeftRoots, 269–270
legislative reform. *See* inside-outside campaigns
Lenchner, Charles, 140–141
Lenin, Vladimir, 17, 29, 255
Lewis, John, 324
Lewis, Penny, 138
liberation theology, 23
Liberty Party, 235–236
Lightfoot, Lori, 177
Lincoln, Abraham, 231, 236
Lindeman, Leah, 99, 106, 112
lineages
of collective care, 223–224

lineages (*continued*)
　of disruption, 122–124
　and the mastery/improvisation dynamic, 323–324
　of strategy from below, 39–40
　of strategy models, 9–12, 306–311
Liss, Jon, 166–167
listening and narrative shift, 143
Living United for Change in Arizona (LUCHA), 154, 164
local campaigns and the momentum model, 200
lockouts, worker, 55
Long Friday, 122
long-term planning
　by California Calls, 158–160
　experimentation, evaluation, and goal-setting for, 273–275
　intergenerational strategy, 24, 288, 300–301
　movement cycles and, 290–292
　by strategy model, 301*t*–304*t*
　and structural reforms, 294–295
　See also Powell memo; vision
Lopez, Jose, 90, 91, 92–93, 94
Lorenz, Edward Norton, 38
Louisiana, slave uprising in, 240
L'Ouverture, Toussaint, 239
love, organizing from, 91, 95

Machiavelli, 33–34, 278
Make the Road New York (MRNY), 80–86, 88, 89–96, 220
Malm, Andreas, 255
managed capitalism, 14, 58
Mann, Michael, 50, 52
March for America, 81–82, 88–89, 192, 282
Marom, Yotam, 37, 39, 139, 319
marriage equality, 47, 146–147, 148, 198–199, 201, 217
Marxist theory of power, 56
mass incarceration, 65–66
mass organization. *See* base-building
mass training, 11, 200
Massachusetts Constitution, 234–235
maximalism, 252, 257
McDonald's workers, 178, 186
McGhee, Heather, 282
McKibben, Bill, 193–194, 195

Meinster, Mark, 107, 176
member engagement
　and base-building, 84, 86–87, 103, 106
　and collective care, 217
　and electoral change, 154, 156, 163, 164, 168
　and momentum, 200
　union stewards as resource for, 267
member recruitment. *See* recruitment
Mendez, Yaritza, 92
mental warfare, 281
methodological sectarianism, 317–318
Michels, Robert, 94
Michener, Jamila, 295, 296
Middlebury College students, 193
Midwest Academy, 35
military and police power, 50–51, 64–67, 238–240
military strategy, 32, 34, 35, 284
Milkman, Ruth, 138
Milley, Mark, 50
Mingus, Mia, 224, 260
minimum wage campaigns, 55, 173–183, 186–187, 296–297
misinformation dissemination, 262
Mitchell, Maurice, 160, 161, 162, 252, 257, 260–261
momentum model, 11
　abolitionists' use of, 237–238
　common elements of, 198–201
　environmentalists' use of, 190–198
　key components of, 207*t*–208*t*
　lessons learned, 309–310
　and the Sanders presidential campaign, 204–205
　strengths and weaknesses of the, 201–203
　use of other models with, 206
Momentum (training institute), 198, 199, 206
moral panics, 281–282
moral rightness, 5, 120
moral vision, 19–20
moral warfare, 281
Mothers Against AIDS, 214
movement cycles, 290–292
movement ecosystems, 157, 298–300, 301*t*–304*t*, 314
Movement for Black Lives (M4BL), 120, 202, 206, 220, 223–224
movement moments, 125, 199–200

movement upsurges, 222
MoveOn.org, 141, 223, 274
Muñoz, Carolina Bank, 109
Muste, AJ, 109
mutual aid. *See* collective care

NAACP, 7
Naidu, Suresh, 274
Nakhoda, Zein, 251
naming enemies or targets, 143
Nammacher, Greg, 253
narrative shift, 10
  abolitionists' use of, 233–234
  electoral change and, 169
  inside-outside campaigns' use of, 186
  key components of, 150*t*–151*t*
  lessons learned in, 308
  in the momentum model, 11
  Occupy Wall Street's use of, 137–149
  racial neoliberalism's use of, 135–137
  teacher union's use of, 101
  telling history and articulating the "we," 21
National Campaign for Jobs and Income Support, 115
National Education Association, 102
National Labor Relations Act (NLRA), 108, 110, 131, 297, 310
National Welfare Rights Organization (NWRO), 115, 126
NationsBank, 315
neoliberal-progressive alliances, 254–255
neoliberalism, racial. *See* racial neoliberalism
New Deal, 58, 61, 62, 115, 297
New Georgia Project (NGP), 152–153, 155–158, 164
New Organizing Institute, 275
New Party, 154
New Virginia Majority (NVM), 164, 166–167
New York
  drug laws in, 65
  electoral change in, 165
  emancipation law of, 235
  home-care workers' pay raise, 184
  immigrant workers' strike for pandemic relief, 78–79
  "Walking While Trans" law, 91–92
  Working Families Party in, 160–162
  See also Make the Road New York

New York Caring Majority, 27
Newton, Arielle, 291, 292
Nixon, Richard, 61, 64, 65, 66
nonviolent tactics, 39–40, 51, 54, 201, 322
norm breaking and disruption, 124
north stars, 23–25, 255
Northrop, Michael, 190
Nurse, Sandy, 139
nursing home workers, 25–26

Obama, Barack
  and the 2008 financial crisis, 29
  environmental policies of, 191, 193, 194
  and formation of the Tea Party, 62
  and the March for America, 88–89
  pragmatism of, 18
  progressive disillusionment with, 168
Ocasio-Cortez, Alexandria, 252
Occupy Wall Street (OWS) movement, 137–149
  Chicago Teachers Union's joining of, 175
  disruption by, 120
  leadership and, 319–320
  narrative shift by, 308
O'Connor, John J., 216
OODA (observation, orientation, decision, action) loop, 280–283
open bargaining, 101, 112
organizational culture, 259, 272, 315–316
organizational diversity, 298
organizational structure, 82–83, 93, 106, 257, 258
organizer development, 92–93
organizers. *See* leaders and organizers
organizing, sustainability of, 222–223
organizing approach to electoral politics, 163, 164
Ossoff, Jon, 152
Otpor, 203
overdogs
  alliances among, 256
  dark arts use by, 279–283
  disruption by, 123–124
  exploiting divisions among, 241, 312, 322
  ideological power of, 46
  instilling fear in, 118, 125–126
  long-term planning by, 287
  military and police power use by, 50–51

overdogs (*continued*)
  policy feedback loop use by, 295–296
  strategy of, 5, 12–15
  tactics of, 55
  technology and data use by, 277–278
  See also racial neoliberalism
Overton, Joseph, 144
Overton window, 144–145

Page, Cara, 224
Palantir, Inc., 277–278
Paris Agreement, 197
Pateriya, Deepak, 164
Payne, Charles, 83
Pearce, Russell K., 249
People for Bernie, 141
People's Action, 146
People's Climate March, 190
Phillips, Steve, 155, 164
pillars approach to momentum, 195, 200–201
Pinochet, Augusto, 64–65
Pitkin, Daisy, 222, 300
Piven, Frances Fox, 54, 119, 125, 292, 320
plant closings, 293
pluralist theory of power, 56
police power. *See* military and police power
policy details vs. moral vision, 19–20
policy feedback loops, 183, 282, 295–298, 309
policy power, 275
political campaigns and the momentum model, 201–202, 204–205
political power, 48
  abolitionist movement's use of, 231, 234–237
  and collective care, 222
  of corporations, 45–46
  of labor unions, 111
  of racial neoliberalism, 61–62, 71t
  welfare rights movement's use of, 120
  See also electoral change; inside-outside campaigns
political quilters, 299, 316
Political Research Associates, 278
politics, prefigurative, 26–27
Polletta, Francesca, 272
poor women of color and welfare rights, 114–120, 124, 129, 132
post-structuralist theory of power, 56

poverty and mass incarceration, 66
Powell memorandum, 17, 59–60, 67–68, 287–288
power
  analysis of, 312
  of groups, 297
  internal dynamics, 260–261
  levels of, 274–275
  and progressive policy priorities, 297–298
  racial neoliberalism's use of, 71t–72t
  theories of, 56–57
  See also specific types of
Power Resources Approach, 57
pragmatism/utopianism balance, 18, 29
Prakash, Varshini, 196, 197, 202
prefigurative politics, 26–27
The Prince (Machiavelli), 278
principled struggle, 270, 314
prison population, 65
problems vs. issues in community organizing, 87–88
process, in strategy, 34–35
Professional Air Traffic Controllers Organization (PATCO), 69–70, 128
Progressive Dane, 154
Project Confrontation (Project C), 35–37
Promise Arizona, 148
Proposition 13 (California), 158, 159, 160
protest, over-reliance on, 221, 322–323
protest vs. disruption, 9, 120, 307
psychological operations (psych ops), 280–283
Public Higher Education Network of Massachusetts (PHENOM), 24
public opinion. *See* momentum model; narrative shift

Quakers, 21, 23, 232, 233, 235, 237

racial capitalism, 136, 242
racial justice framework, 160–162, 262
racial neoliberalism
  and the 2008 financial crisis, 28–29
  defined, 14
  in Democratic Party reforms, 70–71
  disruptive power of, 69–70
  economic power of, 62–64
  emergence of, 58

examples of use of power by, 71t–72t
military power use for, 64–67
political power of, 61–62
and the Powell Memo, 59–60
solidarity power of, 67–69
working class support of, 135–137
See also overdogs; Right wingers
racism, conflict over, 261–262
racism and the welfare system, 114, 115, 118, 128, 132
radical abolitionism, 237–238
radical flank effect, 197
Radical Republicans, 170, 236
Raise Chicago campaign, 174, 175, 176
Ramirez, Ana, 78–79, 87
Randolph, A. Philip, 104
Ransby, Barbara, 299, 316
Razza, Connie, 300
reaction analysis, 88–89
Ready for Warren, 141
Reagan, Ronald, 69–70, 128, 135, 210
Reconstruction era, 170, 229
recruitment
  and collective care, 222
  in community organizing, 86–87
  and fighting authoritarianism, 321
  by labor unions, 107–108
  in the momentum model, 200
  and rejecting ideological litmus tests, 318–319
  by the Right wing, 311
  into the welfare system, 119
reforms, structural. *See* structural reforms
Reich, Adam, 274
relationship building, 87
religion
  and abolitionism, 232, 233, 235, 237
  and the Christian-neoliberal alliance, 69
  vision and, 21, 23
representation
  in labor unions, 108–109
  in movements, 261–262
Republican Party
  anti-slavery position of, 236
  Equal Rights Amendment and, 68
  and Georgia elections, 155
  immigrant rights and moderates from the, 249–250
  immigration policies of, 67
  political power of, 61–62
  white working-class support of the, 136
research by labor organizations, 105
restorative justice practices, 102
reverse engineering, in strategy, 37
Ricker, Mary Cathryn, 100, 102, 111–112
Right to the City (RTC) Alliance, 260
Right wingers
  grassroots component of, 13–14
  and ideological power, 59–60
  and political power, 61–62
  recruitment by, 311, 319
  vision of the future of, 19–20
  See also racial neoliberalism
Rivandeneyra, Camila, 79
Robinson, Cedric, 136
Robinson, Edwin, 23–24
Robinson, Rashad, 146
Rockefeller, John D., 190
Rockefeller, Nelson, 65
Rockefeller Brothers Fund, 190–191
Rolling Stone magazine, 195
Rollins, Sonny, 268
Romanow, Lissy, 199, 200, 206
root ideas, 19–21, 142
Rove, Karl, 199
rule breaking and disruption, 124
Rules for Radicals (Alinsky), 6, 278
Rumelt, Richard, 37
Russian troll farm, 262
Rustin, Bayard, 130, 299
Ryan White CARE Act, 214–215

saliency and narrative shift, 144
Sanders, Bernie
  electoral change and, 168
  former Occupy activists in campaign of, 141
  identity narrative of, 142
  momentum-style political campaign of, 201–202, 204–205
  vision and messaging of, 20
Sanders, Beulah, 117, 130
Sarsour, Linda, 262–263, 318
SB 1070 (Arizona law), 249
Scharmer, Otto, 38
Schlafly, Phyllis, 68–69

Schneider, René, 64
Scott v. Sandford (Dred Scott decision), 242
Seattle $15 minimum wage campaign, 180–181
Seidel, Emil, 48
self-interest, in base-building, 87
Serbia, 203
Service Employees International Union (SEIU), 26, 175, 253, 269, 324
service provision, by community organizations, 89–90
sexism, 114, 128, 261–262
Shapiro, Vivian, 215
shared values. *See* values
shareholders' interests, 62–63
Shenker-Osario, Anat, 144
Sherman, Rachel, 271, 272
shop stewards, 106, 267
Shuttlesworth, Fred, 36
Silicon Valley data use, 284–285
Silver, Beverly, 292
Simowitz, Kevin, 41
single-issue momentum campaigns, 202
Sinha, Manisha, 232, 237–238, 240
Sioux Tribe of Standing Rock, 47
slavery, abolition of. *See* abolitionist movement
Smalls, Chris, 255
Smalls, Robert, 3–4, 12
smart repression, 323
Smith, Sabrina, 158, 159–160
Smucker, Jonathan, 146, 147
social conservatives, 68–69
Social Democrats (Germany), 18–19, 41
social justice, as source of vision, 21, 23
social media, 199–200, 262–263, 293–294
Socialists in Office Committee, 165
Society for the Abolition of the Slave Trade, 230
solidarity power, 51–53
  in the abolitionist movement, 229–230
  and fighting authoritarianism, 320
  and the Haitian Revolution, 239
  of labor unions, 106
  of Make the Road New York, 84
  within movements, 263
  of racial neoliberalism, 67–69
Solnit, Rebecca, 220

solutions, identifying, 143–144
Sonti, Samir, 205
South African apartheid, 256
Southern Christian Leadership Conference (SCLC), 35
Southern plantation system, 236–237, 241–242
Spade, Dean, 220, 260
spirituality and vision, 21–23
St. Paul Federation of Educators (SPFE), 98–102, 106, 111–112
Stand UP! Chicago campaign, 175
Standard Oil, 190
state, nature of the, 296–297
state abolition laws, 235
State Power Caucus, 162
states' rights narrative, 242
Stephan, Maria, 51
strategic capacity, 266–270, 271–272, 275–276, 314–317
strategies
  from above vs. from below, 13, 33
  cause and effect in, 37–39
  within coalitions, 319
  combining, 6–9
  common polarities of, 33–34
  connections between, 318
  cross-movement, 298–300
  dark arts use in, 279–283
  definitions of, 31–32
  elements of, 32–33
  examples of, by form of power, 76*t*
  experimentation and data use in, 283–287
  importance of, in underdog movements, 4–6
  lessons learned, by model, 306–311
  long-term planning of, 287–289
  of overdogs, 12–15
  of Powell and Lenin, 17
  relationship of, to vision and conjuncture, 40–42
  seven models of, 9–12
  tactics and, 35–37
Strategy Chart, 35, 183, 312
strategy hubs, 313–314
Strategy Idol method, 275
strategy teams, 270–272
Strike Debt, 140

strikes
   air traffic control strike, 69–70, 128
   disruptive power of, 121, 122, 124, 125, 126, 130, 131
   economic power of, 49
   for equal pay, 122
   by teachers, 175–176, 183, 186
   See also labor unions
structural power, 57, 275
structural reforms, 160, 294–295
student debt, 140
Student Non-Violent Coordinating Committee (SNCC), 83, 123, 125
successful failures, 293–294, 298
Sun Tzu, 35
sustainability of organizing, 222–223, 225
Sweeney, Tim, 213–214, 215–216, 217–219, 221

tabletop exercises, military, 284
tactics
   of Atwater, 61–62
   escalation of, 105–106
   and the momentum model, 196, 202
   outside vs. inside, 174
   of overdogs, 55
   and strategy, 35–37, 41, 75
   of underdogs, 54
targets, identifying and naming, 143, 178
Taylor, Jerry, 279
Tea Party, 29, 62, 138, 278
teachers' strikes, 175–176, 183, 186
team building, 270–272
Teamsters union, 121, 267
technology and data use
   by authoritarians, 323
   for electoral change, 159, 164
   by overdogs, 277–278
   by underdogs, 284–287
   by unions, 273–274
tenant organizations, 122–123, 285–286
Tennessee Industrial Renewal Network, 293
Terán, Raquel, 154
Thatcher, Margaret, 135
Thatcherism, 19, 28
Theory U, 38
Thiel, Peter, 277
Thigpenn, Anthony, 158
Thirteenth Amendment, 236

This Is an Uprising (Engler), 198
Thomas-Müller, Clayton, 192, 193
350.org, 193–199, 201, 203
Tillmon, Johnnie, 114–115, 116, 118, 130
time, as element of strategy, 32, 42. *See also* long-term planning
Tisch, Joan, 214
top-down vs. bottom-up strategies, 13, 33, 317
"Total Strategy" plan for South Africa, 256
tradition. *See* lineages
training, organizer, 269–270. *See also* mass training
Training for Change, 251
Trans Immigrant project, MRNY, 91–92
transformational change
   collective care as seed for, 221
   combining multiple strategies for, 6–9, 241
   electoral change for, 153–155
   importance of strategy for, 5
   and movement ecosystems, 298, 299
   seven strategy models for, 9–12
   See also long-term planning; vision
transformational vs. transactional organizing, 164
transformative justice, 224, 260
transformative scenario planning, 288–289
trauma, conflict over, 259–261
trickster traditions, 39
troll farm, Russian, 262
Trump, Donald
   alliances formed to defeat, 29, 251, 255, 298
   anti-Muslim travel ban of, 283
   articulation of the "we" by, 21
   attempted coup of, 50, 123–124
   conditions for emergence of, 18
   defeat of, in Georgia, 152
   mass constituency of, 13
   narrative shift by, 142
   tactics of, 62
   union leader's proposal to meet with, 256
trust, in team-building, 271
Truth, Sojourner, 235, 241
Tubman, Harriet, 228
Tufekci, Zeynep, 293, 322
Turn It Around (film), 267

Ufot, Nsé, 152–153, 155–157, 169

underdogs
  adoption of overdog strategies by, 282–283
  disruption by, 54–55, 122–123
  exploitation of overdogs' divisions by, 241, 312, 322
  ideological power of, 46–47
  importance of strategy for, 4–6
  lineage of strategies of, 39–40
  long-term planning by, 287–289
  military and police power use by, 51
  overdogs' weakening of strength of, 279–280
  policy feedback loop use by, 296–297
  seven strategy models for, 9–12
  solidarity power of, 52–53
  strategy of, compared to overdogs' strategy, 15
  tactics of, 54
Underground Railroad, 229, 230–231
undocumented workers, pandemic relief for. *See* Excluded Workers Fund
Union of Southern Service Workers (USSW), 206, 324
union stewards, 106, 267
UNITE HERE, 163, 164, 273–274
United Auto Workers (UAW), 122, 125, 130
United Electrical Workers Union (UE), 176
United Farm Workers (UFW), 49, 120, 270
United We Dream, 275
unpaid care work, 121–122
unprogrammed time, 268
UPS strike, 121
upsurges, movement, 108, 222, 290–291, 292, 294, 307
U.S. Chamber of Commerce, 17, 67–68
U.S. Senate election in Georgia, 152–153, 157
utopianism/pragmatism balance, 18, 29

Valdés, Javier, 90, 91, 92
values
  and alliances, 255–256
  conflict over, 252–253
  family values, 68
  and narrative shift, 137, 139, 142, 143, 145
  and the Occupy Wall Street movement, 139
  strategy guided by, 25–26
VanDassor, Leah, 98–99, 100–101, 102, 109, 112

vision
  conflict over, 252–253
  conjunctural analysis and, 28–30
  demands and, 294
  effect of, on strategy, 40–41, 42
  and inside-outside campaigns, 181
  and movement ecosystem, 299–300
  and narrative shift, 145
  north stars and, 23–25, 255
  power of, 26–28
  root ideas and, 19–21
  shared values and, 5–26
  sources of, 21–23
  of the welfare rights movement, 131–132
Voss, Kim, 271, 272
voter mobilization. *See* electoral change

Walker, Wyatt Tee, 35–37, 39, 41
"Walking While Trans" law (New York), 91–92
Walmart, 49, 109
War on Drugs, 65–66
warfare, psych ops in, 280–281
Warnock, Raphael, 152
Warren, Dorian, 131, 311
Warren, Elizabeth, 140–141
Washington, Harold, 48, 170
"we," articulation of the, 21, 25, 91–92, 142, 149
wealth inequality. *See* Occupy Wall Street (OWS) movement
Weinbaum, Eve, 293
Welch, Jack, 62–64
welfare rights movement, 114–119, 127, 128–130, 131–132
white supremacy, 29, 60, 62, 241–242, 282. *See also* civil rights movement; racial neoliberalism
Wiekerson, Sandra, 175
Wildfire (training institute), 258–259
Wiley, George, 129
Williams, Steve, 27–28
women of color and welfare rights, 114–120, 124, 129, 132
Women's Day Off, 122
women's rights, 68–69, 114–115
Wong, Winnie, 140–141
Woodly, Deva, 53, 223

Worker Power, 163, 164
workers
 building the power of, 307
 economic power of, 49
 home-care, 27, 184
 immigration policy and, 67
 lockouts used against, 55
 Occupy Wall Street's influence on, 140
 racial neoliberalism support by the, 135–137
 successful failure and, 293
 See also labor unions; minimum wage campaign; strikes
Working Families Party (WFP), 154, 160–162, 164–165, 166, 169
workplace mapping, 104
Wright, Erik Olin, 298

Youngblood, Patrick, 274
youth climate activists, 193–194, 196

Zurara, Gomes Eanes de, 232

Publishing in the Public Interest

Thank you for reading this book published by The New Press; we hope you enjoyed it. New Press books and authors play a crucial role in sparking conversations about the key political and social issues of our day.

We hope that you will stay in touch with us. Here are a few ways to keep up to date with our books, events, and the issues we cover:

- Sign up at www.thenewpress.com/subscribe to receive updates on New Press authors and issues and to be notified about local events
- www.facebook.com/newpressbooks
- www.twitter.com/thenewpress
- www.instagram.com/thenewpress

Please consider buying New Press books not only for yourself, but also for friends and family and to donate to schools, libraries, community centers, prison libraries, and other organizations involved with the issues our authors write about.

The New Press is a 501(c)(3) nonprofit organization; if you wish to support our work with a tax-deductible gift please visit www.thenewpress.com/donate or use the QR code below.